Corrupting Youth

Corrupting Youth

POLITICAL EDUCATION,

DEMOCRATIC CULTURE, AND

POLITICAL THEORY

· *J. PETER EUBEN* ·

PRINCETON UNIVERSITY PRESS

PRINCETON, NEW JERSEY

Library of Congress Cataloging-in-Publication Data

Euben, J. Peter.
Corrupting youth : political education, democratic culture, and political
theory / J. Peter Euben.
p.   cm.
Includes bibliographical references and index.
ISBN 0-691-01202-4 (cloth alk. paper) — ISBN 0-691-04828-2 (pbk. alk. paper)
1. Political science—Greece—History.   2. Democracy—Greece—History.
3. Politics and literature—Greece—History.   4. Political plays, Greek—History and
criticism.   5. Political socialization.   I. Title.
JC73.E93   1997   321.8′01—dc21   96-54911   cip

This book has been composed in Times Roman

Princeton University Press books are printed on acid-free paper and meet the guidelines for
permanence and durability of the Committee on Production Guidelines for Book
Longevity of the Council on Library Resources

Printed in the United States of America

1   3   5   7   9   10   8   6   4   2

1   3   5   7   9   10   8   6   4   2
(pbk)

TO THE MEMORY OF

MY GRANDFATHER JOSEPH FEINGOLD

MY SISTER JULIE ANN EUBEN FRIEDFELD

MY COUSIN ELLEN ROTH REISMAN

MY FRIEND AND COLLEAGUE RICHARD GORDON

ALL OF WHOM DIED OF

TERRIBLE ILLNESSES

WITH A COURAGE THAT CONTINUES

TO GIVE STRENGTH TO THE

MANY WHO LOVED THEM

And this thinking, fed by the present, works with the "thought fragments" it can wrest from the past and gather about itself. Like a pearl diver who descends to the bottom of the sea, not to excavate the bottom and bring it to light but to pry loose the rich and the strange, the pearls and the coral in the depths, and to carry them to the surface, this thinking delves into the depths of the past—but not in order to resuscitate it the way it was and to contribute to the renewal of extinct ages. What guides this thinking is the conviction that although the living is subject to the ruin of the time, the process of decay is at the same time a process of crystallization, that in the depth of the sea, into which sinks and is dissolved what once was alive, some things "suffer a sea-change" and survive in new crystallized forms and shapes that remain immune to the elements, as though they waited only for the pearl diver who one day will come down to them and bring them up into the world of the living—as "thought fragments," as something "rich and strange," and perhaps even as everlasting *Urphänomene.*

—Hannah Arendt, paraphrasing Walter Benjamin

• *C O N T E N T S* •

I

There is much talk these days about corrupting youth: about who is responsible for their supposedly bizarre tastes in music and dress, their addiction to drugs, television, and promiscuous sex, their hedonism and contempt for authority, their general selfishness and irresponsibility, and their indifference to or cynicism toward public life, the public good, and public education. The harrowing immoralism of the movie *Kids* seems but a mild exaggeration of what has been done to or has happened to them.

One variant of this general complaint focuses on the "politicization" of secondary and higher education and the displacement of "classical" texts in the education of the young, or at least those of the young who go to elite private schools, selective public schools, or four-year colleges and universities. Here the contest is over what students should read and why they should read it, who should teach them, how, where, and for how long. The more general question behind these concerns is about the purpose of especially public education in a more or less liberal democratic polity. Is the purpose of such an education to "inculcate" citizenship or teach technical skills, focus on the liberal arts and the cultivation of character or on vocational training to insure "productive" workers? Who appropriately sets the terms of this debate? Who should have a significant voice or even the final word in it?

In many respects these questions and concerns are as old as our Republic. Mostly they remain white noise. But at times such as our own, their hum becomes a full-throated lament. Then it becomes evident once again how much of our self-fashioning and representation of "who" we are, hoped to be, and blessedly were not (e.g., a class society) is tied to our conception of education.

This book is meant to participate in the current debate. But it does so in a particular if not peculiar way, since its points of reference are Athenian democracy, Socrates, and classical drama and political theory.

As for the first, I suggest certain historical parallels between the sophistic challenge in fifth-century Greece, which, perhaps for the first time in the West, forced people to think systematically about education as a distinct activity and our own educational crisis. That the challenge occurred in the context of debates over the meaning of democracy and in the midst of recriminations—wonderfully parodied in the *Clouds,* where the debate between Old and New Education sounds like that between the National Association of Scholars and their multiculturalist critics—over who is corrupting the young adds substance to the parallel. As for Socrates, he is the one most memorably accused of corrupting the youth, a charge he turns against his accusers, thereby raising the question of what we mean by corruption and what is presupposed by the claim that someone or some force is corrupting the young. Since I will take Socrates as a paradigmatic political educator of a democratic polity (at least most of the time and until the final chapter), the charges against him and his response to them frame the issues of this book.

In regard to classical texts, I am less interested in making an abstract argument for their "usefulness" than in attempting to demonstrate it by thinking about contemporary political and theoretical issues through and with them. Most of the time I focus on a particular issue and text (such as rational actor theory and *Oedipus Tyrannus*), but in one case, that of *Antigone,* my intention is simply to indicate how generative such a text can be.

There is of course something problematic about relying on Athenian democracy, Socrates, and classical texts as a point of reference. Why yet again "privilege" what has been privileged all along, and just at a time when there are good reasons to think with and through other societies, figures, and texts? More pointedly, why have recourse to a democracy that was far less democratic than its defenders (who have in fact been very few indeed) suppose it to be? And is it not incongruous, even dangerous, to insist on parallels between a small premodern city-state and a modern state? Surely such parallels can be manufactured only by sacrificing historical precision and institutional specificity. For instance, the closer one looks at Greek religion, modes of warfare, communication, the economy, and kinship structures, the more surface similarities dissolve into a disquieting otherness or straightforward irrelevance.

J.G.A. Pocock tells the story of how Renaissance humanists, who were drawn to the study of antiquity by the expectation that they could find exemplars by which to model their own lives, found that the more closely they studied the past they revered, the more it receded before them, until its particularities overwhelmed any possible relevance for the sixteenth century. The techniques of historical scholarship they developed to mine the wisdom of the Romans undermined their initial assumption and purpose. Moreover, their refusal to accept what their scholarship revealed and persistence in trying to mimic the past led to a pedantic academism that provoked writers like Bacon and Hobbes to reject the past in the name of a self-sufficient modernism.[1] The moral drawn by Quentin Skinner, as well as by Pocock, is that reading classical texts and authors as if they were contemporaries talking to us about our world, rather than to a set of historically specific issues in the language of their contemporaries, is a self-defeating enterprise that also leads to political and theoretical absurdities.[2]

There is much to be said for and against such theoretical asceticism, but this is not the place to say it.[3] What does need saying is that my juxtaposing of classical

---

[1] J.G.A. Pocock, *The Ancient Constitution and the Feudal Law* (Cambridge: Cambridge University Press, 1957), pp. 4–5.

[2] Quentin Skinner, "Meaning and Understanding in the History of Ideas," *History and Theory* 8 (1969): 3–53.

[3] See Margaret Leslie, "In Praise of Anachronism," *Political Studies* 18, no. 4 (1970): 433–47. I have elaborated some of Leslie's points in the introduction to *Greek Tragedy and Political Theory* (Berkeley: University of California Press, 1986), pp. 3–6.

and contemporary democracy and ancient and modern texts presumes both alienness and familiarity, and that my occasional indifference to Skinner's caution is purposeful rather than inadvertent. My argument, which is perhaps most relevant to the aims of public education in the United States, is that unless "classic" texts can speak to contemporary political and theoretical issues they will wither, and our students will have a more impoverished sense of political and intellectual possibilities than they would have had otherwise. This is not a warrant for the casual appropriation of texts but an argument for an informed loosening of the constricting prerogatives of specialists who, by hoarding the insights these texts provide, disable them as works of civic education.[4]

My shorthand way of raising this issue is to ask whether we can and should take Socrates out of the academy and put him back, if not in the streets, then at least in front of a far wider audience and constituency. Of course, there is a sense in which this is "my" Socrates, not because he is a convenient cipher for whatever views I fancy—indeed, in many ways he is a pest—but because I come to my reading of the *Apology, Gorgias,* and *Protagoras* (as well as *Oedipus Tyrannus, Antigone,* and *Clouds*) with a specific set of questions about the relationship between academic and civic education in a democratic culture. Though specific historical allusions in the dialogues are crucial, and though I will make much of the tension between the dramatic and historical dates of the *Protagoras* especially, I am, with the possible exception of chapter four, less interested in the "historical" Socrates than with the figure who plays various roles in dramas by Plato.

As this indicates, this book is also about the relationship between Socratic/Platonic philosophy and radical democracy. I will suggest the ways in which Socrates expanded a democratic tradition of accountability and self-critique into a way of doing philosophy that remained parasitic upon, if not respectful of, that tradition, even when he found fault with it. This is not only the case in the *Apology* but with the *Gorgias* as well. Both explore the dependencies of radical (as distinct from liberal) democracy and philosophy.

I say "explore" because I do not think the relationship between philosophy and democracy is stable, let alone resolved, in either dialogue. What I do think is that Socrates considered a factious marriage between them better than an outright divorce. Of course, any claim that a "philosophically informed" citizenry is necessary to sustain a radical democracy requires that one be clear about what "philosophically informed" entails. If it entails too much, if it means that citizens must "be" philosophers, and if Socrates is indeed right about the dependency of radical democracy on philosophy, then such a democracy seems utterly quixotic. Evidence that Plato may have come to this conclusion is present in the *Protagoras,* where he moves away from Socrates and democracy toward a more "professional" idea of philosophy, which attenuates its connection to political life.

---

[4] My exemplar is William Arrowsmith's translation of Aristophanes' *Clouds* (New York: New American Library, 1962).

In general, I will resist the conclusion about the incompatibility of philosophy and democracy, though I recognize its force and the danger of folding one into the other, as well as the dim prospects for radical democracy in a bureaucratized state that is both too large to be of human scale and too small for the globalized economy with which it must deal. I also acknowledge the element of self-aggrandizement in any argument by an "intellectual" about the importance of intellect for politics. Indeed, I will read the *Clouds* as parodying precisely such claims.

This book is also intended to participate in the debate over educational reform and make an intervention in what is known as "the culture wars." What I argue in chapter one, and illustrate in subsequent chapters, is that recourse to Athenian democracy, Socrates, and classical drama and philosophy pushes us to ask different questions, deepen the ones we do ask, and reminds us that our practices are answers to questions we no longer remember to be such. More specifically, such recourse refocuses current controversies by foregrounding the question of the political education of democratic citizens.

In regard to the culture wars, I argue that conservative canonists are largely mistaken in regarding Plato (let alone Greek drama and Socrates) as weapons in their arsenal against their multiculturalist critics and that their didactic co-optation of those texts saps them of their generative capacity to educate the young. Indeed, I will suggest the existence of an unholy alliance between those conservatives who rely on what I regard as one-dimensional readings of classical texts to justify the cultural power they deny having, and those of their multi-culturalist critics, who accept their readings and reject those texts based on them. But I also want to indicate why and how Plato and Socrates can be valuable partners for those challenging the dominant voices in our culture, even when those voices "speak Greek." It is not just that there is a deeply radical impulse in Socratic and Platonic political philosophy, but that multiculturalists can, and perhaps should, take at least some of their inspiration from the tradition they (rightly) contest, as Socrates did in regard to Athens. In this sense Socrates' accusers may be correct in saying that he "corrupts" the youth, as conservatives may be in their accusations against multiculturalists. Of course, in both cases there are at least two questions: is Socrates and are multiculturalists corrupting youth or responding to developments and forces that have developed largely independent of them; and, more important, what sort of narrative constitutes the terms in which one can define corruption?

I have few illusions about how far my strategy can go in dissipating the polemical posturing of the culture wars. Insofar as the contest is over turf and power and based on resentment (as is the *agōn* between New and Old Education in the *Clouds*), invoking canonical texts in the way I do will seem blasphemy to some and refurbishing the master's tools to others. Still, there may be some use in blurring the battle lines and calling for a truce, if only because commercial and technological imperatives may, if the war continues, relegate both sides to an academic backwater toward which they are already moving.

II

Most of these chapters began as talks presented at various colleges and universities that were kind enough to invite me to lecture. To say I have benefited from the response of these various audiences and the smaller conversations that followed is an understatement. With remarkably few exceptions, I was asked questions that needed to be asked, challenged in ways that made me think harder and purge at least some of my rhetorical excess, and directed to literatures or made aware of sensibilities about which I was largely ignorant.

I have been blessed with patient, responsive, erudite, and deeply thoughtful friends. Though I mostly work alone, rarely imposing my writing on others, virtually every idea in this book has been vetted by them. There are friends of long standing such as Stephen Salkever, Tracy Strong, Wendy Brown, Laura Slatkin, Terry Ball, Arlene Saxonhouse, Hanna Pitkin, John Schaar, Sheldon Wolin, and Ann and Warren Lane with whom I have been talking about politics, classical texts, teaching, and political theory for many years, and newer friends like Josh Ober, Jeff Isaac, Bill Connolly, Terrell Carver, Gillian Robinson, Jane Bennett, Gary Shiffman, and George Kateb, all of whom have discussed some of the ideas in this book with me. Don Moon and George Shulman are marvelous interlocutors on all human subjects. Though we often disagree, their ability and willingness to see the possibilities of my ideas before I do, their constant encouragement and probing queries, are among the treasured gifts friendship brings. Then there are my former students, now friends, who will no doubt recognize some of their own ideas unacknowledged for which I apologize: John Wallach, Paige Baty, Mark Reinhardt, Chris Rocco, Val Hartouni, Shane Phalen, Melissa Mathes, Gabe Brahm, Michael Janover, Sara Monoson, Melissa Orlie, Steve Rugare, Billy Robinson, Kent Dannehl, and Mark Nechodom. I know this is an obnoxiously long list of people but I thought it best to spread the blame.

I also want to thank Princeton University for awarding me a Laurence S. Rockefeller Visiting Fellowship at the University Center for Human Values. The warmth and generosity of the center's director Amy Gutmann and what I came to call "my fellow fellows" was exceptional, given my constant complaints about analytic philosophy, the deontological-consequentialist debate, liberal hegemony, the food, weather, and anything else that came to the mind of this nearly-dead white male. One of the pleasures of being at the center was a chance to renew my friendship with Alan Ryan and deepen one with George Kateb. I am not sure how, given our very diverse backgrounds, Alan and I came to complete each other's jokes, but we do and at least *we* think we're funny. Some of my most treasured moments at Princeton were arguing with George Kateb. We disagree about Emerson, politics, individualism, and liberal democracy, and no one can say "The Political" with such scorn. But I have gotten much from our conversations, though he thinks they are the wrong things.

Penultimately my year at Princeton coincided with the third year of my daughter Roxanne's matriculation there as a graduate student in political philosophy and Islamic Studies. Our frequent walks were often about our mutual work and I have benefited considerably from the clarity of her intelligence and her inquisitiveness.

Finally, I wish to thank the anonymous readers at Princeton and Cornell University Presses for a number of astute criticisms and valiant attempts to keep me on something like the straight and narrow.

III

The chapters that follow are something more than separate essays and something less than the chapters of a book. They develop a point of view cumulatively rather than an argument sequentially. Each takes up an issue broached in chapter one and elaborated both politically and theoretically in Plato's *Apology of Socrates,* which I consider in chapter two. All address either directly or indirectly the relationship among democratic politics, political theory, and political education. Each moves between ancient and modern preoccupations or texts, simultaneously drawing parallels and providing contrasts between the crisis of Athenian civic identity and our own.

Though three chapters have appeared other places, none has simply been reprinted. In one case, that of chapter three on the "Battle of Salamis," I have updated some of the references and elaborated or clarified several points. In the case of chapters five and eight, I have rewritten the beginning and end, changed some of the argument, and inserted cross-references to make this more of a book.

Chapter three, "The Battle of Salamis and the Origins of Political Theory," appeared in *Political Theory* 14, no. 3 (August 1986): 359–90, published by Sage Publications. Chapter five, "When There Are Gray Skies: Aristophanes' *Clouds* and the Political Education of Democratic Citizens," first appeared in the *South Atlantic Quarterly* 95 (Fall 1996): 881–918, published by Duke University Press. Chapter eight, "The *Gorgias,* Socratic Dialectic, and the Education of Democratic Citizens," appeared in Josiah Ober and Charles Hedrick (eds.), *Demokratia: A Conversation on Democracy, Ancient and Modern* (Princeton University Press, 1996), pp. 327–59. I want to thank each for permission to reprint revised versions of these essays.

I would be terribly remiss if I did not thank the staff at the Word Processing Center, particularly Cheryl Van De Veer and Zoe Sodja. Their ability to decipher what passes for typing with my numerous crossing-outs, scribbled inserts, and enough arrows for an archery camp, certainly qualifies them for counterintelligence work. I am grateful for their patience and for their intelligence.

Corrupting Youth

Imploding the Canon: The Reform of
Education and the War over Culture

I

The issue of corrupting youth is part of the current debate over the nature and purpose of public education. At stake in that debate is the definition of a national identity and the possibilities of American democracy. What is different, even distinctive to the current debate dubbed the "Culture Wars" by conservative public intellectuals, is the apocalyptic rhetoric of Armageddon and battle. It is as if, having lived so long and found such moral comfort in the bipolarity of the cold war, we could not do without it, even if that meant shifting the battle lines from the international to the national arena, as of course it had partly been in the McCarthy era.[1]

The new war is being fought over many issues and on many fronts: over affirmative action, prayer in the schools, and immigration policy; over the relationship between race and IQ, textbooks and standardized tests; over levels of public support for public education and multicultural curriculum. The battles go on in local school boards, in Congress and the Supreme Court, by those who have removed their children from public schools, those who would like to but cannot, and those who remain committed either by default or in principle to public schooling. Whatever their respective politics and diagnoses of our educational ills, almost all participants agree that the public school system as now conceived and functioning is failing, whether because of the skills and values it has failed to inculcate or the ones it has, because it has been asked to do too much or cannot do even the rudiments. Either in despair or with relief people are coming to regard schools as places of discipline and confinement.[2]

Perhaps the most obvious manifestation of the disaffection with the public school system as now constituted is the proposal for a voucher system. The one rejected by California voters in 1993 (and which has reappeared in modified form in 1996) would have given each child a $2,600 voucher from the state public

---

[1] McCarthyism itself has become a contested mythology. Conservatives either say it wasn't so bad or that it was bad but not as bad as the McCarthyism of the left as represented by political correctness.

[2] The ideal citizen is literate, drug free, and disciplined in schools that emphasize the basics and authority. (See the discussion of this in David M. Steiner, *Rethinking Democratic Education: The Politics of Reform* [Baltimore: Johns Hopkins University Press, 1994], chap. 1) In *The Bell Curve: Intelligence and Class Structure in American Life* (New York: Free Press, 1994), Richard J. Herrnstein and Charles Murray equate citizenship with civility by which they mean "deference *or* allegiance to the social order befitting a citizen" (p. 254, emphasis supplied). Examples of civility vary from mowing the lawn and personal hygiene to generally being neighborly and law abiding. They too invoke Greek political thought (especially that of Aristotle). See their chaps. 12 and 22.

education budget toward tuition at participating private and religious schools with at least twenty-five students. Proponents argued that only drastic action could reverse a decade or more of miserable failure by the public school bureaucracy, which seemed capable of turning out drug-ridden, violent, promiscuous youth without any respect for authority or America.

With typical hyperbole William Buckley likened the disease infecting our educational system to AIDS. Just as people refuse to accept the cure of a blanket prohibition against certain kinds of sex and dirty needle use to control that horrifying disease, so people refuse to accept the voucher system.[3] The "cure" for an "ungovernable" educational system ruled by heavy-handed bureaucracies mired in regulations that discourage change and risk, buffeted about by politics and dominated by special interests, is privatization, the market, and an entrepreneurial government.[4] Unrestricted school choice would force fundamental restructuring of a school system that is "monopolistic, archaic, inefficient, prevents competition and is bereft of incentive for improvement" because it would restore performance and accountability. Those schools that were insufficiently entrepreneurial, that is, "flexible, adaptive and innovative,"[5] schools that were not meeting the needs of their students, were not delivering a quality educational "product," and did not "offer the best deal" and the highest "return on investments"[6] would simply lose students to the competition and "go out of business."[6] The campaign manager for the California voucher proposition compared the situation of public schools to the condition of the U.S. Postal Service. Before competition from Federal Express there was no next-day delivery service. The same for schools.

There is much that could be said about voucher plans in practice (as they are in Minnesota and Milwaukee) and as proposed, as in California.[7] One could, for instance, provide some historical perspective insofar as the present debate echoes that in the late nineteenth century when the movement to make education more efficient and businesslike culminated in Taylorism.[8] Then too the impetus for reform was the influx of immigrants and fear of multiculturalism. Scientists and social scientists, together with the "culture of professionalism"[9] they imitated

[3] William Buckley in the *National Review* 26 (March 18, 1988): 65.

[4] See David Osborne, "Government That Means Business," *New York Times Sunday Magazine* (March 1, 1992): 20; and John E. Chubb and Terry M. Moe, *Politics, Markets and America's Schools* (Washington, D.C.: Brookings Institution, 1990), and David Kearns and Denis Doyle, *Winning the Brain Drain* (San Francisco: Institute for Contemporary Studies, 1988), who argue for business aggressively setting the new educational agenda so that reform can be driven by competition and "market discipline."

[5] See Laura A. Locke, "The Issue of 'Choice': A Voucher Initiative Goes to the Voters," *California Journal* 24, no. 6 (June 1993): 13–15.

[6] See John Hood, "What's Wrong with Head Start?," *Wall Street Journal* (Feb. 19, 1993): A14.

[7] See the succinct analysis in "Markets Can't Fix Schools' Problems," in a "Counterpoint" column by Robert H. Carr in the *Wall Street Journal* (Thursday, May 2, 1991): A17.

[8] See Raymond Callahan, *Education and the Cult of Efficiency* (Chicago: University of Chicago Press, 1962).

[9] Burton Bledstein, *The Culture of Professionalism, The Middle Class and the Development of Higher Education in America* (New York: Norton, 1978).

and certified, presented themselves as providing a nonpartisan standard for public behavior and citizen "training" that would "make" foreigners over into Americans, or at least keep them from polluting America.

One could also point to evidence that parents do not seem particularly concerned with the academic content of their children's education and to the likelihood that as economically poor students or those with average academic ability come to be "at the mercy of schools of last resort" there will be a further inscription of class divisions and radical inequalities of power, all sanctified by the "natural" workings of the market and in the name of freedom.[10]

Or, finally, one could point out the curious symmetry between the probable consequences of the voucher system and identity politics, even though many of the supporters of the voucher system are implacably hostile to multiculturalism on the grounds that it fragments American society. If one is worried about the "balkanization" of American culture, then the voucher system is part of the disease, not the cure. To the extent that the force of the market rationalizes parental distrust of "the other," that is, of different races, ethnicities, classes, or religions, we can look forward to a resegregation of American society that will make identity politics look like nationalism.

Given the concerns of this book, perhaps the most striking aspect of the voucher debate is the questions and issues that are not asked or raised, namely those having to do with the civic function of education. To blame Reagan (and perhaps Bush) for showing contempt for democracy by ridiculing politics as they practiced it, corrupting public discourse, assimilating politics to the market, fostering privatization of public tasks, and refusing to provide funds to reform the conditions under which schools are now forced to operate is too easy. It ignores the fact that not all supporters of the voucher system are laissez-faire conservatives and it misses what may be the most disconcerting aspect of the debate as a whole: that *critics* of the voucher initiatives do little more than gesture in the direction of the antidemocratic consequences of the system. Somehow questions about the role of public schooling in the educating of democratic citizens have become marginalized.

A similar conclusion emerges from the polemics between multiculturalists and canonists. Here again the issue of politically educating democratic citizens is largely peripheral, buried under an avalanche of charges by conservatives that multiculturalists and their allies are politicizing higher education and countercharges by the latter that they are merely responding to a situation that is already politicized.[11]

---

[10] Steiner, *Rethinking Democratic Education,* p. 8.

[11] Both sides feel themselves besieged because their points of reference are different. Conservative canonists look at elite universities and see political correctness silencing their friends. Multiculturalists and their allies look at the Republican-dominated polity (to which Clinton has adapted) and feel themselves surrounded by an aggressively self-righteous moralism. Insofar as Patrick Buchanan's speech at the 1992 Republican Convention signaled the closing down of public discourse, the university remained one of the few venues for political views that were no longer legitimately presented elsewhere. David Bromwich discusses what happens in the academy when political discourse im-

In the remainder of this chapter I want to cast the two debates in a way that focuses on the issue of political education, connect the rhetoric of reform with that of the culture wars, implode the canon in ways that skew the usual battle lines, and make a distinction between a political and a politicized education that might, at the very least, give depth to what often degenerates into name-calling. My point of reference in this endeavor is democratic Athens and Socrates.

II

"Our nation is at risk" begins the report that set the tone and terms for the educational reform debate of the past decade.[12] The report, addressed to Secretary of Education Bell and "to the American people" by the Reagan-appointed National Commission on Excellence in Education chaired by David P. Gardner, then president-elect of the University of California, was anointed by the *New York Times* as a founding document, analogous in its "singular economy of language and thought" to the Constitution itself. The *Times* called the report "one of the most significant documents in the history of American public education" and saw it as "the most visible symbol of the need to improve primary and high schools since the Russians put Sputnik into space."[13]

Our nation was at risk because we were losing our once "unchallenged preeminence in commerce, industry, science and technological innovation." This was due to a "rising tide of mediocrity"[14] in our schools that was corroding the educational foundations of our society, threatening our "prosperity, security and civility" and so "our very future as a nation and a people." If a foreign power attempted to impose on America the mediocre educational performance that exists today, we might have viewed it as an act of war. As it stands, we have allowed this to happen to ourselves and so have, in effect, "been committing an act of

---

plodes. See his *Politics by Other Means: Higher Education and Group Thinking* (New Haven: Yale University Press, 1992).

[12] David P. Gardner, *National Commission on Excellence in Education* (Washington, D.C.: U.S. Department of Education, 1983). The Gardner Report was the impetus for over a hundred commissions established to work on school reform. For a discussion of these commissions, see Ira Shor, *Culture Wars* (Chicago: University of Chicago Press, 1992), chap. 4.

[13] *New York Times* (April 27, 1988): B10. According to the *Times,* the government sold or gave away 220,000 copies and 5 to 6 million more were distributed through newspapers and periodicals. President Bush was not so congratulatory when, in April 1991, he declared that "Eight years after the National Commission on Excellence in Education declared us a 'nation at risk' we haven't turned things around in education. Almost all our education trends are flat." Echoing the language of the report, he complained that we were still "idling our engines" and went on to blame poor education and undereducated workers for our economic woes. On the impact of the report see Ernest Boyer, "Reflections on the Great Debate of 1983," in *Phi Delta Kappan* 65, no. 8 (April 1984): 525–30, and "A Nation Still at Risk," *Newsweek* (April 19, 1993): 46–49.

[14] Bromwich points out the irony of a report lamenting intellectual mediocrity being presented to a president "whose every unprompted utterance was a testimony to the amiability of thoughtlessness, and who, at the end of two terms characterized by immense popularity and an abuse of constitutional power, narrowly averted impeachment by a profession of total incompetence and memory loss" (*Politics by Other Means,* p. 224).

unthinking, unilateral educational disarmament," thereby squandering all the achievements in the wake of the "Sputnik challenge."

Instead of moving forward, we have been standing still and "History is not kind to idlers" in the competition for "international standing and markets" in products and ideas. Thus the risk is not only that the Japanese make more efficient automobiles, that the South Koreans built the world's most efficient steel mill, or that American machine tools are being displaced by German products, but that these developments "signify a redistribution of trained capability through the globe. Knowledge, learning, information and skilled intelligence are the new raw materials in international commerce" and so for us even to keep our "slim" competitive edge in world markets requires that "we dedicate ourselves to the reform of our educational system for the benefit of all." Learning is "the indispensable investment required for success in the 'information age' we are entering" (p. 7).

But the report is concerned with more than matters of commerce and industry. It worries about "the intellectual, moral and spiritual strengths of our people which knit together the very fabric of our society," about individuals who, lacking appropriate kinds of skill and literacy, will be effectively disenfranchised from participating "in our national life," and about an equivocal commitment not only to excellence but to equal educational opportunity as well (pp. 7–8). What can the dissipation of a shared national vision portend for an educational system that has been a part of that vision and the means for realizing it? Unless "we" are willing to reaffirm our commitment to educational excellence, our ideals will be transformed: individual freedom will become self-indulgence or egotism, pluralism will become indifference, and equality will mean mediocrity. Especially American education must be committed both to unity and diversity. Without shared values, sentiments, and experience, cultural and individual differences will cease to be disagreements about what is shared. When and if that happens, we will simply be unable to talk to each other.

The ideal they admire was enunciated by Thomas Jefferson: "I know of no safe repository of the ultimate powers of the society but the people themselves; and if we think them not enlightened enough to exercise their control with a wholesome discretion, the remedy is not to take it from them but to inform their discretion."[15] And the commission is clear that this means *all* the people. "We do not believe that a public commitment to excellence and educational reform must be made at the expense of a strong public commitment to the equitable treatment of our diverse population." They are committed to the twin goals of equality and quality "in principle and in practice." Anything less would deny young people their chance to learn and live "according to their aspirations and abilities" and lead "either to an accommodation to mediocrity or the creation of an undemocratic elitism" (p. 13).

To remedy and reverse this educational decline and to implement Jefferson's

---

[15] Letter to William Charles Jarvis, September 28, 1820, in Paul Ford, ed., *The Collected Works of Thomas Jefferson* (New York: Putnam, 1905), 12:1630.

vision, they propose a "Learning Society" where all would have a chance for an education that enhanced career goals as it improved the overall quality of life. In this society education would go beyond traditional institutional sites and designated times. Diplomas and universities would be the beginning, not the end of learning, which would go on in homes and workplaces, in libraries and museums, in "every place where the individual can develop and mature in work and life" (p. 14).

These are noble sentiments. Given the president to whom they were addressed and the general political climate, they are courageous ones as well. Thus the report's reliance on military and economic language may be part of a strategy aimed at achieving humane ends in an inhumane time, when the president of the nation was himself a man of limited education. If defense receives attention and funding, then it is a good idea to make education part of the defense effort. If what matters most is winning the cold war, then make education a weapon in it. If economic growth, reindustrialization, and beating the Japanese are endorsed by the entire political spectrum, then remind everyone how essential education is to those aims. If businessmen are the sages of the time, then it is sagacious to present schools as a business or as preparing people for it. To be heard by the powerful, one must speak their language and to their concerns.

That such strategic considerations may have been present is indicated by what the report did not say, but which was said by virtually everyone else. The report does not blame teachers for the educational decline and, in fact, recognized the need to make teaching a more rewarding and respected profession. Nor does it conclude that better management and more "efficient productivity" in the schools can solve the crisis. Still more impressively, it avoids blaming the decline of the economy on the failures of our educational system as do other reports[16] and it recognizes the fact that students are part of a larger culture which shapes what schools are asked to do and their capacity to do it.[17] And while the report does not endorse a Freirean project of literacy as a liberatory process, it understands literacy in a less positivistic way than, say, E. D. Hirsch does. Finally, it does not blame everything wrong with American education on 1960s radicals, Marxists, and feminists, as do later litanies of lament.

But there is a danger in speaking the language of power to get the ear of the powerful.[18] Cooperation can slide into co-optation, and respectability is too often purchased at the price of principle. Then diagnosticians may become part of the

---

[16] In 1983, *The Business–Higher Education Forum Report* (Washington, D.C.: American Council on Education, 1983) argued that the decline of schools was the major cause of the decline of American industry. As Ira Shor suggests, this explanation ignores the flight of capital, multinational corporations evacuating the unionized northeast for cheap labor, the huge military budget, and low level of social investment in roads, bridges, transport, housing, and services, and the refusal of industries to modernize. (See *Culture Wars,* pp. 122–30.)

[17] As Alan Ryan has noted, even the failures of the American educational system imply ambitions that few other societies have ever entertained *(New York Review of Books* [February 11, 1993]: 13). Indeed such utopian ambitions cannot help but lead to disappointment and disillusion.

[18] Perhaps the most subtle discussion of the issue can be found in Thomas More's *Utopia.*

disease, their reports part of the risk rather than an adequate response to it. Something like that happens with the Gardner Report.

The report speaks in two voices: one material, technological, military, and quantitative; the other cultural, spiritual, and political, which it reconciles abstractly without fully recognizing the tensions between them. And the voices are not equal. For all its virtues, the Gardner Commission's language is dominated by metaphors drawn from battle and commerce, cold war ideology, and the technological ethic of efficiency. Thus it is not surprising that the report conceives of education in instrumental terms. In contrast, the democratic sentiments tend to become somewhat perfunctory and largely decorative.

If it is the military, business, and technological voice that defines why our nation is at risk, then what sort of vision of education becomes appropriate? If we are losing the war for economic supremacy because we have become a nation of idlers, and if we are engaging in "unilateral educational disarmament" by squandering the gains in student achievement made in the wake of the Sputnik challenge when all efforts were concentrated on science and technology with military potential, then the solution is clear. We must rearm[19] ourselves by reviving the coordination of science, engineers, government, and private enterprise that marked the post-Sputnik era. National security requires nothing less. If our survival is at stake, then all academic pursuits must be judged by their contribution to that end. If we do not speed up our educational productivity in the same way that we need to speed up our industrial productivity, we will be left behind by the Japanese, pushed aside by the Germans, and left defenseless by the Russians. If education is "one of the chief engines of society's material well-being" (p. 17), we need to build bigger, more efficient engines to keep or improve our slim competitive edge in world markets.[20]

In these terms the primary role of the humanities (outside of their decorative function) is to help in those adaptations necessary to create a more efficient fighting force to combat the decline in education and of America in the world. This is most evident when the report seems to be endorsing the opposite sentiment.

The report quotes "some" people as concerned that an overemphasis on technical and occupational skills as the aim of education will leave little time "for studying the arts and humanities that so enrich daily life, help maintain civility and develop a sense of community." These same people believe that the "humanities must be harnessed to science and technology if the latter are to remain creative and humane, just as the humanities need to be informed by science and technology if they are to remain relevant to the human condition" (pp. 10–11). This formulation contains an instructive asymmetry. It suggests not an equality

---

[19] Since the language of war had been used before in the "War on Poverty," the commission was able to use a rhetoric recognizable by liberals and conservatives alike.

[20] Whether they were aware of it or not, the image of a machine echoes Benjamin Rush who argued for a national university, which would be an efficient machine for "melting" the "youth of all the states" into a unity (quoted in Carl F. Kaestle, *Pillars of the Republic: Common Schools and American Society, 1780–1860* [New York: Hill and Wang, 1983]).

between the humanities and science/technology, but a hierarchy in which the purposes of the former serve those of the latter. In these terms and given the military metaphors, "civility" can only mean politeness and good form rather than an active, informed, and critical citizenry. And a sense of community is unlikely to be established by humanists or in humanistic terms, if the humanities and "softer" social sciences exist primarily to serve technological, commercial, and scientific imperatives. Power within the academy will follow those imperatives and devolve to those disciplines and scholars who contribute most to the educational war effort, and be taken from those who criticize or repudiate it.[21]

The commercial/technological/business emphasis in the Gardner Commission Report helped legitimate more aggressive claims by business to set the educational agenda of the 1980s. The Hunt Report, *Action for Excellence,*[22] argued that "businessmen, in their role as employers, should be much more deeply involved in the process of setting goals for education in America, and in helping our schools realize those goals." Examples of this were the $22 million grant Monsanto Corporation gave Washington University Medical School to fund research leading to marketable biomedical discoveries, a faculty member turning over patent rights of an invention to Allied Chemicals for $2.5 million following which the corporation bought two million dollars of stock in the firm founded by the professor,[23] and the Whittle Corporation's commercials for Burger King and Snickers on Channel One shown to eight million students daily, as part of what has been admiringly termed "the commercial penetration of a student market worth 80 billion dollars annually."[24] And, finally, there is the New American

---

[21] In *The Degradation of Academic Dogma: The University in America, 1945–1970* (New York: Basic Books, 1971), Robert Nisbet argued that since World War II American universities were dominated by roles which destroyed the idea of a community of scholars "founded upon the rock of dispassionate reason." By the late 1940s and early 1950s universities were expected to play the role of "higher capitalist, chief of research establishment, super-humanitarian, benign therapist, adjunct government, and loyal revolutionary opposition" (p. 8).

[22] *Action for Excellence: A Comprehensive Plan to Improve Our Nation's Schools,* Task Force on Education for Economic Growth, Education Commission of the States, Washington, D.C., 1983. Despite the collapse of the nation's largest experiment in private management of public schools (in Hartford at the beginning of 1996), public education is becoming, in the words of the *New York Times,* "an enticing market for private businesses." The CEO of Eduventures regards public schools as "a very big industry with enormous potential for growth." (See Peter Applerome, "Lure of Education Market Remains Strong for Business," *New York Times* [January 31, 1996]: 1.) In a later essay in the *Times* (March 24, 1996): sec. 4, p. 4, Applerome reports that the Second National Education Summit included more chief executives than educators, which no doubt encouraged Colorado's Governor Roy Romer to speak of students as products and corporations as customers who should have something to say about the sort of products graduates should be.

[23] See the discussion in Benjamin Barber, *An Aristocracy of Everyone: The Politics of Education and the Future of America* (New York: Ballantine Books, 1992), pp. 198–206.

[24] When the Whittle Corporation enters the schools, Jonathan Kozol argues, "it is selling something more important than the brand names of its products. It sells a way of looking at the world and at oneself. It sells predictability instead of critical capacities. It sells a circumscribed job-specific utility" and develops a mind to be receptive to a market mentality. (See his "Whittle and the Privateers," *Nation* 255 [September 21, 1992]: 272.)

Schools Development Corporation's plans to replace teachers with Electronic Teaching Centers.[25]

Given all this, what can one say about the call for "higher academic standards"? No one advocates lowering standards. The issue is what vision of the schooling and education animates the demand? Whose standards for whom, for what ends? How diverse and qualitative will the criteria be by which "success" is measured? Quantitative emphasis on attendance, dropout rates, and test scores, and prescriptions for longer school hours, more days in school, and more uniform national standards of measurement is not promising.

Much of the Gardner Report's sense of urgency and rhetorical power depended on the existence of the cold war. The reference to Sputnik, allusions to unnamed enemies (who could they be?), and the overall military language in a period of bellicose international posturing linked the call for educational excellence to national security imperatives. But now that the cold war is over, those imperatives are no longer so imperative. Neither is an educational agenda justified in its name.

The ending of the cold war not only removed an important rationale for educational reform, it also exacerbated the educational crisis by removing an admittedly pallid and negative but still useful construction of national identity. We were not the Soviet Union, not tyrannical, not godless, and not undemocratic and could, whatever else was wrong with us, take common comfort from those facts. But if, as Hannah Arendt argues, national identity and education are inextricably mixed here as nowhere else in the world,[26] then the crisis in education is a crisis of national identity and the "problematizing" of such identity intensifies the crisis, which is one reason why already present conflicts, such as those over multiculturalism, the canon, and the politicization of the university, have become so polemical and so public.

If Arendt is right in arguing that the present educational crisis affords an opportunity to see through what have become inadequate answers to questions we have forgotten were ones, then we have a chance to rethink what is involved in the education of democratic citizens. This rethinking might begin with the Jeffersonian sentiments quoted but then marginalized by the Gardner Commission. If the people possess the animating and limiting power in our nation, how can we inform their discretion without the informers assuming that power for themselves? If we are responsible for educating the people, who is the "we" and by what authority is the responsibility "ours"? Are there forms of political education that honor both the authority implied by education and the political equality demanded of a vigorous democracy? If public education is "the great means of forming an American identity," then these questions about political education are also questions about American self-fashioning in the late twentieth century.

---

[25] If Socrates is right in supposing that we teach our character as much as a subject matter, what is one to make of replacing teachers with electronic teaching centers?

[26] Hannah Arendt, "The Crisis in Education," in *Between Past and Future: Eight Exercises in Political Thought* (New York: Penguin, 1968), pp. 173–96.

III

The Gardner Commission speaks about "our" common literary heritage, about "our" nation at risk and about "we" Americans. The presumption is that all benefit from an inheritance that belongs to us all, perhaps even that we all have somehow contributed to it and are responsible for it. It also presumes that we are nearly equal members of the nation that is at risk such that we all have roughly equal amounts to lose if it is unable to meet the challenges detailed by the commission. Finally, it assumes that the story of our heritage is the same for us all and that it is one story: of progress, enlightenment and reason, of increasing liberty, equality, and abundance, of the triumph of civilization and culture over primitivism and barbarism. But this story is now vigorously contested, characterized, and chastised as a "functionalizing history," which obscures the deformations within the form, the violent suppressions erased by the victors, and the barbarism done in the name of civilization. Contesting the story means challenging groups whose power is legitimated by it and the vision of education they endorse. The counternarrative reminds us of slavery and genocide, of Chinese laborers and battered women, of silent presences and subjugated knowledges. If "we" are to celebrate "our" literary heritage and the achievements of Western culture by pointing to the French and American revolutions, to the Parthenon and King Lear, to democracy and philosophy, we cannot point past Auschwitz, the Gulag, and the Inquisition.

The purported danger of these counternarratives and the identity politics they legitimate or represent is the encouragement of a fragmentation that threatens paralysis and civil war. "If we repudiate the quite marvelous inheritance that history bestows upon us," Arthur Schlesinger Jr. warns, "we invite the fragmentation of the national community into a quarrelsome spatter of enclaves, ghettoes and tribes." The "cult of ethnicity" is exaggerating our differences and intensifying racial and national antagonisms.[27] James Atlas regards multiculturalism as "a harbinger of anarchy."[28]

At stake is the existence of the Union. But this civil war is not between North and South, but between the whole and its parts, between our identities as citizens and our particular ethnic, racial, and sexual identities. If we permit the social fabric to unravel, as it will if our particularities dominate our politics, we will, so these critics aver, become Eastern Europe, thus reversing the self-defined historical trajectory of American exceptionalism. Tom Paine thought that we "had it in our power to begin the world all over again"; Noah Webster, that for America to "adopt the maxims of the Old World would be to stamp the wrinkles of old age

---

[27] Arthur Schlesinger Jr., *The Disuniting of America: Reflections on a Multicultural Society* (New York: Whittle Communications, 1991), pp. 137–38.

[28] James Atlas, *The Battle of the Books: The Curriculum Debate in America* (New York: Norton, 1992), p. 135.

upon the bloom of youth, and to plant the seed of decay in a vigorous constitution."[29]

This "problematizing" of the "we" has become one battle in the culture wars. While the Gardner Commission had relied on military analogies and on a cold war mentality to provide urgency to its analyses and legitimacy for its prescriptions, much of this reliance was rhetorical and strategic. But the language of war in the debate over the canon is something else and something more. The "new barbarians," we are told by Dinesh D'Souza, "have captured the humanities, law and social science departments" of many of our universities. The "unholy alliance" of "multiculturalists, feminists, radicals, poststructuralists, new historians and other varieties of leftism" have breached the gates and stand triumphant in the citadel.[30] "The Barbarians are in our midst," Alan Kors warns. "We must fight them a good long time. Show them you are not afraid; they crumble."[31] "Resistance on campus," D'Souza warns, "is outgunned and sorely needs outside reinforcement."[32] William Bennett sees great books as part of the "arsenal of the West";[33] George Will calls Lynne Cheney, past director of the National Endowment for the Humanities, the "secretary of domestic defense."[34] "The foreign adversaries her husband Dick must keep at bay," Will assures us, "are less dangerous, in the long run, than domestic forces with which she must deal." Kors exhorted those of his colleagues committed to reason and civilization to "become the monasteries of the new Dark Ages, preserving what is worth preserving amid the barbarian ravages of the countryside and the towns of academe."[35] Civilization itself is at stake. If we let the domestic barbarians win and permit the destruction of Western values such as the family, reason, morality, and discipline, we will be unable to confront foreign barbarians, which will leave us, William Lind argues, besieged by Islam now as the Viennese were by the Turks in 1683.[36]

---

[29] Quoted by Kaestle in *Pillars of the Republic,* p. 6.

[30] Denesh D'Souza, "The Visigoths in Tweed," in Patricia Aufderheide, ed. and introd., *Beyond PC: Towards a Politics of Understanding* (St. Paul: Gray Wolf Press, 1992), p. 11.

[31] Quoted by Joseph Berger in "Scholars Attack Campus 'Radicals,'" *New York Times* (November 13, 1988): A22. As Berger notes Kors's remarks and others like them sounded more like calls to battle than the measured evaluations of a scholar, and the applause he received was more typical of a political rally than of an academic conference.

[32] D'Souza, "Visigoths," p. 22.

[33] See William J. Bennett, "Education for Democracy," in *Our Children and Our Country: Improving America's Schools and Affirming the Common Culture* (New York: Simon and Schuster, 1989).

[34] In his review of John Carey's *The Intellectuals and the Masses,* Ian Hamilton discusses how the English cultural elites, resentful that the new literacy was controlled not by them but by new vehicles of popular entertainment which they saw as degrading the human spirit, "affected disdain for the mob and evoked apocalyptic visions of the imminent deluge of barbarism." By castigating the "malodorous rabble" unappreciative of their leadership, they "recaptured a notion of their own centrality. They would become warriors on behalf of an imperiled life of the imagination" (*London Review of Books* [July 23, 1992]: 14).

[35] Quoted by Jacob Weisberg, "NAS—Who Are These Guys Anyway?," in Aufderheide, *Beyond PC,* p. 85.

[36] William Lind, "Defending Western Culture," *Foreign Policy,* no. 84 (Fall 1991): 40–50. Lind

What is so astonishing as well as suspect about all this is how decisions about (usually first-year) curriculum became the subject of heated public debate. Why did decisions that are usually the issue of desultory compromises reached in the relative anonymity of faculty committee meetings suddenly become the center of such apocalyptic posturing, wild historical analogies, and extravagant prophecies?[37] Such excess invites a symptomatic as well as a substantive reading of the multiculturalism-canon debate.

For all their complaints (to be considered here) that the left has politicized the university, the complaint itself is often motivated by a politics of a fairly cynical kind. From Spiro Agnew's vice-presidential candidacy and Reagan's gubernatorial campaigns in California to Dan Quayle's and Newt Gingrich's imprecations against the cultural elite, university bashing has been a politically profitable strategy. But while this strategy has been effective in gaining power over the university, it has not necessarily been effective in gaining power inside it. In these terms the conservative "attacks" on the university may be a concerted effort to achieve the kind of dominance over higher education they have achieved in other domains.

In saying this I am not dismissing "conservative" criticisms of higher education, many of which are not distinctive to conservatives, and some of which I share. There are indeed serious problems with higher education. They include faddism, presentism, impatience (which leads to the Koran being read in a week as part of a survey course), self-righteous and ignorant dismissal of texts not read or read hastily, and a failure to recognize what the critics owe to what they are criticizing. But the seriousness of these criticisms is compromised by the critics' own self-righteousness, their denial that there is any such thing as cultural power or that if there is it comes to them "naturally" as the transmitters of what is best and highest, and by defensive reiteration of what may be outworn pieties.

This said, I have no desire to perpetuate either the tone or terms of the polemic over the canon. Indeed, I want to recast the terms of the debate in ways that make room for the articulation of views that defy the labeling polarities that have too often forced people into alliances they do not want and positions they do not respect.[38] To this end I will defend the canon against some of its critics and use it

---

interprets the cold war as a civil war within the West. Its end allows a united front against external enemies. But this front requires that we vanquish the enemies within who are not communists but those intent on destroying Western culture as the basis of Western power. (For a theoretical articulation of the argument see Samuel P. Huntington, "The Clash of Civilizations?," in *The Clash of Civilizations?: A Debate: A Foreign Affairs Reader* [New York: Council on Foreign Relations, 1993], pp. 22–49.)

[37] "In this war against Western culture, the one chief object of attack within the academy is the traditional literary canon and the pedagogical values it embodies. The notion that some works are better than and more important than others, that some works exert a special claim on our attention . . . is an anathema to the forces arrayed against the traditional understanding of the humanities." Roger Kimball, *Tenured Radicals: How Politics Has Corrupted Our Higher Education* (New York: Harper and Row, 1990), p. xii.

[38] Though I use "multiculturalists" and "canonists," I do so uneasily since I know that they misdescribe, sometimes perversely so, the various points of view within what is posited as a single

against some of its defenders. I want to defend "the" canon because, from one perspective, dismissing it is too easy and American, too congenial to too many cultural prejudices. Alexis de Tocqueville argued that it was the tradition of Americans to be antitraditional, which implies that those who wish to overthrow all canons may be reenacting an American ritual even as they suppose themselves contesting American identity. And if his claim that the rejection of all authority and tradition leaves men and women isolated and powerless individualists susceptible to the quiet despotism of the administrative state and majority opinion, then we should be somewhat skeptical of arguments intended to liberate us from cultural authority and traditions, especially if the rich associational life Tocqueville thought would mitigate this susceptibility is now less strong. As this suggests, authority is not the opposite of freedom and tradition is not necessarily opposed to liberty. We need to distinguish between traditions like those analyzed by E. P. Thompson and Lawrence Goodwyn that sustain democratic practices and empower the poor and those that do not, and between canons that enhance political freedom and democratic authority and those that do not.

But I also want to implode the canon against some of its defenders since I believe that their reading of canonical texts often misses the way those texts warn us against what canonizers do to and with them. Too often "great books" are seen as texts which must be read "rightly" if "we" are to reclaim our "cultural inheritance," which, on this assumption, flows like an electrical current or is passed on like genes.[39] Those who fail to teach the right lessons or read canonical texts as

---

position. Thus multiculturalism has become an epithet and an abstraction, reified beyond the strategic purposes for which it was initially and contentiously embraced by its proponents. The term underestimates the diverse positions within particular ethnic groups (say the disagreement over "cultural skinning" among Asian Americans), blurs differences of experience, cultural position, and arguments about what multiculturalism means and what the canon should be that goes on both within the various "hyphenated" groups (Asian, African, Native, and Latino-Americans) and between them, and lumps together these groups with feminists, postmodernists and radicals who have distinct if sometimes overlapping agendas, arguments, and proposals. The problem of misdescription becomes more formidable insofar as multiculturalists insist on a multicultural way of talking and "thinking" about multiculturalism and find the sometimes smug insistence on reasoning a way of begging the question.

A similar diversity exists among canonists. Some are perfectly comfortable acknowledging the historical dimensions of canonicity and the fact that it is a form of social power. Others emphasize the transhistorical truths the canon purportedly embodies, claiming that, as the best that has been thought and written, canonical texts are the foundation of Western civilization. Here again familiar categories of left and right, liberal and conservative, democratic and elitist have been straitjackets and stereotypes. (Their inadequacy is suggested by the inclusion of Marxists and socialists as opponents of the canon despite the fact that Gramsci and Lukacs had extraordinary respect for classical education, as Irving Howe has reminded us, and that the newly renamed *Socialist Review* has recently run articles critical of political correctness and multiculturalism.) (See Irving Howe, "The Value of the Canon," *New Republic* 88, no. 7 [February 19, 1991]: 40–47.)

[39] Frederick Crews, "Whose American Renaissance," *New York Review of Books* (October 27, 1988): 68. Given this image of education Joan Wallach Scott's question (in her "The Campaign against Political Correctness: What's Really at Stake," *Change* 23, no. 6 [November–December 1991]), about whether elites really want critical thinking for the masses of students rather than a prescribed education passively received, is apt. See Bromwich's discussion of George Will's sentiments on this matter in *Politics by Other Means*, pp. 68–70.

giving contradictory lessons are relativists, inattentive readers, or perverts[40] who distort the canon and undermine the reason for having one in the first place. As I noted in the preface, at times there seems to be a peculiar alliance between canonists who insist on one true reading and multiculturalists who dislike that reading and dismiss the text because of it. Something like that is present in Carolyn Heilbrun's otherwise appropriately skeptical review of James Atlas's *Battle of the Books* when she quotes "someone" who, with only a slight exaggeration, claims that "great books courses teach young men to be warriors the first semester, priests the second."[41]

One reason canonical texts such as the Bible or Iliad are "great" is that they stimulate the kinds of moral and political controversies some canonists seek to minimize. If politicizing something (such as gender roles or racial classifications) means regarding them as "man"-made and so subject to human design rather than inscribed in nature, then the "greatness" of canonical texts and even the reason they become canonical may lie in their politicalness—in the kinds of interpretative controversies they stimulate and the conflicting view of human nature, action, or goodness they perpetuate. If true, then one cannot reduce these texts to a single meaning without destroying their capacity to provoke thought and stay alive, still less control their meaning for various audiences. Indeed many of the controversies prominent in the canon debate may be already inscribed in the plots, themes, arguments, and dramatic settings of the texts being celebrated or criticized.[42] That means two things: that conservative canonists who lament the politicizing of higher education ignore the way the texts they venerate create an educational atmosphere they deplore; and that radical anticanonists may not recognize the degree to which the texts they excoriate are as much allies as antagonists in their fight against the master canon or the democratization of cultural authority.

IV

Although there are plenty of antecedents and previous examples of culture wars in American history, perhaps the first "salvo" in the present one was Bennett's *To Reclaim a Legacy: A Report on the Humanities in Higher Education,* published in 1984 when he was director of the National Endowment for the Humanities.[43]

---

[40] Gerald Graff in *Beyond the Culture Wars* tells the story of how Eve Sidgwick's not yet written conference paper on "Jane Austen and the Masturbating Girl" was criticized by Roger Kimball in the *New Criterion.* The critique was picked up by the popular press and became a cause célèbre before it existed (see pp. 156–57).

[41] In the *New York Times* (December 25, 1992): B3.

[42] See Kenneth R. Johnston, "The NEH and the Battle of the Books," *Raritan* 12, no. 2 (Fall 1992): 118–32.

[43] In *To Reclaim a Legacy: A Report on the Humanities in Higher Education* (Washington, D.C.: National Endowment for the Humanities, 1984), p. 32. (Hereafter, page references will be given in text.) It is astonishing how many of the phrases used in the Report are repeated verbatim in the

Bennett presented his report as complementary to that of the Gardner Commission. What they did for elementary and secondary education he would do for higher education (particularly the humanities): bring about "a number of long-overdue changes" and put "higher education in the public eye" (p. ii). As he described it, the fundamental task was to provide (or rather restore) a "vision and a philosophy of education" that could be a guide and standard for changes that would respect the specific missions of different kinds of educational institutions. Fortunately the roots, substance, and inspiration for that vision were located in the same place: in the words of Walter Lippman that prefaces the report, "the central, continuous and perennial culture of the Western world." Unfortunately almost no students have "even the most rudimentary knowledge about the history, literature, art, and philosophical foundations of their nation and their civilization." The result is intellectual drift and moral confusion. Unless we teach students that we are all "part and product of Western civilization," that our principles of justice, liberty, consent of the governed, equality under the law" are "directly descended from the great epochs of Western civilization" and are "the glue that binds together our pluralistic nation" and the nations of the West, our students cannot be "participants in a common culture, shareholders in our civilization."

This is our past. As such it must form the core of a college curriculum. It is the legacy to be recovered and reclaimed so we can understand "America and all of its people." "If their past is hidden from them," Bennett concludes without a trace of irony, "they will become aliens to their own culture, strangers in their own land."

Because we have ignored this legacy or dismissed it on ideological grounds, we have become confused about what is worth caring for and cultivating, which lives and actions are worth emulating, and which books and ideas are worth studying. The legacy teaches both *that* there are standards of judgment independent of time, place, and circumstance and *what* those standards are. In the absence of such teaching we are left with a destructive dialectic of moral relativism and ideological absolutism. "To subordinate" texts and courses to "particular prejudices," to choose the latter or shape the former "on the basis of their relation to a certain social stance" as was done in the 1960s and continues to be done by those who would reclaim *that* legacy, is to pervert the vision and aims of education to a political rather than a cultural agenda, to fragment rather than unite our nation and the West and dissociate us from the wellsprings of civilization.

Many of the concerns and themes presented *sotto voce* here become the de-

---

subsequent controversies over higher education, the humanities, and curriculum reform at both the secondary and university levels. What was an argument has become an incantation, repeated even by those who have little respect for humanistic learning. Indeed, one of the ironies of the call for reform of education is that the humanities have been losing enrollments and that departments, such as philosophy and classics, have been or are in jeopardy of being closed down. Even if some of the blame can be placed on the aridity of much analytic philosophy and philology, the decline amidst the celebration should give us pause.

clamations by conservative polemicists like Kimball, D'Souza, Allan Bloom,[44] and Bennett himself. Here, for example, is Roger Kimball:

> What we are facing is nothing less than the destruction of the fundamental premises that underlie both our conception of liberal education and a liberal democratic polity. Respect for rationality and the rights of the individual, a commitment to the ideals of disinterested criticism, color-blind justice, and advancement according to merit, not according to sex, race, or ethnic origin; these quintessentially Western ideas are bedrocks of our political as well as our educational system.[45]

Multiculturalism rejects or undermines every one of these principles and commitments. It "wag(es) war against Western culture," "assaults the mind," and trumpets a "politically motivated betrayal of literature."[46] Indeed the very idea of literature as a distinct realm of experience is rejected in the name of a "radically egalitarian conception of culture," which fosters "ideological separatism" and irrationalism at the expense of reason and objectivity. In fact, multiculturalism relentlessly and monotonously politicizes all aspects of education and culture leading to a crippling divisiveness within the nation and university.[47] Here the historical trajectory of the eighteenth century will be reversed and the new world will mimic the old or the new one coming to be in the dissolution of Yugoslavia.

For Kimball and his fellow soldiers, universities and colleges are the citadels that need defending and great books are the threatened treasures within them. Institutions of higher learning are places where the achievements of Western culture are celebrated, taught, and exemplified, where enlightenment and civilization are spread, and where the disinterested search for truth finds a singular home and support. To choose inferior works like *The Color Purple* on the basis of intellectual affirmative action or because special interest groups push them is to deny oneself the depth and variety of experience and profound insights into the human condition a well-educated person gets by reading the *Republic, The City of God, The Inferno,* or *Lear.* Not to choose books for their intrinsic merit, their self-evident virtues, and their capacity to reveal truths about human nature, or to pervert those texts by writing an essay on the masturbatory girl in Jane Austen or to discuss the Godfather as a metaphor for American business is to compromise Western civilization at precisely a time when it is threatened by the dominance of electronic media, the equalization of all values, and pervasive moral drift. Some canonists are cultural Darwinists: great works have selected themselves because of their aesthetic qualities, their power of imagination and language, their craftsmanship and reasoning capacity. Though they have not been selected for

---

[44] Bloom seems to me a special case. His view of the canon and great books is more skeptical and subtle than that of most others who see him as an ally. Furthermore, his polemicism has a different aim from theirs, and he puts his argument in a theoretical framework while they do not.

[45] "The Periphery of the Center," in Paul Berman, ed., *Debating PC* (New York: Dell, 1992), p. 65.

[46] Ibid., p. 82.

[47] Kimball, *Tenured Radicals,* and "The Periphery V. The Center: The MLA in Chicago," in Berman, *Debating PC,* pp. 61–84.

political reasons (since that would imply politicizing the university), they have salutary political and moral teachings.

Perhaps the most repeated canonist charge is that an unholy alliance of post-modernists, Marxists, feminists, and multiculturalists are "politicizing" the university. They have made race, class, and gender the litmus test for who should be hired and what should be taught, by whom and in what way, and made member-ship in "an oppressed" group determine the legitimacy of what is said, leaving white males to defend their right to speak on such issues as race or gender instead of having to defend the cogency of what they say. That this amounts to a strategy of silencing from groups that complain about being silenced just adds a little irony to the process. But universities and colleges are distinctive as places where people give reasons and make arguments, the legitimacy of which are at least potentially independent of race, class, gender, sexual preference, or ethnicity. The unholy alliance politicizes the university in another way: using it as an instrument of social transformation. For canonists, no university can be part of a political movement, and no serious intellectual endeavor can honor prejudice and parti-sanship above truth and impartiality.

Nor should colleges and universities mirror the social divisions of society, what Kimball terms "ideological separatism." In fact, they must *not* do so, but rather provide a place for rational nonideological discussion of them. What dis-tinguishes universities from political institutions is precisely their ability to stand back from the demagoguery and vituperation characteristic of political conflict. To bring such conflicts into the university, as happened at City College of New York, is to substitute competing indoctrinations for education. It follows that the university is not a representative assembly where different interests compete for power and influence, but a place for reasoned debate. It is a community of scholars, not a community of power brokers.

Canonists tend to posit the 1950s as an idealized moment before the deluge of the 1960s when universities became politicized.[48] The 1950s are described as a time when applicants were selected on the basis of academic merit rather than affirmative action, where faculty were teachers committed to the search for truth and students respected authority in the family (which exemplified family values), the schools, and the nation, in contrast to the 1960s, whose explosion of demo-cratic activism is demonologized even by those who present themselves as medi-ators in the culture wars. "In their attempts to redress injustice," James Atlas writes, "the radicals of the 1960s unwittingly helped to perpetuate it; the assault on the curriculum has undermined the foundation of learning on which our soci-ety rests."[49]

---

[48] Neil Jumonville argues that contrary to the later interpretation of themselves, the New York critics "were not committed political and cultural radicals in the 1930s who were pushed into neo-conservatism by the antinomian uprising of the young in the '60s. . . . Instead, even in the 1930s these intellectuals had clear tendencies toward what later became neoconservatism" (*Critical Cross-ings: The New York Intellectuals in Postwar America* [Berkeley: University of California Press, 1991], p. xiii).

[49] Atlas, *Battle of the Books*, p. 135. Throughout the debate there is an assumption that at some

Posed less polemically, there is substance to these worries. Canonists are right to regard those multiculturalists who wish to discard the canon as presently constituted or those who think there should be no canons at all as reenacting an American ritual even as they contest "American" identity. They are also right to warn about the dangers of a suffocating presentism as in David Harlan's promise that "poststructuralist culture will force texts to answer our questions, derive from our needs, be couched in our terms."[50]

And they are right to argue that "great" works cannot be reduced to political usefulness (even if such "usefulness" covertly legitimates their canonization) and that the "greatness" of texts lies in their aesthetic qualities and generative imagination, the brilliance of their craft, and their capacity to make other worlds or points of view so vivid that "our" life seems, for the moment at least, foreign, unnatural, or absurd.[51] Works like the *Iliad* and *Oresteia* give voice to silence. They save expression from slipping beyond the reach of memory and provide solace in wisdom against the heart's oppressions and evasions.[52] Finding space for action against the invasiveness of paralyzing grief, they make it possible for humans to accept responsibility for a world they did not make and inspiration to remake the parts they can less cruel, more free, and more just. If one wanted to maintain hierarchies of cultural power, *Antigone* and *Lear,* Plato's *Republic* and Exodus, Augustine's *Confessions* or Dante's *Inferno* are unlikely candidates for the job. Thomas Hobbes complained that the reading of Aristotle and Cicero caused the English Civil War. As usual he exaggerated. But he did know something both canonists and their critics sometimes forget.

Additionally, canonists are right to warn us about using race, class, and gender to legitimate who can teach in what way and about what. Not only does it stereotype "people of color" constricting them to certain fields (such as Afro-American Studies), and presume that those who have undergone oppression can speak about it with unchallengeable authority so that skeptical questions are themselves labeled oppressive;[53] it also leads to cases like that of *The Education of Little*

---

time and some place things were very different—more harmonious, purer, and better. But one could argue that precisely because education has been so important in forging a national identity and that in America the idea of a nation has itself been so contested from our very beginning that education has always been a volatile issue. Or if not from the very beginning, certainly since the waves of immigration in the nineteenth century as ethnic "enclaves" sought to have schools that sustained their cultures. One would have thought that contemporary multiculturalists were the first to make such claims, but in fact they are doing what previous generations of immigrants did (as detailed studies of the urban public schooling attest).

[50] Quoted in Stephen Watts, "The Idiocy of American Studies: Poststructuralism, Language, and Politics in the Age of Self-Fulfillment," *American Quarterly* 43, no. 4 (December 1991): 654.

[51] Bromwich, *Politics by Other Means,* p. 95.

[52] See Adrian Poole, "War and Grace: The Force of Simone Weil on Homer," *Arion,* n.s., 2 (Winter 1992): 1–16.

[53] The situation is complicated. On the one hand, we know that people are sometimes wrong about their own experience and that the oppressed do not automatically have the deepest understanding of the culture that oppressed them. On the other hand, their experiences have always been interpreted for them and their views consistently subjugated to restatement or dismissal. Indeed, that is one thing we

Tree[54] and the confirmation of Clarence Thomas. *The Education of Little Tree* was presented as the autobiography of an eighteen-year-old Cherokee. Selling more than 600,000 copies and receiving numerous accolades, which praised its "natural approach to life" and ability to "capture the unique vision of Native American culture," it was in fact written by a member of the KKK. And the mere fact of Clarence Thomas's race paralyzed liberal opposition within the black and liberal white communities.

Furthermore, fragmentation can be an educational and political threat. Within the universities specialization increases, as does suspicion of any theoretical integration that might lessen it. Interdisciplinary work usually defines a new specialization rather than lessens it. Within the nation wedges between races and nationalities seem to be deepening with a growing promotion of "self-pity and self-ghettoization" as well as a "patronizing calculus of victimization, a formulaic demand for reversibility, and a clannish standard of political correctness."[55] The politics of identity sometimes paralyzes not only attempts at a coherent curriculum, but at concerted action on issues like poverty, the debt, industrial stagnation, meaningless work, racial and sexual discrimination, environmental degradation, violence, the emotional and financial havoc created by an increasingly older population, and, not least, the crisis in our public school system.

Canonists are right again when they argue that without a common language conversation would be a babble and differences would remain unrecognized and unheard; that without a common culture diverse people would be unable to talk to each other; and that without a sense of a shared fate in the future they would have no need to do so. This does not, as some canonists insist, preclude such a culture or language from being contested. Nor does it mean one must be blind to the structural inequalities of gender, race, and class that turn ostensive dialogues into covert monologues or to the differences between a common and a hegemonic culture. It does mean that diversity depends on a prior unity that constructs differences as related to each other rather than random expressions; that even the most intense disagreements are only so within a particular discourse. "But what is original about Machiavelli," the French philosopher Maurice Merleau-Ponty wrote, "is that, having laid down the source of struggle, he goes beyond it without ever forgetting it. He finds something other than antagonism in struggle itself."[56] What he finds are the grounds that make the struggle possible and worth having; the recognition that if the antagonism crosses some vague but certain boundary, there will be nothing left to struggle for, just as there are lines lovers cross at the risk of destroying their relationship. Similarly, if critics push beyond

---

mean by a people being oppressed. So the question is how to honor the self-interpretation of their experience without essentializing that representation.

[54] Henry Louis Gates discusses the incident in "Authenticity or the Lesson of Little Tree," *New York Times Book Review* (November 24, 1991), p. 1.

[55] Watts, "Idiocy of American Studies," p. 653.

[56] Merleau Ponty, "A Note on Machiavelli," in *Signs,* trans. Richard C. McCleary (Evanston, Ill.: Northwestern University Press, 1964), pp. 211–23.

some limit (a limit those in power are only too ready to define as a challenge to them), either in the university or society, they will destroy the whole they are trying to reform. (This is not to deny that there may be times and places where the whole should be destroyed.)

Moreover, canonists have a point when they insist that the university's common language is one of reason, evidence, and argument. Education is premised on a shared commitment to impartiality and thinking, though if Jacques Derrida is right, our commitment to such an enterprise must include acknowledging its limits of the discourse in which both commitment and critique take place.[57] Penultimately those canonists who object to speaking of "the West" as "a" culture or "a" tradition rightly point to the amalgam of Greek, Roman, Judaic, and Christian traditions as already a diverse culture. That is why cultures can be used against themselves, why the beginning, if not the end, of radicalism is so often using the master's tools, if not to destroy the master's house, then to substantially remodel it. If all this is true, then critics of the West may be drawing on the resources of the culture they criticize, as I will argue Socrates was doing. Emerson's insistence that "the past has baked your loaf" and "in the strength of its bread you would break the oven"[58] is echoed in Irving Howe's warning[59] that criticism must "maintain connection with its heritage or it becomes weightless, a mere compendium of momentary complaints."[60] Finally, canonists are right to insist that the crisis in education is a contest over American identity as represented in "our" history and as a part of Western civilization.

But instead of seeing the crisis as providing an opportunity to confront fundamental questions about the grounds, origins, and practices of education and the university, conservative canonists simply draw up the wagons. Like *Antigone's* Creon, they respond to the presence of plurality and the desire for shared power

---

[57] "The Principle of Reason: The University in the Eyes of Its People," *Diacritics* 13 (Fall 1983): 3–20. See also Adrienne Rich's essay "Toward a Woman-Centered University," which suggests how the sociology of the university, its political position, epistemological commitments, curriculum, and classroom dynamics create a disciplinary structure in which the subordination of women is overdetermined. (Her essay appears in *On Lies, Secrets and Silence: Selected Prose, 1966–1978* [New York: W. W. Norton, 1979].)

[58] Ralph Waldo Emerson, "The Conservative," in *The Works* (London: George Bell, 1894), 2: 268.

[59] Irving Howe, "The Value of the Canon," in Berman, *Debating PC*, p. 162.

[60] In "The Greek Polis and the Creation of Democracy" (in *Philosophy, Politics, Autonomy* [New York: Oxford University Press, 1991], pp. 86–88), Cornelius Castoriadis argues that the reasoned investigation of other cultures and the reflection upon them, the keen interest in other states, the commitment to impartiality that the ethnographer, historian, or philosopher brings to her reflection upon societies other than her own (and perhaps her own as well) "is a reality only within the Greco-Western tradition." In *An Aristocracy of Everyone* (p. 144), Benjamin Barber argues that because pluralist tolerance of multiculturalism has distinctly Eurocentric roots, the special place of Western civilization in a multicultural curriculum is justified. Similarly, Schlesinger insists that "whatever the particular crimes of Europe, that continent is also the source—the unique source—of those liberating ideas of individual liberty, political democracy, the rule of law, human rights, and cultural freedom that constitute our most precious legacy and to which most of the world today aspires" (*Disuniting of America*, p. 127). The problem with these arguments is not that they are false, but that they are too easily made; that they may be true by definition, and may rest on suppressed empirical claims having to do with knowledge of other non-Western claimants.

with the imposition of singularity, structure, and hierarchy, and impugn the motives of those who challenge them. As he becomes more and more incensed by Antigone, Haemon, the people and Tiresias, Creon aggressively asserts that he will not be ruled by women or the young or those who lack sense. Like him, D'Souza and Kimball posit Manichaean polarities that escalate the conflict they purport to deplore but which justify their call for the imposition of rule.

As Creon destroys the legitimate concerns he has and so disables himself from adequately responding to them, so do some canonists vitiate their own best points. Suspicious of dogmatic historicism, they ignore historical precedents and complexities. Impatient with the reduction of great works to being part of a conspiracy of white male power, they simply dismiss the very possibility that the canon is a form of cultural power and historical artifact. Rightly concerned with political indoctrination and preaching in the classroom, their own definition of what politicizing is and who is doing it is so vague and self-serving that only those who already agree with them will be persuaded. In appropriately honoring classic texts, their reading of those texts is too often constricted by a moralistic didacticism that transforms the legacy of "the West" into castor oil. The more general point, which applies to both sides, is made by Katha Pollitt: "Books are not pills that produce health when ingested in measured doses. Books do not shape character in any simple way, if indeed they do so at all, or the most literate would be the most virtuous instead of just the ordinary run of humanity with larger vocabularies."[61]

What is astonishing about many participants in the culture wars but particularly disconcerting in the case of conservative canonists is the indifference to the history of higher education in the United States.[62] The litany of complaints by canonists as well as their allies in the educational reform movement echoes disputes of previous generations.[63] The fears they express and the language they use to express them are similar to those of the late nineteenth and early twentieth centuries when cultural elites worried about the influx of "barbarian hordes" from Eastern and Southern Europe,[64] many of whose children and grandchildren are well represented among canonists. It was to socialize these heterogeneous masses that the canon was abruptly changed from one grounded in Greek and Latin

---

[61] Katha Pollit, "Why Do We Read?," in Berman, *Debating PC*, p. 210. She goes on: "Books cannot mold a common national purpose when, in fact, people are honestly divided about what kind of country they want—and are divided, moreover, for the very good and practical reasons as they always have been."

[62] This is Francis Oakley's argument in "Against Nostalgia: Reflections on Our Present Condition," in Darryl J. Gless and Barbara Hermstein Smith, eds., *The Politics of Liberal Education* (Durham, N.C.: Duke University Press, 1992), pp. 267–90.

[63] For an acute analysis of the evolving discourse about educational reform, see David Tyack and Larry Cuban, *Tinkering toward Utopia: A Century of Public School Reform* (Cambridge, Mass.: Harvard University Press, 1995).

[64] See Lawrence Cremin's discussion of education as the central mode for "stamping a mass of heterogeneous elements with the hall-mark of American citizenship." He is quoting Reverend T. L. Papillon, a member of the Mosely Education Commission. Lawrence Cremin, *The Genius of American Education* (Pittsburgh: University of Pittsburgh Press, 1965), p. 65.

Classics to one based on English. It was not that English works were deemed of a higher intellectual or aesthetic order; they weren't. But they *were* regarded as more efficient in disciplining unruly immigrants by initiating them into the superior culture of the English-speaking races.[65]

There is something like "we lost China" syndrome operating in this ahistoricism. Conservative canonists sometimes look for scapegoats and traitors instead of recognizing that the world has been changed by forces and developments—such as the decolonization movements in the third world countries where emergent national identities positively value histories and practices previously demeaned by the colonizers—beyond their control.[66] Nor, for the same reasons, are they much better at acknowledging that the engine of the domestic changes they despise, such as the fact that commercialization of culture that agitates Hilton Kramer and the contributors to the *New Criterion,* is driven by mechanisms and ideologies such as free-market capitalism promoted by their political allies. Indeed, for all the fulminations against popular culture and predictions of the collapse of civilization once the rigid line between high and low culture is breached, conservative canonists know astonishingly little about such popular culture or who, why, and when distinction between high and low culture emerged.[67] Perhaps the battle over what books to read is to intense because, in Pollitt's words, "while we have been arguing so fiercely about which books make the best medicine, the patient has been slipping deeper and deeper into a coma."[68] If so, then we need an analysis that helps us understand the phenomena, not ignorant diatribes against its existence.

Because they identify historicism with relativism and politicization, canonists tend to ignore the historical dimensions of canon formation. But since the canon changes over time, it cannot be irrelevant to ask why. How and when were the texts that presently constitute the canon chosen? Why these and not others? What were the political imperatives and cultural circumstances that once led people to denounce Melville as a trivial hack but now lead them to celebrate *Moby Dick* as perhaps the greatest American novel ever written? Why was Nietzsche dismissed as a fascist crank just decades before achieving canonical status as *the* theorist of modernity and saint of postmodernity? And why do readings of texts seem to change over time? If great texts speak to us all, why don't they say the same things? Prior to the Vietnam War, Thucydides' *History of the Peloponnesian War* was read as providing lessons that would enable future statesmen to prevent or at least mitigate the excesses to which all regimes, but especially democratic ones, were prone. But after Vietnam, Thucydides became a pessimistic writer for

[65] See the discussion in Graff, *Beyond the Culture Wars,* pp. 149–56.

[66] See Joan Wallach Scott, "The Campaign against Political Correctness: What's Really at Stake?," *Change* 23, no. 6 (November–December 1991): 213.

[67] See, for instance, Lawrence Levine's *Highbrow, Lowbrow: The Emergence of Cultural Hierarchy in America* (Cambridge, Mass.: Harvard University Press, 1988), and Greil Marcus's *Lipstick Traces: A Secret History of the Twentieth Century* (Cambridge, Mass.: Harvard University Press, 1989).

[68] Pollitt, "Why Do We Read?," p. 206.

whom the lesson of history was that there were no lessons; that statesmen were helpless in the face of the implacable logic of war and civil war and the dynamism of democratic power, which achieved unprecedented greatness at the cost of unprecedented suffering. Or worse: people did learn from the brutality of the Corcyraean civil war. But what they learned was how to be ever more brutal. This reinterpretation of Thucydides was not a matter of better translations or new historical evidence, but of a new generation of readers chastened by the experience of a brutal and futile war.[69]

But if judgments of a text's value varies over time as do the readings favored by the most relevant interpretative communities, then any canon is necessarily local, and standards, academic or otherwise, exist in history where they define the obligations and responsibilities of historically situated actors. If, in Stanley Fish's words, values are "fashioned and refashioned in the crucible of discussion and debate then there is no danger of their being subverted because they are always and already being transformed."[70] From this perspective one cause of the recurrent crisis in the academy is the resistance of an old orthodoxy to an emerging one and the consequent dispute between generations about what constitutes common culture, eternal verities, and common sense. In blaming others for what the culture itself has failed to preserve, they recall Aristophanes' *Clouds* where Old Education accuses New Education of abandoning standards and ruining civilization. Like Old Education, conservative canonists would arrest the play of democratic forces in order to reify an uncommon stage in cultural and political history and to elevate a set of tastes to a position of privilege from which they can castigate all other tastes as vulgar and inessential.[71]

To the extent standards and values are renegotiated historical categories, they are already politicized, which means that the complaints by both conservative canonists that radicals are politicizing the university and the call by some multiculturalists, feminists, and "radicals" *to* politicize it, are beside the point: education is already politicized. If the common is always a particular conception of what is common, Diane Ravitch's argument that the spread of particularism throws into question the very idea of American public education, that public schools "exist to teach children the general skills and knowledge that they need to succeed in American society" and to "function as American citizens" begs part of the question.[72]

But Fish's definition is too sweeping and abstract.[73] At least since Max Weber, academics have rightly worried about sanctioning partisan agendas and pon-

---

[69] Similar stories can be told about Popper's "totalitarian" Plato and Barker's "liberal" Aristotle.

[70] Stanley Fish, "The Common Touch, or, One Size Fits All," in Gless and Smith, *The Politics of Liberal Education,* p. 264.

[71] Ibid., p. 260.

[72] "Multiculturalism: E Pluribus Plures," in Berman, *Debating PC,* p. 294.

[73] John Searle argues (in "The Storm over the University," *New York Review of Books* [December 6, 1990]: 18.) that because the humanities have a political dimension in the sense that they, like everything else, have political consequences, it does not follow that the only or even principal criteria for assessing them should be political.

tificating in the classroom.[74] But the charge by conservative canonists that the "left" is politicizing the university is suspect, not only for the reasons Fish gives but for those which underlie Henry Louis Gates's complaint that people who can "with a straight face" protest the eruption of politics into something that has always been political "says something about how remarkably successful official literary histories have been in presenting themselves as natural objects, untainted by worldly interests."[75]

So intense is the conservative canonists' fear of politicization[76] that they are willing to risk instrumentalizing education and proscribing the texts they admire as medicinal. Both sides in the debate try "to produce a desirable kind of person and a desirable kind of society—a respectful, high-minded citizen of a unified society for the conservatives, an up-to-date and flexible sort for the liberals, a subgroup-identified robustly confident one for the radicals."[77]

As I have already argued and will illustrate in subsequent chapters, this is a very peculiar view of texts and how they work in the world, as well of an education based upon them.[78] It is especially peculiar if the texts are Greek drama and Platonic dialogues with their extraordinary capacity to portray and generate conflicting views of the human condition, of goodness, action, and wisdom. For instance, as the initially decorous struggle between Socrates and Gorgias (in the dialogue that bears his name) over the relative merits of rhetoric and dialogue becomes a battle between Socrates and Callicles over who will have power in the dialogic community within the text and in the political one outside it, the idea that truth is derived politically rather than epistemologically is presented with a dramatic power that is not erased by Socrates' victory, which can, to complicate matters further, also be regarded as a defeat.

---

[74] See his "Politics As a Vocation" and "Science As a Vocation" in H. H. Gerth and C. Wright Mills, eds., *From Max Weber: Essays in Sociology* (New York: Oxford University Press, 1964). For a number of historical institutional and cultural reasons Weber's worry about the impact of German professors on students has much greater warrant than a comparable worry about American professors' impact on their students.

[75] "Whose Canon Is It Anyway?," in Berman, *Debating PC*, p. 195.

[76] Of course, some conservatives are delighted that the university is becoming politicized because they now have the power. Thus Norman Podhoretz boasts that since neoconservatives "are the dominant faction within the world of ideas—the most influential—the most powerful," liberal culture "must appease us," while Irving Kristol argues that corporations should fund ideological ventures that support capitalism as against "the unreasonable demands" made by "the undisciplined poor" and their intellectual allies. With them as with others less honest the objection is not that the university is politicized but that it has had the *wrong* politics. (Podhoretz and Kristol are quoted in Jumonville, *Critical Crossings,* pp. 31–32.)

[77] Pollitt, "Why Do We Read?," pp. 211–12.

[78] As Henry Louis Gates reminds us, it is not obvious that the fate of the Republic will be decided by what students read in classrooms or that those who control literature departments or the MLA control the world. There is a substantial gap between the classroom and the streets and the connection between them is, to say the least, highly contingent. Gates is right to be skeptical that paying homage to the marginalized through deconstructive readings of texts "ameliorates a real world wrong." See his *Loose Canons: Notes on the Culture Wars* (New York: Oxford University Press, 1992), pp. 17–19.

If the presence of such conflicts helps explain the abiding value of classic texts, then the legacy William Bennett would have us reclaim is one of struggle and paradox, of difficult, even impossible choices great souls confront and about which they can be terribly mistaken despite or because of their extraordinary gifts. The controversies between the interlocutors in a Platonic dialogue, between the dialogue's text and subtext or argument and drama, and between the various interpretative communities reading it, mean that such texts are ineluctably multivocal and dialogic.

V

Lost in the polemics over politicization is the fact that education in America has traditionally had, as one of its primary purposes, the political education of democratic citizens. The question then is not whether to educate such citizens but how. The answer depends, first of all, on how one understands politics, democracy, and citizenship. If, as with both sides in the culture wars, politics is seen as an essentially corrupting activity or as it is by some liberals as "a remote, alien and unrewarding activity,"[79] then a "political" education is either an oxymoron or peripheral to the larger, more pressing concerns of private individual lives. If citizenship is construed as a legal status defined by rights and the rule of law and negative rather than positive liberty, then a political education must be appropriately circumscribed by these limited aims. Finally, insofar as the dominant theoretical tradition follows Joseph Schumpeter in regarding democracy as the least bad mechanism for assuring a minimum of accountability of rulers to the ruled, so that what matters is not what rulers do with the power they get through periodic elections but the way they acquire power in the first place,[80] then political education becomes a pallid civics course like the ones most of us had in high school. The fact that everyone claims to be a democrat and every nation claims to be a democracy—John Dunn calls democracy "the moral Esperanto of the present nation-state system"[81]—does not amount to much if democracy is devalued in practice or so attenuated in theory as to be unrecognizable as a distinctive form of politics and culture.

The answer also depends on whether there is a distinctively democratic way of educating democratic citizens. What, by way of pedagogy and content, does a

[79] Robert Dahl, *Who Governs?* (New Haven: Yale University Press, 1960), p. 279.

[80] See John Dunn, *Western Political Theory in the Face of the Future* (Cambridge: Cambridge University Press, 1979), p. 26. This "democratic revisionism" points to something that is truer today than it was when Schumpeter wrote *Capitalism, Socialism and Democracy* in 1943, or even in the early 1960s when a number of American political scientists took over some of his specific arguments and much of his attitude toward democratic politics: that the very nature of the modern state precludes more than token accountability, has a minimalist commitment to political equality, and is often actively opposed to the dispersal of power and responsibility. But, of course, one need not identify politics with the state, either historically, analytically, or politically.

[81] Ibid., p. 2.

"democratic" education entail? Should a classroom be treated as a microcosm of the larger culture so that process as well as substance is "democratic"? Is democratic education necessarily reciprocal in ways that the political education in other regimes is not? Or must such education principally rely, as it does in other regimes, on habit and socialization?

The answer also relies on a distinction between a political and a politicized education. As I have so far used the term, to "politicize" something is to "denaturalize" it in the sense of presenting it as something contingent and thus subject to human design. Something of this meaning echoes in the current controversies over politicizing the university. But the primary meaning in the various accusations is indoctrination. In these terms to politicize the university is to transform teachers into preachers, literature into ideology, and searchers for truth into partisans. If one can establish at least the lineaments of such a distinction, it might be possible to get all sides to agree that *A* purpose of higher education is the education of democratic citizens.[82] This would hardly resolve the issues at stake, but it might clarify them.

Lying behind the charge of politicization is a claim that politics effaces reason and that the life of the mind is compromised if not debased by the imperatives of public life. (In the next chapter I shall look at the argument that philosophy is necessarily antipolitical.) There is much to be said for the idea that universities should be committed to reason and impartiality. But to say it requires acknowledging the frequently partisan nature of the claim as revealed, for instance, by the irrational polemics surrounding the claim to reason by conservative canonists and by Creon in his response to Antigone and Haemon in *Antigone*. Thus defenses of reason must observe a diligent solicitude for what is elided or silenced in its name, what is made faint and/or obscure by its light, and what the cost of the achievements may be, including the sense of reflection itself. A commitment to reason and reasonableness must at least countenance the possibility that we are mistaken in supposing that the universe as a history or structure of reason can, when rightly understood, yield a pattern that makes sense of human life and capacities.[83]

---

[82] In focusing on political education, I want to avoid two exaggerations: that political education is the only thing colleges and universities do; and that political education happens primarily in the classroom. Institutions of higher learning have many more tasks than political ones, even if in some important sense they are institutions of social reproduction. Moreover, an exclusive emphasis on the political education of citizens runs the risk of making learning purely instrumental and legitimating the demand for relevance that too often translates into teaching students elaborations of what they already know. In addition, an overemphasis on the university's role in cultivating a sense of political judgment and thoughtfulness is likely to underestimate how much cultivation of those traits is independent of academic learning or, more positively, how much they depend on experience that occurs outside the confines of academic institutions. I share with radical democrats the belief that the active and persistent sharing of power is a necessary condition for enhancing a sense of responsibility and political thoughtfulness.

[83] The language is taken from Bernard Williams's *Shame and Necessity* (Berkeley: University of California Press, 1993).

Toni Morrison makes a similar point when she speaks of "unspeakable things unspoken." Examining *Moby Dick,* she argues that the African American presence in America has shaped the language, structure, and meaning of much of our literature and that the fundamental fact of slavery is there as conscience and moral, as a frame and in the center of our experience as a people. Invisible things are not necessarily not there, and absences can call attention to themselves, just as neighborhoods are often defined by the populations excluded from them.[84] To these omissions attention must be paid.[85]

If the university is the preeminent place for reasoned debate, then it matters who constitutes the terms of debate, and thus who and what is reasonable. If it is a place for impartiality, then it matters who takes part given how often protestations of impartiality mask special pleading, how frequently truth is pinned to power, and how often a particular form of cultural power appears within a universal claim.

Consider in this regard the argument made by Martin Bernal in volume 1 of his *Black Athena: The Afro-Asiatic Roots of Greek Culture* that the Greek self-understanding of the Asian and African influences on Greek culture was replaced by a nineteenth-century German scholars' "Aryan Model," which excised those contributions as part of a racialist agenda.[86] For all the criticisms leveled against the book by classical philologists and historians, and all the misleading use of it made by Afro-centrists, Bernal's point that highly educated, extraordinarily erudite scholars committed to what they took to be the truth co-opted classical Greece for anti-Semitic diatribes remains unrefuted. This was not a case of scholars changing their views in the light of new evidence as Mary Lefkowitz implies in her review of Bernal in the *New Republic.* Nor is the claim she makes "that the open discussion of scholarly research has made it rather difficult to

---

[84] Toni Morrison, "On Unspeakable Things Unspoken: The Afro-American Presence in American Literature," *Michigan Quarterly Review* 28, no. 1 (Winter 1989): 1–34.

[85] Many multiculturalists, feminists, and postmodernists would respect the ideal of a university or college as a community of scholars more if it was less hypocritical and incomplete. Many (but not all) of them value institutions of higher learning as a place for reflection in which students can develop their capacities for independent judgment and critical reflection by having the chance to analyze those long-range, large-scale developments that shape their lives. Some even regard the university as a repository for the accumulated wisdom of generations. And for all their critique of the claims to objectivity, neutrality, and universality, for all the repudiation of Enlightenment ideals, their hope that higher education can alleviate sexism, racism, and homophobia by providing a more impartial comparatively and theoretically more informed view of contemporary practices than is available in more parochial settings presupposes it. What some of them object to is that membership in the "community" and even what counts as scholarship has been narrowly and sometimes self-servingly defined. It was not very long ago that Jews (not to mention women and people of color) were thought to lack the "gentlemanly deportment" (as one professor put it in my company) appropriate for membership in this community.

[86] Martin Bernal, *Black Athena: The Afro-Asiatic Roots of Western Culture* (New Brunswick, N.J.: Rutgers University Press, 1987), and "Black Athena Denied: The Tyranny of Germany over Greece and the Rejection of the Afro-Asiatic Roots of Europe, 1780–1980," *Comparative Criticism* 8 (1986): 3–70. See also the special issue of *Arethusa: The Challenge of Black Athena* 20 (Fall 1989).

conceal or to manufacture facts without arousing the skepticism or the scorn of colleagues" persuasive given how long it took the scholarly community to repudiate them.[87] How long and at what cost did "anthropologists" insist on the smaller size of "the Negroid" brain, versions of which continue in the IQ debates?[88] With what consequences did psychiatrists, neurologists, and gynecologists attribute middle class women's "hysteria" to a malfunction of the womb? Here is the "scientific" conclusion of a male gynecologist in 1875:

> We have been studying woman . . . as a sexual being; and . . . we must arrive at the conclusion that marriage is not an optional matter with her. On the contrary, it is a prime necessity to her normal, physical and intellectual life. . . . The end and aim of women's sexual life is perfected by maternity. . . . Physically, children are necessary to the married woman. The sterile wife is constantly exposed to diseases that the fecund wife is comparatively exempt from. The sterile wife is not a normal woman, and sooner or later this physical abnormality finds expression in intellectual peculiarities.[89]

The point is not to repudiate reason. Nor is it to identify the life of the mind with public life or philosophy with politics. It is rather to resist any polarization and acknowledge their mutual "contamination" while honoring what their differences make possible. Here as with the previous questions about democracy, politics, and citizenship and how to educate democratic citizens democratically, Plato's Socrates can become a significant interlocutor and teacher. His elaboration, dependence upon, and critique of a radical democratic tradition provides a way of seeing the risk to our nation in a different light from that offered by the Gardner Commission or, more generously, building upon their subtext as a way of criticizing the educational economism of their text. Socrates can also help us delineate a vision of democratic political education while warning us of the pit-

---

[87] "Not Out of Africa," *New Republic* 79, no. 6 (February 10, 1992): 29–36.

[88] The most obvious recent case of this is *The Bell Curve*. For critiques see Russell Jacoby and Naomi Glauberman, eds., *The Bell Curve Debate: History, Documents, Opinions* (New York: Random House, 1995). As the editors rightly insist, we need to read the book symptomatically as well as substantively. But *The Bell Curve* is hardly the only book in which one could argue that racism influenced academic scholarship. See, for example, Michael Coe's argument in *Breaking the Mayan Code* (New York: Thames and Hodson, 1992). In "Postscript: The Categories of Professorial Judgment," in *Homo Academicus* (Stanford: Stanford University Press, 1988), pp. 194–225, Pierre Bourdieu argues that there is a clearly visible relation between a "hierarchy of epithets," that is, the adverbs and adjectives used to evaluate student work, and a hierarchy of social origins. Technical aptitudes such as the ability to construct an argument and understand a specialized vocabulary and personal and physical qualities made up the grounds of professorial judgment. This is not a case of purposeful action or conspiracy but of the fact that the academic field itself is structured in a way that makes it unthinkable for teachers and students to recognize the social significance of the judgments. It is because they think that they are operating in a purely academic or even a specifically "philosophical classification . . . that the system is able to perform a genuine *distortion of meaning* of their practices, persuading them to do what they would not do deliberately." Bourdieu calls this transmutation of social truth into academic truth "an operation of social alchemy which confers on words their symbolic efficiency, their power to have a lasting effect on practice" (pp. 207–8).

[89] Bledstein, *The Culture of Professionalism*, pp. 109–110.

falls of such an enterprise. Finally, what (my) Socrates says and does may lead us to think of our common heritage differently, perhaps make it more common than we suppose in a way analogous to Gloria Naylor's story of a young black girl who, returning from a performance, asks: "Mama, Shakespeare's black?" to which her mother replies, "Not yet . . ."[90]

[90] Gloria Naylor, *The Women of Brewster Place* (New York: Penguin Books, 1980), p. 127.

Corrupting Socrates

I

In Plato's *Apology of Socrates* the latter mentions the charge others have made and continue to make that he corrupts (*diaphtheirei*) the young (23D, 24C). Enamored by the way he punctures the pretensions of the various know-it-alls who dominate the city's politics and culture, young men imitate his manner of questioning, thereby enraging those whose authority they challenge. Socrates is thus deemed responsible—Meletus will insist singly so—for corrupting the youth, who, as a result of his teaching and example, become instruments of corruption themselves, spreading the disease of disharmony everywhere. Given the force and range of *diaphtheirō* and its cognates—leading astray and seducing, bribing and spoiling, maiming and killing—the charge amounts to the claim that Socrates is destroying the polis. Given the seriousness of the charge, and the number of times it has been repeated over the years, Socrates has his work cut out for him.

Socrates suggests that the charge of corrupting the youth is a convenient summary of the accumulated prejudices generated by his old accusers, whom he cannot now cross-examine even though they have legitimated the terms of the indictment by his present ones. The specific terms of the indictment charge that Socrates corrupts the young by pretending to be wise, by speculating about things in the heavens and beneath the earth, making the worse or weaker argument appear the better or stronger one, and by being an atheist, and teaching them to be and do the same.

While Socrates cannot cross examine his old accusers, he can question his present ones, directly in the case of Meletus, indirectly in the case of the Athenians who have uncritically absorbed the diffuse biases against him. So he asks Meletus who improves rather than corrupts the young. At first silent (which Socrates claims is a sign of his indifference to and ignorance of the topic), Meletus is eventually goaded into claiming that the laws and judges make the youth better. In fact, everyone does except Socrates. Socrates is incredulous at the claim, not only because of the extraordinary power Meletus attributes to him, but because to corrupt the young, or indeed any fellow citizen, would be to corrupt the world in which one lives, an act of self-destruction since, as Jonathan Schell has said, when the journey and the destination are the same, it makes no sense to spoil the conveyance in which one is riding.[1] Either Socrates corrupts the young inadvertently, in which case he deserves private remonstrance rather than a public trial;

---

[1] See his introduction to Adam Michnik's *Letters from Prison and Other Essays,* trans. Maya Latynski (Berkeley: University of California Press, 1985), p. xxxiii.

or he does so purposely, in which case he is so irrational that he can hardly be the evil force Meletus makes him out to be; or the charges against him are false. Socrates not only denies that he corrupts the young; he inverts Meletus's charge by claiming that he alone does not do so. It is he, not they, who is the true patriot and true Athenian.[2] The *Apology* itself provides a stage on which the conflicting accusations are tested, since what Socrates does to Meletus in the dialogue is what he is accused of doing to others outside it. And since what Socrates does with Meletus—accuse his accuser—is what he also does to his fellow Athenians when he insists that the way they expect him to behave at the trial contradicts their own ideal self-representation as a free people, the question becomes whether instead of the Athenians each making each other better as Meletus says, they are in fact responsible for making each other worse; whether because they are self-corrupting they should be accusing themselves.[3]

The charges leveled against Socrates anticipate those leveled against the multiculturalists by conservative canonists in our own day. He and they are charged with corrupting the youth by seducing them away from their parents and traditional authorities and distracting them from the pursuit of wealth, honor, and power.[4] He and they are accused of not believing in the gods of the city, with being unpatriotic and lacking proper respect for the achievements and sanitized self-representation of their native lands. He and they are accused of making the worse argument the better by engaging in logical shenanigans that trick the youth into transgressing proper boundaries and repudiating normal ways and rightful hierarchies as they are defined by those with political and cultural power, such as the politicians and poets.

One curious result of these parallels is that critics of the canon who confront "the" hegemonic self-understanding of "our" culture may be better students of Socrates of the *Apology* than those for whom Socrates is a canonical figure. The paradox is suggested in *Time* magazine's question: "Why are Western cultural and social values out of favor in the classroom when so much of the rest of the world has moved, during the past couple of years, to embrace them?"[5] insofar as the questioning of those values is itself part of the "Western" tradition (which suggests that the current controversies over the canon is as much about the construction of Western values as it is about whether to embrace "them" or not). It is suggested, too, by Michel Foucault's Socratic aim of trying to grasp the implicit

---

[2] I have argued this in detail in *The Tragedy of Political Theory: The Road Not Taken* (Princeton: Princeton University Press, 1990), chap. 7.

[3] He presents himself as a protector against the youth who have already been corrupt or, if not corrupt, no longer in thrall to the traditional ways his accusers would like to reestablish (*Apology* 39d–e).

[4] "My excellent friend, you are a citizen of Athens, the greatest of cities most famous for its wisdom and power. Are you not ashamed of caring so much for the acquisition of wealth and for reputation and honor, when you neither think nor care for wisdom and truth and the improvement of your soul?" (*Apology* 29d–e).

[5] Paul Gray, "Whose America? A Growing Emphasis on the Nation's Multicultural Heritage Exalts Racial and Ethnic Pride at the Expense of Social Cohesion," cover story, *Time* (July 1, 1991): 12–17.

systems of thought that determine our most familiar behavior without our knowing it.[6]

When Socrates inverts the charge that he alone corrupts the youth, he raises a general question that Meletus answers in a conventional way, which Socrates regards as missing the point and ignoring the problem: how should a democratic citizenry be politically educated? Meletus's traditionalist response—that participation in the conventional practices and institutions of the city make the young better while those who criticize such practices and institutions make them worse—becomes problematic if, as the accusers themselves allege, the youth are already corrupt, or are so skeptical of the legitimacy of cultural norms that going back to the old ways becomes like trying to recapture one's virginity. But Meletus cannot fully understand the question because it was just becoming one.

In the late fifth century B.C., education as a "natural" process in which older male relatives initiated young men into the rituals and practices of public life was being challenged by professional teachers who claimed superiority in imparting skills that would lead to political success. As education became seen as a product of self-conscious human design, questions arose about who should teach what to whom, how, when, and for what purpose. The sophists raised these questions, both by what they said and who they were, noncitizen outsiders.

Most of them argued that virtue was not innate but learned, which meant that privilege was not passed on from fathers to sons like property or physical traits but was earned by individuals as a consequence of their own achievements.[7] Thus power lay not in physical prowess, inherited status, or even wealth, but in having command of the tools of politics, especially of speech. Those who had (or professed to have) such command competed for students against traditional authorities.

Such developments both enhanced and threatened democracy. They enhanced democracy insofar as they further eroded the hold of traditional aristocratic elites with their assumption of "natural" superiority. But they threatened it insofar as the tradition being challenged was a democratic one, to the extent that it established a new elite of wealthy young men able to pay the sophists' fees, and because, as foreigners, the sophists did not have to live with the political consequences of any success their students had in directing Athenian policies. Though they had to be careful not to alienate the citizenry even as they attracted the young because of their iconoclasm, the sophists were not, in Schell's phrase, traveling in the same conveyance as the citizenry.

As Plato's Socrates defines his vocation, he walks the streets of Athens talking to anyone he meets, but is especially anxious to converse with his compatriots since he is more closely related to them (30A). He is closer to them because, for all his eccentricities, he is an Athenian and so he shares their democratic culture

---

[6] See for instance "Two Lectures," in Colin Gordon, ed., *Power/Knowledge: Selected Interviews and Others Writings, 1972–1977* (New York: Pantheon, 1980), pp. 78–108, and "Nietzsche, Genealogy, History," in David Bouchard, ed. and introd., *Language, Counter-Memory Practice: Selected Essays and Interviews* (Ithaca: Cornell University Press, 1977), pp. 139–64.

[7] Such a constructivist view may have been held by Simonides, a sixth-century poet.

if not their fate. But he is most anxious to converse with those who have and believe they deserve to have the power they do, and are, because of this sense of privilege, condescending to their fellow citizens. These scions of political and cultural power are certain that they know what is most worth knowing and are most offended at Socrates' interrogations and, presumably, at his willingness (or boast) to admit that he, unlike them, is wise because he knows he is not wise about what they think they are: what it is that makes someone a good man and an excellent citizen.[8]

The chapters that follow argue that the democratic dimensions of Athenian political culture were a necessary condition for the intellectual critique Socrates made of it, and that there are strong continuities of sentiment and practice between democratic politics and Socratic political philosophy. Both share a critical spirit as well as an impulse toward transformation, which leave them unmoved by claims that a rule is legitimate just because it happens to exist. Perhaps uniquely among political regimes, democracy calls attention to the conventional quality of its own conventions, generates a cultural logic that demystifies the authority of its own practices, and condemns its own denial of equality and inclusion.[9] Just as a Socratic question opens a world of thought, which is also a form of life beyond the project which allowed the question to be posed in the first place, so does political action in a democracy. Such questions and actions pluralize and multiply the world, dividing and subdividing it, demanding more of its interpreters and provoking them to other thoughts and other possibilities for action.[10]

Both Socratic philosophy and democracy provide a space between appearance and reality within which structural deficiencies can be recognized, traditions of cultural critique can be established, and the idea of democracy itself can be rethought and revised. More concretely, the experience of being a democratic citizen called for intellectual abilities that find expression in philosophical argument. "The fundamental point remains," G.E.R. Lloyd writes, "that much Greek philosophy and science presupposes an audience that prides itself on its ability in the evaluation of evidence and arguments; and if we ask where that ability came

[8] See James L. Kastely, "In Defense of Plato's Gorgias," *Publications of the Modern Language Association* 22, no. 1 (January 1991): 109. Socrates says that he examines politicians and artisans as well as the poets. Politicians have a grossly inflated view of themselves and of what they know. Artisans do have useful knowledge (how to make a pair of shoes), but they exaggerate the importance of what they know, claiming more for it than is warranted because they are ignorant of the relative importance of various activities in the living of a good life. Poets (the canonists of their time) may have a kind of inspired wisdom, but they are unable to give an account of what they say and know, though they too think themselves wise, not only about poetry but all of life.

[9] George Kateb argues that this is true of liberal democracy (in *The Inner Ocean: Individualism and Democratic Culture* [Ithaca: Cornell University Press, 1992]), Sheldon Wolin of radical democracy (in "Transgression, Equality, Voice," in Josiah Ober and Charles Hedrick, eds., *Demokratia: A Conversation on Democracy, Ancient and Modern* [Princeton: Princeton University Press, 1996], pp. 63–99).

[10] The argument is made in much more detail by Michael Dillon in his *The Politics of Security and Tragic Denial in the Political Tradition of the West* (London: Routledge, 1996), and Dana Villa, *Arendt and Heidegger: The Fate of the Political* (Princeton: Princeton University Press, 1996).

from, then the experience in law courts and political assemblies provides at least part of the likely answer."[11] And we know that no citizens spent more time in lawcourts and assemblies than the Athenians and that in no city was citizenship more inclusive.[12] No wonder then that *elenchos* so famously identified with Socrates has, as its primary meaning, the examining of an opponent's case. In these terms it is fully appropriate that the *Apology* be my touchstone since it articulates Socratic political philosophy in the context of a trial.

My elaboration of the closeness between democracy and philosophy will move in two directions. I will look at certain democratic practices for anticipations of Socratic political philosophy and at the *Gorgias* and *Protagoras* for their democratic sentiments and democratic subtext. Thus chapter four looks at the preliminary scrutiny (*dokimasia*) of all magistrates by a jury of citizens chosen by lot and the final examination (*euthunai*) carried out and the end of their tenure. Since virtually every Athenian citizen would be a magistrate some time in his life, all would be required to give an account of themselves at some time in their lives, a situation that prefigures Socrates' insistence that they be accountable for their actions and choices in general. Indeed I will argue that institutions of accountability together with drama helped constitute a distinctively democratic tradition of collective reflection and self-critique upon which Socrates could build. In these terms his claim that the unexamined life is not worth living can be seen as a philosophical articulation of democratic practices and a way of making public the thinking process present in the dialogue between me and myself.[13] What made

---

[11] G.E.R. Lloyd, "Greek Democracy, Philosophy, and Science," in John Dunn, ed., *Democracy: The Unfinished Journey, 508 bc to ad 1993* (New York: Oxford University Press, 1992), p. 47. For a complementary argument, see Sara Monoson, "Frank Speech, Democracy, and Philosophy: Plato's Debt to a Democratic Strategy of Discourse," in J. Peter Euben, John R. Wallach, and Josiah Ober, eds., *Athenian Political Thought and the Reconstruction of American Democracy* (Ithaca: Cornell University Press, 1994), pp. 172–97.

[12] I mean inclusive in the power it afforded ordinary male citizens as distinct from elites. Obviously its exclusions are intolerable and chastening for a democrat. The only thing that might be said in defense of the Athenians is that their principle of inclusiveness provided grounds for a critique of their exclusions.

[13] Hannah Arendt, *Lectures on Kant's Political Philosophy,* ed. with an interpretive essay by Ronald Beiner (Chicago: University of Chicago Press, 1982), p. 37. Here is Arendt in "The Crisis in Culture," in *Between Past and Future: Eight Exercises in Political Thought* (New York: Penguin, 1977), pp. 220–21: "In the Critique of Judgment . . . Kant insisted upon a different way of thinking, for which it would not be enough to be in agreement with one's own self, but which consisted of being able to 'think in the place of everybody else' and which he therefore called an 'enlarged mentality' (*eine erweiterte Denkungsart*). The power of judgment rests on a potential agreement with others, and the thinking process which is active in judging something is not, like the thought process of pure reasoning, a dialogue between me and myself, but finds itself always and primarily, even if I am quite alone in making up my mind, in an anticipated communication with others with whom I know I must finally come to some agreement. From this potential agreement judgment derives its specific validity. This means, on the one hand, that such judgment must liberate itself from the 'subjective private conditions,' that is, from the idiosyncrasies which naturally determine the outlook of each individual in his privacy and are legitimate as long as they are only privately held opinions, but which are not fit to enter the market place and lack all validity in the public realm. And this enlarged way of thinking, which as judgment knows how to transcend its individual limitations,

him a threat then was not so much what he said or did but that he spoke and acted outside of prescribed institutional settings.[14] This may explain why he expects his fellow Athenians both to reject his claim about the examined life and to appreciate its import.[15]

The claim that the unexamined life is not worth living implies the necessity of dialogue because only by examining my own life in the context of examining the lives of others will I be able to think at all. In this Socrates seems to be suggesting something analogous to what Arendt calls "representative thinking." Political thought is representative in the sense that one forms a political opinion by "considering a given issue from different viewpoints, by making present to one's mind the standpoints of those who are absent; that is, one represents them." This process of re-presentation is not a matter of uncritically accepting the views of those who stand somewhere else or of becoming somebody or something different or giving up what is my own distinctive standpoint. It is rather a case of "being and thinking in my own identity where actually I am not." The more people's standpoints I have present before my mind while I am considering an issue and the better I can imagine how I would think and feel in their place, "the stronger will be my capacity for representative thinking and the more valid my final conclusions, my opinion."[16]

Representative thinking achieves what might be called an engaged impartiality: engaged because it "represents" a way of being in the world rather than being outside it; impartial because it takes other particular perspectives into account without giving up its own, even if what is its own becomes redefined in terms of more public purposes. The pluralizing multiplicity embodied in representative thinking derives from and is encouraged by the dialogue I have with myself that constitutes thinking. Recognizing the pluralizing and diversifying capacity of dialogue may be a necessary condition for recognizing and respecting the plurality of others. Once we realize that the thinking self can be more than one without losing its unity, we can better understand how a political community can contain differences and still be a community or, even better, why differences must be cultivated rather than tolerated if the community is to remain political.

The claim that the unexamined life is not worth living implies both that an unexamined life is not a human life at all because it lacks coherence and point, and that thinking, no matter what the object thought about or the particular conclusion reached, may be the best way of dealing with corrupting youth and the surest guide for the education of democratic citizens. The latter possibility is present in Arendt's characterization of Adolph Eichmann. Eichmann, she argues,

---

cannot function in strict isolation or solitude; it needs the presence of others 'in whose place' it must think, whose perspective it must take into consideration, and without whom it never has the opportunity to operate at all."

[14] Of course he was also suspect for his affiliations with members of the Thirty whose claims of special privileges were unacceptable.

[15] But Socrates is surprised at the closeness of the vote against him, which may indicate that more of them recognized their culture in the claim than he expected.

[16] The quotations are from "Truth and Politics," in *Between Past and Future,* p. 241.

was not evil in the conventional sense of an Iago or Richard III, but was, on the contrary, an ordinary man who lacked the capacity to see what he was doing because he lacked the moral imagination to see the world and so himself from another's point of view. "He was not stupid," Arendt writes. "It was sheer thoughtlessness—something by no means identical with stupidity—that predisposed him to become one of the greatest criminals of that period."[17] Later, looking back on Eichmann and her analyses of him, she echoes Socrates[18] in wondering

> Might the problem of good and evil, our faculty for telling right from wrong, the just from unjust, be connected with our faculty of thought? . . . Could the activity of thinking as such, the habit of examining whatever happens to come to pass or to attract attention regardless of results and specific content, could this activity be among the conditions that make men abstain from evil-doing or even actually condition them against it?[19]

Arendt is careful not to equate thinking with reason because she thinks that "thinking in its non-cognitive, non-specialized sense is a natural need of human life." It is "not the prerogative of the few but an ever present faculty in everybody; by the same token, the inability to think is not a failing of the many who lack brain power but an ever present possibility for everybody—scientists, scholars, and other specialists in mental exercises not excluded. Everybody may come to that intercourse with oneself whose feasibility and importance Socrates first discovered." Since such thinking is a prerequisite to the exercise of judgment, it is reasonable to expect all sane persons to exercise it no matter how erudite or ignorant, intelligent or stupid they may prove to be.[20]

Arendt regards "thought" as a more inclusive category than reason and, so, a way of criticizing reason's limits without abandoning it. This is similar to Derrida's argument that the university's commitment to reason must include considering the reason for reason, its genealogy and limitations, its strategies of silencing, the intolerance of reasonableness, and the preemptory denial that it can be studied by anything other than its own methods, seen with its own eye.[21] That is

[17] *Eichmann in Jerusalem: A Report on the Banality of Evil* (New York: Viking, 1964), pp. 287–88.

[18] Arendt is ambivalent about Socrates as a comparison of "Thinking and Moral Considerations," *Social Research* 38, no. 3 (Fall 1971): 417–46, and her lectures on Kant suggests. In the former Socrates is less the Athenian citizen refining the opinions of his compatriots than a corrosive thinker who might well have corrupted the youth. Here the aporetic quality of dialogues reveals Socrates to have no positive doctrine. As a result he paralyzed action and undercut all customs and rules of conduct necessary for the measurement and living of a moral life. The latter text gives a much more sympathetic view of Socrates. For my purposes what is provocative about Arendt's ambivalence is that it anticipates Plato's in the *Protagoras,* or so I will argue in chapter nine.

[19] *The Life of the Mind,* vol. 1: *Thinking* (London: Seches and Warborg, 1978), pp. 3–5. See also Elizabeth Marmarck Minnich's elaboration of Arendt's argument in her "From Ivory Tower to the Tower of Babel?," *South Atlantic Quarterly* 89, no. 1 (Winter 1990): 181–94. Katha Pollitt makes similar remarks in "Why Do We Read?," *Nation* 129 (September 23, 1991): 31.

[20] *Life of the Mind,* 1:191.

[21] "The Principle of Reason: The University in the Eyes of Its Pupils," *Diacritics* 13 (Fall 1983): 3–20.

why he, like Arendt, focuses on the notion of thought as something that includes reason but is more encompassing and permeable. In regard to Socrates this means that we need to think critically about critical thinking, and to examine whether Socrates' views are too intellectualist and rationalist while acknowledging the paradox present in such an enterprise.

II

Of course, there is something paradoxical if not self-refuting about using the *Apology* as evidence for there being affinities between Athenian democracy and Socratic philosophy, given the obvious fact that the dialogue presents Socrates as being condemned to death by that democracy.[22] Surely the argument that the political education of democratic citizens and the commitment to reason or intellect are incompatible, even opposed forms of life, seems confirmed at the very moment the two are articulated in Plato's portrait of the life and death of Socrates. The moral and message of the story seem unequivocal: renounce utopian aspiration for philosophical citizens and resist the temptation to transform the irrational rabble into deliberative democratic citizens, either because it cannot be done or because the attempt to do it will lead either to the corruption of philosophy or the death of the philosopher. Better to accept the verdict that democracy and philosophy are necessary enemies.

Except for its exceptional eloquence and grace, Michael Walzer's argument for the necessary and desirable separation of philosophy and democracy is typical in this regard.[23] Walzer argues that there is a necessary opposition between philosophy (including political philosophy) and democracy because philosophers are committed to truth, reason, and values that are universal rather than particular or local. Thus philosophers must dissociate themselves from the common ideas and ideals of their fellow citizens if only, like ancient legislators, to refound the community. Only by leaving the Cave, the Original Position, or Ideal Speech Situation, can the deepest and most general questions about the meaning and purpose of political associations and the appropriate structures for political communities as a whole (rather than in particular) be addressed.

It follows that philosophical validation and political authorization are two entirely different things and belong to two entirely different spheres of activity. Philosophers reason in a world they inhabit alone or that is full of their own speculations; citizens think in a world of opinion peopled by many speeches and

---

[22] I have argued against the self-refuting nature of the claim at length in *The Tragedy of Political Theory*, chap. 7.

[23] Walzer's argument is in "Philosophy and Democracy," in John S. Nelson, ed., *What Should Political Theory Be Now?*" (Albany, N.Y.: SUNY Press, 1983), pp. 75–99. On the general point, see the agreement between Allan Bloom in *The Closing of the American Mind* (New York: Simon and Schuster, 1987) and Benjamin Barber in *An Aristocracy of Everyone: The Politics of Education and the Future of America* (New York: Ballantine Books, 1992). As Walzer is well aware the precise relationship depends on one's conception of philosophy. Pragmatism and certain variants of Neo-Marxism would tell a very different story.

speakers.[24] For the philosopher the result of her reasoning becomes a political and moral touchstone by which to judge the rightness of what the people do and how they live. For her, the people do not have a right to act wrongly. But in a democracy they do, and the right to decide takes precedence over making the right decisions (though not in the case of constitutional rights). For the philosopher, political action must be ontologically grounded, and political knowledge can be knowledge only if it is universal and singular. Yet political knowledge is plural and parochial, shifting and unstable, less the product of orderly design than historical negotiation, intrigue, and contestations of power.

Given this incompatibility between philosophical validation and political authorization, democracy "has no claims in the philosophical realm and philosophers have no special rights in the political community. In the world of opinion, truth is indeed another opinion and the philosopher is only another opinion maker."[25]

Walzer is right to warn against any easy identification of philosophy with democratic politics. And he is right to suggest that politics demands action and closure in a way that philosophical disagreement does not. But I shall argue that democracy does have a special claim on philosophy, a claim that is at once historical, intellectual, and political. And if philosophers have no special rights in the political community, they may have special obligations to it, particularly if it is a democratic community. The question, of course, is how philosophers are to fulfill those obligations democratically, and how one is to distinguish a philosophical critique of democracy aimed at restoring its animating principles from one that masks antidemocratic contempt for the people. This is no simple matter given the many times "friends" of democracy have thought it prudent to save the people from themselves.

Nor am I sure that in the world of opinion the philosopher's opinion is just one among many, though it is surely never the only one or even the best one. This is especially true if philosophy does not so much destroy opinion as reveal how painful it is to recognize the partial truthfulness of any one opinion. Moreover, if opinion, including political opinion, is defended by reasons and arguments as well as by appeals to sentiment and history, and if the practice of giving reasons and arguments to support opinion is itself part of that history, then philosophy becomes, once more, an elaboration of citizenship rather than something necessarily and unalterably opposed to it.

None of this is to deny what I regard as a lover's quarrel between philosophy and politics or the tension between the life of the mind and the education of democratic citizens it adumbrates. But I think the story of Socrates' life and death indicates how those tensions might be eased and why radical democrats need to ease them. As I read them, the *Gorgias* certainly and *Protagoras* maybe hold out the prospect of philosophical citizenship and democratic culture, even as the

---

[24] See Benjamin Barber's argument in "Misreading Democracy: Peter Euben and the *Gorgias*," in Ober and Hedrick, *Demokratia,* pp. 361–76.

[25] Walzer, "Philosophy and Democracy," p. 79.

death of Socrates, which haunts them, is a warning against complacency and a spur to a healthy skepticism of commitments that must nonetheless be made.

III

The chapters in this book are also reflections about teaching, more specifically about the appropriateness of teachers being political educators both inside and outside the academy. Once more the *Apology* introduces the theme, though in a peculiar way.

In the *Apology* Socrates denies that he is a teacher. To us this seems as disingenuous as his professed ignorance of the court language he in fact parodies so effectively. It is also thoroughly perplexing given his claim in the *Protagoras* that choosing a teacher is the most significant decision in a life. Some of his reasons for the denial are straightforward: he has never withheld himself from anyone who wished to speak with him, as if he possessed some precious commodity that should be sold to the highest bidder; he never charges fees, since for him the reward is living among juster fellow citizens. It is when he says that he "cannot justly be charged with causing these men to turn out good or bad, for I never either taught or professed to teach any of them any knowledge whatever" (*Apology* 33B) that we are suspicious. But whatever our response, Socrates' disclaimer, together with the fact that he remains one of the great moral teachers in the West, raises a series of questions about what it means to teach—more particularly, what it means to teach actual or future fellow citizens in a democracy.

In part Socrates denies being a teacher because of the way most people think about teaching and about themselves as teachers (and students). Many suppose that teaching is a matter of transmitting specific doctrines or attitudes so that students come to know what their teachers know and act as their teachers intend them to act. But as any teacher knows, there is a radically contingent relationship between intentions and consequences, between what is taught and what is learned. And as most teachers know, there is a difference between how students understand texts, issues, and themselves as students when they participate in discussions whose terms they help structure and when they do not, or when they are expected to cultivate their own sense of judgment rather than repeat the judgment of others. Of course Socrates had strong views which he thought others would share if only they were not distracted, misled, or confused about the life they were living. But for them to do what he says because he says it, or to be convinced because he is who he is, instead of convincing themselves, is literally self-defeating,[26] because they will not understand their beliefs sufficiently to withstand the seductions of rhetoricians. The highest vocation of a teacher of democratic student/citizens is to encourage people to think about what they are

---

[26] See Foucault's similar remarks in "The Mashed Philosophers," in Michel Foucault, *Politics, Philosophy, Culture: Interviews and Other Writings, 1977–84*, ed. and introd. Lawrence D. Kritzmar (New York: Routledge, 1988), pp. 323–30, though he is clearly *not* concerned with the seduction of rhetoric.

doing and to render independent judgments for the reasons analogous to the ones Socrates gives when he says it would be stupid of him purposely to make his fellow Athenians worse.

The fact that Socrates held strong views strongly, yet sought to teach others to be teachers of themselves so that political education could be reciprocal, helps explain the place of irony and paradox in his teaching. Irony and paradox, like humor, work as a counterpoise to the intensity of erotic attachments, which, however essential for teaching, constantly threaten to undermine it. The tension between proximity and distance, attraction and distrust, reverence and skepticism that Socrates thought necessary for teaching as he understood it was only possible in a dialogue that accepted the presence of power and conflict as an aspect of communication.

Part of the contingency between what teachers teach and what students learn, or between the books students read in classes and the actions they take in the world, derives from the fact that we teach who we are as fully as we teach any idea or text. For Socrates, knowing who we are in the sense of the kind of character we present as we teach is only possible if we are able to be students of our students so we can be teachers of them. Even then there is an instability to our identity as teachers because for Socrates (or Plato), the question "Who are we?" is not simply a self-critical one as it is for Kant, but a self-transformative one as it is for Nietzsche. Only if teaching is dialogic and the risks of revelation and discovery are shared, only when what and how we think are tied to something in our life that does *not* have some final form or the order of narrative, but emerges from intense encounters with real and/or fictive interlocutors, only then might Socrates have allowed himself to agree that he was indeed a teacher.

If we teach who we are as much as any text or doctrine, then teachers and subtexts can work against as well as with textual surfaces and explicit argumentation. Such tensions open up interpretative spaces within which we enter as interlocutors, reframing the issues raised by the *Gorgias* or *Protagoras*. As partners in the creation of a dialogue's meaning(s) we might, like the interlocutors within them, recognize suppressed aspects of ourselves as teachers and thinkers.

Particular conversations, no matter how abstract or analytically precise, are structured by cultural forces and social relations that complicate the specific "substance" of what is being said in ways analogous to the way inequalities in civil society vitiate formal political equalities. Dialogues like the *Gorgias* and *Protagoras* not only dramatize how these forces and relations work with and against the explicit argument, but they allude to political and cultural movements outside themselves which they also recapitulate and resist. Doing so they reveal what makes the enterprise of philosophy and dialogue possible and impossible, and point to the ideal conditions that make conversation cooperative and speech transparent, even while the movement of the dialogue disrupts its own preconditions and so problematizes the ideal.

In Socrates' case the problem of teaching is magnified by the overwhelming legitimacy of the "real" and "natural" against what seems (especially in Aristophanes' hands) his dangerous and silly efforts to delegitimate them. But while the problem may be exacerbated by Socratic dialectic, it is not created by it insofar as the sheer fact of our mortality dictates the limits of our understanding and power, which is one reason why Socrates emphasizes that the kind of wisdom he has is human in contrast to the kind of wisdom claimed by his accusers and by the sophists. They suppose they can "make" someone into something whereas he, recognizing the degree to which "extraneous" considerations that cannot be fully or permanently defined shape all human interactions, does not. Even philosophers are historical beings, constituted by particularities of time, place, and circumstance. For Socrates it is the acknowledgment of such limits that is or should generate a desire partly to transcend them. That is why the fact that a particular view has survived in the past "offers absolutely no certainty that it always will in the future; it may have been vindicated in a thousand elenchi in the past and prove false in the very next one after that."[27] For Socrates there could always be something he had missed and someone, no matter how seemingly ignorant, socially unconnected, or poor, from whom he could learn and whom he could "teach."

Of course all of this is mere talk if Socrates does not himself "really" risk anything. There is no "real" dialogue if his exchanges are simply cases where a respondent, ignorant of certain truths as shown by his false statements, confronts Socrates who already knows the answer and asks questions that will induce it. Then Socrates would possess political and moral expertise and the antagonism between philosophy and democracy would be more likely and substantial. I do not believe Socrates endorses either of the first two positions though I know he is sometimes taken to do so. I am not even sure Plato endorses them though he is almost always taken to do so. And as for the animus between philosophy and democracy, it is already clear that I think it is mitigated by mutual dependence and affinity.

Suppose we could possess the truth, be sure of what we know, and be equally sure that what we know is most worth knowing. How do we teach it to others? Is there some distinctively "democratic" way of educating citizens, something about the way things are taught, what is taught, or who does the teaching that marks democratic teaching off from that appropriate to other regimes? Is habit less important or rote learning less desirable a process in educating a democratic citizenry than the sort of critical reflection Socrates stands for? If democracy especially relies on the independent judgment of its citizenry, however collectively sustained that independence may be, does it follow that the truth can be taught democratically only if citizens are willing and able to teach it to themselves?

IV

These issues have added force if Hannah Arendt is right that we "must decisively divorce the realm of education from others, most of all from the realm of political life" since it is a dangerous mistake to identify politics—the joining with "equals

---

[27] Gregory Vlastos, *Socrates: Ironist and Moral Philosophy* (Ithaca: Cornell University Press, 1990), p. 114.

in assuming the effort of persuasion and running the risk of failure"—with the kind of education that rests on "dictatorial intervention based upon the absolute superiority of the adult, and the attempt to produce the new as a *fait accompli.*"[28] Particularly a democratic polity, where citizens actively share the responsibilities of power, must avoid any implication that citizens can be divided into political children and political adults, though the cumulative impact of democratic revisionism, false consciousness, trilateralism, and certain versions of the ethics of care have done just that. Democrats must reject the tradition of political thought since Plato insofar as it has regarded the authority of parents over children and teachers over pupils as the model for political authority. "Whoever wants to educate adults," Arendt concludes, "really wants to . . . prevent them from political activity," and to coerce them "without the use of force" (p. 177). Arendt's rejection of the enterprise of political education as a disastrous misunderstanding of politics as well as education is part of a larger argument about modernity which she then goes on to qualify in respect to America.

For Arendt the crisis in education is part of the crisis of modernity itself,[29] which is characterized by the loss of common sense, the disappearance of authority, and the increasingly problematic status of answers to questions upon which we relied without even realizing that they were originally answers to questions. Both the crisis in education and of modernity become disasters only if we respond to the newly recognized questions with "preformed judgments" and an aggressive iteration of outward pieties that make us "forfeit the experience of reality and the opportunity for reflection it provides" (pp. 174–75). This is the response of some conservative canonists, of Old Education in the *Clouds* and of Meletus in the *Apology.*

"By its nature" education presupposes authority and tradition in a modern world that is neither structured by authority nor held together by tradition. Children require answers and common sense even though our ways of making sense no longer make sense. In response many are tempted to impose educational blueprints on the young in hopes, for example, of creating the politically correct students of the 1990s or reviving the putatively deferential ones of the 1950s. But this is, for Arendt, a literally inhuman project.

Unlike the young of animals, the child is a newcomer in a human world that was there before him, that will continue after his or her death, and in which he

[28] Arendt, "The Crisis in Education," in *Between Past and Future,* pp. 176, 90–91. (Hereafter, page references may be cited in text.)

[29] Some of Arendt's claims are too sweeping, others involve a specific response to the panic that followed the launching of Sputnik, still others, such as those concerning the decline of standards have become trite, appearing with monotonous regularity in the recent educational reports and conservative commentary on them, though Arendt is adamant, as they are not, that whatever the crisis what she calls "simple, unreflective perseverance, whether it be pressing forward in the crisis or adhering to the routine that blandly believes the crisis will not engulf its particular sphere of life" can only "lead to ruin" (ibid., p. 194). In addition, recent developments such as increasing racial diversity in heretofore racially homogenous nations, ethnic conflicts, and new patterns of emigration and immigration have made America less exceptional. Still, her essay both deepens the debates over educational reform and multiculturalism and, given the importance of Athenian democracy and classical political thought for her ideas, provides a preface for the chapters that follow.

will spend his or her entire life. "If the child were not a newcomer in this human world but simply a not yet finished living creature, education would be just a function of life and would need to consist in nothing save the concern for the sustenance of life and that training and practice in living that all animals assume in respect to their young" (p. 185). It is because children are born into a human world that parents not only summon their children to a biological life but introduce them to a shared cultural life. They, together with teachers, and indeed all adults, must assume responsibility for this world even if they themselves did not make it, and even if they wish it were other than it is. "Education," Arendt writes, "is the point at which we decide whether we love the world enough to assume responsibility for it and by the same token save it from that ruin which, except for renewal, except for the coming of the new and young, would be inevitable" (p. 196).

Respect for the world takes the form of authority. Not to care or respect the world, or take responsibility for it, is to renounce all claims to authority. Yet *to* care for it is to respect the young as sources for renewal and to renounce any attempt to dictate the new. Thus we must be conservative in education to be radical in politics, and sustain traditions for the sake of the new and revolutionary in every child and every action. "The sense of conservation is the essence of educational activity, whose task is always to cherish and protect something— the child against the world, the world against the child, the new against the old, the old against the new." But this conservative assumption of responsibility for the world holds good only for the realm of education and for relationships between adults and children (p. 192). As we have seen, it cannot hold for the political realm in which we act with adults and equals. To be conservative in this realm "can only lead to destruction, because the world, in gross and in detail is irrevocably delivered up to the ruin of time unless human beings are determined to intervene, to alter, to create what is new" (pp. 192–93).

Thus for Arendt, as for Jefferson and Machiavelli, the single-minded effort to preserve the status quo ignores the fact that the human world is necessarily delivered up to the ruin of time. We are always educating for a world that is coming out of joint, always trying to set it right and renew it lest it perish with the mortality of its creators and inhabitants. Each new generation grows into an old world and those who wish to dictate to the young are robbing the newcomers of "their own chance at the new" (p. 177). But just as there is no courage without the risk of death or loss, there is no human world without the risk of the unexpected. The future is a wager with the unprecedented and the attempt to be sure of winning only insures the certainty of losing, as we shall see in chapter nine.

All of this has a special valence in the United States where the crisis of education is revealed with particular clarity and intensity. For we are, as the cliché goes, a nation of immigrants (though not all of "us" chose to immigrate), with many languages and cultures. That means that here schools have had to perform functions which in other nations would be performed as a matter of course at home. Since it is education that turns strangers from the old world into citizens of the new, education and politics are inextricably fused the way they are not elsewhere.

V

Even if we possessed the truth, how, as Walzer might ask, would it be relevant to politics? Is political knowledge grounded epistemologically or politically? When we say someone has political knowledge, are we simply saying that she has knowledge of politics analogous to knowledge of any other activity, or is political knowledge also political in the way it is derived and constituted? Josiah Ober has argued that the possibility of knowledge about politics outside relations of power did "not even enter the ordinary Athenian's head."[30] Political knowledge was socially and politically constituted, part of a "regime of truth" that entailed a more or less coherent set of assumptions and principles about what is right, proper, and true. Such "democratic knowledge" presumed or asserted that social reality was constituted and reconstituted "through collective practices of public communication rather than being given by an external authority or discovered through intellectual effort." The belief that collective decisions made by a large body of citizens were superior to one made by the privileged few has obvious political implications especially if democratic power includes control over the development and deployment of systems of meaning. Could anything be less worthy of being called knowledge in Plato's sense than the enactment formula of the sovereign assembly of the people in Athens: *edoxe tōi dēmōi* (it appeared right to the people). Though I will disagree somewhat with Ober's argument—how much depends upon what he means by "intellectual effort" and on my reading of drama as a "theoretical" institution—he poses the issue with particular incisiveness.

The question of how one could teach the truth, and what truths are most worth teaching become urgent in times and cultures where there is, to adopt Michael Walzer's brilliant characterizations of seventeenth-century England, "a slow erosion of the old symbols, a wasting away of the feelings they once evoked, an increasingly disjointed and inconsistent expression of political ideas, a nervous insistence upon the old units and references—all this accompanied . . . by a more and more arbitrary and extravagant manipulation of them until finally the units cease to be acceptable as intellectual givens and the references cease to be meaningful."[31] With some exaggeration—how much was disputed in Athens, as the *Clouds* suggest, and is disputed now in the debate over the "decline" of Athenian

[30] "How to Criticize Democracy in Late Fifth- and Fourth-Century Athens," in Euben et al., *Athenian Political Thought and American Democracy*, p. 158. See also his "Civil Ideology and Counterhegemonic Discourse: Thucydides on the Sicilian Debate," in Alan L. Boegehold and Adele C. Scafuro, eds., *Athenian Identity and Civic Ideology* (Baltimore: Johns Hopkins University Press, 1994), pp. 102–26; "Power and Oratory in Democratic Athens: Demosthenes 21, *Against Meidias*," in Ian Worthington, ed., *Persuasion: Greek Rhetoric in Action* (London: Routledge, 1994), pp. 85–108; and "Thucydides' Criticism of Democratic Knowledge," in Ralph M. Rosen and Joseph Farrell, eds., *Nomodeiktes: Greek Studies in Honor of Martin Ostwald* (Ann Arbor: University of Michigan Press, 1993), pp. 81–98.

[31] Michael Walzer, "On the Role of Symbolism in Political Thought," *Political Science Quarterly* 92 (June 1967): 198.

democracy in the fourth century—this could be a description of Athens in the later fifth and early fourth centuries.

What is not in dispute is that Athens in the late fifth and early fourth centuries was a democracy in transition. The increasing complexity of such a large city ruling an empire of diverse peoples, then the loss of the war and empire, led to an increasing emphasis on professionalism as a claim to cultural authority and a partial rearticulation of democracy. As society became more diversified and the juridical apparatus grew more complicated, there was "a need felt for more specialized roles and greater permanency of function."[32] If there was not a "decline" in Athenian democracy,[33] there was certainly a change. The significance of public life, while never uncontested, was increasingly contestable, and while democracy was now an accepted fact, what democracy meant and entailed were not. The vigorous debate about the "ancestral constitution"[34] was as much about the present as the past, as often about what democracy "really" was and should do as about who founded it.

One could say that the late fifth and early fourth centuries saw a crisis of political identity in Athens and that the debate over political education explicitly "dramatized" in the *Clouds, Gorgias,* and *Protagoras* and implicitly in *Antigone* and *Oedipus Tyrannus* was both a symptom and the center of that crisis. One could also say that "we" are in a somewhat analogous situation, that our debates over educational reform, the Enlightenment legacy, and the relationship of intellect, reason, and theory to politics finds echoes in these earlier times and texts. In these ways our ethical situation may make us, as Bernard Williams writes, "more like human beings in antiquity than any Western people have been in the meantime. More particularly, we are like those who, from the fifth century and earlier have left us traces of a consciousness that had not yet been touched by Plato's and Aristotle's attempts to make our ethical relations to the world fully intelligible."[35]

I mean "dramatized" in a general as well as specific sense since I will emphasize the dramatic subtext of Platonic dialogues as well as the way tragedy and

---

[32] Claude Mossé, *Athens in Decline, 404–386,* trans. Jean Stewart (London: Routledge and Kegan Paul, 1973), p. 28.

[33] On the debate over whether Athens declined, see Barry S. Strauss, *Athens after the Peleponnesian War: Class, Action and Policy, 403–386* (London: Croom and Helm, 1986); Mogens Herman Hansen, *The Athenian Democracy in the Age of Demosthenes* (Oxford: Basil Blackwell, 1991); P. J. Rhodes, "Political Activity in Classical Athens," *Journal of Hellenic Studies* 107 (1986): 132–44 (who concludes that "after two experiences of oligarchy based . . . on violence everyone accepted democracy but no longer found the old enthusiasm for it," p. 140); Simon Hornblower, "Creation and Development of Democratic Institutions in Ancient Greece," in John Dunn, ed., *Democracy: The Unfinished Journey, 508 bc–ad 1993* (New York: Oxford University Press, 1992), pp. 1–16, who argues that fourth-century democracy was "less democratic but more efficient"; and Sheldon S. Wolin, "Norm and Form: The Constitutionalizing of Democracy," in Euben et al., *Athenian Political Thought and American Democracy,* pp. 29–58.

[34] See the discussion in M. I. Finley, "The Ancestral Constitution," in *The Use and Abuse of History* (London: Chatto and Windus, 1975), pp. 34–59.

[35] Bernard Williams, *Shame and Necessity* (Berkeley: University of California Press, 1993), p. 166.

comedy helped constitute the democratic tradition of self-scrutiny I have argued is a necessary condition for Socratic political philosophy. Although abstracting the words of Greek plays from their contemporary context of performance makes it too easy to overintellectualize them and forget that they were entertainment, there is evidence that the playwrights were officially regarded as political, religious, and cultural educators of the city, and that theater provided the space and opportunity for a more comprehensive structural understanding of public life than was available amid the tumult and press of everyday affairs.

One way the plays educated their onlookers was by dramatizing the cultural exclusions and social inequalities that Athenian democracy presupposed even at the expense of its own stated principle of inclusion. Another came from the way tragedy made the half-visible particulars of everyday life visible as a form of life.[36] In these ways the wisdom tragedy provided helped legitimate the sharing of power and responsibility democracy endorsed.

Old Comedy played a complementary role in the political education of its audience. It raised questions about the limits of human power, the necessity of war, and the litigiousness of the culture, ridiculed the most powerful intellectual and political leaders in the community as if to preserve *isonomia* and *isēgoria,* and dramatized debates over education, democracy as a whole, and the place of humor in politics. In Aristophanes' *Women in the Assembly* (Ecclesiazusae), the question is whether Athenian women could be constituted male if the Assembly voted for it. If the *dēmos* could constitute political realities by legal enactment, and if human intelligence was so powerful that it could tame the sea (as the great choral ode in *Antigone* proclaims it can), then why couldn't men reconstruct the natural world in which they alone were empowered and make women rulers of the city? What were the "natural" limits on what they could do?[37] Other of his plays go after Pericles, Cleon, Euripides, and Socrates in ways that make the last-named's criticisms of the first-named (in the *Gorgias*) seem tame by comparison. And in the *Clouds,* Aristophanes involves spectator, actors, and even himself in a series of reciprocal relationships of spectacle and spectator that seem to parallel rotation in office.

Once again the *Apology* introduces the theme. When Socrates claims that Aristophanes has established the terms and biases that legitimate the present accusations against him, he announces his intention to engage the poetic tradition that had provided much of the public education of his compatriots. When Plato presents Socrates' life and death as a tragedy, he announces his intention of refocusing that tradition as part of a reeducation of democracy, or so I will argue. I will also argue (in the concluding section of chapter eight) that Plato presents Socratic

---

[36] I have argued this at length in my introduction to *Greek Tragedy and Political Theory* (Berkeley: University of California Press, 1986), and chapter 2 of *The Tragedy of Political Theory.* Those arguments (and this one) should have been (and be) more tentative, for the obvious reasons that we do not know for certain how an Athenian audience responded, the sense in which there was "an" audience, what all the performance conditions were, and what some of the contemporary allusions meant (this is especially so in comedy).

[37] See Ober, "Power and Oratory in Democratic Athens."

dialectic not simply as a way of arriving at truth, but as a way of representing it. If the choice of writing dialogues and arguing dialectically "expresses a sense of life and of value, of what matters and what does not, of what learning and communicating are, of life's relations and communications then dialogue becomes exemplary as well as instrumental."[38]

VI

Socrates' claims for thinking and intellect, together with the kind of teacher he represents himself as being, suggest the possibility of a distinction between a political and a politicized education. It is a distinction that provides terms for recasting the current discussion of educational reform and the often futile polemicism of the culture wars by focusing on what these debates should be about: the political education of a democratic citizenry. And it does so in a way that obviates Arendt's concerns about inappropriately importing relationships and purposes from education into politics. Paradoxically, I think Socrates able to provide such terms precisely because he cannot easily be politically or philosophically categorized. He is a democrat skeptical of democracy, a critic of democracy's critics who nonetheless recognizes the force of their criticisms, a teacher who believes in the general diffusion of knowledge into everyday life and the infusion of ordinary experience with theoretical significance but worries that the task is too great. This paradoxical quality may substantiate Josiah Ober's argument that in a vigorous democracy critics become crucial elements in keeping democracy from becoming hegemonic in ways that contravene its own purposes.

Though I think a distinction between a political and a politicized education can bear the weight I rest on it, I want to avoid reifying it, for reasons suggested in the preceding chapter and by Aristotle when, in books 6 and 10 of the *Nicomachean Ethics,* he distinguishes practical from theoretical reason. While the aim of the latter is contemplation of what is unchangeable, the former deals with a contingent political world subject to human design and action. In these terms, to "politicize" something is to claim that it is not natural in the sense of an unchangeable given but is part of a humanly constituted social world.[39] In this sense the evolution of Athenian democracy (to be discussed in detail in chapters three and four) presupposed the "politicization" of what had been regarded as the natural prerogatives of powerful kings and nobles. By insisting that people give an account of their lives and thus undergo a kind of public scrutiny, Socrates is continuing this "politicization."

[38] Martha Nussbaum, *Love's Knowledge* (New York: Oxford University Press, 1992), p. 5. I have made a parallel argument about the dominant form of analytical Plato criticism in "Politics and the Polis: How to Study Greek Moral and Political Philosophy," *Polis* 11, no. 1 (1992): 3–26.

[39] Judith Butler politicizes gender when she argues that gender is a sociocultural construction all the way down, that there is no final ground, original point, or inner essence to it. Rather it is performative, constituted by acts repeated which seem as if they are self-generated instead of generating a self. (See *Gender Trouble: Feminism and the Subversion of Identity* [New York: Routledge, 1989].)

Reifying the distinction would be false to Socrates for two other reasons. It would be false to him insofar as he was raising the question of what politics was and where it went on, when (as he saw it) normal institutional practices were corrupt. If the possible sites and ways of being political are subject to contestation, then so is the divide between political and politicized education. Second, if one is committed to the examined life, then presumably that life too must be subject to examination. There would be something paradoxical about privileging the injunction to examine one's life in ways that exempt it from examination, ignoring, for instance, the possibilities that Socratic thought is too rationalistic, gendered, and phallocentric, that the examined life may be unlivable for most or destructive of what is most valuable about life, or that intellectuals especially need to be suspicious of claims for the intellect, lest they be as guilty as the poets, politicians, and artisans in the *Apology* were of exaggerating the significance of their vocations. Even though the distinction between a political and a politicized education must be permeable and negotiable, this does not negate its usefulness. Indeed in some respects such contestability may enhance it.

A politicized education regards the "objects" of instruction as passive recipients of knowledge which molds them according to some blueprint of the good society. Here what can be taught, who can teach it, and where it can be taught is tightly regulated, and education is close to what we mean by training, socialization, or "indoctrination" in the original unapologetic meaning of that term. Of course every culture, including a democratic one, educates its young to embody certain ideals of action and character and much of that education is a matter of habit and initiation, of social, psychological, and cultural processes that constitute us as the kinds of people we become. But a politicized education—whether posited by revolutionary movements or conservative revanchists—treats the new as if it already existed, which is precisely Arendt's worry when she warns about conflating education with politics and criticizes the authoritarian models in Plato and Aristotle that are based "on an absolute superiority such as can never exist among adults and which, from the point of view of human dignity, must never exist."[40] In these terms a politicized education marks off some class of people as in need of perpetual tutelage due to political incapacity and moral adolescence.

A political as distinct from a politicized education would be deeply respectful of those traditions which empowered democratic citizens but skeptical of those which claimed the exclusive privilege of doing so. It would encourage student citizens to challenge those with power while reminding them of the critical traditions within the dominant culture that makes such critique possible and intelligible. These paradoxes echo Arendt's argument that taking responsibility for the world means being conservative so that we can be radical. In the *Apology* Socrates suggests that caring for one's city means being a radical critic of what the city is or claims itself to be. A patriot would do as he does, ask his fellow citizens whether what they care for most is most worth caring for. Yet in the *Crito* he implies that the more radical the criticism, the greater the obligation to honor the

---

[40] Arendt, "The Crisis in Education," pp. 177, 191.

society one criticizes, or at least those parts of it that nurtured the capacity for critique.

A political as opposed to a politicized education recognizes the temporariness and institutional particularity of the inequality between student and university teacher, and the paradox of having authority over students who are already adults and so our political equals. Such an education aims to teach such students to be thoughtful in a way that exemplifies as it cultivates the capacity for independent yet collegially sustained judgment essential for the active sharing of power and responsibility that should define democratic citizenship. For teachers in institutions of higher learning, the simple task not so simply accomplished is to help students think about what they are doing while acknowledging that, however well informed or expert one may be, there are significant things about the world that we have missed, distorted, or evaded. As I shall argue in regard to the *Gorgias,* and *Protagoras,* and about the Platonic corpus generally, once one engages in dialectic, being a teacher is less a professional role one assumes than a changing position in a dialogic encounter.

Democratic political education must be dialogic whether it is with our student/citizens within the university or our fellow students outside it. In both contexts "real" dialogue must be about its own preconditions in the sense of acknowledging how the will to power often frames if it does not inspire the will to truth, and acknowledge how informal inequalities of power shape the "positions" of interlocutors in ways that turn proclaimed dialogues into covert monologues. Such a two-level dialogue is a way of accepting the combination of authority and inequality present in the classroom, of responding to Arendt's warning not to confound politics and education, and of being alert to subtext and context as well as text. The insistence on dialogue is also an unembarrassed admission of our own historicity. As this implies, dialogue presupposes that truth is neither wholly subservient to political imperatives nor deduced from ontological or metaphysical foundations.

This conception of political education seems to answer most of Arendt's worries as well as those of Richard Flathman who, reframing Arendt, is wary of the illiberalism of civic education, which he regards as "impositional and indoctrinating."[41] While acknowledging that liberal education cannot be neutral, he argues that democratic political education "deepens the ineliminably illiberal character of all institutional education, because it engenders regime's preferred characteristics while combating what is regarded as non- and anti-democratic or anti-civic doctrines and orientations."[42] To identify oneself first and foremost as a citizen is to "conscript oneself" to the state that creates that office; to endorse an ideal for everyone requires you to combat all ideals that challenge its hegemony; to engender pride in those accorded the status of citizens and to participate

---

[41] "Liberal versus Civic, Republican, Democratic and Other Vocational Educations: Liberalism and Institutional Education," *Political Theory* 24, no. 1 (February 1996): 15. Cf. Amy Gutmann, *Democratic Education* (Princeton: Princeton University Press, 1987).

[42] Flathman, "Liberal versus Civic," p. 15.

vigorously in the activities of the office are to encourage guilt in those who default on the duty and shame in those who are denied the status.[43]

Whatever unease one might have with Flathman's arguments about what would exist in the absence of democratic education, about liberalism as setting the terms of discussion, of whether the encouragement of guilt is always pernicious, he, like Arendt, offers significant cautions for any defense of democratic political education.

VII

But why have recourse to Socrates yet again? There is so much that seems missing in his thought and sensibility and so much that seems unattractive about him that Alcibiades' praise of his beauty in the *Symposium* seems wholly ironic. To begin with, there is his dogmatic intellectualism and indifference to the material preconditions (broadly understood) even for living the life he regarded as highest, an indifference hardly erased by the poverty he chose for his family as well as himself, alleviated only by charity from wealthy friends. Then there are his often contemptuous references to the *dēmos* even in the *Apology,* let alone in the *Gorgias* and *Protagoras* or book 8 of the *Republic,* and his brow-beating, manipulation, and feigned deafness to the views of others such as Protagoras. In addition there is his diffidence toward the role of habit and tradition in political education, in contrast to Aristotle and perhaps Plato himself.[44] Finally, there are his repeated "failures" with figures in the dialogues (like Crito, Euthyphro, and Callicles) and political figures outside them, like Critias, Alcibiades, and Charm-

---

[43] Ibid., p. 22.

[44] Socrates' view of thinking largely (though not completely) ignores the role of habit and convention in education in the way Aristotle's did not. (See, for instance, Carnes Lord, "Aristotle and the Idea of Liberal Education," in Ober and Hedrick, *Demokratia.*) One could argue (as perhaps Plato did) that the unexamined life is not livable or livable by a few and at a cost of a dangerous (for most) deracination. But if one believes about Athens what Walzer argues was true of eighteenth-century England, then habit and convention are not much to rely upon. (There are of course different sorts of habits and conventions: different in specificity, origin, and mode of perpetuation.)

When Plato considers education in the *Republic,* he gives relatively little attention to schools. It is the community as a whole that educates since every influence molds the mind and character of the young—music, architecture, drama, painting, poetry, laws, as well as athletics. Similarly, though Jefferson was a great believer in schooling as a place for teaching technical skills and rudimentary knowledge, it never occurred to him that schools would be the chief educational influence on the young. The same was true for Horace Mann and John Dewey. Though Mann's generation built the modern public school system, it also organized many other settings in which education, including political education, might go on: public libraries and lyceums, mechanics institutes and agricultural societies, penny newspapers and dime novels, not to mention other informal sites such as women's literary societies that were self-generating. Dewey too thought all of life educates and that even when talking about deliberate educational institutions, schools were only one along with homes, shops, churches, and neighborhoods. It was only when he concluded that industrialism was destroying these other institutions that he turned to the public school as society's great instrument for shaping its own destiny. Only then did public education become coextensive with the education of the public. On these issues, see Lawrence A. Cremin, *American Education: The National Experience, 1783–1876* (New York: Harper and Row, 1980).

ides. "One chooses dialectic," Nietzsche wrote in *Twilight of the Idols,* "only when one has no other means. One knows that one arouses mistrust with it, that it is not very persuasive. Nothing is easier to erase than a dialectical effect; the experience of every meeting at which there are speeches proves this. It can only be self-defense for those who no longer have other weapons."[45]

There is a second aspect to the question: why Socrates for us now rather than, say, Jefferson or Dewey[46] or, even better, someone more contemporary who knows the distinctive dimensions of our current crisis in education? Athens was not a multicultural society, political theory was not then an academic subject, and teachers and schools in our sense hardly existed. What then is the point of eliding the institutional and historical differences, ignorance of which gives initial plausibility to invoking Socrates but knowledge of which makes his activity seem extremely remote and alien.

There is surely something to these concerns. But there are strategic as well as substantive and pedagogic reasons to think that some of them are overstated or misguided.

To begin with, Socrates remains, for some Western intellectuals and academics, a vision of "us" at our best. An exemplary teacher of extraordinary moral integrity, committed to enlightenment, self-awareness, the search for truth and knowledge, insistent that we think about our lives instead of "merely" living them, he is at once our conscience and our inspiration no matter what our field of study, our methodological commitments or our political predilections. Even those most critical of Socrates on political or philosophical grounds, who regard him as too Platonic or not Platonic enough, too disingenuous, manipulative, misogynist, or misanthropic, too antidemocratic, antipolitical, moralistic, and intellectualistic, find themselves talking about the issues he posed and exhibiting the critical sensibility if not the tools used by "Socrates."

Admittedly whom we are admiring is unclear. In the *Clouds* Aristophanes suggests that the clouds are the perfect deities for philosophers and intellectuals, since their formlessness permits us to project any meaning onto them. We see in their shapes a projection of ourselves and a home for our projects, though how we appear reveals more than we know. (In the end the clouds turn out to be just as indifferent as welcoming to our projects.) The same could be said about readings of the *Clouds* and representations of Socrates. There are those who find this situation intolerable and wish to discover "the historical Socrates," while others find the attempt fated to be disappointed or a largely futile if not superfluous enterprise. Philosophers of an analytic persuasion see him as a protoanalytic philosopher making rigorous arguments of the form they would make (though they do it with a logical sophistication he could not have achieved),[47] while

[45] "Twilight of the Idols," in Walter Kaufmann, ed., *The Portable Nietzsche* (New York: Viking Press, 1968), p. 476.

[46] See Stephen Esquith, *Intimacy and Spectacle: Liberal Theory As Political Education* (Ithaca: Cornell University Press, 1994), chap. 8; and David M. Steiner, *Rethinking Democratic Education: The Politics of Reform* (Baltimore: Johns Hopkins University Press, 1994).

[47] See for instance Vlastos, *Socrates;* T. H. Irwin, *Plato's Moral Theory* (New York: Oxford Uni-

"continental" philosophers see him as a protophenomenologist, nascent her-
meneuticist, and the initiator of or inspiration for the invention of Western metaphysics and/or a profound sickness of soul.[48] Still others, such as Martin Luther
King Jr. and the civil disobedients of the 1960s, find in him a political actor of
moral stature and generative courage.

But it is precisely this ambiguity about "who" Socrates is, and the contests
among his disciples and for his authority, that make him a worthy interlocutor
here and now. Not only is "Socrates" more than every figuration, the remainder
peers back at "the" original with irony and laughter in an erotic dance of reason
and desire that leave his erstwhile admirers behind or frustrated. His ugliness and
beauty seduce and repel us but it is hard to leave him be. He was what Nietzsche
despised but thought, feared, or hoped himself to be.

As is obvious, "my" Socrates is the political educator of democratic citizens, a
figure who can help us think more deeply about educational reform and recast the
current debate over the canon and multiculturalism. Certainly he resists co-
optation by conservatives to legitimate their educational agenda, since he shares
as much with the critical spirit of some multiculturalists as he does with their
conservative critics. Offering a more democratic Socrates might help break the
rigid polarities and self-indulgent polemics that too often characterize the canon-
multiculturalism debate. One burden of this book is to save "Socrates" from his
erstwhile defenders and commend him to his critics.

In a recent essay[49] Carol Dougherty argues that the Athenians did not try to
resolve the multiple narratives of their origins by which they represented themselves as Athenians, but allowed them to remain unrationalized. She goes on to
suggest that the competition over origins was part of a then contemporary controversy over citizenship and the construction of civic identity. As she puts it, "foundation tales of all kinds tend to respond to needs of the present as much as if not
more than they adequately record the past." Her point is not only helpful for
understanding how the discussion of Periclean leadership in the *Gorgias* is less
over whether he is a good leader than about how "Pericles" is to be represented
and what sort of politics various representations of him legitimate; it also helps us
understand the contemporary debates over who Socrates is, over democratic citizenship, and over American civic identity.

As for the radically different institutional and historical contexts in which Socrates lived, it is precisely such differences that can provoke us to see how we live
and offer answers to questions we do not recognize to be such. For instance, the
idea of theorists or philosophers roaming the streets, either literally as a place or
metaphorically in the language they use, as a way of engaging in dialogue with

versity Press, 1977); Gerasimos Santas, *Socrates: Philosophy in Plato's Early Dialogues* (London:
Routledge and K. Paul, 1979); and Thomas C. Brickhouse and Nicholas D. Smith, *Plato's Socrates*
(New York: Oxford University Press, 1994).

[48] See for instance John Sallis, *Being and Logos: The Way of Platonic Dialogue* (Pittsburgh:
Duquesne University Press, 1975).

[49] Carol Dougherty, "Democratic Contradictions and the Synoptic Illusion of Euripides' *Ion*," in
Ober and Hedrick, *Demokratia*, pp. 249–70.

ordinary citizens, seems as nostalgic as the idea of radical democracy.[50] Theory or philosophy, at least as that is conceived of in the United States, is an academic subject: taught in the academy, by people with academic degrees, in a specialized sometimes technical dialect of academese. In these terms philosophy is a course one takes or a subject one teaches, not something one has to do in order to make sense of a life, or of the world. But, of course, as we saw, the Socrates of Plato's *Apology* is in the streets talking to whomever he meets in everyday language (which he admittedly uses in unusual ways), about the preoccupation of their lives (which he induces them to think about rather than merely live). Without ignoring the fact that theory and philosophy have become the kinds of subject they have, it is worth asking what was and is lost by having "Socrates" in the academy. At the very least, the question might help us look more critically than is usually done at the role universities play in certifying professions, sustaining a culture of expertise, expanding bureaucratization and centralized power, all of which can eviscerate democratic citizenship. It might also push academics to make the conditions of their work its subject instead of leaving institutions that sustain our practices immune to the kind of critiques we level at others.

But what about Socrates' "failures," and Nietzsche's complaint that nothing is easier to erase than a dialectical effect? Here I would only say that to decide that something is a failure presupposes that one knows what constitutes success, a far from simple matter in Socrates' case (as I shall argue in chapters eight and nine); and that Nietzsche's own fascination with Socrates speaks against his conclusions, as he perhaps knew it did. But most of the time my aim is Nietzsche's; neither to refute nor uncritically to endorse classical thinkers, but to engage them (in both the lovers' and the military sense) to learn not so much where to go or what to do, as to indicate how we are situated and in what trajectory we find ourselves, so that we may "think about what we are doing."[51]

There is a more disconcerting warning in Nietzsche's criticism of Socrates exemplified in the way intellectuals and philosophers have domesticated the *Clouds*' challenge to them. In *Wir Philologen* Nietzsche argues that a classical education may cripple an appreciation of "the Greeks," since it reflects (in both senses) a "bloodless recollection of the past," is possessed by "nauseating" erudition, and fosters a timid, sluggish, passive indifference to the world, guaranteeing the death of freedom. "What" Nietzsche asked of his contemporaries "would a Greek say, if he could see us?"[52]

The reason for teaching the past, Nietzsche thought, was to provide an example and challenge to later generations. This is not nostalgia but a contest, a

---

[50] This is an exaggeration as the debate over public intellectuals and renewed interest in Dewey attests. In some respects, Socrates is a public intellectual. He is neither in the Assembly nor does he remain private (though he calls himself a "private citizen") but speaks about public matters in public places like the agora. (Socrates distinguishes *idiōteuein* from *dēmosieuein; Apology* 32a).

[51] Arendt uses the phrase a number of times. I have in mind something analogous to Heidegger's *auseinandersetzung* where one aims not at refutation but at an engagement designed to explore the other's thought which one's own thinking makes possible.

[52] I rely on William Arrowsmith's translation in *Arion* 2, nos. 1–2 (Spring–Summer 1963).

struggle with the Greeks to achieve what one does not possess but which one needs, to create what does not yet exist but must if men and women are to live. This demands not droning lectures but a vigorous presentation and presentment of the Greeks, not respectability but "life," not only Apollo but Dionysus. But most of "us" are, appropriately enough, Lockean underlaborers "clearing the ground a little, and removing some of the rubbish that lies in the way of knowledge.[53] But then how do we answer Nietzsche or teach Socrates? I am not sure.

In Aeschylus's *Agamemnon* the chorus turns, in desperation and perplexity, to Zeus, asking him to "cast this dead weight of ignorance finally from my brain." It cannot (or perhaps does not want to) see where the cycle of revenge and death will lead, how it will end, and what will end because of it. The chorus continues its prayer, here in Lattimore's elegant translation.[54]

> Zeus, who guided men to think,
> Who has laid it down that wisdom
> comes alone through suffering.
> Still there drips in sleep against the heart
> grief of memory; against
> our pleasures we are temperate.

This lament poses questions about the conditions of our knowing relevant both to the status of political theory and to the compatibility of the aims and structure and idiom of this book as a whole. What is it that "we" want to know and why? How do we come to know something that changes who we are, and what strategies of evasion do we employ to remain aloof from such knowledge? If wisdom comes alone through suffering, do academic essays teach us wisdom or something else? If temperance comes not from lectures but from the reluctant remembrance of things past, then what, recalling Nietzsche, are we not teaching when we teach the Greeks "academically"?[55]

VIII

If the jury is still out on Socrates, it seems to have arrived at a verdict in regard to Athenian democracy. It was far less democratic than it is celebrated for being, not only because it excluded women from political power, relied on slaves and metics, rationalized empire, and posited a barbarian "other," but because of the

---

[53] John Locke, *An Essay Concerning Human Understanding,* Fraser edition (New York: Dover, 1959), 1:14.

[54] In volume 1 of Richmond Lattimore and David Grene, eds., *The Complete Greek Tragedies* (Chicago: University of Chicago Press, 1959), p. 40.

[55] In *Love's Knowledge* (pp. 19–20), Nussbaum argues that stylistic choices by contemporary philosophers are dictated not by substantive concerns but by habit and pressure of convention, more particularly by what she calls "Anglo-American fastidiousness and emotional reticence, and above all by the academization and professionalization of philosophy," which leads to a narrow rigid notion of respectability. As my question about Socrates and the academy suggests I am sympathetic to her argument and to the contrast she goes on to make between this sense of philosophy and the conception found in the ancient world.

discrepancy between formal political equality and social and economic inequalities that compromised the "purity" of even its most radically democratic institutions. Even if it had been the radical democracy[56] its admirers claim it to have been, that is of little import for our own liberal democracy, which, whatever its flaws, is nowhere near as undemocratic as Athenian society.

Granting this and more, even the scholars who have brought the "imperfections" of Athenian democracy to our attention and dislodged what is actually a fleeting celebration of that democracy[57] conclude that "Athenian citizens participated to an unprecedented degree in the social control of their own society."[58] With its rotation in office and selection by lot, its commitment to *isonomia* and *isēgoria* (equality before and through the law, equality of speech in the Assembly), practices such as the *graphē paranōmōn*, ostracism, *dokimasia, euthunai,* and *eisangelia,* and its general belief in the sovereignty and power of the people (literally *dēmokratia*) as exercised in the local politics of the deme or the city politics of the Assembly, courts, and council, Athens gave more power to the common man than any other society we know and provided a justification for us of why such power should be given to the common people as a whole. It also recognized that such a democracy depended upon the political education that came from living a fully public life, one that included participation in cult and ritual, and in dramatic festivals as well as in political institutions and practices more conventionally defined. Because the citizens were the city, the latter's existence depended at every moment on their perspicacity and wisdom. Without such an education, participatory democracy would become what its ancient and modern critics always suppose it to be: rule by an ignorant mob driven by prejudice and the tyranny of opinion.[59]

Even if we do not seek to "apply Athenian democracy" (whatever that could possibly mean), haven't we learned enough to recognize the vision of ordinary people actively sharing power and responsibility and initiating action as anachronistic or worse—dangerously utopian, antimodern and antiliberal, and insufficiently attentive to the compromised standing of all radical projects in the wake of totalitarianism? If the history of the past two hundred years (since the French Revolution), past seventy-five years (since the Russian Revolution), and the past

---

[56] On the meaning of radical democracy, see C. Douglas Lummis's *Radical Democracy* (Ithaca: Cornell University Press, 1996), and David Trend, ed., *Radical Democracy: Identity, Citizenship and the State* (New York: Routledge, 1996).

[57] On this see Jennifer Roberts, *Athens on Trial: The Antidemocratic Tradition in Western Thought* (Princeton: Princeton University Press, 1994).

[58] The quotation is from Virginia J. Hunter's *Policing Athens: Social Control in the Attic Lawsuits, 420–320 b.c.* (Princeton: Princeton University Press, 1994), p. 149. I chose a quote from Hunter rather than others who conclude the same thing because of the title and concerns of her book.

[59] As Barber argues in *An Aristocracy of Everyone.* This view is shared by ancient and modern "conservatives" even when the latter regard themselves as liberals, as with the contributors to the Trilateral Commission Report. See Michael Crozier, Samuel P. Huntington, and Joji Watanuki, *The Crisis of Democracy* (New York: New York University Press, 1975), chap. 3, where the 1960s are seen as a disruptive upsurge of democratic activity eroding the capacity of "responsible elites" to govern.

five years (with the rise of nationalism and ethnic cleansing) proves anything, it is the necessity of rights, proceduralism, and constitutional guarantees, and the dangers of "fundamentalist projects" such as radical democracy, which are hostile to structural differentiation and social pluralism and attached to a vision of community based on a single conception of the good life.[60]

Even those contemporary activists and writers committed to radical democracy either ignore or explicitly reject classical Athens as a point of departure and reference. While sympathetic to the rediscovery of citizenship, Chantal Mouffe warns against going "back to a pre-modern conception of the political." "We need," she continues, "to be alert to the dangers of a nostalgia for the Greek polis and Gemeinschaft types of community."[61]

Once more these are serious objections. Once more I think them overstated and, in a few instances, misinformed. I turn first to the issue of rights, then to Mouffe's warning, which will speak to the status of citizenship and "the people."[62]

It is undoubtedly true that the discourse of rights has been and can be a means for advancing democracy, as new groups claim access to rights already declared or new rights are demanded in social relations previously regarded as "naturally" hierarchical, such as those concerned with race or gender. But I do think there are good political and historical reasons to be skeptical of the sufficiency and efficacy of rights in the absence of a vigorous culture of civic activism and democratized power. Without these, social, economic, and cultural inequalities erode, if not undercut, formally guaranteed rights such as the right to vote, speak, worship, acquire and protect property, and be assured of a fair trial.[63] Moreover, without providing democratic content to rights, they can be used for antidemocratic ends, less by the democratic majorities so feared by liberal and conservative elites as by legislative and administrative rulings inspired by single-issue minorities using political and legal means to deprive other citizens of rights or restrict their scope. We can see examples of this in the rights to abortion, sexual freedom, and privacy from invasive surveillance.[64] Finally, even rights and constitutionalism create certain kinds of relationships, powers, institutions, and practices, which may then

[60] This argument is made by Jean L. Cohen and Andrew Arato in *Civil Society and Political Theory* (Cambridge, Mass.: MIT Press, 1992).

[61] In her "Preface: Democratic Politics Today," in *Dimensions of Radical Democracy: Pluralism, Citizenship, Community* (London: Verso, 1992), p. 5. In addition see her concluding chapter (written with Ernesto Laclau) of *Hegemony and Socialist Strategy: Toward a Radical Democratic Politics* (London: Verso, 1985).

[62] The most subtle reconstruction of these categories responsive to postmodern criticisms is Kirstie McClure's "On the Subject of Rights: Pluralism, Plurality and Political Identity," in Chantal Mouffe, ed., *Dimensions of Radical Democracy: Pluralism, Citizenship, Community* (London: Verso, 1992).

[63] For the democratic potential of rights see Mouffe's essay "Democratic Citizenship and the Political Community," in her *Dimensions of Radical Democracy,* especially pp. 226–27. For why a vigorous civic culture is necessary for rights to do what liberals want them to see, Steven Lukes's discussion of "the third dimension of power" in his *Power: A Radical View* (London: Macmillan, 1974).

[64] See Sheldon S. Wolin, "What Revolutionary Action Means Today," *democracy* 2 (Fall 1982): 17–28.

be posited as natural or historically necessary. Rights can also be used against dominant practices and any idea or practice can come to be "naturalized" in this way, even radical democracy. (Indeed liberals would argue that is where the charge is particularly apt.) But liberals too often see the language of rights as the opposite of or an alternative to disciplinary practices rather than another form of them, which does not mean all such practices are equal.

Even when rights do what they are supposed to do, guarantee a form of protection and freedom beyond the ordinary reach of legislative and executive power, they do so more because of the success of liberal political education in creating a sustaining culture, than because of particular institutional arrangements like the separation of powers or the existence of a bill of rights.[65] "There is no norm or norms," Cornelius Castoriadis writes, "which would not itself be a historical creation. And there is no way of eliminating the risks of collective hubris." The supposition that one can eliminate such risks by creating a constitution is an exaggeration, if not an illusion. If we can be reasonably certain that the reestablishment of slavery in the United States is extremely improbable, that has less to do with existing laws or constitutions than with "a judgment concerning the active response of a huge majority of the people to such an attempt."[66]

There is another register to the debate over rights, one that leads to the issue of gemeinschaft and to choice of democratic Athens as a way of exploring how a democratic culture can ground a political education capable of containing "democratic" excess[67] democratically while remaining alert to postmodernist concerns about hypostacizing the category of citizen. It is a register admirably presented by Jeremy Waldron.[68]

"In a world crying out for a greater emphasis on fraternity and communal responsibility in social life," Waldron begins, "what is the point of an institution that legitimates the making of querulous and adversarial claims by individuals against their fellows? If human relations can be founded on affection, why is so much made in modern jurisprudence of formal and impersonal rights as a starting point for the evaluations of laws and institutions?" His answer is twofold: "rigid

[65] For two views that emphasize this point but disagree about its implications, see Esquith, *Intimacy and Spectacle,* and Kateb, *The Inner Ocean* (especially chap. 3). Kateb argues that the moral worth of constitutional democracy rests not only on its defense of rights but on the effects of a way of life predicated on rights based individualism. For him rights become a culture rather than a set of formal claims or stipulations and *democratic* individuality's spiritual outgrowth and elaboration of rights-based individualism in a constitutional democracy. Esquith is far more skeptical.

[66] "The Greek Polis and the Creation of Democracy," in David Ames Curtis, ed., *Philosophy, Politics, Autonomy* (New York: Oxford University Press, 1991), pp. 115, 116. One could argue that liberal political education creates precisely a kind of citizen and person most susceptible to the worst kind of communitarian appeals on grounds analogous to Freud's argument on the return of the repressed or Dostoevski's in his story of the Grand Inquisitor in the *Brothers Karamazov.* On liberalism as political education, see Esquith's *Intimacy and Spectacle* and Flathman, "Liberal versus Civic."

[67] It cannot be said too often that the worst political excesses in Athens were committed by oligarchs. A similar case could be made for the excesses of our own "responsible elites."

[68] Jeremy Waldon, "When Justice Replaces Affection: The Need for Rights," *Harvard Journal of Law and Public Policy* 2, no. 3 (1979): 624–47. (Hereafter, page references will be given in text.)

abstract formulas of justice" and "legalistic rights and duties" provide a "fall-back" position in case other constituent elements of social relations come apart; and "impersonal rules and rights" furnish a basis on which people can initiate new relations with other people even if alienated from the affective bonds of existing attachments and community. To illustrate the first, Waldron considers marriage; to consider the second, he looks at the world of Shakespeare's *Romeo and Juliet.*

When we hear a partner complaining about a denial or withdrawal of conjugal rights "we know that something has gone wrong with the interplay of desire and affection between the partners." The bonds of affection and intimacy no longer hold when lovers see themselves as competitors if not enemies. Impersonal rules and rights provide a basis for new moral initiatives, initiatives which challenge existing affections and so provide the chance for "social progress" (p. 631). In Shakespeare's *Romeo and Juliet* there is no public and hence no visible and reliable way for the lovers to coordinate their actions or expectations. They can count only on their own resources because they live in a world in which their relationship cannot formally exist (p. 633). Given that there are always times and places where communication breaks down, actions are misread, and timing fails, where the only hope for success is desperately to assume, with Juliet, "the form of death to the social world in which she was brought up, and to resurrect herself in the giddy space of a world beyond the city walls," shouldn't critics of rights pause before calling for a return to a particularistic communitarian form of politics? "Don't urge us to identify the structures for social action too closely with the affections of existing communities" (p. 634). Recognize the need for a structure of rights, "somewhat apart from the communal or affective attachments," which can be relied upon to survive as a basis for action no matter what happens to those attachments.

Though an individual standing apart from all social relations is unimaginable, the examples of marriage and Juliet suggest why it is a good thing that modern men and women feel able "to distance themselves from, reflect upon, and consciously embrace or repudiate any or all of the relations that constitute their history" (p. 645). Certainly we live in and form communities; "but our communal attachments are never so remote from our capacities as conscious articulate, thinking, choosing, creating beings that we cannot subject them to scrutiny and consideration" (p. 645). This does not mean holding back something from our commitments, only that we can make the effort, when necessary, to wrench ourselves away and construct the necessary psychological distance. For us moderns "intensity, whole-heartedness, and the sense of having identified comprehensively with a project or commitment, are as much features of the commitments that people *choose* and the ones they could give up IF they wanted to, as of the commitments which people *discover* they have and find they cannot question." Indeed having something to fall back on if an attachment fails may be "a *condition* of being able to identify intensely with one's attachments, rather than something which derogates from that intensity" (p. 641).

Athens of course was not a liberal society based on rights, legalism, and an abstract idea of justice.[69] Yet by the last third of the fifth century B.C. there was a sense in which the citizenry as a whole distanced itself from and reflected upon the conditions that constituted its own history and identity as it participated in a tradition of self-scrutiny, that Socrates expanded outside the institutional confines in which it was initiated. This tradition of politicocultural education insisted on communal responsibility in social life *and* legitimated adversarial claims against fellow citizens; it involved myths of common ancestry and familial bonds *and* recognized an extraordinary variety of social forms and relationships. In these terms, the role rights play as a fallback position and creating a space for reconstituting political relationships was played by the people exercising power at different points in different ways and from different perspectives within a democratized society that politicized much of communal life.[70]

What made this work (to the degree it did) was a tragic sensibility alien to Waldron's self-proclaimed modernism, this despite his reliance on *Romeo and Juliet* and reference to Arendt. To Waldron's emphasis on agents capable of "conscious, articulate, thinking, choosing, creating beings" the Greeks would have added a second dimension. Here is Jean-Pierre Vernant:

> In the tragic perspective, acting, being an agent, has a double character. On the one side, it consists in taking counsel with oneself, weighing the for and against and doing the best one can to foresee the order of means and ends. On the other hand, it is to make a bet on the unknown and the incomprehensible and to take a risk on a terrain that remains impenetrable to you. It involves entering the play of supernatural forces . . . where one does not know whether they are preparing success or disaster.[71]

What this suggests is that Athens was a *political* community in which the force of "political" undermines the sort of communitarianism Waldron criticizes. Indeed I suspect that the construction of Athens as an undifferentiated gemeinschaft integrated by a largely uncontested idea of the common good is a serious, if not self-serving, exaggeration.

It is a serious exaggeration because it underestimates the importance of class differences and the contests for cultural and political power they provoked. It also ignores the diversity of local traditions and the fact that an Athenian citizen belonged to a number of political, social, and cultural affiliations, such as demes and phratries, which gave a fluidity and plurality to citizen identity.[72] In addition

[69] But see Eric A. Havelock, *The Liberal Temper in Greek Politics* (New Haven: Yale University Press, 1964).

[70] I do not mean to overstate my case. While a good argument can be made that the movement of democratization provided the space and occasion for political challenges to particular community standards (which in effect were standards that encouraged such challenges), the case for social changes (in regard to gender relations or the status of slaves) is problematic. Then again the case for liberal rights in this regard is also more problematic than Waldron's examples suggest.

[71] Jean-Pierre Vernant in *Tragedy and Myth in Ancient Greece* (Atlantic Highlands, N.J.: Humanities Press, 1981), p. 37.

[72] See Josiah Ober, *Mass and Elites in Democratic Athens: Rhetoric, Ideology and the Power of the People* (Princeton: Princeton University Press, 1989), for a discussion of class and democratic ideology. In several respects this plurality echoes contemporary "postmodern" rights. In "On the

such a construction ignores a literary tradition that represents, and historical evidence that supports, the idea that Athens was a sanctuary for outcasts, exiles, and peoples of diverse ethnicities who later became citizens. The Athenian exclusivist myth of autochthony was in fact part of a more inclusive civic myth in which the Athenians, faced with the ethnic diversity of citizens whose ancestors came from Corinth, Sicily, or Anatolia, assigned them to tribes named after traditional Athenian heroes. While the reforms of Cleisthenes that constituted this civic myth were hardly multiculturalist—immigrants were not encouraged to cultivate their original customs—they did demand that native Athenians renounce many of their privileges and accept equality with those of foreign origin.[73] Penultimately, the vision of Athens as a homogeneous community without respect for plurality ignores the fact of polymorphous sexuality[74] and the social consequences of polytheism. And finally, it ignores the way the Athenians were able to transform the notion of aristocratic honor into a democratic idea of dignity, which seems to have functioned even more effectively than rights now do in protecting even the poorest citizens against physical abuse and political intimidation.[75] If one is interested in maximizing plurality and differences within a strong democratic framework, Athenian political culture is more than an object lesson.

The characterization of Athens as *gemeinschaft* is self-serving to the extent that it delegitimates Athenian democracy as a point from which to question the democratic credentials of liberalism, obscures what may be "our" homogeneity, and fails to emphasize the antidemocratic form differentiation can take.[76] One could argue that the culture of late twentieth-century capitalism, with its aggressive consumerism, market mentality, technical fetishism, and "information highway," is a more homogenizing force than the preoccupation with pluralism and difference would lead one to believe.[77] One could also argue, at least in the case

---

Subject of Rights: Pluralism, Plurality and Political identity" (in Mouffe, *Dimensions of Radical Democracy*), McClure talks about multiple and intersecting group memberships of identities within a social plurality where only one "is that of formal citizenship in the state" (p. 115). Granting the differences between the nation-state and the polis, there are still similarities between her description and the status of citizenship in Athens. There is some controversy about how important demes and phratries were to Athenian identity, especially when compared to other geographic-kinship units in premodern states.

[73] I have taken this argument from Barry S. Strauss, "The Melting Pot, the Mosaic, and the Agora," in Euben et al., *Athenian Political Thought,* pp. 252–64. As he rightly points out the subsequent history of Athenian citizenship is less admirable. The issue is dramatized in Sophocles' *Oedipus at Colonus* (on which see Laura Slatkin, "Oedipus at Colonus: Exile and Integration," in Euben, *Greek Tragedy and Political Theory*), pp. 210–21.

[74] This may be one thing Thucydides' Pericles means when, in the Funeral Oration, he boasts that the Athenians live as they like. That claim, and the idea of life it represents, is the object of scorn by both Plato and Aristotle.

[75] See Josiah Ober, "Power and Oratory in Democratic Athens," in Ian Worthington, ed., *Persuasion: Greek Rhetoric in Athens* (London: Routledge, 1994), pp. 84–108.

[76] There are times and places where the opposite emphasis would be appropriate, where liberalism could (and should) be used to question the democratic credentials of Athenian democracy. But a progressivist myth reinforced by the claim that liberal America is the apotheosis of history suggests that this is not the time or the place for it.

[77] This is not to minimize the political significance of ethnic and national animosities. But that is a

of the United States, that in recent years American society has grown more and more inegalitarian, more divided by extremes of wealth and poverty, education and ignorance, more systematically dominated by corporate power and systemically corrupt, more retarded by mass media that ensure political and cultural immaturity, and more and more openly ruled by elites bent on appropriating the conduct, knowledge, and procedures of public life. In a reversal of the democratization of power that defined the evolution of Athenian democracy, this represents a closing down of public spaces and a narrowing of matters brought before the commons. More and more of political life is being claimed as the eminent domain of professional experts and professors who reappropriate knowledge while forming a caste of initiates.[78]

---

somewhat different matter, and nationalism itself, it could be argued, is a distinctively modern phenomenon and thus part of the homogenization I am talking about.

[78] For the critique, see Wolin, "What Revolutionary Action Means Today." For the way that critique inverts the evolution of Athenian democracy, see Jean-Pierre Vernant, *The Origins of Greek Thought* (Ithaca: Cornell University Press, 1982), pp. 47–48, 51–52.

The Battle of Salamis and the
Origins of Political Theory

No remembrance remains secure unless it is condensed and distilled into a
framework of conceptual notions, within which it can further exercise itself.
Experience and even stories which grow out of what men do and endure, of
happenings and events, sink back into the futility inherent in the living words
and the living deed unless they are talked about over and over again.

—Hannah Arendt[1]

[Philosophy's] claims in respect to politics can be readily summed up as an
imperative: to shield politics from the perils that are immanent to it, it has to
be hauled on to dry land, set down on terra firma.

—Jacques Rancière[2]

IN THIS CHAPTER I want to make an argument and tell a story about the origins of
democratic politics and political theory in classical Athens. It is an argument in
the sense that I have a thesis (actually several) and will offer evidence, mostly
"literary" and "textual," for it. It is a story, not only because the evidence is
uncertain, and because I cannot, in such a short compass assess the evidence we
do have, but because I will be talking about the mythologizing of a historical
event, the naval Battle of Salamis in 480 B.C. where an Athenian-led Hellenic
alliance defeated a greatly superior Persian force.[3] Given the disparity of power
and the enormity of the risk, the sheer fact, let alone the magnitude, of the victory
seemed nothing less than miraculous. When a "city that was no city except in
desperate hope"[4] risked all only to have those hopes realized beyond their most
fervent prayers, it is easy to understand how that victory could have provided a
moment of shared faith and a lasting vision of civic achievement. As far as we
know, Salamis was the only historical event elevated to the mythical status accorded those heroic legends from which tragedy drew its inspiration and stories.
In and through Aeschylus's *Persians,* Herodotus's *Histories,* and Thucydides'

---

[1] Hannah Arendt, *On Revolution* (New York: Viking, 1963), p. 222.

[2] *On the Shores of Politics,* trans. Liz Heron (London: Verso, 1995), p. 1.

[3] Nothing about the story is meant to suggest some simple progression. The texts do not suggest it,
nor would I.

[4] Thucydides 2.74. Here, as elsewhere, I rely on the Crawley translation with some minor
alterations.

History, we can see how the triumph there became a spiritual foundation and an empowering vision of democratic action sustained through emulation and reenactment.[5] In terms of Vernant's discussion of the evolution of the polis (detailed in the next chapter), the victory at Salamis helped open the public arena in both size and substance beyond anything known in the Hellenic world by legitimating the claims to power and authority of the poor whose courage and steadfastness had won the victory.[6]

As this suggests Salamis was interpreted by democrats and oligarchs alike as a democratic victory, so this essay is also about the origins of the Athenian democratic ethos as it relates to the beginnings of political theory.[7] Although Athenian politics continued to be directed by the sons of eminent families for sixty years after Salamis, the triumph there provided the ground and opportunity for the poor to claim for themselves a share of glory and respect the *aristoi* had made their exclusive prerogative. In doing so they gave substance to Pericles' boast (in the Funeral Oration) that the Athenians were an aristocratic democracy, collectively great in words and deed,[8] and provided evidence for Josiah Ober's argument that concepts like *eugeneia* (high or noble birth) and *kalokagathia* (good and beautiful) "were democratized and communalized in the course of the fifth and fourth

---

[5] In *The Origins of Totalitarianism* (New York: Harcourt Brace Jovanovich, 1973 [new edition with added prefaces], p. 208), Arendt writes about such foundations as "promising safe guidance through the limitless space of the future." She elaborates this in section 4 of "What Is Authority," in *Between Past and Future: Eight Studies in Political Thought,* enl. ed. (New York: Viking Press, 1968), pp. 91–142.

[6] Though I do think Salamis had institutional consequences, my emphasis is on the way it helped legitimate what Josiah Ober calls the "demotic control of the public realm." He argues that power is manifest in how discourse is fashioned and sustained more than in narrow legal power residing in particular institutions. Since I think it is precisely such contests for power over discourses that are dramatized in Platonic dialogues like the *Gorgias,* book 1 of the *Republic,* and the *Protagoras,* I am more sympathetic with his view as opposed to that of Mogens Herman Hansen. See Josiah Ober, "The Nature of Athenian Democracy," *Classical Philology* 84 (1989): 322–34 (the quotations are from p. 333), and Mogens Herman Hansen, "On the Importance of Institutions in an Analysis of Athenian Democracy," *Classical et Medievalia* 40 (1989): 107–13.

[7] I will have little to say about the undemocratic practices this democratic ethos presupposed or about the role of Solon's legislation, Cleisthenes' reforms, or the tyrants in the creation of this ethos. On these matters, see W. G. Forrest, *The Emergence of Greek Democracy* (New York: McGraw-Hill, 1966); Martin Ostwald, *Nomos and the Beginnings of Athenian Democracy* (New York: Oxford University Press, 1969), and his *From Popular Sovereignty to the Sovereignty of the Law* (Berkeley: University of California Press, 1986); Christian Meier, *The Greek Discovery of Politics* (Cambridge, Mass.: Harvard University Press, 1990); Josiah Ober, "The Athenian Revolution of 508/7 B.C.: Violence, Authority and the Origins of Democracy," in Josiah Ober, ed., *The Athenian Revolution: Essays on Ancient Greek Democracy and Political Theory* (Princeton: Princeton University Press, 1996); and the essays by Charles W. Fornara and Loren J. Samons II, *Athens from Cleisthenes to Pericles* (Berkeley: University of California Press, 1991).

[8] The idea of an aristocratic democracy has been given contemporary restatement by Joseph Tussman in his *Obligation and the Body Politic* (New York: Oxford University Press, 1960), chap. 4, pp. 105–7, and has been contested by Nicole Loraux in her *The Invention of Athens: The Funeral Oration in the Classical City,* trans. Alan Sheridan (Cambridge, Mass.: Harvard University Press, 1986). Cf. Josiah Ober, *Mass and Elite in Democratic Athens: Rhetoric, Ideology and the Power of the People* (Princeton: Princeton University Press, 1989).

centuries and so made the common property of all citizens."9 The Salamis story was a critical aspect of this process.

I am not only interested in how Salamis helped constitute this democratic ethos. I am also concerned with how "an" event—in this case, the naval victory over Persia—became bounded, memorialized, and culturally inscribed, thereby organizing and legitimating certain forms of Athenian thought and action for three generations.10 All events are placed within larger narratives and are defined by a grid of comparisons and contrasts. Salamis as event and symbol competed for renown and significance with the earlier land triumph at Marathon. Already with Cimon in the decades following the victory, then again with the philosophical critics of democracy in the fourth century, and perhaps among the oligarchs who joined the revolution against the democracy at the end of the fifth century, the status of Salamis (and so of the democratic claims enabled by it) was contested. "We know" Nicole Loraux writes "that in the fifth century" (she is referring to "Cimon and his entourage") a whole "ideological structure was built up around the exaltation of Marathon at the expense of Salamis."11 Two examples of what she calls "a vast propaganda program" is Pausanias's account of how Aeschylus, the combatant of Salamis, sought glory in death from the glory of Marathon alone, and the splitting of Salamis (by Aeschylus among others) into two simultaneous episodes, the known naval battle and the hoplitic Battle of Psyttaleia, "a fiction entirely in the service of tendentious history."12

The establishment of the Salamis legend enables us to see what Clifford Geertz calls "the suspended webs of significance human beings have spun for themselves."13 But perhaps more significantly it also affords a glimpse of a people coming to understand themselves as spinners of their own webs of significance. Initially the victory at Salamis was understood as the jealous and justice-affirming gods exacting retribution for Xerxes' literally unbounded ambition in seeking to enslave the sea and the Hellenes.14 That is Aeschylus's view, and

9 See Ober's discussion of Lysias 30.14 in *Mass and Elite* where Lysias associates *polloi* (typically used in a derogatory way about the Athenian masses) with *kaloi k'agathoi* (moderation and goodness), implying that these aristocratic virtues can be the attribute of any good citizen (pp. 259–61).

10 I mean "inscribed" in a literal as well as figurative sense. "The invention of a prose which would realize the full potential of the word inscribed, the scope of expression available when the world no longer needed memorization to survive, took even longer. Its progress can be marked in the texts of Herodotus, Thucydides, and Plato." Eric A. Havelock, *The Literate Revolution in Greece and Its Consequences* (Princeton: Princeton University Press, 1982), p. 183. See also Walter Ong, *Orality and Literacy* (New York: Methuen, 1982).

11 Loraux, *The Invention of Athens*, p. 161. She suggests that the aristocratic rejection of Salamis was almost an aesthetic revulsion. The battle lacked order and form as opposed to a hoplite battle made in close order.

12 Ibid.

13 Since culture consists of these webs, the analysis of it cannot be "an experimental science in search of laws, but an interpretative one in search of meaning." Clifford Geertz in *The Interpretation of Cultures* (New York: Basic Books, 1973), p. 5.

14 See the messenger's story of how the Persian retreat over the River Strymon ended in catastrophe. *Persae*, 495–514.

largely that of Herodotus, although he emphasizes a theme already present in the *Persae:* that the victory at Salamis (which is the dramatic center of Herodotus's *Histories)* was won by men because of their political culture. With him (but still more with Thucydides), we see the Athenians coming to understand their power (as distinct from their material strength), and so their triumph, as emanating from their democratic ethos.

As the Athenians became "more impressed by human capacity than by divine vengeance,"[15] they became more convinced that political and intellectual power (and powerlessness) derive from the practices men create by and for themselves. It is no accident that the gods are virtually absent in Thucydides' *History* (although the theological structure of *koros-atē-hubris* certainly is not), and that he reveals men as collectively sustaining their lives through their interpretations of words and deeds. He and the actors in his *History* show how meanings are embedded in and constitute political practices. Although such practices are inseparable from the meaning they have for those engaged in them, they are not identical to those meanings. Thus, Thucydides investigates and corrects what he regards as the naive, distorted, and corrupt self-understandings and self-definitions articulated in the political practices of the actors in his *History* and the projected readers of it.[16] Let me offer two examples.

Near the beginning of his *History* (1.20) in the course of showing how ignorant people are of their own history, Thucydides "unmasks" the traditional Athenian interpretation of the tyrannicide by Harmodius and Aristogeiton. This not only corrects the historical "record" (at the expense of exploding a myth of collective hostility to tyranny and passionate devotion to freedom),[17] it reveals human beings as creators of meaning in the context of political struggle.

A few paragraphs later (1.24) he assures us that he is interested in the truest occasion of the war although it was not manifest in speech. Most simply and immediately he means that he will say, and so make known, reasons and causes that were left unsaid or were not known to the participants themselves. But more generally, he suggests that he will rearticulate and redescribe the speeches, deeds, and practices of actors in order to expose the implicit framework by which they give meaning to what they do.

One could say that this self-consciousness was prefigured by the kind of victory Salamis was. One could also say that the powers the threat called forth were

---

[15] The phrase is that of A.W.H. Adkins in *Moral Values and Political Behaviour in Ancient Greece* (New York: Norton, 1972), p. 100. "[T]he victory of Salamis, which Aeschylus saw as a demonstration of divine anger, was no longer anything but the sign of a wrong-redressing people's right to hegemony" (Loraux, *The Invention of Athens,* p. 54). On this, see Lysias 47; Plato's *Menexenus;* 240 and Clifford Orwin, *The Humanity of Thucydides* (Princeton: Princeton University Press, 1994), chap. 4.

[16] See the discussion of these matters in Charles Taylor, *Philosophy and the Human Sciences: Philosophical Papers,* vol. 2 (Cambridge: Cambridge University Press, 1985), chap 3.

[17] M. I. Finley, "The Ancestral Constitution," in *The Use and Abuse of History* (New York: Viking Press, 1975), p. 58. Thucydides mentions the tyrannicide legend again (at 6.53) but now, not coincidentally, the Athenians are more "realistic" in their understanding of motives and events.

the beginning of the end. Nietzsche for one thought "the danger was too great and the victory too overwhelming,"[18] and Thucydides seems to agree, at least to the extent that he regarded Salamis as the true origin of Athenian greatness *and* as initiating (or exacerbating) cultural rhythms that eventually undermined that greatness. It is in and through his *History* that the Salamis legend achieves its apogee (in the Funeral Oration) and its perverse fulfillment (at Melos and Sicily). As he portrays and exemplifies it, the victory there made it possible for the Athenians to think theoretically, and necessary for them to do so when confronting the crises that victory helped foster. The daring at Salamis foreshadows and inspires the Athenian daring Thucydides describes and that describes his *History*. This same daring is preface, problem, and inspiration for Socrates and political philosophy. In these terms, Socrates appears as the supreme embodiment and the severest critic of the Athenian political and intellectual tradition as it was formed by and at Salamis. And Plato's denigration of Salamis (in the *Laws*) appears as the repudiation of that tradition (and of Socrates' partial commitment to it).

To speak of origins as legitimating (and delegitimating) forms of action and character, of men and women as constituting their collective lives through interpretations amid political struggle, and of the beginnings of political theory as implicit in democratic culture suggests that stories about or analyses of origins are political projects as much as they are accurate accounts of the past. This is clear in the debate over the Ancestral Constitution *(patrios politeia)* and to Plato—as true about "the" tradition of political theory as about "the" Athenian political tradition.

During the last years of the fifth century B.C. and the first decade of the fourth, almost all Athenians agreed that the only way to rescue their city from its present calamities and forestall future dangers was to restore the Ancestral Constitution. Although there were some disagreements about what exactly that constitution was and so which institutional arrangements it presently mandated, there was virtually no dispute about the legitimacy or limits of the appeal to antiquity.[19] At least after 399, and for the great majority of Athenians, the origins of their democracy with Solon and at Salamis remained sacrosanct images that provided inspiration and identification with their democratic roots and aspirations.

Of course, some men probably retained oligarchic commitments in private. No doubt others, like Thucydides, regarded Salamis as the foundation of democratic greatness and democratic excesses. And a few others, such as Plato, may well have become disillusioned with conventional politics altogether as he tells the story in the *Seventh Letter*.

As legends become suspect and subject to critical analyses they are seen as disguising the past while commemorating it, as making it more, less, and other

---

[18] Quoted in Tracy B. Strong, *Friedrich Nietzsche and the Politics of Transfiguration* (Berkeley: University of California Press, 1975), p. 169. (Legend has it that Euripides was born on the day of the Salamis victory. No doubt this only confirmed Nietzsche in his judgment of Salamis and of Euripides.) I think Nietzsche has a point. That Salamis was also the impetus for political theorizing and that Plato shares Nietzsche's view of the battle only makes the story more interesting.

[19] Finley, "Ancestral Constitution," 44.

than it "really" was, as suppressing complexity, particularity, and dissonance in the "interests" of clarity, evocation, and inspiration.[20] Sometimes these suppressed alternatives are rediscovered and so renovated by politically disaffected groups or individuals who reinterpret the legend, offer a competing one, or come to regard the very idea of venerating the past and origins as insufficient or pernicious. In the *Republic,* Plato dismisses appeals to past authority and attempts to reground political foundations in cosmology, metaphysics, and ontology. In the *Laws* he offers an interpretation of the past that seeks to reestablish the primacy of Marathon.

The political dimension of origins not only involves particular historical traditions, it also involves "the tradition" of political theory. As political theorists themselves have realized, founding legends not only establish and demarcate a political landscape, they do the same for theoretical landscapes.[21] Political theory, like a particular political society, has its legendary foundations, empowering visions, and paradigmatic figures who provide "guidance through the limitless spaces of the future."[22]

I

The *Persians,* presented in 472 (with the young Pericles as *chorēgos*), is unique among extant Greek drama in honoring a contemporary event in which many of the audience had been participants.[23] That event was the Battle of Salamis. Although the defeat of Persia required many battles, Aeschylus compresses the entire war into this one confrontation, which he distorts in ways that would be obvious to his compatriots. He misrepresents Darius as a prudent king who never left Asia, exaggerates the importance of the minor action on Psyttaleia, portrays Xerxes' retreat from Salamis as the hasty flight of a totally shattered monarch, and virtually invents the disaster at Strymon.[24] Obviously, Aeschylus is not offering a "historical" reconstruction of Salamis.

The setting of the play is not Athens but the Persian capital of Susa. It opens with the chorus, awestruck at the enormous diversity, wealth, and unequaled

---

[20] Plutarch (*Themistocles* 9.4) claims that Themistocles' strategy was highly unpopular.

[21] In both cases the process is a hermeneutic one. The conceptions of origins shape contemporary understandings of politics and political theory while those understandings shape the understanding of the origin, including what an "origin" is and how important origins are in particular and in general.

[22] In fact, one could present the history of political theory as a conflict between two founding legends: the classical vision of founding by men of supreme, often divinely inspired virtu(e), creating a civic brotherhood (but not sisterhood) of patriots; and the liberal vision of social contract in which men (although not women) are defined as preformed individuals who join with others in limited partnerships for largely instrumental ends. Here again the question is how a theoretical event or deed is constituted as moral and memory—whether it appears in intellectual and political rhetoric as exemplar or object lesson.

[23] I have relied on Podlecki's translation of *The Persians* (Englewood Cliffs, N.J.: Prentice-Hall, 1970), but again with my own emendations.

[24] H.D.F. Kitto, *Greek Tragedy* (Garden City, N.Y.: Doubleday Anchor Books, 1954), pp. 35–45, and *Poiesis* (Berkeley: University of California Press, 1966), pp. 92–93.

strength of the armament that has left to cast "an enslaving yoke" (1–50) on Greece *(zugon amphibalein doulion Helladi)*. So great is the power of this "golden race of godlike men" that no natural human force can withstand it, for it is like a "raging flood" and "irresistible wave" (86–92).

But interspersed with pride in the expedition's grandeur we hear about the suffering of those, especially women, who are left behind. Regardless of the outcome, the cost of throwing a yoke over Greece and the Hellespont is to enslave Persian families with their husbandless women.[25] Doubts about the outcome only reinforce these fears. In counterpoint to the wonder at the invincible army are reminders of how the "gods' crafty snare" lures the powerful into a net of ruin. Great power is as much temptation as opportunity, as fearful to its possessors as to the possessors' enemy.

The queen enters, and the fearsome net of ruin takes on detail and substance. In her recurrent dream, which she now recounts, her son is destroyed amid images of dust, torn fabric, and prey to an unnaturally vanquishing predator. Counseled to supplicate the gods and bring the ghost of Darius up from beneath the earth, she starts to leave, but pauses to ask about Athens. Where is it? Why is it so important? How strong and wealthy is it? How does it fight? Who rules it? The chorus tells her Athens is the key to Greece's freedom and that its strength lies less in the size of its army or its wealth than in its way of fighting "in close array" (the hoplite phalanx) and in the fact, which the queen finds barely credible, that the Athenians' courage comes from their freedom rather than from some lord who instills fear for battle.

The chorus's foreboding and the queen's dark dream are made palpable by a messenger arriving with news that "a single stroke" has ruined the great Persian host: That stroke is the defeat at Salamis.

> O name of Salamis, most hateful to my ears.
> Ah, how I lament when I remember Athens.
>
> (284–85)

The queen is sure only greater force could have vanquished the Persian force. But she is wrong. It is the joint efforts of men and gods that have brought the empire low (345–47). And to her query "Do you mean to say that Athens remains unsacked [*aporthētos*]?" he replies, "While her sons still live, the ramparts of the city remain impregnable." As the audience well knew, the city of Athens was destroyed by Xerxes. And yet the city that was no city lived on in the courage and hope for freedom of her citizen soldiers and sailors. The messenger relates how before the battle a mighty shout reached their ears:

> O sons of Hellas, go now and bring freedom to your native land,
> to your children and your wives,
> to the seats of your ancestral gods and
> the tombs of your fathers: now the struggle is for all.
>
> (402–5)

---

[25] Michael Gargarin, *Aeschylean Drama* (Berkeley: University of California Press, 1976), chap. 2, especially p. 18.

Unlike the Persians, who fight far from their land to enslave another, leaving behind both the "Asian earth, their mother consumed in grief and longing," and their real mothers and wives whose fear stretches with the lengthening days of absent men, Greek power and freedom remain tied to the land, household, and ancestral hearth. The Athenians' courage blooms from soil of common ties and inherited pieties, and so their mortal efforts are seconded, even transfigured, by divine energy.[26] Indeed, the victory at Salamis is gained by man *and* given to him by the gods.

In bridging the Hellespont, Xerxes had thought to enslave the sea, lash nature to his mortal aims, transgressing boundaries between land and sea, east and west, Hellene and barbarian, and so confounding divine apportionments of fate and place. But the gods wreak havoc on such mind-diseased men, leaving them, as Xerxes is left at the play's end, defeated and destroyed, his tattered robes a symbol of his once proud army now in disarray, a victim of his own impetuosity and the gods' jealousy. Destroyer of temples, he is now destroyed: having blindly reached beyond himself in thought and action, he has lost the location of life and judgment.

Yet given where the play is performed it is not that Persia should remember Athens but that Athens should remember Persia, for both its political dissimilarities and its human similarities.[27] The superiority of the polis lies in adherence to divinely sanctioned limits that Xerxes has ignored and Athens might come to ignore. All men, whether Greek or Persian, must remember their mortality amid their power and wealth, for only respect for limits makes achievement lasting. Without it, wealth, conquest, and mind defy human finitude, until, reaching for all, men grasp nothing.

For an Athenian audience watching the suffering of a dignified enemy, the *Persae* unites loss and gain in a single instant, bringing to the victors in their exultation a wisdom borne of suffering and loss. The play does indeed celebrate Greek power and freedom and one can certainly find the construction of "the other" in it. But it also warns that sustaining such freedom and power requires the observance of those boundaries of life, place, and action violated by Xerxes.

In Aeschylus the celebration of Athenian power and freedom is central to the play's shaping of the Salamis legend. So, too, is the warning about excess. The play's double vision mirrors the policies of Themistocles and the innovation of the Athenians. For Themistocles' naval strategy was as daring as the willingness of his compatriots to abandon their homes and risk all in a single battle. Yet that daring was aimed at preserving what is ancient, local, and particular.

This balance is augmented and sustained by one between unity and diversity. This, too, marks a contrast between Greek and Persian conceptions of power, freedom, and politics. The Persian army, like the Persian state, is at once too unified and not unified enough. It is too unified insofar as it is ruled by a single

[26] John Finley, *Pindar and Aeschylus* (Cambridge, Mass.: Harvard University Press, 1955), p. 218.

[27] See the discussion in Arnaldo Momigliano, "Persian Empire and the Greek Freedom," in A. Ryan, ed., *The Idea of Freedom: Essays in Honour of Isaiah Berlin* (London: Oxford University Press, 1979). For a very different view of the *Persae*, see Page DuBois, *Centaurs and Amazons* (Ann Arbor: University of Michigan Press, 1982), chap. 3.

man who regards himself as master in all things and treats others as mere posses-
sions. It is not unified enough because it is composed of peoples of such diverse
tongues and traditions that they can only be united by fear and in silence. But the
Greeks, as Aeschylus portrays them in the *Persae,* speak and act while maintaining their freedom and distinctiveness.

The communal quality of the Greek victory is suggested by Aeschylus's refusing to name Greek leaders (although there are unmistakable allusions to
Themistocles), while cataloging Persian princes on three occasions. This refusal
serves at least two purposes: it prevents the play from engaging partisan emotions
that might rob it of "larger significance"[28] and, more important, it emphasizes the
collective nature of the triumph. By making the heroic joy in names suspect
through an "orientalizing refraction," Aeschylus celebrates "the presumptive
unity of democratic action."[29]

Greek power is a function of the Greek freedom it exists to protect and defend.
Part of the meaning of freedom is political autonomy, the right of and opportunity for a city to live by its own laws and constitution *(politeia).* This cannot be
the largess of some superior power any more than individual freedom can be a
revocable grant from a superior. Freedom must be won and rewon by the courage
of citizens. "For to each citizen his city's laws were his charter for freedom, his
safeguard against oppression by a tyrant or by a privileged class, and his guarantee of future liberty."[30]

There is another, apparently paradoxical, dimension to Greek freedom. When,
in a passage quoted earlier (402–5), the Greek commander calls on the Hellenes
to defend freedom (he repeats *eleutheroute* for emphasis) by fighting for family,
ancestral gods, and the tombs of fathers, he is reminding them that freedom
means living where a man feels he belongs, among his own people, gods, and
land. To be free and human is to be among those who share your ways. Linguistic
evidence indicates that the root meaning of freedom is to belong to an ethnic
stock in the sense of plants that come from the same root. Belonging confers
special privileges denied slaves or strangers. Indeed, a stranger in our midst is a
slave, a stranger outside an enemy. Thus, slavery is dispersal; liberation is being
among friends.[31] Moreover, those who share your ways are those whose strength
seconds your own, whether in battle or in adhering to a shared conception of
virtue. In this sense independence presupposes mutual dependence, autonomy
rests on what is shared, and freedom is a function of equality.

The play's teachings about democratic power, unity, and diversity, political
difference and human equality, freedom and limits, are seconded by the physical
and social context of its performance.

---

[28] Gilbert Murray, *Aeschylus the Creator of Tragedy* (Oxford University Press, 1949), p. 126.

[29] Thomas G. Rosenmeyer, *The Act of Aeschylus* (Berkeley: University of California Press, 1982), p. 114.

[30] T. A. Sinclair, *A History of Greek Political Thought* (London: Routledge and Kegan Paul, 1961), p. 35.

[31] See Emile Benveniste, *Indo-European Language and Society* (Coral Gables, Fla.: University of Miami Press, 1973), book 3, chap. 3.

The configuration of the theater encouraged a sense that all life, here exemplified by dramatic action, was public life, open to the view of all, inviting the participation of many. Yet the theater is not limitless. Instead, it clearly outlines a dramatic space "that combines freedom with definition."[32] In that space Athenian history is placed in a mythical setting that generalizes what would otherwise be parochial.

In many respects tragedy was a political institution analogous to the Assembly and Council. But one thing that distinguished it from other political institutions was its "theoretical" character. For although tragedy was part of a religious festival and so reaffirmed the city's rituals, gods, and practices, it also called them into question. Thus, it simultaneously validated the city's institutions and made them problematic, certified its painfully accomplished structure of order and pushed the mind to face the chaos that order purposely exorcised.[33] In this way tragedy enabled its citizen audience to reflect on their lives with a generality denied them in their capacity as political actors. Insofar as it is appropriate and useful to regard these ruminations as theoretical, the Salamis legend was constituted by a choice of themes *and* by the theoretical nature of the political institution that explored them.[34]

Tragedy was also a democratizing institution. Not only did it develop along with other such institutions and practices; it was, in William Arrowsmith's words, a "democratic paideia complete in itself."[35] As such, it enabled Athenians to bring the experience of being democratic citizens to the theater and the wisdom of the theater to the deliberations of the Assembly; it maintained a cultural equality that helped constitute and legitimate political equality and, as the *Persians'* nameless Greeks indicated, collectivized the heroic ethic.

By telescoping the victory over Persia into the triumph at Salamis, Aeschylus helped justify, ratify, and extend the city's democratization in at least two, more particular ways. First of all, by concentrating on Salamis he could not help but remind his citizen audience of the contribution of Themistocles, the architect of that victory. Although the evidence is inconclusive, the political label controversial, and the assumption of direct political commentary in the play no doubt exaggerated, it appears that Themistocles was the leader of the more "radical" democratic party in Athens, and clear that he had fallen into disfavor at the time the play was performed.[36]

---

[32] Rosenmeyer, *Art of Aeschylus*, p. 54. See also Peter D. Arnott, *An Introduction to the Greek Theatre* (Bloomington: Indiana University Press, 1959).

[33] On this point, see Jean-Pierre Vernant, "Tensions and Ambiguities in Greek Tragedy," in Charles S. Singleton, ed., *Interpretations* (Baltimore: Johns Hopkins University Press, 1969), pp. 273–89; and Charles Segal, "The Music of the Sphinx: The Problem of Language in Oedipus Tyrannus," in Stephanus Kresic, ed., *Contemporary Literary Hermeneutics and the Interpretation of Classical Texts* (Ottawa: University of Ottawa Press, 1981), pp. 156–80.

[34] I have argued this in detail in the introduction to *Greek Tragedy and Political Theory* (Berkeley: University of California Press, 1986) and chapter 2 of the *Tragedy of Political Theory: The Road Not Taken* (Princeton: Princeton University Press, 1990).

[35] William Arrowsmith, "A Greek Theater of Ideas," *Arion* 2 (1963): 33.

[36] This is Podlecki's argument in his *The Political Background of Heschylean Tragedy* (Ann Arbor: University of Michigan Press, 1966).

Second, and more important, the singling out of Salamis added to the standing of those who won the victory: the poor who manned the ships. The naval victory at Salamis helped detach aristocratic virtues from social class and reassign them to the community as a whole. Thus, insofar as political privilege had depended on citizen-soldiers adhering to an aristocratic ethos of courage, loyalty, patriotism, and honor in action, the bravery of the citizen-sailors at Salamis eroded (but did not eliminate) the foundations of exclusive privilege, and gave substance to the vision of Athens as an aristocratic democracy. Even the Old Oligarch agrees on the justness of the "poor and ordinary people having more power than the noble and rich since it is the ordinary people who man the fleet and bring the city her power."[37]

II

For all the discrepancies between Aeschylus's treatment of the Persian Wars and the account offered by Herodotus,[38] despite the differences between history and tragedy,[39] and even though each writes for a different generation,[40] Herodotus elaborates the legend of Salamis as it is presented in and by Aeschylus. For both, Salamis is a democratic victory that reveals the link between political culture, power, and freedom. Because both works explore that interface in public performances at Athens, they help constitute a community of democratic self-understanding.

For Herodotus, the celebration of victories such as Salamis is consonant with his aim to preserve "from decay the remembrance of what men have done," and so to prevent "the great and wonderful actions of the Greeks and the Barbarians from losing their due meed of glory" (1.1). Herodotus regards history (and his own *Histories)* as a monument set against time, a mark of what men have been and done, and a story of everything that has come into being through human agency.

And that means that history is about liberation and freedom. For liberation is a precondition for power, power for memorable action, and action is the substance of history. Without the power to act (and action that sustains power), no nation or individual can enter history at all. That is why history preserves the defense and

---

[37] See Pseudo-Xenophon, *The Constitution of Athens,* 1.2.

[38] For instance, Herodotus accords Sparta a more prominent role in the defense of Greece, discusses Greek disunity and reluctance to fight (which is why Themistocles tricks the Greeks as well as the Persians), gives a less flattering portrait of Darius, Xerxes, and Themistocles, is concerned with the antecedents of the war, and gives more attention to battles other than Salamis. (For Herodotus, I rely primarily on the Rawlinson translation with some emendations.)

[39] On the differences and continuities between tragedy and history, see Charles Fornara, *The Nature of History in Ancient Greece and Rome* (Berkeley: University of California Press, 1983), pp. 171ff.

[40] Since Herodotus wrote fifty years after Aeschylus, he was not part of the phenomenon he describes but instead finds in the Persian wars a foreshadowing of the contemporary conflict between Athens and Sparta. On this, see G. W. Fornara, *Herodotus: An Interpretative Essay* (New York: Oxford University Press, 1971), pp. 40–41.

acquisition of freedom, and why in doing so it preserves its own possibility. A nation has no history (or historian) when it is enslaved; as contemporary feminists remind us, the "history" of a subject people is part of the history of its rulers.[41]

But Salamis is not just a victory; it was *the* crucial victory of the war. It is not only a turning point in history, it is the turning point in Herodotus's *Histories*. Until Salamis the structure of his work is based largely on Eastern accounts to which Greek material is subordinated. After Salamis this is no longer so, as if the triumph of the Greeks, especially the Athenians, was a victory of conceptual as well as political and military power.[42]

Why and how was it that Athens came to have such power and became the savior of Greece? The obvious answer is that it had the most ships and men. But this misses Herodotus's point about Salamis, about Athens, and of his *Histories*. For him, as for Aeschylus, power is no more a function of numbers than courage is of fear (though he does emphasize the significance of numbers in his comments on Themistocles persuading the Athenians to build ships in 483 B.C. [7.144] and at 8.86 where he discusses courage and fear). Athenian power derived from the fact that, as citizens of a democracy, the Athenians above all others embodied freedom in their *politeia* and fought for it unstintingly. He elaborates the point through two contrasts: one between Hellenes and Persians, the other between Athens and Sparta.

The contrast between Greece and Persia is a contrast between a conception of government and politics based on freedom, equality, and law and one based on despotism. Although Herodotus presents Xerxes as a generally benevolent despot before his invasion of Greece, the Persian king epitomizes the arrogant man of limitless power. He whips and brands the Hellespont after a storm destroys one of his bridges, despises omens, is willfully cruel, leads an army of mostly slaves who fight only under the lash and out of fear, and seeks to rule the entire world (7.34–35, 56–58). As Otanes says in the famous debate over forms of government in book 3, tyranny allows a man to do what he likes without being answerable to anyone (3.80).

Xerxes' own view of power and politics is clear in his conversation with Damaratus, an exiled Spartan king. The Persian ruler asks whether the Greeks will fight at all, given their poverty of numbers and wealth. Damaratus not only assures Xerxes that they will, but insists that their indomitable courage is the product of wisdom and firm laws that drive out both want and tyranny. Most of all the Spartans (about whom Damaratus is largely talking) will never accept terms that would reduce Greece to slavery, even if they have to fight against hugely superior forces (7.102). Xerxes is incredulous. How could even fifty thousand men stand up to his host, especially if they "were all alike free, and not under one lord"?[43]

[41] Henry Wood, *The Histories of Herodotus: An Analysis of the Formal Structure* (The Hague: Mouton, 1972), p. 30.

[42] H. R. Immerwahr, "Historical Action in Herodotus," *Transactions of the American Philological Association* 85 (1954): 40.

[43] As A. W. Gomme argues (in *Greek Attitudes to Poetry and History* [Berkeley: University of

In fact, as Damaratus says, the Spartans do have a master, the laws, whom they fear more than the Persians fear Xerxes. Whatever it commands they do, and it forbids the Spartans "to flee in battle, whatever the number of their foes and requires them to stand firm, and either to conquer or die" (7.104).

As Xerxes regards courage as contrary to the promptings of nature, he believes men will fight only under compulsion. In these terms power *is* a matter of numbers and is possible only with a tyrant-king who unites men by coercing them. The Greek way is inefficient at best. The idea of equals deliberating collectively in a public arena is unimaginable and absurd.

Because he does not understand Greek politics, he does not understand Greek warfare. Unlike the Persians, the Greeks were citizen-soldiers whose courage and power came from being the free citizens whom their military prowess aimed to protect. The hoplite phalanx, in which each soldier depends on the thrusting spears and shields of his neighbor, sustained the political equality essential for a free citizenry. Conversely, it was political equality that made the Greeks so powerful. In politics, as in combat, there is a special courage that comes from fighting for your own and a special power that comes from the self-confidence of having your own say and acting with others to implement commonly arrived at decisions. Developing a theme in the *Persae,* Herodotus shows us that the power of a collectivity acting together is not proportionate to the strength or capabilities of the separate individuals who compose it, but derives from the constellation of their collective lives. For him it is free speech that creates a condition of life that makes men ready to face death and strong enough to overcome a foe many times more numerous. The proof of this is Athens.

It is also Athens that most fully illustrates the connection between freedom, equality, power, and political culture. Here is the conclusion of the Otanes speech referred to previously. After condemning the rule of one man, he goes on to extol the rule of the many, which has

> in the first place, the fairest of names, equality before the law [*isonomia*]; and further it is free from all those outrages which a king is wont to commit. There places are given by lot, the magistrate is answerable for what he does, and measures rest with the commonalty. I vote [to] . . . raise the people to power. For the people are all in all. (3.80)

Several things are notable about this conclusion. First of all, Otanes suggests that political equality—the sharing of political power—is the guarantee of lawfulness and that lawfulness sustains political equality.[44] Second, the one polis that this best describes is Athens. For Herodotus, Athenian power is based on freedom, and freedom "is an excellent thing: since even the Athenians, who, while they continued under the rule of tyrants, were not a whit more valiant than any of their

---

California Press, 1954], p. 104), Xerxes was right to be scornful, given the infighting among a Greek army composed of separately trained units.

[44] The analysis of the Otanes passages draws on my "Political Equality and the Greek Polis," in M. J. Gargas McGrath, ed., *Liberalism and the Modern Polity* (New York: Marcel Dekker, 1959), pp. 207–29.

neighbors, no sooner shook off the yoke of tyranny than they decidedly became the first of all" (5.78). Free institutions instill an enthusiasm for accomplishment lacking in all other regimes. Third, this freedom is not simply the absence of tyranny, but involves the active participation of the common people in public life. Earlier in book 5, again discussing the growth of Athenian power, Herodotus links that growth not only to the overthrow of tyranny but to Cleisthenes' bringing the common citizens into a more active political role.[45]

The phrase "the people all in all" and the praise of *isonomia,* rather than *eunomia,* shift the contrast from the one between Greeks and Persians to one between Athenians and Spartans. This contrast is, of course, central to Thucydides' *History.* And even though there are substantial theological differences between the two historians, the secular tone of the debate in which this contrast between the two Greek cities is introduced also anticipates Thucydides. It is true that Herodotus, like Aeschylus, shows the humbling of pride through the combined efforts of gods and men. It is also true that he finds sufficient similarities among religious diversity to reaffirm a divinely sustained reality beyond and behind the seeming variety of practices and cultures. And since the gods intervene at every turn of personal and national fortune to restore balance, measure, and order to the cosmos, the Greek victory at Salamis was possible only because the gods permitted and seconded it. To forget this fact in the pride of victory ensures that one's fate will be as Persia's.[46] Yet for all this, parts of Herodotus's *Histories* (such as the debate over forms of government) are so self-contained and secular, and the gods are so often distant from the action, that we are invited to regard politics as an autonomous activity.

With Thucydides this process of secularization goes further, as does the emergence of politics as an autonomous activity and realm. Although it is true that Thucydides' *History* retains the structure of retribution for transgressions found in Aeschylus and Herodotus, his analyses of those transgressions omit the gods. And those who continually invoke them, such as Nicias and the Spartans, are ridiculed for doing so.[47] Perhaps Thucydides' prospective audience would be reminded of Xerxes when they heard or read Pericles proclaim that his compatriots had forced the sea to become the highway of their daring (2.42), or that Athens was tyrant to the sea as well as the cities in its empire (2.65). But Pericles does not expect, and Thucydides does not mention, any revenge by jealous or just gods.[48] That is not to deny that all human things decay and die. But they do so

---

[45] This does not mean Herodotus was a democrat, only that he recognized the role of a democracy as saving Greek cultural life and that he understood Athens to be the dominant political force in Hellas.

[46] That is why the *Persae is* a tragedy and why Herodotus regards freedom as tragic.

[47] The emergence of politics as an autonomous realm was due to the classical, especially the "Athenian *polis* which . . . introduced politics as a human activity and elevated it to the most fundamental social activity." Finley, *Use and Abuse of History,* p. 30.

[48] W. Robert Connor argues that Thucydides' intolerance of myth and story presupposed and demanded an intensely intellectual readership, one willing to contemplate a radical reinterpretation of the past. *Thucydides* (Princeton: Princeton University Press, 1984).

because of human folly, arrogance, and chance, unaided and unseconded by the gods.

As politics becomes an increasingly autonomous activity, the interface of power, freedom, and political culture becomes less clouded by divine intervention and so more precisely stated. The cause of the war was Spartan fear of Athenian, more precisely, democratic power. And the conflict between the two cities was a conflict of political cultures, two kinds of power and two conceptions of freedom.

III

Despite these differences between Herodotus and Thucydides, though the latter's methodological imprecations may be aimed at the former, and however much Thucydides is (selectively) contemptuous of legend, he elaborates and embodies the Salamis legend as constituted by Aeschylus and Herodotus. By what is said and done in the *History* and by what Thucydides says and does in the writing of it, the ambivalences and moral ambiguities of the Salamis legend are played out before us.

But probably not before his contemporaries and compatriots. In part this is because Thucydides presents his *History* not as an *agōnisma* (a piece for momentary public performance), but as a *ktēma* (a written volume possessed by a reader).[49] Whereas Herodotus read his manuscript before immediately present audiences, Thucydides presents himself as a writer, and so his projected audience is temporally and spatially less defined and certain. It is true that he is traditional in his aim of celebrating great deeds, his claims upon the memory of posterity, and the disparagement of his rivals. But how such deeds are to be celebrated, the definition of posterity, and the grounds for disparagement are not traditional. Before Thucydides, poetic speech is preservable speech, whereas vernacular prose was by definition ephemeral because it had a temporary life in the memory of speaker and listener.[50] But he is part of the literate revolution that inverted these priorities, thereby contributing to the development of conceptual thinking we associate with political theory. All this suggests that with Thucydides the legend of Salamis becomes inscribed in a theoretical tradition for which the culture of his fellow citizens was, at a minimum, a necessary condition.

Thucydides regards Salamis as both a paradigm and an object lesson. He admires the intellectual power and political greatness the victory represented and fostered. But he also recognizes the destructive dialectic contained within it. Or, to put it another way, he is too realistic and too remote from the moment of victory to share the feeling of civic faith that animated Aeschylus (and reappears in the Funeral Oration), and too attached to that moment and too critical of realism to accept the Athenian repudiation of Salamis at Melos.

Thucydides' *History* is about power, more specifically about the rise of Athe-

---

[49] Havelock, *The Literate Revolution,* pp. 138–39. I have relied on the Crawley translation with emendations.

[50] Ibid., p. 147; and his *Preface to Plato* (New York: Grosset and Dunlap, 1963), especially p. 54.

nian democratic power. That was the truest occasion of the war and of his work. It is because of Athens that the *History* was written; it is because Thucydides was an Athenian who shared the daring of his countrymen that it was written. In other words, the *History* is itself evidence of the Athenian power it portrays.

Aside from the *History* as a whole, the most elaborate definition and example of Athenian power is contained in a series of speeches by the Corinthians and Athenians at the first Lacedaimonian Congress and in the three speeches by Pericles. Together they delineate Athenian political culture by analyzing or demonstrating the power that issues from it. Once more the legend of Salamis is a unifying theme and preoccupation.

The congress was called by Corinth, and it is the Corinthian speech that is "recreated" by Thucydides. Its rhetorical object is to move Sparta to action by making clear the threat it faces, and to define the nature of the threat. This is done by contrasting the Athenian and Spartan constitutions.

As opposed to the Spartans, the Athenians are "addicted to innovation and their designs are characterized by swiftness alike in conception and execution." Not only are they "adventuresome beyond their power and daring beyond judgment," but in "danger they are utterly sanguine." Constantly moving, Athenians treat their homes as but temporary residences that they leave whenever they are presented with an opportunity to expand their power or wealth. Whether promptly following up a victory or slowly retreating from a defeat, they "spend their bodies ungrudgingly in their country's cause; their intellect they jealously husband to be employed in her service." Here is a people "born into the world to take no rest themselves and to give none to others" (1.70).

In case we think this is simply the polemical exaggeration of a frustrated enemy, Thucydides follows it with a speech by Athenian envoys, whose tone, substance, and purpose confirm the Corinthian portrait. They come forward not to defend Athens against specific accusations, but to render a more comprehensive view in hopes of dissuading Sparta from deciding for war. To this end they make three points. First, they insist Athens deserves what it has, reminding their listeners of how much their city risked and accomplished for a common cause. Second, they want Sparta to think hard about the sort of adversary it will be facing if it decides for war. Third, they maintain that their acquisition of empire was unremarkable, except perhaps for the lack of violence in acquiring it, the legal equality of its members, and the fact that they respect justice more than their right and position of dominance requires them to do.

Central to their objective and to these points is Salamis. (Marathon is mentioned but once.) It was Salamis that saved Greece from slavery and the Athenians who contributed most to the victory, providing both the largest number of ships and the ablest commander (Themistocles). Without their strength and Themistocles, all would have been lost. But most of all, the victory depended on their daring patriotism.

> Receiving no reinforcements from behind, seeing everything in front of us already subjugated, we had the spirit, after abandoning our city, after sacrificing our property (instead of deserting the remainder of the league or depriving them of our services by

dispersing), to throw ourselves into our ships and meet the danger without a thought
of resenting your neglect to assist us. (1.74)

It is obvious from this speech that the Athenians now regard Salamis as a
human victory (the gods are not mentioned), and as an almost exclusively Athenian one. This view is basic to the justification of their empire, their understanding of politics, and their political culture as a whole.

Pericles' first speech defines what is at stake in the prospective conflict with
Sparta, insists on the necessity of war, assays the Athenians' strengths, and as-
sesses the chances of success. As he sees it, Athens is confronted by a choice
between slavery and escalating Spartan demands on the one hand, and freedom
and honor on the other. There is then no real choice: Athens must fight. And it has
a fair hope of success. For while the Spartans are tied to the land by material and
religious dependence, the Athenians are not. That is because (as a result of
Themistocles' policy and of Salamis) Athens is a sea power, and rule of the sea is
a "great thing."

> Consider for a moment. Suppose that we were islanders: can you conceive a more
> impregnable position? Well, this in future should, as far as possible, be our concep-
> tion of our position. Dismissing all thought of our land and houses, we must vigi-
> lantly guard the sea and the city. . . . We must cry not over the loss of houses and
> land but of men's lives; since houses and land do not gain men but men them. And if
> I had thought that I could persuade you, I would have bid you go out and lay them
> waste yourselves to show the Peloponnesians that this at any rate will not make you
> submit. (1.143)

Notice that Pericles is asking his fellow citizens to do what Themistocles had
convinced them to do at Salamis: forsake their houses and land for strategic
reasons. Yet here the forsaking is less temporary and so the result is more permanent. Moreover, it might be argued on good traditional grounds that, except in the
most literal sense, houses and land do make men, and that by abandoning them
for life in a barracks-city and for the sea, the Athenians were becoming like
Xerxes. (That the walls connecting Athens and the Piraeus were built with fragments from ancestral tombs gives another dimension to this shift.)

Notice too that Pericles asks his countrymen to imagine Athens as an island
and then to act in the world in terms of what they imagine, as if human conception could change the world itself. Of course, their imagining is grounded in fact,
and so the world remains some check on conception. (With Alcibiades and Sicily
it is less so, although the greatness of Athenian power and talent was such that it
almost didn't matter.) Pericles did not and could not ask his compatriots to imagine themselves a land power, or to ignore geography. Athenian sea power and the
long walls that made the city virtually impregnable to defeat by land were tangi-
ble realities. But the question was how one regarded these and other such realities: whether one was deferential and accommodated them as natural or divinely
ordained necessities; or whether, on the contrary, one saw them as conventional
limitations that might be overcome and reconstituted according to human design

and by human power. The Spartans were deferential; the Athenians see the world as moments of opportunity for the exercise of political and theoretical power.

The Athenian capacity to think of the world as other than it is is a resource Sparta lacks. This is less a matter of controlling events, as chance intrudes in even the best made plans, than of controlling the subjective effects and affects of chance.[51] For the Athenians, as Pericles epitomizes and speaks of them, in contrast to Aeschylus, Herodotus, and Sparta, men are victims of forces outside themselves only when they let themselves be victims by failing to sustain the preconditions and fact of political and theoretical power. Politics, unlike nature, is permeable to human design.

In one sense this had been "known" before. But the knowledge was shrouded in the religious aura of divinely inspired lawgivers. Now the knowledge is democratized and secularized. The Athenians are collective lawgivers, able to change who they are and so the world around them.

They are also collective theorists. For the capacity to envision the world other than as it is and to reconstitute the world to realize that vision is the basic impulse behind what Sheldon Wolin has called "epic political theory."[52] To the degree that Pericles' Funeral Oration is justified in claiming this as an attribute of the whole people rather than of a few leaders, the city itself emerges as a theoretical actor. And when the plague erodes this confidence in human power to control the subjective impact of events,[53] it also reflects on the theoretical impulse that was part of and an expression of that confidence.

Finally, if what men think about the world can change what the world is or might be, then how one interprets an event helps constitute what that event "is." Pericles does not draw this conclusion, but others such as the sophists do. Or, to put the point another way, Pericles is here suggesting how events become elaborated into legend. The growing awareness that this happens, and that every interpretation implies a political position if not vision, is a premise for the sophists and Socrates, imperialism and liberation, empire and political theory.

Pericles is largely aware of the dangers as well as the opportunities of this new power. He knows (or Thucydides points to) the way "the" Athenian mind, like the Athenian polis, continually expands, thus menacing the very conditions that made its political and intellectual power possible in the first place. It is this danger that lies behind Pericles' statement, "I am more afraid of our own blunders than of the enemy's devices" (1.144). That this fear is well founded is proved by the consequences of Athens' failure to heed his advice. Pericles' foil in

---

[51] See the fine discussion of this point in Lowell Edmunds, *Chance and Intelligence in Thucydides* (Cambridge, Mass.: Harvard University Press, 1975).

[52] See his "Political Theory As a Vocation," reprinted in M . Fleisher, ed., *Machiavelli and the Nature of Political Thought* (New York: Atheneum, 1972), pp. 23–75; and *Hobbes and the Epic Tradition of Political Theory* (Los Angeles: William Andrews Clark Memorial Library, University of California, 1970).

[53] The plague disrupted the balance between confidence and caution so that the swings between them became more violent and the activity increasingly frenetic. That is seen in the change in policy and the change in leadership.

this is Alcibiades, who justifies precisely an adventure Pericles enjoined by claiming, "We cannot fix the exact point at which our empire shall stop" (6.18).

However, Pericles' first speech ends not with his fears but with a call to glory that explicitly invokes the memory of Salamis. "Did not our fathers resist Persia with even less resources than we have and even abandon those they had? Even then they defeated the barbarians and advanced our fortunes to their present height more by wisdom than by fortune, more by daring than by strength" (1.144).

The Funeral Oration continues to develop the contrast between Athens and Sparta, although the emphasis is now on the former's democratic *politeia*. Democracy is now seen as a precondition for victory and the most cherished fruit of it. Because power was shared "by the people all in all," Athens has become great. Its collective courage liberated Athens from preoccupation with life, for the freedom of the world. In the process Athens has become the school of Hellas, imitated rather than imitator, a paradigm for those in future generations who love action.

In Athens freedom, equality, and self-government exist under the law and are sustained by it. "We acknowledge the restraint of reverence; and render obedience to those in authority and to the laws, especially to the ones which offer protection to the oppressed and those unwritten ordinances whose transgression brings acknowledged shame'" (2.37). Athenian power is the offspring of this mutual enhancement of freedom and law. Such power depends more on its democratic constitution than on any technical or narrow military superiority. When called to action, no people fight more bravely or with more spirit than the Athenians. And that is because their commitments are freely given rather than coerced. Their power to thwart the inadvertent drift that dominates "unhistorical" peoples derives from seeing themselves as, and being, individuals who have decided to join their separate intentions into a joint singleness of purpose. Thus, when they fight, it is for a life in which they all share. That life is one of common purpose as well as variety, of grace as well as action. For the Athenian is a versatile amateur (in the original sense) but never a dilettante. He cares for beauty, order, proportion, and balance without being in thrall to them. He is a lover of wisdom, without forgetting the imperatives of the world. Ordinary citizens pursue their work but remain sound judges of public matters and look upon discussion and thought as enhancing action rather than inhibiting it. The Athenian *politeia* presents the "singular spectacle of daring and deliberation, each carried to its highest point and both united in the same persons" (2.40). Citizens of such a polity combine great speech and deed in their activity as citizens, thereby collectively realizing the heroic ideal of the *Iliad,* and carving out a human dimension against the recalcitrant forces of necessity, corruption, oblivion, and powerlessness.

In this eulogy for the Athenian dead, Pericles provides a vision for his countrymen of what they have been and might yet become. Yet the ideal has wider significance and appeal. For the Funeral Oration may also be read as Thucydides' epitaph for fallen Athens. Thus, when Pericles calls on his fellow Athenians to "realize the power of Athens, and feed your eyes upon her from day to day until love of her fills your hearts" (2.43), Thucydides may be inviting us to do the same. When "love of her greatness" breaks upon us, we, like the Athenians, are to "reflect that it was by courage, sense of duty and a keen feeling of honor in action that men were enabled to win all this."[54] Not only the graves of these fallen men but Athens itself will be "eternally remembered upon all occasions on which deed or story shall fall for its commemoration."

With these words the legend of Salamis achieves its apogee. The moment of shared faith unfolds into the democratic mythos of the Funeral Oration. The sailors there are part of a people whose collective achievements rival Achilles. And like Achilles, who is found singing of great deeds even while Homer sings of his, Pericles and Thucydides exemplify a new self-consciousness about the world. With them the polis becomes an object of theoretical reflection.

Pericles' third speech comes after the plague and attempts to reconstitute the unity of purpose dissipated by the fearful interjection of unpredictable and meaningless death. He is only partly successful. Something unrecoverable has been lost. Having been reminded of their individual mortality, Athenians are less susceptible to the Funeral Oration's vision of collective immortality. The oration's celebration of courage, patriotism, and human power are now mere echoes, and Pericles knows it. That is why he now calls for rededication on the grounds that the public good enhances private good, and that, as tyrants, they have no choice. It is why he now speaks of I and you, where he had spoken in the first person plural "we" in the Funeral Oration.[55] And it is why the empire is now seen as an active power confronting its possessor with alternatives almost as grim as those that confront the cities over which Athens tyrannizes. When, in a sentence of superlatives, Pericles almost casually envisages Athenian decline, and when he proclaims that Athenian greatness is no longer tied to its physical existence, he almost seems to understand the plague as a prelude to the collapse of the Salamis legend.

We can read Melian Dialogue as epitomizing the collapse.[56] Not only is the dialogue a startling contrast with the idealism of the Funeral Oration, the justification of empire based on the Athenian contribution to the Greek cause at Salamis is dismissed as "specious pretense." Similarly, the distinctiveness of democratic culture and the idea of Athens as the school of Hellas is jettisoned for a logic of empire that drives all states whatever their political constitution. The ideal common to Aeschylus, Herodotus, and Pericles of power as the product of a

[54] See the suggestive reading of this passage by S. Sara Monoson in her "Citizen As *Erastes:* Erotic Imagery and the Idea of Reciprocity in the Periclean Funeral Oration," *Political Theory* 22, no. 2 (May 1994): 253–76, and Clifford Orwin's analysis of what is elided and obscured by the obstructions of the speech in *The Humanity of Thucydides,* chap. 1.

[55] W. Robert Connor, *Thucydides* (Princeton: Princeton University Press, 1984), pp. 65–66. Orwin argues that this third speech "comprises Pericles' true funeral oration" (*The Humanity of Thucydides,* p. 20).

[56] In their speech at Corinth (1.76–77) the Athenians claim that their power has created the possibilities for a discourse of justice other than sheer domination of the sort whose universal legitimacy they declaim at Melos.

constellation of civic ties among citizens is replaced by an emphasis on material force, which makes the Athenian victory over superior military force at Salamis unintelligible. Once the defender of Greek freedom, Athens now enslaves the Greeks as Persia did, while the Melians express the sentiments that echo those of the Athenians when they confronted Xerxes. Here are the Athenians as reported by Herodotus in words that sound Melian.

> We know . . . that the power of the Mede is many times greater than our own. . . . Nevertheless we cling so to freedom that we shall offer what resistance we may. . . . So long as the sun keeps his present course, we will never join alliance with Xerxes. Nay, we shall oppose him unceasingly, trusting in the aid of those gods and heroes whom he lightly esteems. (8.143)

That the Athenian invasion of Sicily recalls the Persian invasion of Greece, that the debacle at Syracuse drives the Athenians to invoke the gods, hope, and chance, all that they have scorned at Melos, that the battle in the harbor evokes Salamis, that Nicias's second speech (7.69) echoes Aeschylus's description of the battle—all this only adds layers of irony to an already ironic tale.[57]

At Melos the Athenians have forgotten their own words and past. The warnings of Aeschylus and Herodotus unheeded, they embark on an adventure whose literally boundless ambition imitates that of the tyrant Xerxes. In their blindness they are dispossessed of place, continuity, and orientation. Bereft of limits to mind and desire, their ambition pushes them beyond the compass of their experience and the horizon of their foresight, to Sicily and to ruin.

Of course it is not so neat or simple: it never is with Thucydides. What is said at Melos has precedent. Indeed, the Athenian arguments there force us to reread and reassess their speech at Sparta, the speeches of Diotodus and Cleon at Mytilene, the Funeral Oration (and Pericles generally), and Thucydides' *History* as a whole.[58] It was in their speech at Sparta that the Athenians announced a principle of empire repeated at Melos, although there it was hedged with a concern for justice and justification. What is said at Melos echoes Cleon's impatience with distinguishing friends from enemies and with dialogue, as well as Diotodus's reliance on expedience. (It is a reliance whose short-term consequence is mercy but whose long-term result is moral catastrophe.) The Funeral Oration begins by eschewing long-winded reiterations of past victories and proclaims an ambition as wide as the expanding audience it addresses. Pericles begins by addressing those immediately present and ends by addressing posterity. As he does, his principle of greatness enjoins present and future generations to continue the expansion begun by their ancestors.[59] Finally, the Athenian contempt for the past and skepticism toward legend and sentimentality remind us of Thucydides' own methodological strictures in the opening chapter of his *History*. Perhaps the pos-

---

[57] Connor, *Thucydides,* pp. 197–99.

[58] I have argued this in detail in *The Tragedy of Political Theory,* chap. 6.

[59] For an elaboration of this point, see Michael Palmer, "Love of Glory and the Common Good," *American Political Science Review* 76 (December 1983): 825–36.

sibility that his *History* contributes to a process it partly laments adds to its power, poignancy, and tragedy.

The Melian Dialogue, then, is no morality play. True, what Thucydides says in his own voice when concluding his analysis of Corcyra (3.84) echoes what the Melians say to the Athenians (5.91) about the danger of abrogating principles that are the common protection of mankind. But it remains unclear whether this is a lament or a morality. And for all its pleonexia, the Sicilian adventure almost succeeds. That it failed was due to a factionalism that is a symptom and sign of the collapse and final elaboration of the Salamis legend.

IV

The victory at Salamis made political theory possible and necessary. It made theory possible insofar as the Athenian triumph and the subsequent legend enshrined a daring of mind and action that regarded the world as susceptible to human design. It made it necessary insofar as the content of the Salamis legend was itself the cause of the unraveling evident at Melos.

If I am right, then the task Plato's Socrates set himself was the reconstitution of practical and intellectual life and of moral and political discourse. This entailed reestablishing conceptual and political boundaries and instilling a sense of common purpose achieved by a Salamis legend that he believed had become corrupt and corrupting. This was a conservative as well as radical enterprise: conservative because it sought to restore a tradition, albeit a democratic one; radical because it sought to do so on explicitly theoretical grounds. Thus, Socrates calls on Athenians to live up to the principles of the Funeral Oration, while subjecting those principles to moral, political, and theoretical critique.[60]

In these terms Socrates is, and I think saw himself as, the culmination and severest critic of the Athenian political tradition as that was formed by the victory at, and the legend of, Salamis. His daring is distinctively Athenian and democratic, and he knows it. And so his attempt to repair the democracy of his native city is in part at least a reaffirmation of his own vocation. This suggests that Socrates is an Athenian citizen first, even if citizenship was not everything. It

---

[60] See Steven Salkever's persuasive reading of Plato's *Menexenus* ("Socrates' Aspasian Oration: The Play of Philosophy and Politics in Plato's *Menexenus*," *American Political Science Review* 87, no. 1 [March 1993]: 133–43). Salkever argues that the *Menexenus* presents itself as Plato's Socratic counterpart to Pericles' Funeral Oration in Thucydides. It is an alternative understanding that shifts the moral focus from greatness to goodness, from self-creation through military daring to a mythic theocentric origin story, from considerations of how best to maintain a collective civic project to the question of each individual's virtue, from a language of glory, greatness, brilliance, and action to a language of caretaking, healing art, nature, virtue, justice, and freedom. But as Salkever points out, the complex irony of the dialogue makes this shift itself problematic. The philosophical statesman's task seems to be less designing institutions or policies than persuading citizens of the primacy of the good life. His purpose is not to give "unqualified acceptance to any formulation or doctrine that purports to solve the question once and for all," but to insist upon the unending importance of the question itself. In this the alternative creates a kind of *aporia* (pp. 133–35).

also suggests that Socratic philosophy is political philosophy both by choice and by necessity, at least after Delphi and through the *Republic.*

None of this is meant to deny that Socrates is highly critical of the substance of Pericles' vision, or that he (or rather Plato) tries to displace that vision with one in which Socrates' life and death rather than the life and death of Athens take center stage. In the *Apology* and *Crito* (Plato's) Socrates detaches *aretē* from the heroic ethic and reassigns it to philosophical activity. As he does, being great becomes being good, and courage becomes the willingness to suffer injustice rather than commit it. In these altered terms elaborated in the *Gorgias* as we shall see in chapter eight, the purpose of life is not to conquer Syracuse but one's own tyrannical impulses; not to avenge one's friends but to harm no one; not to build an empire but a just city; not to leave great monuments for good or ill but paradigms of right action. Justice is not the interest of the stronger, or of the weaker for that matter. Indeed, it is not really an interest at all, except in the sense that what we do to others we also do to ourselves, and so being moral is also serving the self. (Thucydides had implied this when he juxtaposed the might-makes-right doctrine at Melos with the factionalism at Athens during the Sicilian debate.)

It is to insist that "Socrates" extends the Athenian tradition of critical reflection even as he challenges its previous form and content. That the Athenians have such a tradition is suggested by the way tragedy problematized cultural accommodations, and by Pericles' claims in the Funeral Oration and speeches as a whole. That it needs rearticulation and regrounding is suggested by Meletus's responses in the *Apology,* by the manipulation and ignorance of rhetoricians like (Plato's) Gorgias, and by sophists such as (Plato's) Protagoras.

Meletus, like Old Education in Aristophanes' *Clouds,* would excise the critical component of Athenian traditions in the name of a bogus conservatism. Gorgias and Protagoras, when not primarily interested in serving anyone who pays well, embrace what New Education does in the play; a destructive critique in what is, I shall argue in chapters eight and nine, a bogus radicalism. As an Athenian, Socrates can do neither, any more than Aristophanes can. He cannot uncritically accept the old ways (which are self-servingly distorted anyway), or the unqualified rejection of them. That is why he seeks to reground critical reflection in the life of his city (although in the agora rather than the Assembly or theater) in the individual citizen, in dialogue, and with full recognition that he owes the fact and even substance of his criticism to the city he is criticizing.

Thus, Socrates has a complex relationship to Athenian traditions notably shaped by the intellectual and political daring enshrined in the Salamis legend. That the simultaneous fulfillment and demise of that legend made Socratic political theory possible and necessary can be seen in Socrates' attitude toward self-knowledge, toward the Athenian strategy of Themistocles and Pericles, and in his dialogue with the laws in the *Crito.*

Gnōthi seauton (know thyself) and *mēden agan* (nothing in excess) were traditional pieties that Socrates elaborates in ways that are at once radical and conservative. In the late sixth century B.C. these inscriptions on the Alcmaeonid temple of Apollo were interpreted as a call to piety and moderation, summed up in the

Greek word *sōphrosunē*.[61] But by Socrates' time and under the influence of the sophists, a contested meaning emerged. Rather than being a counsel of restraint and limit, the insistence on self-knowledge, now largely dissociated from warnings against excess, was a call for mortals to remember that, in Protagoras's words, "man is the measure of all things." Socrates' commitment to self-knowledge (in the *Apology)* unites ancient caution with modern confidence. When he insists that intellectual power, reasoning, and thoughtfulness must be the foundation of individual and collective life, he does so in the expectation that men will thereby come to relearn the need for those limits necessary for freedom. If human beings remain aware of their mortality—that is, of their partiality in the dual sense of incompleteness and bias—they will be less likely to forget or neglect their need for others and for dialogue. If they remember that, as mortals they share a common condition of knowing they are creatures fated to die, they might even extend the need to outsiders within such as metics, slaves, and, in a different way, women. Both democracy and Socratic philosophy condemn their own exclusivities.

Both are transgressive in ways that reject the fundamental aristocratic and oligarchic value of exclusivity. In the case of democracy this transgressiveness is a social invasion of a preserve from which the invaders have been previously barred by claims of birth and natural entitlement. In the case of Socratic political philosophy, it is an intellectual invasion that challenges claims to privilege, power, and ideological hegemony.[62] Only with this awareness and these reminders can the Athenians hope to respond to the dual legacy of the daring born at Salamis and enshrined in the legend of victory. Echoing Aeschylus we might say that remembering one's mortality unites loss and gain in a single moment. Following Aeschylus, Herodotus, and Thucydides we could see Socrates as critical of the way Athenian naval power led to an attenuated connection between power and place, when instead of the city representing a place where power was constituted, it became a naval base, and a launching pad for a form of power that was projected abroad rather than embodied in internal deliberations, policy decisions, or degrees.[63] This gives added point to Socrates' question in the *Gorgias* of what will happen to the Athenians after they lose their empire, and to the tension between the dramatic and historical dates of the *Protagoras.*

Salamis made political theory possible and necessary because Themistocles' temporary strategy there helped shape a permanent way of life. As we saw, his urging the Athenians to abandon the city for the ships was opposed by a powerful minority on good traditional grounds. Aeschylus takes the conservative point of

---

[61] See Helen North, *Sophrosyne: Self-Knowledge and Self-Restraint in Greek Literature* (Ithaca: Cornell University Press, 1966), and *Charmides* 164e, where Critias claims to eliminate the ambiguities of "Know thyself." One could argue that he understood its riddles least of all.

[62] See Sheldon Wolin, "Transgression, Equality, Voice," in Josiah Ober and Charles Hedrick, *Demokratia: A Conversation on Democracy, Ancient and Modern* (Princeton: Princeton University Press, 1996), pp. 63–90. As I will argue in the next chapter, the "invasion" is a refusal to accept institutional and cultural limits on where and how people must be held accountable.

[63] Ibid.

view even while celebrating the strategy that conservatives opposed. Although the Athenians left the land, they fought for it. Still, it is probable that Themistocles' strategy helped loosen the hold of place and land.[64] Certainly it established Athens as a naval power and set a precedent that Pericles followed when he convinced his compatriots to abandon their land to the Spartans and to take refuge behind the city's walls and the fleet.

One way to understand this strategy is as a sign and cause of a distancing from those conserving traditions Aeschylus, Herodotus, and perhaps Thucydides regarded as essential for political freedom. Such distancing contributed to the Athenian justification at Melos, which, in contrast to the Funeral Oration, subsumes Athenian actions under a universal law of power and empire. It is present in the debate about and decision to invade Sicily. But it is also present in the increasing abstraction of Pericles' own speeches, and, most notably, in Thucydides' speech, the *History* as a whole.

In these terms the Socratic project is to elaborate an already existent theoretical impulse, while regrounding that impulse in the traditions it threatens to destroy. Only a democratic ethos founded on sentiment and reasoning, on love of one's own, and on justice offers hope in dealing with the dialectic of power revealed in the Salamis legend. The old ways and ideas cannot fully comprehend (in the double sense of mentally grasp or encompass) empire. But in Athens those old ways include a mode of discourse that has enabled Athenians to reflect critically on practices they also lived. It is to this resource of understanding that Socrates appeals in hopes of bringing his fellow citizens back to themselves, to the city, and to "reason," all of which he is also redefining. That is, I think, the challenge he set for himself and for political theory.

This helps us make sense of Socrates' dialogue with the laws in the *Crito;* why, for instance, he calls himself their slave after having been so defiant in the *Apology.* For the laws (as he constructs them) are not only father to the man but the vocation as well. Because they are, who Socrates is and what he does, including his insistence that men justify the lives they might otherwise live unquestioningly, he owes to the traditions and city he criticizes. If his fellow citizens cannot understand what he says and does, who can? Perhaps one reason Socrates refuses exile is that philosophy, or rather Socratic political philosophy as he describes it in the *Apology,* is only possible in Athens.

The *Republic* begins in Athens, more precisely in the Piraeus, and with familiar themes. But as the dialogue proceeds, the Piraeus, which is home to the fleet and sailors, is left far below and so the perspective on those themes radically alters. After book 1, Plato seems less interested in reconstituting Athenian traditions than in constructing a city in speech and among the speakers. Historical legends and concerns with the Ancestral Constitution are replaced by cosmological myths and concern for ontological grounding. Plato does not so much repudi-

---

[64] I do not want to exaggerate. Large sections of the population remained tied to the land. Moreover, the gradual erosion of that attachment can hardly be attributed to this strategy alone. For instance, one would have to consider the alienability of land, the impact of trade and commerce, changes in citizenship laws, and so on.

ate Salamis as ignore the whole context of debate about it. History, as it is defined by Herodotus and Thucydides, is no longer sufficient. When men know themselves to be users of history and creators of their own greatness, all accounts of the past, like all quotations of poetic authorities, are or are believed to be political projections that construct reality rather than give an account of it. (We will see an example of this in the exegesis of Simonides' poem in the *Protagoras*.) When legends lose their hold so that what was once a common self-understanding now promotes conflict, or when the glorious deeds of ancestors are revealed as "in fact" the issue of evil or petty motives, then the grounding of public life and the understanding of reality demand some new form of thought. Or so Plato seems to believe in the *Republic*.

One can understand Plato's project by suggesting the questions he was trying to answer. What can be done about tyrants and tyrannical longings when the glory of tyrannicides is debunked? How is it possible for men to stop short of regarding anything as possible once they regard arrangements as conventional, if not arbitrary? (Of course this does not preclude them justifying conventionalism as "natural.") If, as Thucydides implies, Corcyra really does anticipate Athenian *stasis*, what sense can there be in the Socratic project of reconstituting Athenian traditions by drawing on elided, repressed, or unrecognized aspects of those traditions? What if the attempt to substitute the Socratic legend for the Salamis legend fails, or, more disconcertingly, suppose Socratic questioning turns out to be insufficient, perhaps part of the problem (as Plato seems to indicate in the *Protagoras*)? One "solution" is to shift the terms and world of debate by looking to nature for the right form and shape for the city.

But it is unclear how the ideal state can be realized, where it can be realized (in the soul or in the city), or even whether it ought to be realized. In fact, there are at least two ideal communities in the *Republic* and they stand in tension, if not contradiction, to each other. One is the community of interlocutors led by Socrates, democratic in spirit if not argument. The other, which is the issue of the first community's dialogue, is a rigidly hierarchical society ruled by philosopher-kings. Insofar as this "Platonic" "solution" is as problematic as the dilemma it sought to resolve, insofar as the project and prospect of turning tyrants into philosophers is absurd in principle or extremely remote, one must either turn away from politics altogether or return, in some form, to the Socratic aim of reconstituting the Athenian traditions (and politics generally) from its own unrealized possibilities. In the *Laws*, Plato returns to the Socratic aim and the debate over the Ancestral Constitution, although in very different terms. Surely it is significant that the principal interlocutor (or lecturer) in the *Laws* is an Athenian stranger, not "Socrates."

In that dialogue, the Athenian stranger argues that any state aiming at peace and wisdom needs to avoid the sea, lest its citizens succumb to the sea's temptations of luxury, disunity, and decadence. Remoteness from the sea is a necessary condition for political freedom and harmony. By making a city alien to itself, sea power encourages imperialism and corrodes just and noble habits of life. After the stranger proclaims that states that depend on navies for power give honors to the inferior, Clinias asks whether the naval victory at Salamis saved Greece from the barbarians. The Athenian stranger both denies the importance of the victory (in favor of the land battles at Marathon and Plataea) and insists that the battle made the Greeks morally worse, even if it did allow their physical survival. Echoing Socrates' criticisms of Pericles in the *Gorgias* he says: "I . . . affirm that it was the land-battle of Marathon which began the salvation of Greece, and that of Plataea which completed it: and we affirm also that, whereas these battles made the Greeks better, the sea-fights made them worse" (707c).[65]

V

With these words Plato rejects the Salamis legend in favor of Marathon and of an Athens uncorrupted by naval power and democratic activism.[66] In his final writing, he presents Salamis as an object lesson not only to his contemporaries but any "tradition" of political theory that considers Plato as its beginning point, which is one reason why Rancière argues, "The whole political project of platonism can be conceived as an anti-maritime polemic."[67] The irony, of course, is that the virtues of the Marathon generation, like Spartan or Cretan virtues, could not have generated political philosophy. That Plato knew that too leaves us uncertain about his ultimate judgment either of democracy or of the activity he has been interpreted as defining. As this uncertainty attests, political theory is a tradition of activity whose empowering vision contains within it an immanent critique of its own possibility and prospect.

In the following chapters I will suggest how much of this critique builds on democratic practices it also rejects and in later chapters try to reclaim the democratic dimensions of Platonic (Socratic) dialogues. In the next chapter on *dokimasia* and *euthunai* (the scrutiny and accountability of officials), I will suggest how Socrates elaborated concrete democratic practices into a philosophical way of life that retained its political origin and purposes.

---

[65] Bury's translation from the Loeb edition of *The Laws*.

[66] "The speech [the alternative Funeral Oration in the *Menexenus*] not only relegates Salamis to second place in importance behind Marathon . . . but treats Salamis along with Marathon merely as indications that Greeks could defend themselves against Persians—leaving aside the extraordinary character of the sea battle at Salamis . . . namely, that it showed the Athenian polis to be entirely separate from the Athenian earth and the Athenian regime to be located entirely in the spiritedness of Athenian citizens" (Salkever, "Socrates' Aspasian Oration," p. 139).

[67] *On the Shores of Politics*, p. 1.

Democratic Accountability and
Socratic Dialectic

It is not easy Socrates for anyone to sit beside you and not be forced to give
an account of himself [*didonai logon*].

—Theaetetus 169A

As I SUGGESTED in chapter two, the death of Socrates at the hands of Athenian
democracy is regarded as definitive not simply of a historically specific enmity
between Athenian democracy and Socratic philosophy, but of a necessary if not
desirable opposition between philosophy "per se" and democracy "per se."[1] For
Michael Walzer philosophers must dissociate themselves from the common ideas
and ideals of their fellow citizens in part because philosophical validation and
political authorization are two entirely different things.[2] For Allan Bloom they
must be separate in order to protect politics from the potentially corrosive consequences of philosophy's disregard for conventional pieties and to protect philosophers from both the corrupting blandishments of power and the ignorant contempt for the philosophical vocation held by *hoi polloi*.[3] Beginning with a
different politics, Benjamin Barber comes to a similar conclusion. Though Socrates no doubt loved Athens "he did not love democracy. Nor did he believe that
men had a right and a responsibility (let alone the capacity) to govern themselves
in common. That a man might be better off ruling himself badly than being ruled
wisely by another more prudent man—the central tenet of democracy—was simply beyond the philosopher's ken."[4]

There are a number of particular reasons why this characterization of Socrates'
trial and so his relationship to Athenian democracy is more problematic than

---

[1] There are of course exceptions, John Dewey being the most notable. It is perhaps a coincidence
that proclamations about the death of philosophy and of theory as a toolkit are accompanied by the
further erosion of a vigorous democratic politics.

[2] In *The Company of Critics: Social Criticism and Political Commitment in the Twentieth Century*
(New York: Basic Books, 1989), Walzer seems to qualify his earlier argument, calling Socrates of the
Apology a "connected critic" engaged in an "ideological critique" which ties him to his fellow citizens. Walzer rejects the vision of Socrates as a misunderstood solitary figure who braved the implacable hostility of his fellow Athenians. In fact, he had numerous friends, including evidently many (but
not a majority) of the jury. Unlike Plato he did not separate himself from his compatriots but engaged
in continual dialogue with them (pp. 4–5, 12–17, 187–8).

[3] Allan Bloom, *The Closing of the American Mind* (New York: Simon and Schuster, 1987), and his
"Interpretative Essay" in his translation of the *Republic* (New York: Basic Books, 1968), pp. 307–
436.

[4] See *An Aristocracy of Everyone: The Politics of Education and the Future of America* (New
York: Ballantine Books, 1992), p. 186.

these arguments indicate. There is the closeness of the vote which surprises Socrates, his claim that he would have been able to convince them of his innocence if given more time, the fact that he was allowed to say whatever he liked for his entire life, and what seems his purposeful provocations which enhanced his chances of conviction and sentence of death, as if only by dying could he continue the questioning he did during his life. But there is also a more general reason why the opposition assumed by Walzer, Bloom, and Barber is more polymorphous than this. It has to do with the continuities and analogs between Athenian democratic practices and Socratic political philosophy as we hear it described in the *Apology*.

In a recent series of essays[5] Josiah Ober has made a parallel argument about the opposition between what he calls "democratic knowledge" as exemplified by the enactment formula of the Athenian Assembly—*edoxe tōi dēmōi* (it appeared right to the people)—and "counterhegemonic discourse" as embodied in elite critics like Thucydides, Plato, and, more problematically, Socrates. While Athenian civic ideology constructed the identity of the city by promulgating a specifically democratic way of learning about and acting in the public realm, these critics offered a technique of constructing an oppositional identity through mastery of different although equally political sorts of knowledge. Where the former agreed on the significance of liberty for all citizens (especially freedom of public speech), and that collective decisions of the citizenry were inherently wise, their critics regarded such principles as politically ruinous. The people were too easily duped and preoccupied by the moment, their views too superficial and unreflective, for wise decisions to issue from them.

Ober regards the presence of such critics and the willingness of Athenian democracy to tolerate their criticisms as essential to its being a democracy, because without them democracy would become a hegemonic discourse unable to realize consistently its distinctive virtue of revisibility.[6] What marks democracy off from other regimes is its willingness to rethink and reform itself, to contemplate and endorse change in its political culture. In order for this to happen, democracies need interventions from critics, and in the case of major revisions, critics who are, in some sense, outside the dominant culture.

In many respects I share Ober's characterization of Athenian democracy. I would, however, change the accent marks by emphasizing the degree to which Athenians institutionalized self-reflection and self-critique and the degree to which elite critics (including Plato) remained dependent upon and incorporated aspects of that tradition even as they criticized it. Thus I will suggest that demo-

---

[5] See the citations in nn. 6, 9, and 38.

[6] Ober, "Civic Ideology and Counter-Hegemonic Discourse: Thucydides on the Sicilian Debate," in Alan L. Boegehold and Adele C. Scafuro, eds., *Athenian Identity and Civic Ideology* (Baltimore: Johns Hopkins University Press, 1994), pp. 102–6; "How to Criticize Democracy in Late Fifth- and Fourth-Century Athens," in J. Peter Euben, John R. Wallach, and Josiah Ober, eds., *Athenian Political Thought and the Reconstitution of American Democracy* (Ithaca: Cornell University Press, 1994), pp. 149–71; and "Power and Oratory in Democratic Athens: Demosthenes 21, *Against Meidias*," in Ian Worthington, ed., *Persuasion* (London: Routledge, 1994), pp. 85–108.

cratic and elite cultures are more reciprocal than Ober sometimes suggests. My reasons are analogous to the ones that lead me to think Walzer's opposition between philosophy and democracy is overstated, Barber's choice between ruling oneself badly and being ruled wisely by another misses the Socratic challenge that ordinary men can rule themselves wisely, and that it is possible and perhaps necessary to have "philosophical" citizens. Whether this is a democratic position in Barber's sense, or a counterhegemonic argument that in fact promotes democracy by its criticism of it in Ober's sense, and why such a distinction might make a contemporary difference, will become clearer in what follows in this chapter and in chapter eight on the *Gorgias.*

In this chapter, however, I want to elucidate my argument that the democratic political culture of Athens was a necessary condition for the intellectual critique Socrates makes of it and that there were strong continuities of sentiment and purpose between democratic politics and Socratic political philosophy. In many respects this is an alternative iteration of the argument made in the previous chapter. But in another sense it involves a shift of emphasis since I want to look at two specific practices, *dokimasia* and *euthunai,* which helped constitute a culture of scrutiny and accountability which was itself part of a democratization of power and responsibility. If I am right in suggesting that Socrates draws upon these practices and their underlying culture when he demands that citizens give an account of their lives, and if this culture was pivotal in the democratization of Athens, then Socrates can be read as expanding and refashioning those practices and that culture. In these terms what made him a threat was less what he demanded than that he demanded it outside "normal" institutional structures and that he demanded it of everyone with whom he came in contact. One could say that by generalizing and extending the culture of accountability Socrates made an implicit set of convictions explicit.

As these remarks indicate, this chapter looks back to chapter two and the charge that Socrates was corrupting the youth, to the conditions of his trial, to what he is doing when he engaged his fellow citizens in conversation, to what it means to think about what one is doing, and to the difference between a political and a politicized education. It also recapitulates not only the dialectic between Athenian democracy and Socratic political theory described in chapter three, but Otanes' argument about the dangers of unanswerable power: "when a ruler can do whatever he wants and not be held to account for it."[7] Penultimately the chapter also looks forward to the chapters on drama, which provide a "theoretical" counterpart and critical complement in the culture of accountability. By theoretical counterpart I mean that the dramatic festivals provided time and place to look at the significance and coherence of everyday decisions in more comprehensive terms than the press of everyday politics allowed. By critical complement I mean that, though drama helped constitute the culture of accountability, it also challenged the narratives and civic ideology that legitimated certain ac-

---

[7] Herodotus 3.80. When Aeschylus describes Xerxes as *ouch hupeuthunos polei* (*Persae* 213), he emphasizes how crucial accountability is in a democracy as opposed to a tyranny.

counts at the expense of others, or, in more contemporary terms, it dramatized certain counternarratives. This is especially true of comedy, as I shall suggest in the next chapter.

Finally, this chapter also complements chapters eight and nine on the *Gorgias* and *Protagoras*. While it explores democratic anticipations of Socratic political philosophy, they read backward from the dialogues to the democratic practices they exemplify even when they explicitly criticize them.

In the end Athenian democracy and "Socrates" are historically specific phenomena, though it is probably impossible to disinter their historicity from the multiple incarnations with which they have been blessed and to which they have been subjected. This chapter (and this book) is one of those incarnations. It is offered as a provocation and an invitation to gain a certain kind of distance from what may, with the disrepute of Marxism and socialism, be a narrowing of political and theoretical vision, and from what seems to be a further attenuation of democratic politics. As I suggested in chapter two, one could argue that in recent years American society has grown more inegalitarian, more systematically dominated by corporate power, involved in a class war in which only one side is fighting, and more and more ruled by elites bent on appropriating the conduct, knowledge, and procedures of public life. If so, then this reverses the democratization of power as that evolved in Athens in the fifth century B.C. That evolution represented the opening of public spaces and an enlargement of what was brought before the commons. Rather than more and more of political life being claimed as the eminent domain of professional experts and professors who reappropriated knowledge while forming a caste of initiates, the movement toward democracy largely delegitimated claims to exclusive political knowledge by kings and nobles.[8]

II

Before any Athenian citizen could assume office and before he could step down at the end of his tenure, he had to undergo a preliminary scrutiny (*dokimasia*) and a final accounting (*euthunai*) before a jury of his countrymen chosen by lot.[9]

---

[8] For the critique, see Sheldon S. Wolin, "What Revolutionary Action Means Today," *democracy* 2 (Fall 1982): 17–28. For the way that critique inverts the evolution of Athenian democracy, see Jean-Pierre Vernant, *The Origins of Greek Thought* (Ithaca: Cornell University Press, 1982), pp. 47–48, 51–52. The issue of professionalism arises with the prominence of the sophists. I will discuss it in chapters eight and nine.

[9] On the *dokimasia* and *euthunai,* see Aristotle's *Constitution of Athens* 55.3–4, Demosthenes 57.66–70, Lysias 16.9, 26.3, 25, 31; Martin Ostwald, *From Popular Sovereignty to the Sovereignty of Law: Law, Society and Politics in Fifth-Century Athens* (Berkeley: University of California Press, 1986), pp. 12–13, 40–51, 55–62, 77–83; Marcel Piérart, "Les euthunoi athéniens," *Antiquité Classique* 40 (1971): 526–73; Jennifer Roberts, *Accountability in Athenian Government* (Madison: University of Wisconsin Press, 1982); Mogens Herman Hansen, *Athenian Democracy in the Age of Demosthenes,* trans. J. A. Crook (Oxford: Basil Blackwell, 1991), pp. 218–24; R. K. Sinclair, *Democracy and Participation in Athens* (New York: Cambridge University Press, 1988), pp. 77–79;

Since virtually every male citizen would be a magistrate some time in his life, this meant that at some point he would have to give an account of his life, and that Athenian democracy was premised on such mutual accountability. Although the *dokimasia* and *euthunai* were not the only ways in which a magistrate could be called to account, they were "the most obvious and formal manifestations of the generalized power of the Athenian masses to review the actions, behavior and political status of all citizens."[10]

The *dokimasia* which any Athenian elected or selected by lot was required to undergo, was intended to establish the legal qualifications for holding office. This it did by asking a citizen who his father, mother, and grandparents were, what their demes were, where their tombs and shrines were located, whether he looked after his parents, paid his taxes, and performed the required military service. When these questions had been put, the candidate produced witnesses to confirm his answers, after which anyone who wished to could submit evidence that might speak against his being accepted for office. In turn, the candidate had a right to defend himself against such charges with a defense that might include giving an account of his whole life.[11] Then a jury selected by lot from the jury rolls of six thousand (itself selected by lot) would vote to accept or reject him. (In the case of the *Boule* or Council, the organization itself voted.)[12]

Almost certainly the *dokimasia* was not used to judge the competency of a prospective magistrate or "correct" a supposed misfit between office and man.[13] In both aristocratic and democratic cities it was taken for granted "that any citizen who had the proper legal credentials to be eligible could serve whether by election or by lot."[14] It is almost as certain that the *dokimasia* sometimes expanded beyond any formal, specifically legal purposes to become an inquiry into the career, character, and life of the candidate. Thus one scholar concludes that the *dokimasia* "was a comprehensive inquiry, covering not only the candidate's

---

David Whitehead, *The Demes of Attica 508/7–ca. 250 B.C.* (Princeton: Princeton University Press, 1986); Josiah Ober, *Mass and Elite in Democratic Athens: Rhetoric, Ideology and the Power of the People* (Princeton: Princeton University Press, 1989); C. Hignett, *A History of the Athenian Constitution to the End of the Fifth Century B.C.* (London: Oxford University Press, 1958), especially pp. 205–8; Douglas M. MacDowell, *The Law in Classical Athens* (London: Thames and Hudson, 1978), pp. 160–72; P. J. Rhodes, *The Athenian Boulē* (Oxford: Clarendon Press, 1985), pp. 199–210, as well as his *Commentary on the Aristotelian* Athenaion Politeia (Oxford: Clarendon Press, 1981); G. Adeleye, "The Purpose of the Dokimasia," *Greek Roman and Byzantine Studies* 24 (1983): 295–306, and Louis Gernet "L'institution des arbitres publics à Athènes," *Revue des études grecques,* 52 (1937): 389–414.

[10] The quotation is from Ober, *Mass and Elite,* p. 327. There were other institutional and cultural components besides *dokimasia* and *euthunai* that made up the culture of accountability. For discussions of *eisangelia,* ostracism, *graphē paranomōn,* see Hansen, Ostwald, and Roberts, cited in the previous footnote.

[11] See Virginia J. Hunter, *Policing Athens: Social Control in the Attic Lawsuits, 420–320 B.C.* (Princeton: Princeton University Press, 1994), pp. 106–9.

[12] See the details in Rhodes, *The Athenian Boulē.*

[13] See Lysias 26.13, 21–24; Aristotle *Athenaion Politeia* 55.3; Demosthenes 57.67; and A.R.W. Harrison, *The Law of Athens,* 2 vols. (Oxford: Oxford University Press, 1968).

[14] See the discussion in Ostwald, *From Popular Sovereignty,* pp. 79–82.

legal qualifications but also the probity of his life, both public and private."[15] (Though there is evidence that a *dokimasia* could function as a repository of innuendo, rumor, and gossip and that accusers used it to further personal vendettas or political grudges, we must be careful not to let our standards of law and evidence define what they would not see as "abuses" or "extraneous" considerations).[16]

The political dimension of *dokimasia* most likely became more prominent and significant after the reforms of Ephialtes in 462/1 B.C., which transferred judicial power from the aristocratic Areopagus to the *dikastērion* (popular courts), and in the wake of the brutal oligarchic revolutions of 411 and 404 B.C. After these upheavals the *dokimasia* was used to eliminate those with oligarchic sympathies even after amnesty explicitly forbade such political retribution. Between 411 and 405 virtually any connection with the oligarchs would be used for disqualification. But after the passing of the Patrocleides decree only those who were active supporters of the Thirty were eliminated, though other grounds were usually adduced.[17]

Within thirty days of leaving his position, anyone who had carried out a public function or had charge of public funds, including priests, ambassadors, trierarchs, members of the Council and Areopagus, and all officials (except jurors), had to undergo a review by the *euthunoi*, a board of state examiners (one from each of the ten tribes) who were chosen by lot and sat in the agora to hear charges of misconduct.[18] A *euthunai* had two stages corresponding to narrower and more expansive notions of rendering an account. The first involved an audit of public expenditures conducted by *logistai* (auditors) and assessed by ten *synēgoroi* (speakers), again selected by lot.[19] The concern here was misappropriation of funds or bribes (which is why *euthunai* applied even to those who had no administrative duties that involved direct handling of money). After his accounts were inspected, a man was brought before a jury in which *logistai* presided and *synēgoroi* presented the case against him if his accounting appeared unsatisfactory. Even if no fault was found, a herald invited anyone who wished to make an accusation to do so.

The second stage was more inclusive. It was conducted by the ten *euthunoi* who sat in the agora for three days during which anyone wishing to accuse any man whose investigation by the *logistai* had recently been completed could hand his charge in writing to the *euthunos* of the tribe to which the accused man belonged. The charge at this stage usually referred to neglect or positive misuse of power. If the *euthunos* thought the charge had merit, he delivered a formal

---

[15] Adeleye, "The Purpose of the Dokimasia," p. 30.

[16] On this see Sally Humphreys "Social Relations on Stage: Witnesses in Classical Athens," *History and Anthropology* 1 (1985): 313–69; Hunter, *Policing Athens;* Ober, *Mass and Elite;* and MacDowell, *The Law in Classical Athens.*

[17] See Roberts's discussion of Lysias, in *Accountability in Athenian Government,* p. 21.

[18] See the discussion in Hansen, *The Athenian Democracy,* chap. 8.

[19] Though all commentators agree that there was a change from the fifth to the fourth century when the power of the *euthunoi* was divided there is less agreement exactly when it happened or why.

condemnation, which was passed on for trial—to the tribe judges if it was a private matter, to the *thesmothetai* if it was public. Only after the *euthunoi* had cleared the official of any misconduct—whether personal malfeasance, having acted detrimentally to the welfare of another citizen or the city as a whole— could he travel, transfer property, be adopted into a different family, or make a votive offering to a god.[20]

Dokimasia and *euthunai* were embodiments of a generalized culture of accountability.[21] In this culture people were scrutinized and held accountable anytime they proposed or opposed an action or decision. Every time the assembly voted on someone's proposal, or a jury in a political trial acquitted or convicted on the basis of arguments someone had made as prosecutor or defendant, they were subject to a generalized form of *euthunai*. Similarly, insofar as one's way of life, character, and past history came to be deemed crucial to assessing the motives and soundness of what he, as a prospective official, was likely to do, such an individual was subject to "an informal but effective dokimasia."[22]

The culture of accountability evolved as a reaction against monopolistic claims to power. Whether it is Aeschylus's portrait of Zeus as a tyrant who "rules alone, is harsh and is accountable to no one" or Otanes reminding his listeners that unaccountable power destroys political society and the one who would rule, scrutiny was seen as a way of making power responsible by making it accountable.

The question of course was accountable to whom? The answer given by the Athenians was, to the people and the democratic culture that sustained such practices as *dokimasia* and *euthunai*. But there is another question: exactly why should one limit power? Is it only to keep the powerful in check? Or is there a sense that the absence of power corrupts just as surely as its undue concentration, so that democracy becomes not just limiting power but multiplying its sources, the occasions for its use, and the people who share in it. It was this sharing of power that Herodotus believes to be the source of Athenian greatness and freedom as we saw in the preceding chapter. If I am right, then accountability is more than elites being held accountable by the people; it is the people being accountable to each other and to themselves.[23] In these, more radically democratic terms, citizenship becomes the opportunity to initiate as well as react, and political

---

[20] See the discussion in Roberts, *Accountability in Athenian Government,* p. 18.

[21] In many respects the Greek idea of accountability has the same range, breadth, and ambiguity as our own. To render an account is to provide a story or description of events or situations as well as to explain oneself (often to a superior). To give an account is to give reasons (i.e., on this account I am going). Things (or someone) of no account lack importance, worth, value, and consequence. To call to account is to hold someone responsible or blame them: to take account of is to consider, include, recognize; something unaccountable is unforeseen, incalculable, or mysterious.

[22] Ober, *Mass and Elite,* p. 329.

[23] A.H.M. Jones wrote that while Athenian democracy was founded on the principle that "all citizens could be trusted to take their part in the government . . . on one point the Athenians were distrustful of human nature, on its ability to resist the temptations of irresponsible power" (quoted in Roberts, *Accountability in Athenian Government,* p. 7). This is true, but too negative and only part of the story. For the idea of power as collective capacity, see Arendt's discussion of Periclean Athens in *The Human Condition* (Chicago: University of Chicago Press, 1958), secs. 27–28.

judgment is developed through the experience in judging the life and character of litigants, assessing their social and political status as well as that of their families and friends, and determining the ramifications of their failed public obligations.

Of course, there is a darker side to this "severe attitude toward accountability":[24] a policing of people's lives (at least insofar as they are public beings) and an inhibition of leadership. For instance, we do not know how many talented Athenians were deterred from active political involvement by the practice and ideology of accountability.

These are real concerns, but we should be skeptical of the politics and of the theory that would make them definitive. The modern state precludes more than token accountability when it does not systematically constrict it. Add to this a preoccupation with leadership and an indifference to a vigorous notion of citizenship, a minimalist commitment to political equality, and an aggressive opposition to the dispersal of power and responsibility, and complaints about the deleterious consequences of democratic accountability become somewhat suspect. Like the Athenian *dēmos,* most citizens of modern states are threatened by elite power, though now it is a confluence of professional, academic, and corporate elites who often walk, talk, and act like oligarchs while proclaiming a (very abstract) fealty to democracy. Of course they, like their oligarchic progenitors, *do* worry about "governability," and "overloading" the system with political and economic democracy. Democracy seems to them plagued by discontinuities and instability, by inefficiency and incompetence. Even at its best democracy seems too time-consuming and cumbersome, too formless and amateurish to deal with the complexities of modern political life. But it is precisely the demands for political efficiency, competence, stability, and coordination that lead, whether by design or not, to increased state power, unrepresentative bureaucracies, and elite control of democratic civic ideology.[25] Indeed, with only slight exaggeration one could argue that with the depoliticization of public concerns such as education and prisons, and in the narrowing of public space and discourse (despite Clinton's sporadic efforts to the contrary), we are, as I have suggested, witnessing a process that precisely reverses the movement toward democratization that occurred in Athens in the fifth century B.C.

Besides, we should remember that, for better or worse, members of the juries and nonspeakers in the Athenian Assembly, as well as those who generally remained apart from public life, were not subject to the same intense scrutiny. Moreover, as contemporary defenders and critics of democracy agree, freedom as well as equality distinguished democratic regimes. Thucydides' Pericles claims that citizens in Athens live pretty much as they please and say what they want.[26]

---

[24] The phrase is Roberts's. She makes the general argument, elements of which can also be found Hunter's *Policing Athens* and L. B. Carter's *The Quiet Athenian* (Oxford: Oxford University Press, 1986), though he has little to say about the fifth century.

[25] See the discussion of efficiency in David Stockton, *The Classical Athenian Democracy* (New York: Oxford University Press, 1990), pp. 112–16.

[26] *Zen hos bouletai tis kai parrhēsiazesthai.* See the discussion in Robert W. Wallace, "Private

Plato agreed with the description, though he did not share Pericles' evaluation of it. Book 8 of the *Republic* argues that democracies lack decorum and form because in it distinctions are transgressed. Whether in regard to people or ideas, high and low are confounded, knowledge is equated with mere opinion, and life as a whole is a veritable bazaar of goods (in all senses of that word). No one is immune to the corrupting influence of democratic culture. Even the most "natural" relations such as those between children and adults, slaves and freemen, men and women are affected. Socrates of the *Apology* may have believed democracy capable of reform and reconfiguration but the Socrates of book 8 surely did not.[27]

III

The culture of accountability evolved as part of the democratization of power and responsibility that took place from the sixth to the late fifth century B.C. One way to characterize this development is to see it as an expansion of an aristocratic ethos that emphasized both an agonistic conception of political and social life and an intensely egalitarian spirit.[28] Even in the exclusive society of warrior-aristocrats, power became the concern of all citizens rather than the property of one man or one *genos* (clan). This shift meant that decisions were brought *es to meson,* to the middle, center, shared ground or public.

Another way to think of the change is to see it as a redefinition of social and intellectual space where the city became centered on communal spaces, the agora and the public hearth, as problems of general concern began to be debated. Where the royal citadel had been, there arose temples open to public worship. Over the ruins of the palace on the "acropolis" (literally the highest point in the city) the polis was consecrated to the city's gods. "What this urban framework in fact defined," Jean-Pierre Vernant writes, "was a mental space; it opened up a new spiritual horizon. Once the city was centered on the public square, it was already a polis in every sense of the word."[29] But it was not yet a democratic polis.

Yet a third way to characterize this democratization of power and responsibility is to see it in terms of the preeminence of speech as an instrument of power and element of authority. *Political* speech was no longer the ritual words,

---

Lives and Public Enemies: Freedom of Thought in Classical Athens," in Boegehold and Scafuro, *Athenian Identity and Civic Ideology,* pp. 127–55.

[27] See Sheldon S. Wolin, "Norm and Form: The Constitutionalizing of Democracy," in Euben et al., *Athenian Political Thought,* pp. 29–58. For reasons I give in the penultimate section of chapter eight, I am uncertain about this characterization of Plato.

[28] Jean Pierre Vernant, *The Origins of Greek Thought* (Ithaca: Cornell University Press, 1982). I chose Vernant because his brief but lucid description of these developments is particularly useful. But his argument is hardly uncontested. Some other authors who traverse similar terrain are Ostwald, Davies, Meier, Ehrenberg, John Finley, M. I. Finley, Cynthia Farrar, Hignett, Bowra, Forrest, and Cartledge, among others.

[29] Vernant, *Origins,* p. 48. This is obviously a highly schematic rendering in which continuities between archaic oligarchies and classical democracies were a much more complex tangled process.

precise formula, or inspired declaration received from a god by initiates who simply pronounced what justice was. It now involved open debate and argument. The very existence of such debate presupposed a public audience to whom it was addressed and who could be expected to judge what it heard by voting for one of the parties or policies presented to it. However limited that audience might be, and however much *archē* (power, initiative, sovereignty, rule) remained in the hands of an aristocratic elite, the crucial principle was that human choice measured the force of words.[30]

Similarly, political life involved the publicness or publicity given to the most important aspects of collective life. The emergent domain was public in two related senses: it was an area (both physically and intellectually) of common interest as opposed to private concerns, and of open practices openly arrived at as opposed to secret procedures. This insistence on openness meant the progressive appropriation by the community as a whole of the conduct, knowledge, and procedures that had been the exclusive prerogative of king or clan. Power was now visible, its workings exposed to public view.

This process of politicization created an ever widening circle with access to the spiritual world previously reserved for the aristocracy of priests and warriors. Such expansion involved a qualitative as well as a quantitative transformation. In becoming elements in a common culture, knowledge, values, and intellectual abilities were themselves brought before the public and submitted to criticism and controversy. Rather than being preserved in family traditions as private tokens of power, their exposure to what Vernant calls "public scrutiny" fostered exegeses, conflicting interpretations, controversies, and heated debates. Especially at Athens, discussion, debate, and polemic became the rules of the political *and* intellectual game. The law of the polis, as distinguished from the absolute power of the monarch, required a "rendering of accounts." Decisions and values could no longer be imposed by the authority of personal and religious prestige; they had to demonstrate their validity by processes of a *"dialectical* sort."[31]

Democracy extended and deepened this process and these principles further, which is why Aristotle acknowledges that there is a certain affinity between the general idea of a polis and democracy.[32] It was distinguished by who was allowed to do what with what justification and purpose. More specifically, it was distinguished by its answers to eight questions:

1. What did it mean to be a citizen of Athens? Who was a citizen and who was not and by what means were new members to be included in the citizen body?

2. What was the form (method, place, and frequency of meeting) and social composition of the decision-making bodies that determined state policy?

---

[30] If man is not yet, in Protagoras's words, "the measure of all things," he is now the measure of some important things. On Protagoras's aphorism, see Cynthia Farrar, *The Origins of Democratic Thinking: The Invention of Politics in Classical Athens* (New York: Cambridge University Press, 1988), chaps. 3–4.

[31] Vernant, *Origins,* p. 52. The emphasis is mine.

[32] See the *Politics,* 1281a 16–17, 1286a 26–35.

3. Who had the power to propose measures to these decision-making bodies and who had the right to debate those measures once they had been proposed? Who was entitled to speak and who actually spoke? Were there any consequences if something was said by someone who was not of high social standing or great wealth?

4. What were the limitations upon the implementation of decisions? Who was able to limit what and on what grounds?

5. What was the social standing and wealth of those responsible for carrying out decisions? How were they selected and how extensive were their powers?

6. What was the social standing of those responsible for legal judgment? What were the grounds and justification for such judgments?

7. Who was thought to educate whom about public matters? To what degree was education regarded as being inborn or a matter of class rather than learned by the living of a public life?

8. In general how widely shared was power and responsibility and what justification was offered for that sharing?[33]

The general answer to these questions is that by the second half of the fifth century the ordinary Athenian male citizen had attained substantial political power. By 400 B.C. there were no property qualifications for citizenship, the primary decision-making bodies were the citizen Assembly, the legislative bodies of lawmakers (*nomothētai*), and the popular courts. All of these bodies met openly, and some, such as the Assembly and courts, met frequently. With few exceptions (the ten generals being most notable), positions of power were decided by lot and rotated frequently. The agenda of the Assembly was determined by the Council whose members were selected annually by lot from the entire citizen population, and discussion in the Assembly was open to every citizen, even if members of the elite normally took a leading role. Decisions of the Assembly were subject to review only by the people's courts, whose decisions were final. And, as we have seen, all magistrates were subject to intense public scrutiny either formally or informally.[34] (The introduction of state pay for most forms of government service made government accessible to ordinary citizens.)[35]

Democracy not only involved the sharing of power and responsibility; it also included recognizing oneself as a holder of power. In the Funeral Oration Pericles holds up Athenian power to those who constitute it as if to make his fellow citizens aware of themselves as having power and, by so doing, further enacts what he is describing. The erotic and aesthetic dimensions of power in the oration, echoed in Thucydides' description of the Athenians watching their enor-

---

[33] I adopt the first six questions from Ober, *Mass and Elite*, p. 54; the last two are my own. While I obviously owe much to Ober, I think he sometimes "oversociologizes" politics.

[34] See Ostwald's discussion of the Solonic origins of these developments, *From Popular Sovereignty*, p. 3–15, and of the extension of popular power to the *hēliaia*, in sovereignty, p. 55–56.

[35] See Ober's discussion of the relationship between elite, honor, and democratic dignity in his "Power and Oratory in Democratic Athens: Demosthenes 21, *Against Meidias*." Ober argues that the dignity of citizenship represented the intersection of individual freedom, political equality, and security against violation of one's bodily integrity.

mous armament depart for what would be the disastrous expedition to Sicily, seems to be, among other things, an effort to make the intangible dimensions of collective power momentarily visible.

Insofar as democracy's willingness to contemplate change and rethink and reform itself can be regarded as "an innate characteristic of democratic political culture,"[36] and to the degree, as conservative critics were right to insist, that democracy lacked form and boundaries,[37] the very process of development Vernant outlines is democratic. This is not to deny the significant degree of stability and continuity in Athenian democracy, but to elaborate what went with it—a dynamic that, according to the Corinthians in Thucydides, characterized Athenian democratic culture.[38] The transformative aspect of Athenian power is captured in Claude Lefort's claim that one unprecedented feature of democracy is that the locus of power becomes "an empty place" because no individual or group can be consubstantial with it. It cannot be represented or embodied in institutions, though it can sometimes be seen to be present there. Democratic power is always more than the moment and outside the boundaries that would give it definition and aim.[39]

IV

What is the relationship between the culture of accountability distinctive to democratic Athens and the account Socrates demands of his interlocutors and gives his own life?[40] Where can he be placed in the democratization of power and responsibility this culture helped constitute and embodied? In what respects does Socratic political philosophy, particularly as it is portrayed and described in the *Apology,* elaborate processes like *dokimasia* and *euthunai,* and to what degree does it and he depart from them? Do these departures help us understand why people accused him of corrupting the youth?

It seems clear that, in the most general terms, someone undergoing a *dokimasia* or *euthunai* was expected to give an account of his past and present deeds as proceeding from an ethos with which a jury would be sympathetic. More particularly, he had to persuade them that he was a good citizen and patriot who had served the city well in the past and could be expected to serve it well in the future. And he had to prove that he had acted morally, in the sense of not misap-

---

[36] Ober, "How to Criticize Democracy in Late Fifth- and Fourth-Century Athens," p. 149.

[37] See Wolin's discussion of Athenian democracy in "Norm and Form."

[38] The daring and restlessness are integral to Athenian greatness and thus the scale of the war, which affords Thucydides the opportunity to make the claims he does for his own work. I have argued this at length in *The Tragedy of Political Theory: The Road Not Taken* (Princeton: Princeton University Press, 1990), chap. 6.

[39] See his *Democracy and Political Theory* (Minneapolis: University of Minnesota Press, 1988), pp. 16–17.

[40] On this, see Miles Burneyat's discussion in his edition of *The Theatetus of Plato* (Indianapolis: Hackett, 1990), pp. 26–29.

propriating either the city's funds or its trust. To accept a bribe was to break that trust in a particularly destructive way. Insofar as the press of time and complexity of certain issues left some citizens without resources for sound judgment, trust in a particular proposer was essential for trusting a particular proposal. A bribe destroyed this conflation of man and policy, since someone who was bribed spoke for another who was not present and in a voice that was not his own. Thus the anonymous or absent man on behalf of whom an orator was speaking was hidden from public view, as were the true sentiments of the bribed speaker, meaning they were both unaccountable. A trusted adviser to the people who sold out a trust built over many years was selling his good name as well as betraying the *dēmos* who had come to trust him. That is why anyone who accepted a bribe for public speaking was liable to indictment under *eisangelia*,[41] a legal process specifically designed for cases involving treason. The fact that bribe-taking politicians perverted the connection between character and policy and corrupted the reciprocal gratitude that bound the interests of mass and elite explains the "vehemence and prevalence of attacks on opponents as bribe takers."[42]

It also helps explain the importance attached to *parrhēsia* (speaking frankly), which finds expression in Socrates' demand that people say what they really mean, rather than hiding behind what others say or what they think they should say.[43] It also explains his animus against professional orators and rhetoricians. Now if we extend the idea of elites being accountable to the masses to citizens being accountable to each other, as I think Socrates does in the *Apology* (as well as in the *Gorgias* and *Protagoras*), then bribery destroys the lateral bonds of citizenship as well as the vertical bonds that unite elite and masses.

The communal pride in and emphasis on *parrhēsia* also helps explain the suspicion of Socrates and why he was so often identified with the sophists of whom he was so critical. Though no one accused Socrates of taking bribes, he was accused of corrupting the young, in part because of his manipulative "insincere" speech. Being attentive to the particular character of his interlocutor and general and particular context of conversation meant "adapting" to circumstance in a way that makes him appear (and perhaps be) disingenuous. Indeed, from one point of view, Socratic irony seems analogous to false speech, in the sense that it is not straightforward and direct. There are so many junctures in the dialogues where Socrates seems distant, outside, or not fully present that if he is not lying, he is certainly wearing a mask, or playing a part, hiding or reconfiguring his identity as he plays his multiple roles before his various audiences.

Of course that is exactly what actors did in the theater where Sophocles was known for *his* irony. So even where Socrates seems to violate a democratic

---

[41] On *eisangelia,* see Ostwald, *From Popular Sovereignty,* and Hansen, *The Athenian Democracy.* On bribery see Barry Strauss, "The Cultural Significance of Bribery and Embezzlement," *Ancient World 2* (1985): 67–74.

[42] Ober, *Mass and Elite,* p. 329, and Strauss, "The Cultural Significance of Bribery."

[43] On *parrhēsia* as a Platonic and democratic value, see S. Sara Monoson, "Frank Speech, Democracy, and Philosophy: Plato's Debt to a Democratic Strategy of Civic Discourse," in Euben et al., *Athenian Political Thought,* pp. 172–97.

principle—frank speech—he can be read as co-opting another. Here, as with his demand for accountability, he removes a democratic practice from its conventional setting. Here, as with his opening speech in the *Apology* where he disclaims any knowledge of speaking before juries even as he brilliantly parodies what he is not supposed to know about, he reveals an intimate knowledge of practices he problematizes, thereby pushing his compatriots to examine and scrutinize what they do unthinkingly out of habit.

The culture of accountability meant that citizens were incessantly judging each other's lives insofar as how they lived affected how they performed their responsibilities as citizens. One of the favorite words used (mostly) by critics to characterize Athenian democracy was *polupragmosunē,* meaning assertiveness, an inclination to endless activity, or, more pejoratively, meddlesomeness. A *polupragmōn* was someone who is active (or overactive), constantly initiating something new, always restless and impatient with what exists. Though both verb and noun were sometimes used in self-characterization by Athenian democrats (Pericles says someone who minds his own business is *apragmōn,* that is, has no business at all), they were generally used to describe persons or a people who meddled in matters that did not concern them, or who constantly disturbed the peace of others.[44] In the *Republic* injustice is defined as not minding your own business, and litigiousness, which, together with imperialism was regarded as a prime symptom of *polupragmosunē,* is said to emanate from the lowest element of the soul and state and be the cause of continual disunity. Yet in the *Apology* Socrates likens himself to a *polupragmōn* when he says: "Perhaps it may seem strange to you that I go about in private giving advice in many things and meddle, but do not venture in public or come before the Assembly and give advice to the city."[45] He justifies this by saying that his ceaseless questioning is done to improve his fellow citizens. Whether he is being ironic or not, that ceaseless questioning is itself typically Athenian. Indeed the Corinthian characterization of the Athenians—to which I have alluded—as never being at peace with themselves or allowing others to live in peace seems a perfect description of Socrates. With his restlessness, his distinctive mode of accosting people, his incessant cross-examining, and his remarkable intellectual activism and curiosity, it is no wonder that one commentator was "forced" to conclude that "his commitment to intellect itself reflects Athenian values, in contrast with the traditionalism of full-fledged *apragmosynē."*[46]

This not only echoes Vernant's discussion of democracy's evolution earlier in this chapter; it also recalls the arguments in chapter two by Lloyd about the political origins of philosophical terms, as well as Castoriadis's that "philosophy was born in and through the polis and is a part of the same movement which brought about the first democracies."[47] Both philosophy and democracy reject

---

[44] See Frederick G. Whelan, "Socrates and the 'Meddlesomeness' of the Athenians," *History of Political Thought,* 4, no. 1 (February 1983): 3–29.

[45] The translation is Whelan's.

[46] Ibid., p. 28.

[47] Vernant (*Origins,* pp. 59–60) argues that philosophy never resolved the tension between its

claims to validity and legitimacy of rules, representations, and institutions just because they happen to exist. Until Plato, both reject an extrasocial source of truth and justice, while asserting the capacity of the community and of human thought to institute themselves explicitly and reflectively. "The struggle for democracy," Castoriadis goes on, "is the struggle for self-government" which entails explicit "self-institution" and which "presupposes putting existing forms into question." The same is true about philosophy. Philosophy is not about "What is Being or what is the meaning of Being, or where is there something rather than nothing etc." All these questions are secondary in the sense that they are all "conditioned" upon the emergence of a more radical question: "What is it I ought to think (about being, about physics, about the polis, about justice, and so on, and about my own thinking?)"[48] It is only with Plato and afterward that philosophy ceases to be practiced by many dozens of independent thinkers and becomes ossified. "With the fall of democracy and the Stoics, philosophy becomes rigidified in schools and given more and more to commentary and interpretations."[49]

In Castoriadis's terms, what is of paramount importance for us about democratic Athens is not any particular institution established at any particular time, but the continuous process of democratic self-institution (which I am suggesting was itself institutionalized). And what is of paramount importance about philosophy in the period before Plato "is to be found not so much in its 'contents' but in its maintaining an open debate and a critical spirit." Though often denying it in particular or in principle, philosophy in fact "reinsaturates de facto the philosophical agora."[50]

The phrase "philosophical agora" is particularly apt when we recall that the *euthunoi* set themselves up in the *agora,* and that Socrates of the *Apology* calls others to account there. His description of himself as a "private citizen" and his refusal to speak in the Assembly has been taken to indicate philosophy's alienation from politics. But if the agora is a public place where even traditionally defined political activity took place, then Socrates' choosing to be there rather than in the Assembly cannot, by itself, mean that he is being apolitical. If one believes, as Socrates apparently does, that the conventional forums of politics are corrupt, then what "politics" is and where it "properly" goes on is itself contestable. More than that, if Ober is right about democracy being a regime uniquely committed to revisability, if Wolin is right about its suspicion of forms and structure, and Castoriadis is right about democracy as a continuous process of self-institution, then the unconventional way Socrates does "politics" is itself recognizably part of a democratic culture.

---

double origins—initiations into the mysteries and the disputations of the agora, between a sense of secrecy peculiar to the cults and the public argument that characterized political activity. I do not think this form of the tension exists in the Socrates I am portraying, except for the important but elusive role of irony.

[48] Cornelius Castoriadis, "The 'End of Philosophy'?," in David Ames Curtis, ed. and trans., *Philosophy, Politics, Autonomy* (New York: Oxford University Press, 1991), p. 21.

[49] Ibid., p. 22. As will become clear in chapter eight I do not subscribe to this view of Plato.

[50] Ibid., p. 23.

While Socrates may not have given advice in the Assembly, he did fulfill all the responsibilities of citizenship as he reminds his audience in the *Apology*. He has a family and children, has taken part in military campaigns, took up the supreme magistry, and, as president of the city on the day of the battle of Arginusae, braved the fury of many by refusing to initiate illegal proceedings against the generals, just as he refused the directives of oligarchs to arrest the innocent Leon of Salamis. Moreover, in the *Apology* he gives an account of his life, describes making others (especially those with cultural and political power) give an account of theirs, and insists that his accusers and jurors as well as "listeners" give an account of theirs, all in terms that echo a *dokimasia* and *euthunai*.

Still, there is no denying that "philosophical agora" would have seemed as paradoxical and oxymoronic to Socrates' contemporaries as it does to us. That it would suggests what was distinctive and provocative about his project.

Although scrutiny and accountability constituted a generalized cultural norm, in most instances candidates chosen by lot or elections probably had no accusations made against them.[51] And one could, as I have indicated, avoid scrutiny altogether if one chose not to stand for office or limited one's political participation to a minimum.[52] In these respects scrutiny especially was limited by place, time, and space. But Socratic scrutiny observes no such boundaries. He interrogates anyone he meets, not only about their particular fitness for office, but their fitness for life. He relentlessly cross-examines claims to knowledge and authority in ways that were prohibited in the *dokimasia* and *euthunai*. While he is concerned that his fellow citizens prove themselves worthy of sharing power and responsibility, he believes that such proof lies in their ability to think about what they are doing and their capacity to render an account of how they came to believe what it is they believe and why they believe it. Rendering such an account has nothing to do with witnesses and little to do with recounting past achievements (though Socrates occasionally challenges someone to say what they have done in the past to justify their claims in the present). While witnesses were an essential part of official scrutiny because they corroborated the character of the defendant, Socrates rejects such testimonies as irrelevant. And he rejects recounting of one's past deeds for reasons similar to the ones that made him believe that the fact that a particular view had survived past dialectics was no guarantee that it would in the future. "It may have been vindicated in a thousand elenchi," Gregory Vlastos writes in a passage quoted in chapter two, but "prove false in the very next one after that."[53]

---

[51] MacDowell, *The Law in Classical Athens*, p. 168.

[52] Unlike an ordinary trial an accusation in the *dokimasia* could be made on the spot without previous notice and, even if the vote went against a candidate, he was not subject to punishment but excluded from office. Still, if Pericles represents common opinion when he asserts that one who has no concern for politics is not worth much, this would be a more severe punishment in Athens than it would in a liberal polity.

[53] Gregory Vlastos, *Socrates: Ironist and Moral Philosophy* (Ithaca: Cornell University Press, 1990), p. 114.

Socrates wants his fellow citizens to think critically about the doctrines and concepts they have received from others, about the prejudices and traditions they have inherited, and about their own thought.[54] Thinking for him actualizes the human capacity to question, to think even about thinking itself, to see things from multiple perspectives and move between languages and sensibilities. Thinking keeps us from submitting to our own conceptual and political constructs because it depends upon and makes manifest a pluralization of human life, which cannot be recognized in tyrannies where people are turned into "one subjected subject."[55]

Dokimasia and *euthunai* were not about incompetence or ineptitude. Issues of stupidity, ignorance, or political inexperience did not arise because anyone chosen by lot (as well as election) was thought capable of carrying out their political responsibilities. But Socrates *is* concerned with competency, stupidity, ignorance, and political inexperience, as illustrated in his challenge to Callicles to prove that he has done things that make him fit for public life. But the fact that Socrates believed that democratic assemblies, courts, elections, and sortition did not guarantee moral and political knowledge needed to promote a common good does not mean that he believed oligarchy was any better,[56] or that he believed that knowledge must be grounded epistemologically rather than politically.

It is often argued that because democracy is a regime founded on *doxa* the "refutation of opinions is the breath of [its] public life."[57] Since Socrates rejects not just this or that opinion but opinion itself as a guide, it follows that he must be antidemocratic. But Socrates' sense of the insufficiency of opinion does not (at least in the *Apology*) commit him to something that is not opinion, but rather to opinions that are better informed and more completely thought through. At least there, Socrates continued to judge "within and through a regime of social knowledge and truth."[58] To quote Ober again: "For the Athenians, the idea that all knowledge was political, i.e., implicated in relations of power, was a truism. Neither the possibility nor the normative desirability of apolitical forms of knowledge about society or its members even entered the ordinary Athenian's head."[59]

I do not know if, when, and how it entered Socrates' head. At least in the *Apology, Gorgias,* and *Protagoras* he seems to hold out the prospect of philosophical citizenship and politicized philosophy. Such paradoxical notions are made conceivable by a democratic culture, which Socrates believes requires such notions to realize its aspirations of sharing power and responsibility. That his

[54] This is Hanna Arendt's gloss on *logon didonai* in her *Lectures on Kant's Political Philosophy,* ed. with an interpretive essay by Donald Beiner (Chicago: University of Chicago Press, 1982), p. 41.

[55] Elizabeth Kamarck Minnich, "From Ivory Tower to Tower of Babel?," *South Atlantic Quarterly* 89, no. 1 (Winter 1910): 190.

[56] See Terence Irwin's "Socrates and Athenian Democracy," *Philosophy and Public Affairs* 18, no. 2 (Spring 1989): 202.

[57] Castoriadis, "End of Philosophy," pp. 6–7. The metaphor of the "breath of life" will resurface in my use of George Steiner's discussion of translations in chapter seven.

[58] Ober, "Power and Oratory," pp. 90–91.

[59] Ober, "How to Criticize Democracy," p. 158.

conviction and sentence problematize the project seems to me quintessentially Socratic, even if the story is told by Plato.

There is one more possible analog. "To keep faith with Socrates' strangeness," Gregory Vlastos writes, "some way has to be found to save both the assertion of his ignorance and the implied negation of it," to acknowledge the fact that Socratic knowledge is "full of gaps, unanswered questions, . . . surrounded and invaded by unresolved perplexity."[60] It seems to me that Socrates' elaboration and extension of Athenian democratic practices in ways that allowed him to critique what he relied upon provides a political response to the imperative Vlastos presents. It was a way of keeping political norms from becoming normalizing while disturbing the complacency of those in power who thought their prerogatives fully deserved. In these terms Socrates completes but also competes with Vernant's story of democratization.

I am not certain why Socrates suddenly appeared to be such a danger that he had to be tried and condemned; whether it was his connection with the brutal oligarch Critias, some generalized animus against the sophists with whom he was assimilated, a "natural" bias against intellectuals, or a matter of his purposely provoking the jury so he could continue to do by his death that which he had done in his life. But one thing that may have been significant was the way he "used" familiar things in an unfamiliar way—more specifically, the unboundedness of his scrutiny, the way he would call someone to account at any time and in any place without communally legitimated sanction. Who was he to call others to account? He was not selected by lot nor elected. He held no official position. What arrogance to be the self-chosen gadfly of the city. What effrontery to the democratic institutions of Athens. But not, I am suggesting, an affront to democratic culture in which accountability and scrutiny figured so prominently. For better or worse Socrates thought such processes should be extended *if* radical democracy were to be "successful." For him, Barber's opposition between ruling oneself badly (whatever that might mean) and being ruled wisely by another is a false one. Perhaps the people themselves could become wise, though it would be a difficult task for which conventional democratic practices were insufficient, even if the principles underlying those practices pointed the way to "success." It was this task, assumption, and act of faith that animated Socrates' view of himself as a political educator.

Earlier I dismissed the policing dimension to the culture of accountability as a distraction. That was far too glib. For a culture of accountability to be something more than a mode of policing there needed to be some generative tension between it and a Dionysian politics of disruption. That was, in part, supplied by comedy and tragedy.

---

[60] Vlastos, *Socrates,* p. 3, and "Socrates' Disavowal of Knowledge," *Philosophical Quarterly* (1984) 35: 18–19.

When There Are Gray Skies:
Aristophanes' *Clouds* and the Political
Education of Democratic Citizens

Lord heap miseries upon us yet entwine our arts with laughter's low. . . . In
the name of the former and the latter and of their holocaust. All men.

—James Joyce[1]

I will argue that the theater is the natural art form of a democracy; that it
promotes a kind of thinking necessary to a democracy; and that our leaders
both of the left and of the right thereby have a stake in promoting it.

—David Ives[2]

I

Democratic Athens was as much a culture of performance and spectacle as it
was one of accountability and self-scrutiny. This meant that theater "stood
alongside other public forums as a place to confront matters of import and moment" and that politics, law, religion, athletic contexts, music, and poetry were
public and performative so that one form of cultural expression merged easily
with another. Even aspects of what we regard as "family" life, such as rites of
passage, weddings, and mourning the dead were theatrical, as were symposia
where music and poetry were presented. And the plays themselves both refer to
and enact ritual and artistic practices as if to acknowledge their debt to other
manifestations of the performance culture that helped constitute Athenian
democracy.

It also meant that the sense of theatricality was transitive, generalized, and all
pervasive in the sense that the Athenians were "imbued with a sense of event, of
things said and done in the context of the moment and a critical distance from it."
Where we view participation in a ritual and going to the theater as different
experiences involving opposed attitudes to the world, Athenians viewed such
events "as a continuum of performance."[3]

And it meant that Athenian politics were profoundly theatrical. Whether it was
speakers in the Assembly using the power of the spoken word to appeal to the

---

[1] From *Finnegan's Wake* (London: Harper Collins, 1992), pp. 259, 419.
[2] "The Ancient Greeks Did It: Why Can't We?," *New York Times* (February 26, 1995): sec. 3, p. 13.
[3] The quotations are from Rush Rehm, *Greek Tragic Theatre* (London: Routledge, 1992), pp. vii, 3–5.

reason, emotions, and morality of their compatriots like an actor did in the theater, the way the concavity of the Pnyx established a relationship between the speakers and audience analogous to that between actors and spectators in the theater, how the rebuilt Council chamber (at the end of the fifth century) established seating around the speakers platform on the model of the caves surrounding the orchestra in the theater, the highly theatrical aspects of the legal system, or the general "theatrical flair" of political debate and argument, Athenian public life was "a kind of lived performance."[4]

Insofar as it engendered critical reflection on Athenian policies, characters, and cultural norms, the culture of performance helped constitute the culture of accountability and self-scrutiny. But in another sense it stands against the policing mechanisms scrutiny and accountability imply. To the extent comedy parodied conventional political forms and practices, it parodied the culture described in the previous chapter. More specifically, the *Clouds* includes sarcastic references to Athenian litigiousness (as when Strepsiades does not believe a map of Athens because he can see no lawcourts), and shows its principal characters scheming to manipulate the legal system for self-serving ends. In this vision, *dokimasia* and *euthunai* take on a different guise. More generally, comedy's own excesses—its scatology, bombast, ridicule—escape and confront (how much is a matter of dispute) the "normalizing" imperatives of accountability, even as, from another point of view, comedy holds those, such as members of juries and speakers in the Assembly who escape them, accountable through parody. In all these ways one could say that comedy both pluralized accountability while provoking an unease about accountability's purity of purpose and result.[5]

That the culture of performance and comedy in particular built upon a tradition of self-scrutiny and accountability it also "critiqued" (through parody in the case of comedy) imitates the relationship between Socrates and Athenian democracy as I have portrayed them in chapters three and four. That the culture was as generalized as it was suggests why we must look at the performance dimensions of the *Apology* and of Socratic political philosophy as a whole.

Most obviously "Socrates" is a character in a Platonic drama, one of whose aims is, as I argued in chapter three, to make Socrates' life and death rival if not replace that of Achilles and of Athens. It is no accident that Socrates invokes Achilles as he defends the integrity of what we have come to call (because of him) the philosophic life, or implicitly disputes what it means to be great in word and deed as Pericles had claimed Athens was in the Funeral Oration. Even when Socrates most firmly insists on the straightforwardness of his speech and lack of guile as he does in the beginning of the *Apology,* he is clearly performing before

---

[4] Ibid., p. 5, and chap. four.

[5] Robert Connor has argued (in "Festival and Democracy," in Josiah Ober and Charles Hedrick, eds., *Demokratia: A Conversation on Democracy, Ancient and Modern* [Princeton: Princeton University Press, 1996]) that "Dionysiac worship does more than provide a temporary venting mechanism for a highly rigid society." Rather it makes it possible "to imagine an alternative community, one open to all, where status differentiations can be limited or eliminated, and where speech can be truly free." I am suggesting that this is particularly true of comedy.

an audience. And does not his irony constitute a kind of mask, which, like the masks of tragedy, allowed the actor to explore the fusion between different identities, states of being, or categories of experience such as male and female, divine and human, stranger and friend, outsider and insider? And if "the mask makes possible the mimetic representation of the myths in dramatic form"[6] is there a way in which Plato's Socrates does something similar to the democratic myths of his culture? Of course, the mask is also a sign of the audience's willingness to submit to illusion, play, and make believe, and to invest emotional energy in that which is marked as both fictional and Other.

Socrates is as connected to comedy as to tragedy. Like Socrates, comedy detached its audience from the charms and chains of national narcissism, defusing patriotic tirades and puncturing official ideology. While Pericles (in the *Funeral Oration* in Thucydides) called upon his compatriots to fall in love with their city, Aristophanes put them on guard against the seduction of self-love and the self-aggrandizement such love encourages. "One must make the Athenians laugh at the praise that they are so happy to address to the city and to the democratic system," Nicole Loraux writes, "both on the tragic stage and on the speaker's platform of the dēmosion sēma."[7] Comedy also raised the question of the limits of human power and the possibly "constructed" nature of "nature." Thus, in the *Ecclesiazusae* (Women in the Assembly), the question was whether Athenian women could be constituted male if the Assembly voted for it. After all, if the *dēmos* could constitute political realities by legal enactment, and if human intelligence was so powerful that it could tame the sea (as the chorale ode in "praise" of man in *Antigone* and Pericles' boast in the Funeral Oration proclaim it can), then why couldn't men reconstruct nature so that women would be rulers of the city?[8] Other comedies raised similar questions about war and peace, wealth and poverty, Athenian litigiousness, public poetry, demagoguery, and the possibly corrosive effects of new philosophical teachers and teachings.

I concentrate on the *Clouds* because it dramatizes as it reiterates the themes of this book. Thus the conflict between Old and New Education in the play as well as the spatial/aesthetic/political/social opposition it presents between what is high and low echoes the contemporary debate over the canon and educational reform. Similarly, the parody of Socrates returns us to chapter two and Plato's *Apology* where Socrates is charged with corrupting the youth by disbelieving in the gods of the city, making the worse argument appear the better, and transgressing proper boundaries by investigating things that would be best left alone. The play

---

[6] The quotation and the argument come from Charles Segal, "Spectator and Listener," in Jean-Pierre Vernant, ed., *The Greeks,* trans. Charles Lambert and Teresa Lavender Fagan (Chicago: University of Chicago Press, 1995), pp. 201–2. Segal is not concerned with Socrates or democracy here so I am using him for my purpose.

[7] Nicole Loraux, *The Invention of Athens: The Funeral Oration in the Classical City,* trans. Alan Sheridan (Cambridge, Mass.: Harvard University Press, 1986), pp. 302–11. The quotation is from p. 306.

[8] See the discussion in Josiah Ober, "Power and Oratory in Democratic Athens: Demosthenes 21, *Against Meidias,*" in Ian Worthingon, ed., *Persuasion: Greek Rhetoric in Action* (London: Routledge, 1994), pp. 85–108.

gives substance to these complaints, which is why Xenophon as well as Plato regards the *Clouds* as setting the terms for Socrates' later accusers and the general animus against him.[9] Moreover, given its thematic preoccupations as well as the kind of play it is, the *Clouds* raises questions about the relationship between philosophy and democracy raised in chapters two, three, and four even as it helps constitute a tradition of self-critique I have been arguing mediates the purported incompatibility between the two. Penultimately I chose it because by uniting comedy and tragedy, it is a dramatic hybrid and so reenacts the social tensions and contradictions of Athenian society without trying to rationalize them.[10] Finally, I chose the play because it makes the extraordinary suggestion that what is low, mockery, irreverence, ridicule, parody, and scatology has an ethical and political significance rivaling that of both tragedy and philosophy.[11] From its earliest beginnings, philosophy "looks up" to the heavenly mysteries while also perceiving what lies hidden "in the depths."[12] The *Clouds* plays with and against this double quest for the remote and invisible by providing a vantage that is at once imitative and skeptical of these philosophical impulses.

II

In what sense can we speak of comedy as a mode of democratic political education? What is the connection between comedy and democracy and in what sense did it educate its citizen audience? These questions are parasitic upon another: did comedy challenge powerful figures, policies, and cultural norms, or were its anarchic, transgressive, and radical impulses generally domesticated by the desire of the playwright to please the audience and judges of the plays, by the need to "reassert and reaffirm" the "traditional norms of society tragedy put at risk," and by the "controlled environment" of "state sponsored religious rituals allotted

[9] See the excellent discussion of Plato's and Xenophon's understanding of the *Clouds* as initiating the criticism of Socrates in Terence Irwin's "Socrates and Athenian Democracy," *Philosophy and Public Affairs* 18, no. 2 (Spring 1989): 184–205. The version of the *Clouds* we have is a revised one. The original (which won third prize) was produced in 423; the revisions were made in 418/17. This, of course, makes the *Clouds* an atypical comedy in that it was (probably) circulated without being performed. Nonetheless, I think its atypicalness highlights crucial qualities of Aristophanic comedy in general.

[10] See the discussion in the introduction to David Konstan's *Greek Comedy and Ideology* (New York: Oxford University Press, 1995), pp. 3–11.

[11] As one recent critic put it, the *Clouds'* skōmmata (joking, mockery) "aim at ethical criticism and pointedly hold disgraceful behavior up to public scrutiny through humiliating ridicule, much as Aristophanes claims to do through his comedies to his city's benefit." Anthony T. Edwards, "Aristophanes' Comic Poetics: TRUX Scatology, SKŌMMA," *Transactions of the American Philological Association* 121 (1991): 171. Edwards goes on to argue that the ethical ground from which *aidōs* springs is "the impulse to avoid public humiliation, affronts to one's honor and self esteem, resulting either from an objective failure to satisfy accepted public standards or from criticism that one has fallen short of such expectations" (p. 174).

[12] B117 in Hermann Diels and Walter Kranz, eds., *Die Fragmente der Vorsokratiker,* 5th ed., 3 vols. (Berlin: Weidmann, 1922), pp. 50–52. See also Segal, "Spectator," p. 192, on the significance of the fragment.

the appropriate time and space within the civic festival calendar and communal civic space"?[13]

It is certainly true that the Greeks regarded laughter as ambiguous and volatile, as much a matter of laughing at as of laughing with.[14] *Skōptein* and its cognates means both joke with reference to play, fun, humor, and mock or deride in ways that dishonor. So there *was* a need for social practices to contain the antagonism that ridicule created in a society with so strong a sense of shame from exploding the social fabric entirely.[15] As a civic institution assigned a specific place and time, comedy helped do this. Yet I suspect that the attempt to contain laughter and ridicule was at best imperfect, and that a continual tension remained between the spirit of celebratory, playful release and the force of divisive antagonism; between circumscribing what could be said where, and the constant possibility that laughter would transgress whatever rules and boundaries had been set up to contain it.[16] Moreover, the quarantining of comedic effects would seem to vitiate the explicit claim Aristophanes makes for his significance as a political educator. And, as I suggested, Plato and Xenophon certainly thought the *Clouds* had consequences outside the theater and the confines of ritual.[17] Finally, if comedy did indeed help constitute a radically democratic culture of self-scrutiny and self-critique, then the fact that Aristophanes challenged aspects of that democracy is hardly proof of a conservative reluctance to transgress accepted norms.

There are other considerations specific to the *Clouds* that should make us wary of accepting the domestication argument. For one thing, the play lacks the joyous celebratory ending (posited by virtually all critics) essential to resolving the tensions generated in and by comic dramas. Whatever inversions and transgressions take place remain in place, or at least unresolved. For another thing, since the *Clouds* is, as I indicated, a hybrid of tragedy and comedy, it cannot simply reinforce the norms tragedy puts at risk.

---

[13] Paul Cartledge, *Aristophanes and His Theatre of the Absurd* (Bristol: Classical Press, 1990). See also n. 78.

[14] See Harry Levin, *Playboys and Killjoys: An Essay on the Theory and Practice of Comedy* (New York: Oxford University Press, 1987).

[15] On this topic see Stephen Halliwell, "The Uses of Laughter in Greek Culture," *Classical Quarterly* 41 (1991): 279–96; A. M. Bowie, *Aristophanes: Myth, Ritual and Comedy* (Cambridge: Cambridge University Press, 1993), chaps. 1 and 5; Simon Goldhill, "Comic Inversion and Inverted Commas: Aristophanes and Parody," in Simon Goldhill, ed., *The Poet's Voice: Essays on Poetics and Greek Literature* (New York: Cambridge University Press, 1991), pp. 161–222; and Thomas K. Hubbard, *The Mask of Comedy* (Ithaca: Cornell University Press, 1992).

[16] In many respects this tension recapitulates a more general one between a highly agonal politics and precesses of collective deliberation that require some mediation of such agonism. For a parallel argument, see Dana R. Villa, *Arendt and Heidegger* (Princeton: Princeton University Press, 1995). Cf. Bonnie Honig, *Political Theory and the Displacement of Politics* (Ithaca: Cornell University Press, 1993).

[17] Plato's *Apology* 18a–19c. Malcolm Heath in *Political Comedy in Aristophanes* (Göttingen: Vandenhoeck and Ruprescht, 1987) suggests that by insinuating that the charges against him were based on comedy, he meant "to discredit the prosecutors' case" (pp. 9–10), and Arthur Kingman Rogers, in *The Socratic Problem* (New York: Russell and Russell, 1971), p. 86, argues that in the *Apology* Socrates implies that Aristophanes was merely trading on a calumny current for some time.

At bottom I think the domestication argument rests on the assumption that juries of ordinary men chosen by lot to judge the plays could not have honored plays that mocked their own leaders and political commitments. If they did, however, it must have been because they were too unsophisticated to discern the nuances that mocked them. They were either suffering from a version of working-class Toryism, victims of an irresistible power of an overarching aristocratic value system,[18] or were seduced by the crude buffoonery and obscenity of comedy. But in any case they were oblivious to anything intellectual in the play or didactic about it. In effect this argument divides the audience into the sophisticated, knowing few, and the crude, manipulated many. Thus, one of the most perceptive commentators on the *Clouds* argues that when Aristophanes complains in the parabasis about being forced to rely on theatrical tricks in the second version to make it more appealing but then shifts back and forth between references to each version in ways that leave us uncertain which version is being discussed at any point, he is "deliberately playing with the audience, winking at its more perceptive members while deliberately confusing the majority."[19] And it is pretty clear who these more perceptive members are; people like "us."

But it may be that the play warns against just such an interpretive strategy insofar as it mocks the pretensions of intellectuals and philosophers. Indeed, it seems to display each character projecting himself onto the clouds according to his own half-sublimated desires and half-acknowledged ambitions, as if to warn interpreters that they are in danger of doing the same thing to the *Clouds*. For both characters and philosophical readers, the clouds are ciphers; goddesses for atheists, nature for conventionalists, and foundations for antifoundationalists. Both the clouds and poets use their powers of mimetic illusion to engage and mirror men's fantasies and follies. At least they do so until the end when both turn moralistic; or so it seems.

What then about the initial set of questions concerning comedy as a mode of democratic political education? Simon Goldhill expresses the current consensus when he argues that "democracy is the very condition of possibility for Aristophanic comedy."[20] But Nicole Loraux suggests that the converse is also true; that comedy was essential to democracy because, in my terms, it helped to constitute a tradition of self-critique. Loraux's remarks also point to both the differences between and the complementarity of comedy and tragedy as modes of political education.

III

Unlike tragedy, comedy was brought in from the periphery and below, from the countryside and the agora to the center of the polis, as a supplement and perhaps

---

[18] Compare Loraux's argument on this issue (*The Invention of Athens*) with Ober's "Power and Oratory in Democratic Athens: Demosthenes 21, *Against Meidias*."

[19] That is Hubbard's argument, *Mask of Comedy,* p. 101.

[20] Goldhill, "Comic Inversion," p. 183.

as alternative to tragedy.[21] What makes this history particularly relevant to the *Clouds* is that Strepsiades, the old man whose oppressive debts lead him to study the new learning and then to insist his son do so when he fails, has the same history. He is a farmer and rustic brought into the city and a way of life he finds confusing and uncongenial. But, comedy also had a different sense of time, space, and event. While tragedy placed contemporary events and individual actors in a remote mythical past, comedy by contrast was firmly anchored to the moment of performance, openly topical, and unequivocal about its objects of ridicule—Pericles, Cleon, the war with Sparta, the sophists, and Socrates. And unlike tragedy, comedy's treatment of such issues as sexuality, war and peace, the relationship between mind and body or right and wrong, or education and nurture was embedded in the concrete, particular world of ordinary people.[22] While comedy sometimes "gestured toward the universal," it was pulled down and back, as tragedy was not, by the gravitational pull of needing to cope with the exigencies of everyday life.[23] Comedy's different sense of time is also suggested by far more radical shifts of language, plot, character and action than even a tragedy such as *Oedipus Tyrannus,* with its roller coaster of emotions before the king learns the truth about himself, could sustain. [24] Moreover, comedy used language and engaged topics in ways that were permissible in no other venue. In this regard it was perhaps a unique expression of *parrhēsia,* the right to speak freely to power, to say almost anything to anybody.[25] Comedy ridicules gods and politicians, generals and intellectuals, mocks the *dēmos*'s favorites and critics of the dēmos, resorts to violence and verbal abuse, thrives on uninhibited sexuality and constant references to excrement and flatulence, and exults in general vulgarity.

Finally, comedy could transgress "the fourth wall" between stage and audience in a way tragedy never could. Tragedy heightens the emotional intensity of the

[21] I am speaking of Old Comedy. On the differences between Old Comedy and New Comedy, see E. W. Handley's discussion in P. E. Easterling and B.M.W. Knox, eds., *The Cambridge History of Classical Literature* (Cambridge: Cambridge University Press, 1989), chap. 3, parts 10–11. On the point about the recognition and place of comedy, see Dora C. Pozzi, "The Polis in Crisis," in Dora C. Pozzi and John M. Wickersham, eds., *Myth and the Polis* (Ithaca: Cornell University Press, 1991), pp. 126–63, and Jeffrey Henderson, "The Demos and the Comic Competition," in John J. Winkler and Froma Zeitlin, eds., *Nothing to Do with Dionysos?* (Princeton: Princeton University Press, 1990), p. 313.

[22] But these "ordinary" people are caricatured every bit as much as Socrates, which means that their ordinariness is as generic and exaggerated as his extraordinariness. It is interesting that critics who think Socrates is caricatured and Aristophanes grossly unfair to him do not make the same point about the *dēmos*.

[23] Oliver Taplin, "Fifth Century Tragedy and Comedy: A Synkrisis," *Journal of Hellenic Studies* 106 (1986): 164.

[24] There is a compelling logical plot and an air of inevitability to Oedipus's self-discovery that is absent in the *Clouds*.

[25] Again see Sara Mononson, "Frank Speech, Democracy, and Philosophy: Plato's Debt to a Democratic Strategy of Civic Discourse," in J. Peter Euben, John R. Wallach, and Josiah Ober, eds., *Athenian Political Thought and the Reconstruction of American Democracy* (Ithaca: Cornell University Press, 1994), pp. 172–97.

spectator's reaction by enhancing the power of the fiction that what is taking place on stage is "real." Thus the chorus in tragedies does not directly[26] call attention to the play being a play but masks the fictional quality of the action, providing a spatial and emotional mediation between the protagonists and the audience. Indeed, the audience in the seats watches another audience (the chorus) on stage that accepts the action as reality and is emotionally involved in it. But comedy would break the spell and the audience's concentration, calling attention to the fictive character of the (often absurd) actions on stage. Actors speaking of themselves as performers rather than characters would refer to stage and scenery instead rather than the dramatic setting, and so make the audience aware of itself as spectators and as a spectacle being observed. Thus when New Education invited Old Education to look at "the flaming homosexuals" in the audience, the spectators would become a spectacle and be reminded that they were an assembly of citizens.[27] In comedy the audience was especially active; laughing and applauding, hissing and booing, drumming the wooden benches when the spirit moved them, or calling out as the fancy took them.[28]

The interaction between play and audience was institutionalized in the parabasis, a break midway through the play where the chorus directly addresses the audience in its name and that of the poet. But if comedy's self-awareness was to this extent generic, and Aristophanes was "the most metatheatrical playwright before Pirandello,"[29] then the *Clouds* is his most self-aware and most metatheatrical play. For the play we have is a revision in which Aristophanes himself talks to his projected audience about the inadequacies of the original *Clouds,* which had left him humiliated with its third place award. By having the playwright talk about that audience, about the nature and status of comedy in a democracy, and about his own talents as a dramatist, the *Clouds* becomes a narrative in which the history of its performance intersects with its thematic preoccupations. One might even say that the *Clouds* is Aristophanes' most Socratic and sophisticated play. One might also say that in this case the playwright becomes as much a spectacle as spectator, as much a creature caught up seemingly unawares in the inescapable web of comic discourse as the omniscient author of it. Thus he becomes implicated in the human condition he shares with his fellow citizens on stage and in the audience.[30]

The *Clouds* is different in one other way: as I mentioned, it blurs the lines

---

[26] When Strepsiades farts in imitation of a clap of thunder, Socrates tells him to leave that filth for the comic stage. When the clouds arrive, Socrates tells Strepsiades to look at them over the theater of Dionysus. When Strepsiades complains that he can't see them, Socrates instructs him (326) to look along the entry way onto the stage. On this see James Redfield, "Drama and Community: Aristophanes and Some of His Rivals," Winkler and Zeitlin, *Nothing To Do with Dionysus,* pp. 314–35. On the complex ways in which seeing and being seen work in the play and theater, see Hubbard, *Mask of Comedy,* chap. 1 and Bowie, *Aristophanes,* chaps. 1 and 5.

[27] I say not directly because it does indirectly as when the chorus in *Oedipus Tyrannus* asks, "Why shall I dance?"—that is How can I remain a part of a religious festival if the Gods are rejected?

[28] On this see Cartledge, *Aristophanes,* p. 9.

[29] This is Taplin's claim in "Fifth Century Tragedy and Comedy," 164.

[30] Ibid., pp. 14–15, 164–65. The fact that the poet speaks in his own name is hardly distinctive to this Aristophanic comedy.

between comedy and tragedy. Not only is the opening song of the chorus formally closer to tragedy than comedy, but there is no sympathetic comic hero, and the violent, unforeseen, and discordant ending does anything but bring the previous action into a harmonious whole as was traditional. Indeed, the final mood generates "ironic gloom of intellectual despair" as much as joy. Appropriately enough, given its characters and themes, the *Clouds* is a dramatic hybrid.[31]

IV

The *Clouds* focuses on the sophistic challenge to traditional education. What is so disconcerting about the tone and substance of the contest between that tradition and this New Education is how exactly it anticipates the issues and polemics of our own culture wars as I have analyzed them in chapter one. Old Education's aggressive traditionalism insists that existing practices are natural, present identities are fixed, and established hierarchies are necessary; his apocalyptic prophecies and ranting against promiscuous sex, self-indulgent youth, wayward teachers, the decline of standards, and disrespect for authority are all summed up in the call for "Decorum, Discipline, and Duty,"[32] reminiscent of a National Association of Scholars pamphlet. But the play is not much more sympathetic to either the romanticizing of multiple identities, moral libertinism, and transgressive politics, or the denigrating of hierarchy, authority, and traditions, let alone to the deconstruction of the natural that mark some forms of postmodernism.

Socrates' airiness suggests another central theme of the play and a concern of this chapter: the relationship between political theory or philosophy and democratic culture. Scholars have been sharply divided over the meaning of this vision of Socrates. Some have read it as malicious antiintellectualism, and the identification of Socrates with his sophistic opponents as sheer perverseness, the dire consequences of which are alluded to in Plato's *Apology*. But others, with the *Symposium* in mind, have seen unobvious but nonetheless profound affinities between the two, and read the *Clouds'* Socrates as distancing himself from sophistic teachings, and Aristophanes as committed to the kind of self-awareness that is typically Socratic. Yet neither view quite confronts perhaps the most radical implication of the portrait of Socrates: that what intellectuals, theorists, and philosophers regard as disagreements of substantial import are, with some justice, regarded by the ordinary citizen as the narcissism of petty differences. As Gerald Graff reminds us, for our students, "A Roland Barthes and an Allan Bloom would seem far more similar to one another than to people like themselves, their parents and friends. In their eyes a Barthes and a Bloom would be just a couple of intellectuals speaking a very different language from their own

---

[31] That is Hubbard's conclusion (*Mask of Comedy*, p. 112). He goes on to suggest that the ending reveals the comic poet's uncertainty about his role as intellectual mentor.

[32] This is William Arrowsmith's translation of 960–62. Here and in general I rely on his extraordinary translation of *The Clouds* (New York: Mentor Book, New American Library, 1962). Arrowsmith takes considerable liberties with the text but they almost always work. I have taken liberties with his text by trying to make his modernization even more contemporary. Unfortunately Arrowsmith's edition has no line numbers so I refer to pages. (Some page references are given in text.)

about problems they have a hard time recognizing as problems."[33] Perhaps academic culture is so tightly enclosed, its language sensibilities and problems so remote from those of ordinary citizens that the differences between Rawlsians, Arendtians, Straussians, and Habermasians seem casuistic at best.

But this is all too serious and somber, too cerebral and philosophical, which is to say it misses half the point and all the fun. In the *Symposium* the long night is almost over but Socrates is still talking. Near the end of his speech and the dialogue he suggests that comedy and tragedy spring from the same roots.[34] "To this they were constrained to assent, being drowsy, and not quite following the argument. And first of all Aristophanes dropped off to sleep." So fascinating was the first theory of comedy that the most eminent comic poet of his time, or perhaps any time, was put to sleep by a philosopher's lecture on the comic spirit.[35]

Undaunted, I propose that we look at the opening scene of the *Clouds* with its portrait of Strepsiades and contrast it with our initial impression of Socrates; carry this contrast through to the *agōn* between Old and New Education;[36] look at how the *Clouds* negotiates the oppositions it constructs as a way of returning to our principal concern, the education of democratic citizens.

V

The play opens with Strepsiades tossing and turning in his sleep, restlessly awaiting the dawn. He is driven to distraction by his son's debts and by his nostalgia for his own rustic past. Those were the good old days before the Peloponnesian War and Pericles' policy that had forced farmers to abandon their land and take shelter behind the city walls. For Strepsiades this meant removal from the rhythms of nature and rural life that had given the shape of purpose to his existence. The Corinthian characterization of the Athenians as a people who came into the world to give no rest to themselves or anyone else suggests a city that deliberately turned its back on the agricultural traditions[37] that had "grounded" it.

---

[33] Gerald Graff, quoted in Catherine R. Stimpson, "On Differences: Modern Language Association Presidential Address 1990," in Paul Berman, ed., *Debating PC* (New York: Dell, 1992), p. 54.

[34] "It is a fact that, though we know of well over 100 fifth century playwrights, we do not know of a single one who produced both tragedy and comedy," Taplin, "Fifth Century Tragedy and Comedy," p. 163.

[35] Robert W. Corrigan, "Comedy and the Comic Spirit," in his edited book, *Comedy: An Anthology* (Boston: Hougton Mifflin, 1971), p. x.

[36] I follow Arrowsmith in using these terms to describe the opposition, but other ways of formulating it include; philosophy versus sophistry, the just or stronger argument versus the unjust or weaker one, the moral argument versus the immoral one. These ways of putting it seem to me to beg the questions the play is trying to raise so I choose the "more neutral" one, though I understand that it, like the others, presumes a reading of the entire play.

[37] Thucydides 2.70–72. See William Arrowsmith's "Aristophanes' *Birds:* The Fantasy Politics of Eros," *Arion, n.s.* 1 (1993–94): 116–67.

It alone would be free of the cycle of nature and inherited cultural forms.[38] Strepsiades is the product of that attitude and policy, and the *Clouds* an ironic commentary on it. For the restlessness that the Corinthians define as a cultural trait we see played out on the smaller stage of everyday life in the twitching of bodily movements. No grandiloquent phrases here, no exultation in imperialist ventures, no mesmerizing visions of collective power—just a man who can't sleep well seemingly because he has been removed from his former life. (I say seemingly because the self-destructive nostalgia of Old Education later in the play puts us on guard against nostalgia of any kind.)

Strepsiades lives the philosophical opposition between nature and convention posited by the sophists and Platonic characters like Callicles, whose epistemological, moral, and political challenges to conventional beliefs are, in the first instance, physical, sensual, and geographic. Their rejection of a natural (ontological, theological, or metaphysical) grounding for political and moral life, or their appeal to nature as a way of rejecting conventions deemed natural, has confounded Strepsides' life. When Thrasymachus in the *Republic* and Callicles in the *Gorgias* look to nature to justify aggressive behavior, the opposite of what is commonly regarded as the conduct mandated by nature and the gods,[39] or claim that "nature" is socially constructed either by the strong to legitimize their domination or by the weak to prevent such domination, it has consequences for the way in which fathers and sons act toward each other. As the newly educated Pheidippides later asks, if laws are man-made then why should beating your father be less privileged than its opposite? This is a question of some force in a culture where Zeus had murdered Kronos for power, and Oedipus had (albeit unknowingly) killed *his* father and, coincidentally, replaced him in public and in bed.

Strepsiades not only has been literally forced off the land, but also is figuratively uprooted and socially displaced by his marriage to a city girl with aristocratic tastes and lineage. Unsurprisingly the two fight over their son's name.

> She, of course, wanted something fancy, some upper class high-horse handle with hippos in it. While I naturally wanted to give him the fine old name of Pheidonides in honor of his thrifty grandfather. We, we haggled and at last agreed on a compromise name: Pheidippides. She gushed over the baby: "Just imagine. Some day he'll be an important man, just like his Uncle Megakles, and drive in his purple robes up to the Akropolis." And I'd put in, "Ha, drive his goats from the hills, you mean, dressed like his dad in a filthy smock."[40]

---

[38] This is an exaggeration. These older values remained a part of Athenian life, reasserting themselves with particular force in times of crisis. But the point remains that, compared with archaic Athens and the rest of Greece, these traits do define the Athenians.

[39] The moral history of this period and the role of the sophists in it has been told by Adkins, Heinemann, Guthrie, Untersteiner, Kerferd, Solmsen, and Havelock. Nietzsche has spawned a quite different tradition from both the moral decline and the moral improvement/Greek enlightenment arguments, which has, through the influence of Foucault, Derrida, and Lyotard led to a spate of recent studies of the sophists and rhetoric written mostly by professors of literature.

[40] Arrowsmith's translation, p. 21.

Given the Greek belief that the validity and efficacy of language is guaranteed by its "magical, homeopathic relationship to the things of the world," words possess their own nature and structure unmediated by any artificial grammar, syntax, or rhetoric.[41] This gives an "ontological" dimension to the couple's debate over what sort of life their boy will lead, his class affiliation and political alliances, his dress and deportment, his friends and their values. The parents eventually compromise on "Pheidippides" (meaning "cheap aristocrat"), an oxymoron that combines the worst of both worlds and resolves nothing.[42] But the name indicates a new conception of language introduced or elaborated by the sophists. If words can be made up, so can things, such that rhetorical skill becomes the ultimate power in the world, as Gorgias claims when he asserts that he could convince an assembly of a medical diagnosis against the most expert doctors. But even more troubling is the prospect that words and things have no direct or singular connection, that the world is unanchored, leaving us up in the air with Socrates self-indulgently and condescendingly looking down on others.

The circumstances of Strepsiades, his wife (who has obviously married beneath her station), and especially their son indicate that the older world of fixed identities and places romanticized by the old man no longer exists, and that democracy is largely responsible for its disappearance. Democratic culture blurs the lines between classes status and places, making boundaries permeable and identities unstable. Democracy, together with this changed status of language, has consequences for comedy as an institution and genre.

It is not simply that comedy, like all drama and public life, relies on language, but that the idea of speech as a form of power and the relationship of that power to violence is the play's subject.[43] When language becomes an extension of violence, as New Education argues and demonstrates, the celebration of civilization as the triumph of persuasion over force becomes problematic. More than that, insofar as all arguments just and unjust alike rely on the capacity to speak, the position taken by New Education is not only self-defeating but, more pointedly, makes comedy impossible. For comedy plays on words that play on words, and at least part of its role in the education of democratic citizens is to counter rhetorically the narcissism Loraux laments and to play out, in the confines of stage and theater, potentially destructive impulses toward violence and revenge.

In any case, Strepsiades is a man preoccupied with his body, or at least with the lowest parts of it: stomach, anus, and phallus. The lofty sentiments of the Funeral Oration have no more meaning to him than the scientific claptrap Socrates pronounces. They are equally irrelevant to his life, which is preoccupied with getting rid of his goddamned debts and keeping his horsy son from bankrupting him. Strepsiades is relentlessly literal-minded, bringing every thought down to

---

[41] George B. Walsh, *The Varieties of Enchantment* (Chapel Hill: University Press of North Carolina, 1984), p. 80 and chap. 5.

[42] Only at the end are the parents united, this time as victims of their son's new education.

[43] The issue is discussed at length by Daphne Elizabeth O'Regan in *Rhetoric, Comedy, and the Violence: Language in Aristophanes'* Clouds (New York: Oxford University Press, 1992).

earth with a resounding thud, as if his body and worries weigh upon him with such force that he cannot raise his sights or his mind.[44]

Socrates seems to be everything that Strepsiades is not. Where the latter is all body, Socrates is all mind; while Strepsiades has no lofty thoughts, Socrates seems to have nothing but; where he seems stupid and gullible, Socrates seems sophisticated and smart.

We first hear about Socrates not by name but by vague reputation as one of those philosophers who live in the dirty little hovel called a Thinkery (*phrontistērion*).[45] What Strepsiades knows about the Thinkery is that the intellectuals and professors who live in it can prove anything to anyone. He has heard that they teach something called just, philosophical, or moral logic, which he does not pretend to understand or care about. What does interest Strepsiades is the other immoral Socratic/sophistic logic that will enable him to escape his debts. While the father knows only this about the Thinkery, the son knows more—the names of these ashen-faced, flabby, barefoot pedants, these disgustingly miserable, utterly fraudulent charlatans (*aiboi, ponēroi, alazonas, ōchriōntas, anupodētous*) who run the place, Socrates and Chaerephon—and he wants nothing to do with them. So Strepsiades has no choice. He will become a student and save himself, though he knows going in that he lacks the talent for it.

Strepsiades' kick at the Thinkery door disrupts a delicate experiment aimed at discovering how many flea feet a flea could broad jump. Not only has Socrates already solved this problem, but he has gone as far as to resolve the age-old metaphysical conundrum of whether gnats fart through their mouths or behinds.[46] But best of all, Socrates has demonstrated how food can be miraculously manufactured out of nothing by distracting some gullible student with a pretentious experiment, deftly stealing his cloak, and selling it to buy food. Strepsiades is not only impressed, he is overwhelmed. Anyone who has closely studied the asses of gnats can certainly vanquish the asses in the lawcourts; anyone who can manufacture something out of nothing by chicanery and stealth is his kind of professor. "Why Thales was an amateur compared to this! Throw open the Thinkery. Unbolt the door and let me see this wizard Socrates in person. Open up. I'm mad for education" (p. 29).

We are less so. It is not merely that these pompous professors waste their time on utterly trivial matters they take to be of great moment or that they are too clever for their own good and so far removed from life that they look dead; but that, as the cloak-stealing episode suggests, their lofty ideas and high-minded

---

[44] Perhaps "thud" is the wrong word given the way Strepsiades understands Zeus's thunder (see Arrowsmith, p. 45).

[45] The fact that Socrates is introduced so indirectly may be evidence that Aristophanes is less concerned with the specific person than the generic intellectual/philosopher. Of course, some traits of Socrates must have been specific to him for the joke to work but it is his being an Athenian that is probably crucial for an Athenian audience.

[46] This is dramatically connected with the discussion of Zeus's thunder and sophistic speech in ways that link purest thought (*noēma*) to the lowest bodily functions.

studies are a spectacular cover for petty manipulations. Their motives are no different from those of Strepsiades; they only disguise them better and so cheat more successfully. If we think of cloaks metaphorically—it is the first thing Strepsiades has to give up upon entering the Thinkery—as man-made garments that shield us from the elements and cover our nakedness, Socrates' stealing of them represents a stripping away of convention and tradition.[47]

When we first meet this wondrous figure he is suspended in the air, his head in the clouds, looking down from his lofty perch on his students, who, with their noses to the ground and asses in the air are double majors in geology and astronomy. When Socrates is asked why he has his head in the clouds, he pompously replies I "walk on air and look down upon the sun from a superior standpoint . . . [because] only by dangling my mind in the heavens and mingling my rare thought with the ethereal air could I achieve exact knowledge in a survey of all that is above" (p. 33). Though bewildered by all of Socrates' mumbo-jumbo, Strepsiades asks him to teach him sophistic logic so he can evade his debts, for which he promises, with his own peculiar logic, to pay anything. As surety he swears by the gods. That turns out to be a mistake, since, as Socrates assures him, belief in the old gods is merely vulgar prejudice. The real gods or goddesses, rather, of philosophers (as of all quacks, prophets, charlatans, poets, dandies, astrologers, and men of leisure who have their heads in the air or somewhere darker) are the clouds.[48] It is to these goddesses that intellectuals owe their skill at fraud and casuistry and their prodigious vocabulary (not to mention their postmodern Rawlsian-Foucaldian-Habermasian refinements). And the clouds are unusually useful goddesses since their formlessness allows each of us to comprehend them after our own fashion and in our own image. We see in them the shape of our ambitions, while others see a caricature of those ambitions. Just as we project our pursuits and desires onto the world and see the world as legitimating them and reflecting us as we would like to be seen, what others see is the shape of our real motives, unrecognized or denied. That is what happens with the clouds and in the *Clouds*.

If you are looking for female (or male) "companionship" (read: horny), then you appear to others as a centaur; if you are respectful of lobbyists (read: those who defraud the government), you appear as a wolf; and if you are an academic dedicated to truth and reason (read: to maximize your institutional power and impose your views on your field), you will appear as a snake. Because the play ends with the clouds mouthing Aeschylean pieties, commentators have concluded that Aristophanes' wants to show Strepsiades and the audience that crime does not pay.[49] But, as I shall argue in detail later, I read the play's conclusion as inconclusive and so this interpretation as problematic. Better to say that the *Clouds,* like the clouds, can assume many shapes, all of which mirror the follies

---

[47] Cloak stealing was one of the few offenses for which a man could be summarily executed by the Eleven because it was deemed a direct attack on another citizen's honor and integrity.

[48] Notice that poets and philosophers have the same gods (or goddesses).

[49] The most persuasive case for this is made by Charles Segal in "Aristophanes' Cloud-Chorus," *Arethusa* 2 (1969): 143–61.

of the human imagination. Better to conclude that the play plays with those in the audience, leaving it open to their own political and interpretative projections [50] although they had best be prepared to have them thrown back in their faces caricatured and unmasked. Better still, we might regard these goddesses not as Aeschylean surrogates but as deities of comedy.

"Naturally," these puffed-up chameleonesque windbags prefer Socrates to any other theorist or educator. For he is the most superannuated of philosophers, the great bird-dog of culture, the most incorrigible purveyor of bullshit, and the consummate flapper of tongues. Yet the clouds also present themselves as fertility spirits associated with the rustic life for which Strepsiades longs and as teachers of the audience (*didaxomen*) like the comic poet himself. Here, as in the naming of Pheidippides and the battle between the Old and New Education that follows, the terms and boundaries of human life—body, mind, spirit, animal, human, and divine—are, quite literally, up for grabs.

They are both very funny: this boorish old farmer with his gastronomical vision, two-digit IQ, and desperate search for an easy way out of his worldly problems, and the otherworldly pretentiously prattling intellectual who thinks he is superior to everyone. Yet they are not as different from one another as each supposes. Socrates pulls off the business with the cloak and there is a certain gift in Strepsiades' ability to find concrete reference and recognize the airy nonsense that Socrates spouts. But neither knows himself or the other well enough, and their putative opposition is itself a danger, as we shall see.

Strepsiades turns out to be a hopeless student, and Socrates' promise that he will be "reborn"[51] goes for naught. He cannot follow what Socrates says or do what Socrates says he must do to master the logic that will save his ass.[52] His memory is so bad that he only recalls those situations in which someone owes him money. He has no talent for speaking or patience with learning meter since he has no interest in entering polite society for which such learning would qualify him. Furthermore, he is totally befuddled by the analytic word games Socrates plays. (This Socrates is less a gadfly than a bedbug, like those in the Thinkery mattress Strepsiades is forced to lie on and which make a meal of him.) He concretizes to absurdity every concept, idea, and argument Socrates presents to him. He reduces philosophical speculations about measurement into a worry about whether the flour man's scales are honest; he thinks Socrates' pontifications on how to keep time by tapping one's fingers means giving someone the finger; and he cannot see why the female duck is a duchess or that baskette is feminine. Since Strepsiades cannot think for himself or decide what to think about, this Socrates, like the one of the early dialogues, cannot help him.

Having failed to become a philosopher himself, Strepsiades has only one recourse: convince his son to become one. The son thinks his dad is off his rocker,

---

[50] See the discussion in Hubbard, *Mask of Comedy,* p. 89.

[51] There is a sense in which this is true insofar as the father becomes child of the son and sophistry is seen as powerful enough to change the "natural" sequences of things.

[52] Compare Strepsiades "I admire you but I don't follow you" (Arrowsmith, p. 44) with Crito's similar confusion in the *Crito.*

but finally agrees out of (what will be his last act of) filial piety. Strepsiades wants his son tutored in both logics, though of course his primary interest is in having Pheidippides learn the immoral one. Socrates calls on the two logics to come forward and compete for Strepsiades, a contest that parallels the struggle over the boy's name, and that between Socrates and Strepsiades over the meaning of the clouds. Socrates himself leaves the stage, which suggests that the initial opposition between him and Strepsiades is not identical with the *agōn* between the two kinds of education.

VI

As the play makes clear, the competition is not merely for this particular son, but for the city's sons, and so for the future of Athens. It is a struggle over how the past will be remembered and constructed, and so how the present is to be understood. It is over what vision of the city and what concept of democratic culture, moral imagination, and political education will prevail, and over what elements of a tradition are renewable and what can be clung to only at the cost of repression and disaster. In times of crisis the question is not simply who will define what is right or wrong, but who will define the discourse in which such claims are recognized as either being right or wrong. Whose statements or arguments will be heard and taken seriously, even if ultimately rejected as wrong, and whose will not be given a hearing because they are construed as insane, immature, perverse, or otherwise beyond the pale?

The crisis in education and political identity has implications for comedy as well. For the license of Old Comedy presupposed a climate in which the city could accept mockery of almost everything it took seriously. Comedy "tested the limits of festivity—and thus the limits of the experience of laughter as a force for communal release and play—by constantly and irreverently toying with subjects on which life outside the festival depended."[53] But radical questioning (with its affinities to Socratic *elenchos*) has always been risky, even in a democracy which recognizes its significance as a form of self-education.

Whatever the stakes, the competition itself is great fun. At first the antagonists jab wildly at each other. Right (Moral, Old) Education and Just Logic (*dikaios logos*) calls his opponent a swaggering peacock, precious pederast, and cheap stunted runt, as moronic as the audience of citizens who, having made him so popular and powerful, have left the schools of Athens deserted as the young wander the streets trying to "find themselves," moving from one new-age religion to another or to the numbing world of corporate law and international finance. They take their moral cues from Bart Simpson, Beavis and Butthead, Howard Stern, *Hard Copy,* the *National Inquirer, Barron's Weekly,* or the *Wall Street Journal* rather than from the great books and the accumulated wisdom of the past.

[53] Halliwell, "Uses of Laughter," p. 296.

Wrong (Immoral, New) Logic (*adikos logos*) and Education promise to deflate the Old Education's hot air balloon with a post postmodern ultraunorthodoxy.[54] He will do so before an audience of what *he* calls "sophisticated gentlemen." The truth is, there is no naturally sanctioned, divinely prescribed justice. (How *did* Zeus become powerful? Just answer that. Go ahead.) He will prove that dishonor is honorable, abuse is welcome, and things thought wise are merely the fossilized rantings of Dead White Males. "Times change. The vices of your age are stylish now." And style is everything.

The battle rages only a little less wildly after the chorus leader intervenes to formalize this spontaneous aggressiveness as a debate. Old Education speaks first, as befits his age (and irrelevance). He extols the good old days of family values, traditional discipline and docile students. In those days, children learned the three R's, read great books, and respected the authority of parents and political leaders (just like the 1950s). They knew their place and their duty. Students kept their hair short and one color, and listened to Mozart or Bach rather than to the Stones, hip-hop, blues, or rap; young women were virgins when they married and so were protected and respected by men. Those were the ways and the values of the generation that had defeated the Persians at Marathon. Not one of them was a cheap shyster lawyer or prestige-seeking, status-conscious, who's-the-smartest-of-them-all disputatious academic. They were men of vigor and physique, of courage and honor, of moral discernment and virtue. If Pheidippides will follow Old Education, he will be a credit to his family and the city (not to mention to his race).

Behind this caricature is a version of the education that most of the Athenian audience had experienced, one in which the young learned the time-honored ways of their ancestors through imitating the models and absorbing the myths drawn from the great body of lyric and epic poetry. Grounded in custom and experience, it provided a venerable ideal of character and action. But this same audience would also have experienced the erosion of this education and of the world from which it emerged and upon which its intelligibility depended. Old Education thinks a mere description of the traditional ways will suffice, just as Strepsiades will later think that the mere fact of his son's beating him is enough to condemn Pheidippides.[55] Both are wrong. The world has changed. The old ways must be defended by arguments, which leave the old men vulnerable, if not helpless, since (as Burke and Oakeshott could have told them) by being forced to make an "argument," Old Education and Strepsiades have lost before they begin. It is a predicament that Old Education implicitly acknowledges when he speaks in the past tense. Worse than that, his revealingly detailed warning about the impression of young boys' buttocks being left in the sand not only implicates him in the promiscuity he excoriates, but raises questions about the status of the ancestral ways he celebrates.

---

[54] The Greek suggests something contrived or newly invented (like the word Thinkery).

[55] See C. T. Murphy, "Aristophanes and the Art of Rhetoric," *Harvard Studies in Classical Philology* 49 (1938): 52–67.

It is this hopelessness that drives Old Education to adopt an aggressive senti-mentality, which is useless in convincing Pheidippides to adopt the way of life being endorsed; it all sounds like reactionary propaganda and for the same rea-sons that the shriller pamphlets of the National Association of Scholars do in the current debate over multiculturalism. But nothing puts the dilemma Old Educa-tion faces more starkly than his injunction to Pheidippides to honor his parents. What can that mean to a son whose parents come from different classes and ways of life? Honoring one entails dishonoring the other. (Of course, Pheidippides will eliminate this "cognitive dissonance" by *dishonoring* both.) He cannot follow the admonition to honor his parents because to do so presumes what does not exist: social stability, singular identities, and cultural homogeneity. In these terms the ease with which Pheidippides is transformed from a self-indulgent young aristo-crat into an ascetic sophist who can make the worse argument "appear the better" and "twist" the truth for selfish ends suggests not so much the power of the New Education as the weakness of what opposes it.

Sophistry (philosophy, the New Education, or unjust *logos*) can barely restrain himself for at least two reasons. The first is that he has a far superior and much easier vision of the good life, one based on the pursuit of unlimited pleasure, one that is, to boot, sanctioned by the gods. To be self-indulgent *and* pious at once is no mean thing.[56] But even more than that (or perhaps it is part of the pleasure) is the second reason: the sheer joy of demolishing everyone else's conception of a good life by extolling the superfluousness of morality itself. He is not only not embarrassed by being termed the immoral logic, he revels in it, and makes it a selling point. He glories in his reputation as the first to devise "A Method for the Subversion of Established Social Beliefs and the Undermining of Morality" (p. 91). To top it all off, what sophistry calls "these little inventions of mind, this knack of taking what might appear the worse argument and making it better" have proved extremely lucrative. Nihilism pays.[57] Attacking The Moral Argu-ment, he shows the contradictory nature of its precepts. Old Education had dis-missed baths as a sign of softness, for example; yet Heracles, the greatest of all Greek heroes, is the namesake of hot baths. Old Education had likewise been contemptuous of the Athenian preoccupation with politics and had extolled the greatness of Homer, yet it is Homer who praised Nestor's passion for politics. The most glaring contradiction, however, especially given the themes of this play, is the example of Kronos and Zeus. Although New Education is accused of threatening traditional Athenian education—as dramatized by Pheidippides beat-ing his father and promising to do the same to his mother—the old order was itself founded on patricide, so an "Athenian father who played Kronos to his son's Zeus was merely playing a traditional role."[58]

Old Education rambles on and on about moderation, yet he cannot produce

---

[56] Martha Nussbaum suggests that he has no conception of goodness at all. See her "Aristophanes and Socrates on Learning Practical Wisdom," *Yale Classical Studies* 26 (1980): 43–97.

[57] This separates him from Socrates' asceticism, which so disgusts Pheidippides.

[58] Barry S. Strauss in *Fathers and Sons in Athens: Ideology and Society in the Era of the Pelopon-nesian War* (Princeton: Princeton University Press, 1993), p. 160.

anyone who has ever profited from it. How could Pheidippides be expected to emulate a life so filled with contradictions? Why would he want to, given what he would have to give up—the pleasure of satisfying his natural desires unstintingly and without fear of reprisal. In the *Republic,* the shepherd Gyges finds a magic ring that makes him invisible. Armed with the ring he does what any red-blooded man would do: seduces the queen, kills the king, and gets all the money, sex, and power he wants. (He is right in valuing two of the three.) Sophistry is the magic ring. It creates a verbal fog bank around human actions, rendering one immune to retribution and punishment. This is accomplished by "proving" that "natural" distinctions among realms, activities, and persons are conventional, if not arbitrary.[59] The most explosive and impressive example of sophistry's ability to destabilize (or reveal already destabilized) moral discourse is its strategy of making the worse, weaker, or inferior (*hēttōn*) argument appear the better, stronger, or superior (*kreittōn*) one.

These Greek words have a physical as well as a moral sense and were, among aristocratic circles in Athens, virtually indistinguishable. Given a heroic ideal that honored physical and martial excellence above all things, to be stronger was to be better and vice versa, an identity that grounded *nomos* (law, custom, convention) in nature (*phusis*). Although the phrase "law of nature" was probably first coined by Callicles in Plato's *Gorgias* as an attack on democratic equality, something like it had been taken for granted until the sophists made explicit a separation between nature and convention that emerged (only half articulated) with the increased politicizing and democratizing of Athenian life. As what had been the private prerogatives of kings and priests were brought out into the open and made public, what had been "the way things are and must be" became subject to debate and interrogration. Before the sophists men made laws and societal arrangements with divine inspiration. But this made no sense if the gods themselves were human inventions. Then laws and societal arrangements had to be justified in human terms, such as those used by Protagoras in his Great Speech to be discussed in chapter nine.

As we saw in the previous chapter, part of this democratizing process involved the increasing significance of speech. For one thing, the power of speech was regarded as independent of social class, which physical prowess was not. For another, persuasion and deliberation became, as I indicated earlier, recognized alternatives to violence and were viewed as the special achievement of democracy. But when, as in the *Clouds* and its debate, words become weapons rather than an alternative to them, or they work like drugs in leaving their listeners powerless to resist them,[60] then everything associated with the triumph of

[59] On the one hand, the declaration that *phusis* is distinct from *nomos* entails neither a denigration of the latter since it still distinguishes us from animals or the conclusion that all laws are morally equal (or outside morality) because they are all conventional. On the other hand, the removal of nature as a ground and sanction for belief and action does and did leave *nomos* vulnerable to sophistic attack.

[60] In the debate over the fate of the rebellious Mytileneans Cleon accuses his fellow citizens of being so in love with verbal displays and susceptible to the aesthetics rather than the substance of

speech, including the polis, democracy, and comedy itself, becomes deeply problematic. Consequently the violent ending of the play, in which the outraged Strepsiades burns down the Thinkery is a logical as well as dramatic extension of New Education's use of language.[61]

To the degree that speech is nothing but deception and a strategy for domination, comedy itself cannot possibly perform its institutional role as an educator of the audience. It is not just that the ideal of a democratic citizenry making independent judgments as part of a process of deliberation becomes utterly impossible to realize but also that comedy's playing on and with words, like its social and cultural radicalism, is only possible if there are some stable meanings and cultural continuities, and if persuasion and deliberation remain the civilized alternatives to violence and war.

No one wins the debate between Old and New Education. Neither side can win if political life and comedy are to persist. One can no more go back to the old ways than one can restore one's virginity or, in our time, speak of "nature" naively. Things are too politicized. Yet the new way in which everything is politicized is no way at all. What is to be done?

VII

The battle between philosophy/sophistry, the Immoral Argument/New Education and the Old Education ends when the latter, convinced that the punishment for adultery (reaming a radish up the offender's rectum) is meaningless since everyone, including the great tragic poets, the city's most respected statesmen, and the entire audience, practices buggery, has no choice but to throw in the towel and run into the Thinkery.

As for Strepsiades, his son unfortunately proves a far more adept pupil than he was. Pheidippides emerges from his studies so white-faced and smart-assed that his proud father feels safe in ridiculing the audience as well as his creditors. Sure that his son is invincible, he is unaware of how vulnerable that invincibility leaves him.

Initially, everything goes according to plan, although we know from the chorus's moralizing that "this poor man's Socrates" will soon learn that crime does not pay, that you reap what you sow, that no man is an island, and that there are no atheists in foxholes, or when a father is being beaten by his son. And sure enough, the celebratory graduation dinner breaks down into mutual insults whose

---

argument that they are unable to adhere to a settled policy. The irony is that he is the most violent man of his time here defending a harsh penalty of death to all of the Mytileneans no matter what their politics, and is using speech to persuade them not to be so enamored of speech. (See Thucydides 3.37–48 and O'Regan, *Rhetoric, Comedy, and Violence,* on how this plays out in the *Clouds.*)

[61] It is worth remembering that Strepsiades got himself in the predicament so his violence is a result of his own greed and lack of moral principle. It was because of such a possibly violent reaction that both Gorgias and Protagoras (in the Platonic dialogues named after them) take such pains to proclaim their innocence (Gorgias claims rhetoric is a neutral instrument) or disguise what they are doing (which Protagoras does at precisely the point when he insists he is being honest).

tone and substance recall the equally rancorous confrontation between the New and Old Education. And, as with that earlier contest, the chorus intervenes to set up a more formal *agōn,* now between father and son, to be judged by the audience in the theater.[62]

During dinner Strepsiades asks his son to sing songs from the works of the great poet-educators of Greece, as is customary. But Pheidippides will have nothing to do with these boring, bombastic bullshitters, and instead recites a passage from one of what his father calls "Euripides' slimy tragedies where a brother screws his sister." Furious, the father berates the son, and the son returns the compliment in spades *and* justifies the "outrage" as natural and necessary, after first extolling the virtues of his New Education, which gives him the power to destroy the moral order as a preface to doing so.

Pheidippides never dreamed how sensual the sound of words could be, never imagined the rapturous pleasure he would get from hearing himself talk, never once anticipated the thrill of sabotaging the established order.[63] He owes everything to Socrates who transformed him from a stuttering horse lover into a man of such consummate philosophical subtlety and profundity that he can easily prove why beating one's father is justified. Did not his father beat him for his own good? So Pheidippides beats his father for Strepsiades' good. Is there not a saying that old men are boys writ large? Then it follows that old men deserve to be beaten more since at their age they have less of an excuse for the mischief they commit. When Strepsiades invokes all that he has so far disparaged—Zeus, nature, and law—his son responds as did the New Education: law is man-made, the product of powerful words, revocable and reversible by any eloquent man who can convince the Assembly that sons should have the right to administer corporeal punishment to their wayward fathers. Nor will appeals to nature help Strepsiades: look at the permanent state of open warfare between rooster fathers and sons as between those of other animal species. And as for Zeus, remember Kronos.

Strepsiades has no choice but to admit defeat on behalf of the older generation, thereby echoing the capitulation of Old Education in the earlier debate. At first he blames his troubles on the chorus of clouds. Why did they mislead him, or at least not warn him? The clouds insist that the guilt is his, since they but tempt men to give in to their dishonest dreams, drawing forth their illicit desires so that, like Aeschylean protagonists, men can become wise through suffering. At last, Strepsiades realizes that he could only have evaded his obligations to his creditors by destroying the very social fabric that guaranteed Pheidippides' filial obligations to him. Rebuffed by a son who revels in his new self and worships Socrates rather

---

[62] Throughout the play the audience is appealed to and asked "to judge" what is happening before it (e.g., by Amynias one of Strepsiades' creditors who asks them to be witnesses, by Strepsiades who appeals to the audience when his son is hitting him). Of course, plays themselves were judged and Athenian citizens spent considerable time in various courts as suggested earlier.

[63] Like Socrates earlier and Strepsiades later (as he stands on top of the Thinkery with ax and torch in hand), Pheidippides too talks of being able to look down on others and the common conventional way (*tōn kathestōtōn nomōn*).

than Zeus, and who infuriates the old man beyond limit by threatening to beat his mother, Strepsiades doesn't enter the Thinkery as defeated Old Education did. He burns it down. There are, after all, some brute facts in the world, some things that words cannot extinguish, and fire is one of them. Standing on top of the Thinkery, a torch and an axe in hand, Strepsiades first chops down the house of the logic choppers, then sets it ablaze. Now it is he who "walks on air and looks down upon the sun from a superior standpoint."

VIII

Where is Aristophanes in the play? With whom, for what, and where does he stand in the opposition between Strepsiades and Socrates and the *agōn* between Old and New Education?

Surely not with the narrowly materialistic, dumb immoralism, and rustic gullibility of the finger-giving, farting, crotch-grabbing, phallus-waving country bumpkin Strepsiades. Here surely is a dramatic invention created merely for ridicule, obscene in our legal sense of being without redeeming social value. Of course he is a caricature—not an ordinary Athenian as some commentators have argued in order to show Aristophanes' contempt for democracy and affinities with Socrates—at whose bodily fixation we are intended to laugh. But we can also laugh with him and at those who laugh at him.

After all, compared with the airy pomposities of philosophers, there is a certain integrity to Strepsiades' boorish grounding of concepts in the everyday world: his supposition that students with their noses to the ground are looking for truffles, that geometry is good for surveying lots, and that the map he sees cannot be one of Athens since there are no lawcourts visible; his desire, upon viewing the map, to have Sparta moved further away from Athens; and his repeated attempts to find (usually gastronomical) meaning in astronomical and philosophical speculations. Many of us have such thoughts, although we are wise or cautious enough not to speak them.

Moreover, comedy and Strepsiades share a history. Both have moved from the country to the city,[64] so comedy may understand and represent predicaments like his with particular insight. If it does, it may be able to help him (and others in similar straits) understand the contradictions of his life, perhaps even to help him laugh at them and so give rise to second thoughts about resorting to violence to end them. Strepsiades, "at a loss" in every sense of that phrase, is thus susceptible to the crackpot schemes of intellectuals and the pretentious prattle of philosophers or anyone else who promises to save him from the hybrid world in which he owes money and to which he owes his confusion. Surely this is not an unfamiliar situation. To the degree that comedy can save people from themselves and this manipulation by making them more attentive to the seductions around them, it can help sustain the vitality of a democratic citizenry. Political education is not a matter of foisting a particular agenda on an audience, but of helping them think

[64] See the discussion in Pozzi, "The Polis in Crisis."

about what they are doing, and what others are trying to do to them, sometimes in their name, often for their supposed benefit.

But what about Socrates? I want largely to bypass the extensive scholarly debate over how much the character Socrates is like the historical Socrates—whether what we hear him saying represents his own views or an amalgam of often contradictory philosophical positions; whether one can reconcile the animus Aristophanes seems to display toward Socrates in the *Clouds* with his seeming affection for him depicted in Plato's *Symposium;*[65] and whether Aristophanes can be blamed for creating the atmosphere of suspicion that led to Socrates' death—and to assert that "Socrates" is, like Strepsiades, a caricature[66] of the self-important superior intellectual who looks down on the people. Still, he can no more be dismissed than Strepsiades can, because he, too, shares something with the comic poet.[67]

To the degree that one can call the Athenians as a whole an "intellectual" people, then what is caricatured and mocked in Socrates is a shared cultural trait that is exaggerated in, but not unique to, one particular man.[68]

The play presents philosophers and intellectuals as pretentious quibblers, destroyers of people's beliefs and lives, and self-aggrandizing purveyors of esoteric knowledge, which they only teach to initiates who can afford the fee and who actually learn how to steal people blind through the power of words. They are dramatized as impatient and imperious, constantly alert to everyone's assumptions but their own, with their heads only in the clouds, oblivious to what is obvious. Their logic chopping is useless, and their interpretations—theological, political, and literary—merely project themselves onto the world even as they proclaim their neutrality, objectivity, and impartiality. Philosophy is autobiographical in ways that become clear only when caricatured by an Aristophanes or a Nietzsche.

Perhaps worst of all, these intellectuals and philosophers try to exempt themselves from the ignorance they are so ready to attribute to others. To object that this cannot be true of anyone who, like Socrates, claims to know that he does not know is to ignore how this becomes yet another, more mystifying ploy by which philosophers claim the superior ground they seem to be giving up. But comedy,

---

[65] See Plato's discussion of laughter (in *Philebus* 48c–d) as the opposite of the Delphic "Know thyself." I am making something close to the opposite case.

[66] There is a sense in which Socrates was a real person and Strepsiades is a character invented by Aristophanes. But that will not quite do since "Socrates" is also a character and Strepsiades is a caricature of sentiments of "real" people. On the Aristophanic Socrates as an accurate portrait of Socrates "first sailing," see Paul A. Vander Waerdt's "Socrates in the Clouds," in his edited volume *The Socratic Movement* (Ithaca: Cornell University Press, 1994), pp. 48–86.

[67] See Edward's excellent discussion ("Aristophanes' Comic Poetics") of Socrates' warning to Strepsiades not to do the sort of things comic poets do (line 296) since that will disrupt his teaching and their speech.

[68] Pericles talks about the Athenians as a school of or paradigm for Hellas. He also claims and exemplifies a kind of intellectual power for the city that distinguishes it from all others. I have argued this in *The Tragedy of Political Theory: The Road Not Taken* (Princeton: Princeton University Press, 1990), chap. 6.

or at least this one, permits no such claims and allows no such mystification, and in this, as in other ways, it is antihierarchic and egalitarian. In a statement that might be a commentary on the role of the cloak in the *Clouds,* James Redfield argues that the "great instruments" of Old Comedy "are obscenity and scatology, which remind us that we are all naked under our clothes." Individuals are deprived of their dignity but in the process, "mankind in general," embodied in the audience, recovers a sense of power and liberty.[69] When cultural forms or great political and intellectual leaders are ridiculed, we are reminded that neither culture nor those leaders are our creation and so both can be recreated.[70]

But I am not sure Redfield is entirely right about the *Clouds,* because here everyone becomes a spectacle before everyone else: the chorus and characters on stage; the characters who, stepping out of their role, talk directly to the audience about themselves as actors and refer to the theater in Athens;[71] Aristophanes, when he comes forward to address the audience in the parabasis and the audience when he looks out at them; New Education when invites his opponent to tell him what kind of men he sees in the audience. No one escapes being part of the spectacle—as if Aristophanes were imitating the rotation in office that was so central to Athenian democracy—and so no one escapes the mocking that accompanies the ignorance of being human. Each moment of superiority, of laughing at others and ridiculing their foibles, is imperceptibly reversed.

This includes the city as well as the comic poet who is its educator. For the vices ridiculed in Aristophanes' comedies and laughed at by the audience "are in fact the vices of the audience."[72] In the parabasis the audience of citizens is berated for its political ineptitude and its failure to give Aristophanes his due. Yet this spectator of society/audience becomes a spectacle himself when his "personal hopes, ambitions, feelings, and disappointments are witnessed and laughed at by the audience."[73] So everyone becomes a member of the comic event, sharing in the fallibility, vulnerability, and imperfect self-knowledge it reveals.

There is one more thing about the democratic community comedy creates in the theater and presumably helps constitute outside it. Comedy assumes that the people are capable of self-awareness and self-critique, that thinking can and perhaps must be an aspect of democratic citizenship.

All this points to the affinities between Socrates and Aristophanes. Most generally, as I have suggested several times, comedy helped constitute a tradition of democratic self-awareness and self-critique that may well have inspired Socrates' political philosophy. It certainly grounds the exaggerated intellectualism contained in Socrates' injunction that the unexamined life is not worth living, a

---

[69] Redfield, "Drama and Community," p. 328.

[70] Perhaps such vilification served as a kind of cathartic ostracism marking the sense of civic danger of the overly powerful man in a way that lessened his power and so the necessity of exile.

[71] Of course, insofar as this is mandated or expected by the audience, it becomes part of the dramatic illusion rather than a break with it.

[72] Hubbard, *Mask of Comedy,* p. 14.

[73] Ibid., pp. 14–15.

proposition that would have been laughed out of court instead of taken seriously by a people who did not already see themselves as in some sense "intellectuals." Thus it is not surprising that Aristophanes had some sympathy with Socratic intellectualism, or that one could say about Socratic questioning what was said about the *Clouds:* "It transfers the last word to the audience," which is left to enact its own part but a little more reflectively than before.[74] One could also show how the play evinces "Socratic" irony, and how the shared risks of dialogue unite the interlocutors in a recognition of their mortality much as the comic event does. One might even suggest that Socrates shared the risks of dialogue as Aristophanes did the risk of laughter and ridicule.

Moreover, Aristophanes and Socrates both saw themselves as political educators of a democratic polity. Each was concerned with the corruption of language and sought to teach their compatriots how to judge speech and speakers, as we shall see in chapter eight on the *Gorgias.*[75] Both show why it was necessary to move beyond a narrow self-interest, although they certainly differed about what was worth a citizen's attention and care. By precept and example, both sought to provide a more comprehensive framework within which their fellow citizens could understand what they were doing to others and themselves. And both could be caustic critics of the *dēmos,* knowing well enough that ordinary people could be antiintellectual, intolerant of difference, and irrational. But neither concluded that the *dēmos* required institutional limits on its power or rule by "responsible elites" to save the *dēmos* from its excesses.[76] What they did conclude was that a democratic polity had need, most of all, of political education.

The problem for Aristophanes was to find a mode of speech that was tied to but not weighed down by physical desire, a way of thinking that was sensual and concepts that remained connected to their physical grounding in place and body. In terms of the portrait of intellectuals, it means their owning up to their worldliness and anchoring their free-floating ideas, which would otherwise spin off into absurdity. In Aristotelian terms, it means carving out a political language that mediates our being both beasts and gods, at once natural and cultural. In terms of the *Clouds* it means connecting Socrates and Strepsiades in a way that they are not in the play. I think Aristophanes regarded his revised version of the *Clouds* as doing something like this, or at the very least as dramatizing why such an alliance was essential to a democratic citizenry. I also think he believed that by educating the audience in the theater to judge the rhetoric of comedy he would be assisting his fellow citizens in judging the rhetoric of demagogues, orators, and philosophers outside it. This mode of speech would be one that recognized the power of language to change character and the world, but that used such power responsibly in terms of the traditions sustaining a democratic culture. The sense of possibility

[74] O'Regan, *Rhetoric, Comedy, and Violence,* p. 132. But see Nussbaum's criticism of this view and of a "democratic" Aristophanes in "Aristophanes and Socrates on Learning Practical Wisdom."
[75] The preoccupations of the *Clouds* and the *Gorgias* are remarkably similar.
[76] That is the assertion of a report to the Trilateral Commission by Michael Crozier entitled *The Crisis of Democracy* (New York: New York University Press, 1975).

that attends the recognition of the world as open to the shaping hand of human power can too easily initiate a dialectic capable of destroying the culture that made such power possible in the first place. One can see this in Thucydides' *History* as words lose their meaning, and in the counsel of New Education in the *Clouds*. If the medium of both politics and comedy is speech, then the comic poet is necessarily committed to maintaining its "integrity." He seeks to keep it connected to things in the world, but free to confront (and mock) the categories by which we make such connections and construct that world, and to ridicule and provoke without turning language exclusively into a weapon that bludgeons rather than persuades or convinces. After all, if speech is simply war by other means, what is to stop someone from burning down the theater along with the Thinkery?

This mode of speech would also be a form of political knowledge that is not just knowledge about politics, but knowledge that is political in origin and texture.[77] Let me use Machiavelli by way of illustration of the point though it is a point very much like Ober's considered in chapters two and four and like the one I will elaborate in chapter six. In *The Prince,* the political theorist is likened to a landscape painter. Unlike the prince and the people, who are frozen in their positions, the theorist is able to stand on the mountain with the prince to see the people below and to stand with the people in the valley to see how the prince appears on high. This double perspective is the theorist's special claim to knowledge and power. Unlike in Plato where the "ground" of politics is only on high (the *Republic* is a path upward), high and low in Machiavelli are equally valid sources of political knowledge. It is this double perspective that makes the theorist valuable to the prince and allows him to mediate between the prince and the people, showing both the need each has for the other and thereby constituting them as a whole. I want to suggest that Aristophanes (or rather the play) is making a similar claim: the *Clouds* as a form of speech mediates between classes and between the double capacity of "Socratism" and "Strepsiadism."

IX

This view is at odds with the still dominant reading of the *Clouds*. Responding to that view will allow me to return to questions broached in the opening section and to comment on the play, and comedy, as a mode of democratic speech and education.

The prevailing view of the *Clouds* is that it sides with Old Education because, as a conservative by class, choice, and institutional position, Aristophanes thought (or could not help believing) that the sophists were corrupting Athenian

---

[77] *Sophia* is a dominant theme through the play but especially in the parabasis. For a general discussion of how Aristophanes uses it and how the use of *sophos* in regard to *both* forms of education plays upon the ambiguity of a word that designated cleverness in the narrow sense of technical skill as well as worldly knowledge in general; see Hubbard, *Mask of Comedy,* pp. 94–96.

education and politics.[78] From this point of view, the play endorses the burning down of the Thinkery and oppressive legislation against intellectuals generally, seeks to convince the *dēmos* to accept the guidance of the rich and well-born, and shows a "love of simple virtues" and of "the good old times."[79] Indeed, even if this love were not Aristophanes' personal predilection, it would have been imposed on him by his social role because being "commissioned to speak for the solidarity of the audience" rendered him necessarily "hostile to all innovations, including those that might improve society." Although Aristophanes might complain about the current state of things, his most intense ridicule was reserved for those intellectual and political leaders who would ameliorate it. Thus he was a critic of critics, a celebrator of the grotesque only against a background of commonsense normality, which he does everything he can to reinforce. The final scene, in which the clouds reveal themselves as traditional deities who punish wrongdoing, clinches the argument. As Strepsiades takes full revenge on those who have outraged the gods (urged on by the Koryphaios), both the cosmic and the political order are reestablished. Justice triumphs, morality rules, and the old farmer, "put in touch with the rustic energy of his background," is "restored to himself."[80]

As I have already argued, there are good reasons to be suspicious of this reading and so the political portrait of the playwright upon which it rests. They have to do with the clouds being goddesses of poets as well as philosophers, Old Education's rejection of comedy, Aristophanes' boasts (in the parabasis), and the impotence of Old Education, who winds up throwing himself into the arms of his

---

[78] See A. W. Gomme, "Aristophanes and Politics," *Classical Review* 52 (1938): 97–109. For a very different view explicitly critical of Gomme and implicitly of my argument here, see "The Political Outlook of Aristophanes," appendix 30, in G.E.M. de Ste. Croix's *The Origins of the Peloponnesian War* (Ithaca: Cornell University Press, 1972). Ste. Croix argues that Aristophanes "had an essentially *paternalistic* attitude toward them [the *dēmos*]," "resented" their political power, and thought it "intolerable when ignorant and ill-educated men demanded a share in the delicate art of government" (p. 357, emphasis in original). Ste. Croix relies on all of Aristophanes' plays, taking various passages to be propositions representing the author's views. His strongly political reading is a useful challenge to the kind of position I take here, but I think his interpretation of the various texts unpersuasive. The specific argument I refer to here is from Redfield, "Drama and Community," p. 331.

[79] This quotation is from Redfield, "Drama and Community," p. 331. There is a lively controversy about whether Bakhtin's notion of carnival (see especially *Rabelais and His World,* trans. H. Iswolsky [Cambridge, Mass.: Harvard University Press, 1968]) helps illuminate or obscures the function of comedy in Athens. Bakhtin argues that during carnival the norms of the everyday world are suspended, polarities, hierarchies, and oppositions based on power, status, and sex are inverted, and the traditionally subordinate groups get to exercise ritual authority over their superiors. During such times, limits were suspended and the forbidden practiced, as men and women were released from the obligations that otherwise circumscribed their lives and sustained the established order. But the festival at Athens offered institutionalized competitive displays; it was not a matter of the oppressed or repressed revolting, but the opportunity for citizens of a radical democracy to confront and perhaps rethink their decisions and loyalties. Bakhtin thought carnival liberating but his critics (such as Georges Balandier and Max Gluckman) have argued about carnival as Redfield does about comedy—that it is a ritual release of protest that allows power to consolidate itself even more effectively. I think this overstated, though not entirely mistaken.

[80] The language is Charles Segal's in "Aristophanes' Cloud-Chorus," p. 157.

enemy for dumb reasons. But there are other, perhaps more powerful reasons to reject what might be called the "Platonic" Aristophanes.[81] The first arises from a general consideration of the connection between elite and popular culture; the second, from Aristophanes' identifying himself with what he supposedly repudiated; and the third, from the play's ending.

A major assumption of those who believe Aristophanes to be a conservative and the *Clouds* an endorsement of Old Education is that Athenian democracy was controlled by elite families and elite culture. It is an argument made by both "conservatives" who wish to explain how the marvelous artistic achievements of the Athenians could coexist with a mobocracy, and "leftists," who find in Aristophanes little criticism of oligarchs but much of the *dēmos*.[82] As Josiah Ober has argued (using a particularly apt image, given the previous discussion), however, the discursive basis of Athenian society "was not given on high and was not a unique product of elite culture, but rather was established and constantly revised in the practice of public debate."[83] Ober is specifically referring to public oratory, but I think his point can be extended to include Old Comedy which was in its own way part of that oratory. What he says about a juryman deciding a case of *hubris*—that he had no juridically given external model of appropriate behavior but had to judge within and through a regime of social knowledge and truth—is also true of a juryman deciding on the prizes to be awarded to comedies. For both were part of a regime in which their decision participated in articulating a public world either by strengthening the existing assumptions about social categories and behavior or by revising them. Given such power, the central political and cultural ideals of the aristocracy are at once transformed, co-opted by, and delimited within a public environment of democratic politics. When Aristophanes turns our gaze to Socrates and the new aristocratic elite formed by sophistic education, he is turning the power of the people on targets that embody the continuing threat by aristocratic pretensions to superiority, including the new elite tied to wealth rather than heredity.

Second, the play is replete with *sophos* and its cognates, especially in the parabasis. There Aristophanes insists that he speaks truth without limit or restraint, that the *Clouds* is the wisest of all his plays, and that he has written it for the *sophoi* who appreciate its clever new ideas. He seems to ally himself here with the new ideas that the rest of the play ridicules. This is not to deny a conservative element or sympathies, but to insist that these are not the play's only

---

[81] See Nussbaum's argument that "Aristophanes and Plato are both critical of Socrates for the same reasons: his neglect of the importance of habituation, his intellectualism in denying the reality of *akrasia* (weakness of will, incontinence, without power over oneself), his not restricting questions to those who would not be corrupted by it. . . . Plato and Aristophanes," she concludes, "believe that for the ordinary man questioning is destructive without being therapeutic" ("Aristophanes and Socrates," p. 88).

[82] See the discussions by Ste. Croix, in *The Origins of the Peloponnesian War*, and Kenneth Dover, in *Aristophanic Comedy* (London: Bratsfford, 1972), both of whom make this argument about his politics. (Cf. Henderson, "The Demos and Comic Competition," p. 306.)

[83] Ober, "Power and Oratory," pp. 102–4.

sympathies and that, to put it anachronistically in Arendtian terms, we may need to be conservative in education to be radical in politics.

If it is legitimate to appropriate Ober's view of oratory for mine of comedy, and if I am right to see Aristophanes' understanding of himself as a political educator in Arendt's terms, then the ending of the *Clouds* upon which the conservative view rests can be read differently.

One thing is that Pheidippides is left unregenerate and pointedly absent from the ending. If all is supposed to return to normal and order to be restored, something is rotten in the city-state of Athens. Moreover, given that the clouds have continually changed their shape and that the *Clouds* has relied on verbal equivocation and unexpected turns in action, plot, and character, one should be careful about accepting the ending as any permanent shape or form. And while it is true that the "ceremonial aspect of the festival, the highly articulated structure of the plays themselves, provided a frame of containment for comedy's challenge"[84] so that whatever destabilizing surprises posed in and by the play are circumscribed by ritual stage and theater, this play stretches the form to the limit and challenges the frame itself. This is not only because the caricature of Old Education who represents "the good old times," "simple virtues," and "normality" is too powerful to be put to rest outside the theater (as Plato's *Apology* suggests), and not only because the play itself is so innovative; but because its ending is virtually unique in its uncomic aspects and is absolutely unique in its self-consciousness about its own form and purposes.

I do not want to deny how much fun it is to watch (or even to be) Strepsiades taking his revenge by turning the kiln-shaped Thinkery into a real oven while parodying Socrates' pretentiousness. (It is a little like seeing a snob sitting in a proctologist's waiting room.) But the ending is not like the festive celebration and joyous ordering of what has gone before, typical of final scenes in comedy. It is, rather, as abrupt as it is violent, and the burning is as much an act of futility as of defiance and revenge. Indeed, as I have noted, the ending resembles that of a tragedy, which makes this play, like its characters and Athens, a hybrid.[85]

Nor would I deny that the play is condescendingly critical of the glib aggressive immoralism of New Education or that it dramatizes the cost of denaturing practices and relationships and the myopia of New Education in encouraging conditions that make its own existence problematic. But as I have suggested, the play does not endorse either form of education; instead it provides a stage on which the absurdity of both positions and the partisans of each in the audience are ridiculed. By caricaturing each side, the play provides a middle ground and an occasion for laughter so as to free its audience not only from a fascination with its city but from a more particular fascination with party and class. For what the *Clouds* dramatizes is the dangerous political dynamic among sophistic intellec-

---

[84] Pozzi, "The Polis in Crisis," p. 148.

[85] In *Aristophanes' Old-and-New Comedy*, vol. 1 (Chapel Hill: University of North Carolina Press, 1985), p. 338, Kenneth J. Reckford argues that Aristophanes combined Old and New Comedy as he did tragedy and comedy in the *Clouds*. Old Comedy "he thought was what his precursors had performed and what his rivals, had they known better, could have outgrown."

tuals, their students who form a new class of revolutionary aristocratic elite youth united in elite clubs opportunistically using democratic rhetoric to assume power, and the sometimes violent reaction of their fathers.

X

But I do not want to claim too little for comedy by claiming too much for it. Comedy is not philosophy or theory. It is far funnier and can do things that philosophy and theory cannot. While it can dramatize the predicament of its characters, and thus help its citizen audience recognize and live with their own hybrid identities, it offers no solutions and prescribes no cures, though whether and how that is a deficiency is much debated these days.

Nor do I want to ignore what the Greeks never did: the moral ambivalence of comedy. Humor and laughter can be playful and infectious and can defuse potentially explosive situations. But it can also be derisive and caustic, creating tension and animus or used to shame miscreants. We have all been in situations where a joke breaks the ice or tension, where self-mockery is charming, gentle ridicule amusing, and we couldn't help laughing even when we were angry or resentful. But we have also been with couples whose bantering had a disquieting edge to it, or in situations where a joke seemed inappropriate or "bombed," or where self-mockery revealed much more than intended.

Nor, finally, can I point to any comedy and say with certainty that it led to a specifiable change in policy attitude or mood. I do not know for sure that Aristophanes' comedies had any effect on the political fate of Cleon, the standing of Euripides, or the relationship between men and women or fathers and sons, though evidence suggests he did have a profound influence on attitudes toward intellectuals like Socrates. But we can be more certain that this play suggests that irreverence and mockery may provide a ground for political critique, and that effrontery and excess can be an impulse for ethical insight. In the end Aristophanic comedy is like the dung of Strepsiades' rustic beginnings: at one and the same time rude and offensive *and* fertile and productive.[86] In this there is a lesson for democrats and political educators of democratic citizens.

[86] See Edwards's discussion in "Aristophanes' Comic Poetics," p. 179.

Antigone and the Languages of Politics

There is no true freedom without risk.[1] —Merleau-Ponty

I

THIS CHAPTER is about the languages of politics. I am less concerned to define politics than to ask about the force of "political" in phrases such as political order, political power, political knowledge, and political wisdom. Can we say what is distinctive to the domain or field of politics without being overly historicist or hopelessly ahistorical? Is politics defined by who does it (men as opposed to women, adults as distinct from children, coreligionists as distinguished from dissenters or heretics), by where it is done (in prescribed institutional settings), by subject matter (war or taxes), or by its ground so that political knowledge is political not simply because it is about politics but because it is derived politically rather than epistemologically? And why do we want to bound the field of politics or secure definitions in the first place?

There is something paradoxical about trying to define politics. It is captured by the argument that what is political is itself a political issue. Think, for instance, about the current debate over the politicization of the university discussed in chapter one; or of how issues such as sexual harassment have become political; or of analyses of the way power functions to keep an issue from becoming political in the first place. I call it paradoxical because to claim that what is political is a political question asserts that politics cannot be defined even as it does so. It is this paradox that leads me, rather clumsily, to entitle this chapter the language*s* of politics.

The fact, if that is what it is, that the very contestability of what constitutes politics may be distinctive to it, suggests that a political society is at once bounded and radically plural, a home that is unsettling, and a realm of being that is constantly becoming. Perhaps such complexities provide impetus for Rawlsians to embrace of a thin theory of the good, Habermasians to retreat from commitment to a Hegelian-Marxist theory of emancipation to a procedural rationality and, from a different perspective, to postmodernist celebrations of proliferating identities, transgressiveness, and disruptive genealogies.

This chapter is also about certain aspects of the relationship between language and politics as defined by Thucydides in his portrait of civil war at Corcyra, where, "to fit in with events, words too had to change their usual meanings. What used to be described as a thoughtless act of aggression was now regarded as the

---

[1] In *Signs*, trans. Richard C. McCleary (Evanston, Ill.: Northwestern University Press, 1964), p. 210.

courage one would expect to find in a party member: to think of the future and
wait was merely another way of saying that one was a coward." It is not that
language became more ambiguous, but that, in times of crisis, the Corcyraeans
were stuck with the same old words that provided a beguilingly harmonious
lexical surface over a "subterranean battlefield"[2] where men fought over the
meaning of words with the same ferocity that they fought each other. Paradoxically the shared vocabulary that seems to ground the city contributes to its disin-
tegration precisely because it is shared. This paradoxical quality of language, its
strange capacity to create and destroy, is a second reason why my title refers to
language in the plural.

The question, of course, is how "abnormal" civil war is, how different the
relationship between language and politics is there from more "normal" circumstances. It is a question urged on us by Thomas Hobbes as well as by Thucydides.

Thomas Hobbes translated Thucydides and there is evidence that the latter's
portrait of civil war provided a historical referent point and mythic dimension to
his own description of the English Civil War and was, in this way, an inspiration
for his vision and of the state of nature. The exigencies of civil war transmuted
into the fearful state of nature provide a dynamic and logic that leads to a teleology of crisis management and a politics which puts a premium on order, mastery,
and rule (in both senses). In *Leviathan* our choice is clear: the linguistic and
political chaos of the state of nature or the absolute security of absolute
sovereignty.

It is no accident that the sovereign is the great definer or that Hobbes thought
words could redeem us from our not so original sin of seeking for ourselves the
foundation of good and evil. If all goes as it ought, logically and prudentially, the
sovereign (with the essential assistance of the new and clear sacred text entitled
Leviathan) will define the sum total of what is, if not knowable, then publicly
sayable. If it all goes perfectly, Hobbes will have created the mental and political
space within which the project of security becomes the beginning and the end of
politics. Then it will be axiomatic that our instinct for self-preservation, self-
defense, and fear of violent death will rule all and, being beyond question, set the
terms for them. Whatever politics is allowed, posited, or projected as being, it
will be bounded, captured, fixed, and determined by a rigorous economy of security.[3] Who then would be so mad or suicidal to question the "fact" that freedom
(and anything of value) is only possible after law and order have been
established?

Hobbes's project is more prescription than description, aiming to make us talk,
speak, and act as calculating (and so calculable) beings. We need to accept this as
our nature even though Hobbes knew well enough that some men are moral

---

[2] The phrase and some of the phraseology in this paragraph are drawn from Laura Slatkin's "Sophocles' *Antigone* and the Paradoxes of Language" paper presented to the American Philological Association, Chicago 1991. Her analysis of the play has had a substantial influence on my own even where
our interests differ. I have discussed the civil war at Corcyra at length in *The Tragedy of Political
Theory: The Road Not Taken* (Princeton: Princeton University Press, 1990), chap. 6.

[3] Michael Dillon, *The Politics of Security: Toward a Political Philosophy of Continental Thought*
(London: Routledge, 1996).

beings despite it all, and that very few of us are always the self-conscious preda-tors essential for our consent to sovereign authority. Still, we need to think of ourselves as egoistic self-interested beings, since only if we do will we know what to fear and what to love, what is right and what is wrong, what, in short, has to be policed, warred against, and excluded for us to secure our security.[4] We need fear to establish the thought within which all thought takes place so that departure from it becomes as mad as insisting two plus two is five.

Hobbes never gives us much hope that humans could live in harmony with each other or that they can be instructed to understand the world in ways that allow them to be in harmony with it.[5] We remain tied to a condition we cannot wholly escape or entirely remake (despite Hobbes's gargantuan efforts), and which we cannot ultimately determine because our actions stimulate chains of reactions to which we must constantly respond. The state of war shadows our peace of mind and public safety. At the heart of his thought is an uncertainty about his certainties, an intellectual hesitancy about claims that have to be ac-cepted if the edifice is to stand and our survival and salvation be assured. Given that Hobbes translated Homer and Thucydides, it is unsurprising that there re-mains a tragic dimension to his thought not found in Enlightenment thinkers who posited the harmonies Hobbes hoped for but thought unlikely, and by the tradi-tion of metaphysics which from Plato to Kant and Hegel strove to secure the mastery of thought over the contingency tragedy took as a condition for human life.

But Hobbes did allow himself the indulgent thought that once the sovereign had established *Leviathan* as the new Scripture to be taught from lecterns and pulpits, the sovereignty of its language rather than a sovereign king would sustain the commonwealth. It is a thought that makes Foucault's choice of Hobbes as the symbol of what he regards as a now distracting preoccupation with the central-ized state somewhat curious. Hobbes, like Foucault, was concerned with the way "discourse" constitutes a field of objects, how power (through language) circu-lated like blood through the body to its farthest extremities, and how norms become normalizing, though he applies a very different moral valence to these processes. More than that, Foucault's own reversal of Clausewitz's dictum about war being politics by other means also links him with Hobbes, though again they have very different targets.[6]

Hobbes and Foucault give added urgency to the question raised by Thucydides' description of *stasis;* how wide is the divide, how clear is the dis-tinction between the normal and perverse or corrupt in the relationship between politics and language?

---

4 See David Johnston's discussion of how Hobbes's vision of egoistic man was prescriptive and how, anticipating failure in making those consumed by invisible spirits into rational calculators, he invested the sovereign with supernatural powers sufficient to intimidate even those not afraid of violent death, *The Rhetoric of Leviathan* (Princeton: Princeton University Press, 1986).

5 Bernard Williams, *Shame and Necessity* (Berkeley: University of California Press, 1993).

6 See Foucault's "Two Lectures" and "Truth and Power," in Colin Gordon, ed., *Power/Knowledge: Selected Interviews and Other Writings, 1972–1977* (New York: Pantheon, 1980), pp. 78–108, 109–33.

The same question is posed by George Steiner's notion of "divisive facsimile." With *Antigone* as his example, he argues that a situation, where "living beings using 'the same' language can mean entirely different indeed irreconcilable things, is present to a greater or lesser degree in all speech, but most dramatically in exchanges between men and women."[7] For him contests such as those over the meaning of piety, honor, friendship, profit, love, sanity, knowledge, and even life and death we find in *Antigone* are not distinctive to times of crises even if the intensity may be.[8] This too leads me to talk about the languages of politics.

Though Steiner does not himself make the connection, one can understand the controversies over the play's meaning in terms of the contest over language between Creon on the one hand and Antigone, Haemon, and Tiresias on the other. As what Steiner calls "an emblematic text" that inspires intense controversy, *Antigone* amplifies "normal" problems of interpretation and translation analogous to the way civil war "amplifies" the lexical tension in speech. That no translation is wholly commensurate with the original seems rooted in the singularity of every speech act. "None can transfer to another tongue the entire sum of implication, tonality, connotation, mimetic inflection and inferred context which declare the meanings in meaning." Something always gets lost or elided, subtle but decisive magnitudes alter scale, things are added or transposed, cadences rescripted in ways that make each speech a dialect and a unique presence in a language game whose rules are not quite seen for what they are. "Speech," to quote Steiner once more, "is as intimate to the pulse of man's [or woman's] being . . . as breath. No man [or woman] can reduplicate perfectly, can substitute for another man's breath," which is one reason why *pneuma* and *logos,* "the breath which inspires or blows us into being" and "the word,"[9] are so closely meshed in theological and metaphysical speculations. If speech and action are central to politics, then the issue of translation, and interpretation, recapitulates the themes of speech and silence present in the play and the possibility of political deliberation outside it.[10]

These issues about politics and language, like the other issues considered in this book, are present in the *Apology*. When Socrates proclaims himself a "private citizen" he emphasizes his paradoxical status as one who does "politics" outside established institutions and in unconventional ways (though as I argued in chapter four the agora was a place where conventional politics happened). The questions he asks his compatriots and the language he uses to ask them, though in some respects Athenian, nonetheless seem strange to them, at once tangential and

---

[7] George Steiner, *Antigones* (New York: Oxford University Press, 1984), pp. 234, 242.

[8] This has consequences for the question of how much Thebes was seen as a mirror of Athens as opposed to being an anti-Athens. Victor Ehrenberg in *Sophocles and Pericles* (Oxford: Blackwell, 1954) and Bernard Knox in *Oedipus at Thebes* (New York: Norton, 1970) see a fairly close identity and regard what happens on stage as a parable for what happens outside the theater. Froma Zeitlin takes the opposite view in "Thebes: Theater of Self and Society in Athenian Drama," in J. Peter Euben, ed., *Greek Tragedy and Political Theory* (Berkeley: University of California Press, 1986), pp. 101–41.

[9] Steiner, *Antigones,* pp. 202–3.

[10] As Hannah Arendt argues in *The Human Condition* (Chicago: University of Chicago Press, 1958).

offensive, distracting and irrelevant. Recall that one of the accusations against him is that he makes the worse *logos* (speech or argument) appear to be the better and vice versa, thus spreading disorder and disharmony in the city. By refusing to embrace accepted distinctions, settled practices, and rightful authority and by encouraging his students to do likewise, Socrates is, given the force and range of *diaphtheirō* discussed in chapter two, creating the conditions for civil war. To realize fully the moral charge such an accusation carried, we need to recall how pervasive the image of fraternal equality was in Athenian public discourse.[11] If all Athenians were born of a single mother and this common origin made them citizen brothers and so "relatively" equal, then civil war was fratricidal and, insofar as it destroyed political equality, particularly antidemocratic.

Socrates not only rejects the charge that he corrupts the youth, he turns it around by defining corruption as thoughtlessness, smugness, and self-congratulation. Thus his effort to have his fellow Athenians render an account of what they do and how they live their lives without permitting them recourse to notions of necessity, naturalness, or obviousness is a way of combating corruption as he understands it. Where they "go through the motions," he wants them to see their implicit moral choices and to recognize and thereby make subject to scrutiny the unseen forces that shape who they are as citizens and individuals. He accepts the fact that such demands are disruptive and so he rejects the identity of corruption and disorder. Indeed, the disorder encouraged by examining one's life seems to be a precondition for democratic politics.

In this Socrates stands against *Antigone's* Creon and with the play as a whole. This is hardly surprising if, as I have asserted, a significant dimension of Socrates' practice of philosophy was an elaboration of democratic culture, and if tragedy was a significant constituent of that culture.

As I indicated in chapter two, tragedy was a mode of political education that dramatized both the cultural accommodations upon which Athenian democracy rested, and the structural consequences of the political developments and choices that had occurred or were occurring. In making the half-visible particulars of everyday life visible as a form of life, it anticipated Socratic dialectic. By putting recognizable actions on stage and so on trial before the citizenry who had decided upon them but were now reconstituted as an audience reflecting on what they had done, tragedy contributed to the democratic tradition of self-critique and self-scrutiny. As such, it mediated what for us is a (sometimes generative) tension between theory and practice, or philosophy and politics. It also provided a historically specific, but nonetheless provocative, instance of democratic political education while giving texture to the distinction between a political and politicized education.

In this, tragedy was a complement to comedy, as I argued in the preceding chapter. There, I presented the contest between Old and New Education and between Socrates and Strepsiades as raising a question about the location and nature of what might be called, with obvious anachronism, "public reason." In

---

[11] See Carol Dougherty, "Democratic Contradictions and the Synoptic Illusion of Euripides' *Ion*," in Charles Hedrick and Josiah Ober, eds., *Demokratia: A Conversation on Democracy, Ancient and Modern* (Princeton: Princeton University Press, 1996), pp. 249–70.

the *Clouds* the question of public reason is dramatized spatially between what is high and low. In *Antigone* it is played out horizontally in a contest between Antigone, Haemon, and Creon.[12] That contest dramatizes many of the issues present in the debate between "postmodernists" and "modernists" over the role of reason in public life. If, as in mythical Thebes, public reason is itself essentially contestable and epistemic moral and political standards are inextricably intertwined, then conflicts are not just conflicts about particular beliefs or even principles, but about the principles of adjudication themselves. What is at issue is the character of political life as well as the meaning and scope of accepted political values.[13] But even if this is the condition of mythical Thebes, is it also the condition of historical Athens and of public life generally? Or can the audience sustain public reason because it has taken to heart the vision of corruption it sees on stage?

Steiner's idea of divisive facsimile has bearing on these questions insofar as his argument about translations and speech acts suggests that any hope for communicative transparency is illusory and self-defeating. My appropriation of his idea to describe interpretative controversies about the play is also applicable to interpretative controversies over dialogues like the *Gorgias* and *Protagoras*. But just as one ought, on Socrates' authority, to resist the equation of disorder and corruption Creon embraces, so ought we, also on Socrates' authority and perhaps Plato's as well, to resist the temptation to regard these dialogues as "incomplete" and so defective. As I argued in chapter one, this incompleteness as represented by the dialogue's fissures, inversions, and turnings, by the tensions between their dramatic and historical contrast, as well as between their explicit argument and structural subtext, is politically and theoretically generative in ways that confound any conservative effort to subordinate them to a political agenda or a multiculturalist dismissal of them as the product of one.

Though this argument is central to the book as a whole, it is the particular focus of this chapter, which considers three contemporary controversies as a frame for a detailed consideration of the play and the theme of politics and language.

II

The first theme concerns the status of reason and the possibilities of deliberative democracy that follow from it. Among contemporary social and political theorists few would defend reason's purity or sovereignty.[14] Almost all acknowledge reason's unavoidable entanglement in history and tradition, society, power, and

[12] Since the audience sits on high (as Socrates does in the *Clouds*), watching the action below, and generational and gender hierarchies operate in and around the play, there is an important vertical dimension present here as well.

[13] See the discussion by James Bohman in "Public Reason and Cultural Pluralism: Political Liberalism and the Problem of Moral Conflict," *Political Theory* 23, no. 2 (May 1995): 253–279.

[14] There are exceptions to this generalization and I will discuss them in the following chapter on Oedipus and rational choice theory.

interest as well as its roots in the body and desire. The question raised in chapter one is how entangled reason is—how "grounded" must it be (in both senses)—and what conclusions can be drawn from the fact of its historicity.

One possible response is that of "postmodernists."[15] Here one engages in a genealogical critique of logocentrism, metaphysics, universalism and foundationalism of all sorts in the name of localized truth and the invasiveness of the will to power, the preconceptual and unconscious at the heart of the will to truth. Postmodernists stress (and sometimes celebrate) heterogeneity and heterotopias, fragmented or plural selves, floating signifiers, and epistemologically and morally decentered subjects. Finally, they insist on the primacy of the aesthetic dimension of language, the rhetorical dimension of philosophy, and the need to reject totalizing theories and universal intellectuals for particular intellectuals providing assistance to local resistance.[16]

A different response has been given by Jürgen Habermas. Habermas acknowledges the impurity of reason and the failure of the original Enlightenment project but thinks that redefining reason as communicative action can both salvage the part of that project while retaining the critical capacity of reason. Thus the embeddedness of reason is not sufficient grounds to give it up, any more than acknowledging that the rhetorical aspects of language need vitiate distinctions between truth and falsity, or between communicative practice of everyday life where language functions as a medium for dealing with concrete problems and poetic discourse where the urgency of the decision is absent and the innovative world creating power of language is allowed free reign.

Habermas defends "the modernist project" against its overly ambitious defenders and its postmodern detractors by reconceptualizing the idea of enlightenment and the possibility of emancipation. That reconceptualization entails maintaining allegiance to notions of moral agency and rational action while acknowledging a permanent shift in philosophical sensibility and an irreversible process of differentiation of spheres of validity and discourse that requires rejection of Kant's assumption that moral validity can be fully grasped by a self-consciously reflective individual. Once we appreciate the need to locate the deliberative subject in the space of interactive communication and acknowledge that meaning is arrived at dialogically, we can recast the ideals of autonomy and practical reason in ways that vindicate Kant's cognitivist and universalistic claims without being committed to the idea of a monological subject as the ground of ethical reflection and justification. In this "communicative theory of meaning," rationality and validity emerge from and remain ineluctably tied to human action because the truth and goodness of a claim can only be established and adjudicated (without coercion) through public debate. Thus Habermas's uni-

---

[15] Because he regards the desire to be postmodern as itself an aspect of modernity, William Connolly argues against using the term. See *Political Theory and Modernity* (New York: Basil Blackwell, 1988), chap. 1.

[16] See Jürgen Habermas's lectures in *The Philosophical Discourse of Modernity,* trans. Frederick Lawrence, introd. Thomas McCarthy, and McCarthy's introduction (Cambridge, Mass.: MIT Press, 1990).

versalism (as distinct from Kant's) is procedural, having to do with how we argue about a range of determinate issues that can be decided in a way that is mutually acceptable to all participants. Rather than stipulating a specific normative standard, this universalist principle specifies the preconditions essential for justifying any substantive principle. By so doing, it continues to value the autonomous moral agent, at least to the degree that it rejects the existence of moral authority external to the wills of rational agents. But it is an intersubjective autonomy in which each participant is impartially concerned with the ends that can be willed in common. In these terms, each participant must, when examining the validity of proposed norms, see the world from the perspective of all others, since it is the consequences of those norms "for the needs and interests of those affected that constitute the relevant reasons in terms of which the issue of normative validity must be decided."[17]

As this suggests, Habermas denies any interest in offering a normative political theory. Rather he regards himself as simply providing a "reconstruction of actual conditions, under the premise that in everyday communicative practice, sociated individuals cannot avoid *also* employing everyday speech in a way that is oriented toward reaching understanding." Whenever we mean what we say, "we raise the claim that what is said is true, or right, or truthful." Such a claim is implicit in our very engagement with others and with it "a small bit of ideality breaks out in our every day lives." That an argument which appears valid today may not be tomorrow or that individuals can decide to manipulate others and act strategically does not undermine the fact that everyday praxis oriented toward understanding is "permeated by idealizations" that "simply inhere" in the medium of everyday language in which social reproduction takes place. These idealizations are as close as we can (or ought) to come to consensus about the right action or good life given the irreducible pluralism that has come to define our condition. Thus we have no alternative except to locate the normative basis for social interaction in the rational structure of communication itself.[18]

Unless, of course, one rejects the Kantian project as a whole. Then the necessary preconditions for ideal speech may appear as otherworldly as Platonic Forms, and the emphasis on rational agents as confounding the classroom and the agora, depoliticizing morality while underestimating the tyranny of reasonableness. Seen from the vantage point of *Antigone,* Habermas's version of procedural rationality and the technical abstractness of his language seem homologous to and thus reifying the "system's world" at the expense of the "life world," whose integrity he is committed to maintaining. From that point of view, one might

---

[17] See Jürgen Habermas, "Discourse Ethics: Notes on a Program of Philosophical Justification," in *Moral Consciousness and Communicative Action,* trans. Christian Lenhardt and S. W. Nicholsen (Cambridge, Mass.: MIT Press, 1990), pp. 43–115, and Ciaran P. Cronin's "Introduction to Jürgen Habermas," in *Justification and Application: Remarks on Discourse Ethics,* trans. C. P. Cronin (Cambridge, Mass.: MIT Press, 1993), pp. xi–xxix.

[18] See Jürgen Habermas, "What Theories Can Accomplish," in Max Pensky, ed. and trans., *Jürgen Habermas: The Past As Future, Interviews by Michael Haller,* foreword by Peter Hohendahl (Lincoln: University of Nebraska Press, 1994), pp. 99–120.

wonder whether his distinctions between spheres of activity and levels of analysis are too sharply drawn, and whether he has too quickly renounced the possibility of a substantive morality. It may be that such a morality is possible even in our radically plural world, though it would have to be pre-Kantian non-Aristotelian morality, one intimated, I shall suggest, in Sophocles' *Antigone*.

From the perspective of the play, discourse ethics too easily banishes passion, rhetoric, and theatricality and is insufficiently attentive to the constructive (but not functionalizing) role dissonance and agonism play in politics. It underestimates how much moral and political life has to do not only with understanding shared premises, but establishing shared experience, how often the "same" words, including words for deliberation, mean quite different things to people who live in the same and yet in different worlds. Indeed *Antigone* is full of words for deliberation, reasoning, and knowledge, which the various characters fight over only to have the play reveal them as either reductive or self-serving. Creon in particular insists that his views and politics are *to phronein* (i.e., right-thinking, sensible, and reasonable), while those of everyone else are *anous* (i.e., irrational, without sense or judgment). But not only Creon: *every* speaker "dwells on the thing he thinks is rational or wise."[19] From this point of view even a revised Kantian project is too Apollonian, too oblivious to the way instinctive forces move men and women to reason. The one person who seems to embody the voice of reason and makes a case for what might anachronistically be called deliberative democracy is Haemon, and his arguments are framed by his love of Antigone and his hatred for his father.

But the world of the play is not the world of the audience, at least insofar as mythical Thebes is a scene of displacement, in which the dynamic of corruption and perversion in the household and city plays itself out on stage so that it will not play itself out in the lives of the citizen audience[20] (much as Hobbes hoped that the power of his rhetoric would stimulate people to take the world apart in their imagination so they would not do so in fact). But if the actors watching the play can, because of their experience in the theater, resist the play of forces that consumes the characters on stage, then there may be room for something akin to a Habermasian project in the sense of providing a criterion for justifying when one can reasonably break off being reasonable in the face of some actor who rejects contestation of his claims. It may even be that the conditions of performance and the experience of theater and theatricality contribute to, are even necessary conditions for, the deliberation that took place in the assemblies and juries that marked Athenian democracy.

---

[19] See Robert F. Goheen, *The Imagery of Sophocles'* Antigone: *A Study of Poetic Language and Structure* (Princeton: Princeton University Press, 1951), pp. 84, 105; and Elizabeth Van Nes Ditmars, *Sophocles'* Antigone: *Lyric Shape and Meaning* (Pisa: Giardini Editori E Stampatori, 1992).

[20] The argument is Froma Zeitlin's "Thebes: Theater of Self and Society in Athenian Drama." She goes on to suggest that Thebes is a world from which no escape from tragic conflict is possible, as opposed to Athens, which can institute a future outside and beyond the world of the play. While I still think her argument strong, I am less persuaded by it than I had been in part because for Thebes to be a warning there must be a possibility that Athens could become what Thebes already is.

But since Thebes is not simply another place but a stage in Athens where people confronted recognizable figures, issues, and attitudes—toward leadership, power, justice, speech, friendship, piety, technological progress, sexual and generational conflict, love, madness, empire, and sophistic education—the audience sees itself as much as it sees something that is not itself. So the audience exists in a tension between two worlds, proximate to yet distant from the cultural terms in which democracy happens. If the perversities of Thebes are distanced without being banished, if the contests between characters, passions, and principles are familiar to the audience because it is part of their intensely agonal politics, then we need to be careful about both sanitizing "deliberation" *and* dismissing it as an un-Nietzschean charade.

The issue can be put this way: what role does reason play in deliberations if standards of rationality are themselves subject to deeply conflicting interpretations?[21] Does *Antigone* provide us with a view of reason as defective, or does it provide us with a case of pride and stubbornness "masquerading" as and perverting reason? Is what we see not "true" reason but a "semblance" of it? Or do the very terms of this distinction beg the question?

Despite the fact that Hobbes is a problematic liberal, his social ontology has helped constitute the discourse of modern politics in both the domestic and international spheres.[22] It is this definition that is presently being challenged by a new generation of international relations theorists. The issues that concern them intersect with those I have just discussed in regard to Habermas, though he is not very sympathetic to the realist and neorealist targets of this often postmodernist inspired critique of international politics.

I have referred several times to Arendt's argument that in times of crisis people come to recognize that what they do and say are answers to questions they no longer realize to be such, because "answers" seemed embedded in the nature of things.[23] But when what was settled becomes unsettled and unsettling, certainties once "justified" by reference to nature, human nature, or the nature of the international political system are seen as "man"-made and historically specific, or worse, arbitrary and manipulative. Defenders of the old ways and concepts resent having to justify what was obvious, while their critics are often contemptuous of this resentment and of the depoliticizing move of recurring to nature, necessity, or "metanarratives." Something like this is happening to the idea of security in international relations and, partly because of that, to the idea of political order itself.

If it is true that "this is an era of increasing disorder," it is hardly surprising that there is a substantial rethinking of order as topic concept and objective.[24] Nor,

[21] Bohman, "Public Reason and Cultural Pluralism," p. 254.

[22] The classic work remains Kenneth Waltz's *Man the State and War: A Theoretical Analysis* (New York: Columbia University Press, 1959).

[23] See her essay, "The Crisis in Education," in *Between Past and Future: Eight Studies in Political Thought,* enl. ed. (New York: Viking Press, 1968).

[24] See Jonathan Friedman, "Order and Disorder in Global Systems: A Sketch," *Social Research* 60, no. 2 (Summer 1993): 205–34.

given the demise of a relatively stable bipolar world, is it surprising that the concept of security has itself become insecure. The end of the cold war has meant the end of any clear demarcation between friend and foe, while the diffusion of power into new national and economic entities and the rise of cultural national-ism (as well as identity politics) has made it unclear what is to be secured or incorporated into some larger international framework or order. Similarly, it is less clear who has the authority to define what must be secured, and which voices and peoples need to be quieted or constrained through the exercise of the sover-eign power by the state or the policing mechanisms of the culture.[25] If who "we" are is constituted by who we are not, if, to use the current jargon, the center and self are defined against what is marginal and other, then the blurring of bound-aries leads to a proliferation of what is strange and so must be secured. This may be one impetus for the apocalyptic posturing in the current culture wars discussed in chapter one. It is certainly part of the explanation of why Creon insists on bringing as many and as much possible within his "zone of security."

James Der Derian has suggested that "no other concept in international rela-tions packs the metaphysical punch or commands the disciplinary power of secu-rity." This is both because it establishes the thought within which thought about politics takes place and because "security"—national and personal—continues to justify the spending of billions on weapons' development, limits dissent, and depoliticizes issues by placing them beyond contestation and the play of power.[26] If Der Derian is right about the concept of security, then challenging the dis-course of security and order brings us back to Hobbes's social ontology—his portrait of a state of war as prior to history and language and independent of political choice—which continues to provide a foundation for the metaphysics and politics of security and order whether domestically or internationally.[27] While Haemon's argument for collective wisdom provides the dramatic focus for the issue of deliberative democracy, Creon's preoccupation with order and mas-tery and his demand to set the terms in which political questions can be posed and insanity understood provide the focus for the debate over security.

There is one further contemporary debate that frames the argument of this chap-ter though in a different way than the other two. The debate is over gender and it is different for three reasons. First, given Seyla Benhabib's feminist critique/ elaboration of Habermas and feminist critiques of the gendered nature of security studies,[28] it cuts across the other two. Second, because Athenian society defined women as passionate and erotic rather than "reasonable" beings, they were

[25] See Ronnie D. Lipschutz, ed., *On Security* (New York: Columbia University Press, 1995), chap. 1.

[26] In "The Value of Security: Hobbes, Marx, Nietzsche and Baudrillard," in Lipschutz, *On Secu-rity,* pp. 33–62.

[27] This is not to argue that Hobbes was a liberal.

[28] See, for instance, J. Ann Tickner, *Gender in International Relations* (New York: Columbia University Press, 1992), and the Special Issue of *Millennium: Journal of International Studies,* "Women and International Relations," ed. J. Ann Tickner 13, no. 3 (Winter 1988).

threats to security unless appropriately sequestered. Third, unlike the debates over Habermas or public reason and security, Antigone as character symbol and *Antigone* as drama have played a direct and occasionally significant role in current feminist controversies over the relationship between public and private life and the distinctiveness of "a" woman's voice.[29]

In 1982 Jean Bethke Elshtain argued that *Antigone* could teach feminists to approach the modern bureaucratic nation-state from a standpoint of a skepticism that "keeps alive a critical distance between feminism and statism, between female self-identity and a social identity tied to the public-political world, revolving around the structures, institutions, values, and ends of the state."[30] Given a state that "monopolizes and centralizes power and eliminates older less universal forms of authority; that structures its activities, and implements its policies through unaccountable hierarchies; that erodes local and particular patterns of ethnic religious and regional identities; that standardizes culture, ideas, and ideals" and overrides all "standards of decency" in the name of *raison d'état*, feminists should regard themselves as daughters of Antigone. For Elshtain that means recognizing that, as a group, women experience their social world differently from men as a group, and that transforming women into people whose public identity primarily defines them loses what is distinctively valuable about women's experience and erases a counterhegemonic discourse. To be "emancipated" by the state in order to participate in its life is doubly problematic (pp. 47–48, 52).

Elshtain believes that women can embrace ideals and values from the social world of women severed from male domination and female subordination if they do not view women's traditional identities as devoid of vitality or simply reactions to male power. What she sees in Antigone is someone who passionately and heroically insists that "primordial family morality precedes and overrides the laws of the state." Creon must be defied for there are matters "that are so basic they transcend *raison d'état*, one's own self-interest, even one's life" (p. 53). Political necessity cannot be allowed to triumph over loyalty to a brother or family honor, cannot presume to "dictate to the human soul" or establish the

---

[29] The debate over Antigone goes on in a number of registers. For instance, there is a philosophical tradition often starting with a commentary on Hegel: see Luce Irigaray, "The Eternal Irony of the Community," in Richard A. Cohen, ed., *Face to Face with Levinas* (Albany, N.Y.: SUNY Press, 1986), pp. 231–56; Lacan's *Le séminaire de Jacques Lacan, livre VII: L'éthique de lay psychoanalyse (1959–60)* (Paris: Editions de Seuil, 1986), chaps. 19–21; Derrida's discussion of Hegel in *Glas*, trans. John P. Leavey Jr. and Richard Rand (Lincoln: University of Nebraska Press, 1986). Though Martha Nussbaum is also a philosopher, her philosophical sensibility is somewhat different. See her discussion of *Antigone* in *The Fragility of Goodness* (Cambridge: Cambridge University Press, 1986), chap. 3. For analyses by political theorists, see, for example, Ann Lane and Warren Lane, "The Politics of *Antigone*," in J. Peter Euben, ed., *Greek Tragedy and Political Theory* (Berkeley: University of California Press, 1986), pp. 51–62, and Arlene Saxonhouse, *The Fear of Diversity* (Chicago: University of Chicago Press, 1993), chap. 3.

[30] "Antigone's Children," *Democracy* 2, no. 1 (April 1982): 46–59. (Hereafter, page references will be given in text.)

priority of abstract political obligations over "values of family and particular loyalties, ties, and traditions."

But it is not just what Antigone defends that Elshtain admires; it is also how she defends it. Antigone's is "a robust voice, a bold voice; woman as guardian of the prerogatives of the *oikos,* preserver of familial duty and honor, protector of children, if need be, their fierce avenger" (p. 55). With Antigone as their guide and inspiration, women can reclaim, explore, and articulate the social world where human life is nurtured and protected and tap a deeply buried human identity where "we are first and foremost not political or economic man but family men and women."

I am not interested in assessing Elshtain's reading of the play here or the politics she bases on it since I will do so in my reading of the play. I would only note here the irony of linking maternal thinking to Antigone (as Elshtain does) given the literal meaning of anti-*genē,* given who *her* mother (and father) are, and given that she is doomed to die childless.[31]

Since Carol Gilligan, if not before, feminists have been concerned with whether, why, and how "women" speak in a distinctive voice, how that voice is silenced, intimidated, disrespected, or constructed by male power and whether an ethic of care can be defended without becoming complicit in reifying hierarchies between activities and spheres that have justified women's exclusions from power.[32] Was there a "woman's" voice based on their "women's" experience as "women" (however that was defined) that made them, if not a saving remnant analogous to Marx's proletariat, then a counterhegemonic force against the gendered politics of the state and international political system such as Elshtain suggests? Could one say they possessed an identifiable epistemology or standpoint (or a commitment to standpoint theory) or academic style—less aggressive and hierarchic and more responsive—a moral sensibility more oriented toward maintaining relationships than to endorsing abstract principles of justice? Could and would all this culminate in a politics of peace rather than war, and a new mode of theorizing more firmly "embodied" in the everyday world in which women lived?

Similarly the slogan "the personal is the political" epitomized as it dramatized feminist challenges to the division between public and private life and to conventional definition of what politics was, where it went on, and who was doing it. Whether one argued for a revaluation of women's traditional activities or wanted to break the hold of that tradition, either by having men share in it or enabling

---

[31] See the critique of Elshtain by Valerie A. Hartouni, "Antigone's Dilemma: A Problem in Political Membership," *Hypatia* 1, no. 1 (Spring 1986): 3–20. Hartouni's analysis helps explain the paradoxical sound of "political actress."

[32] See Carol Gilligan's *In a Different Voice* (Cambridge, Mass.: Harvard University Press, 1982); and the critiques by Kathy Ferguson in *The Feminist Case against Bureaucracy* (Philadelphia: Temple University Press, 1984); and Joan Tronto, *Moral Boundaries: A Political Argument for an Ethic of Care* (New York: Routledge, 1993). (Judith Butler, Wendy Brown, Joan Scott, and Seyla Benhabib [among others] have completely recast the terms of this debate.)

women to be free of it, it was clear that the division between public and private seemed, no matter how historically specific the separate spheres were defined, to sustain the literal and symbolic inequality of women and their relative powerlessness.

For some feminists the fact that women gave birth and were nurturers meant they thought "maternally."[33] Thus they would be less likely to support destructive policies and, being closer to nature, would resist the ethic and metaphysic of mastery—whether of nature, others, or events—that had defined malestream Western politics and metaphysics. On some such premise, one could even argue that women thought through the body in a way men did not and so possessed an awareness of the world men lacked.

Such views remain attractive to some feminists despite criticisms that they reinforce biological determinism; that valorizing women's voices, activities, or an ethic of care where women lack equal cultural and political power is a trap; that the category of "woman" is itself an "essentialist," politically suspect, ahistorical abstraction whose "normalizing" paradigm is of middle-class white heterosexual women with children in a traditional family; that they both underestimate the way male privilege continues to construct female sexuality and gender and the many ways women have of contesting this construction; and that they ignore the way *men* are constructed.

III

Critics have argued that *Antigone* has "a double center of gravity,"[34] by which they mean that there are two tragic figures in the play, Creon and Antigone. And of course they are right. But from a somewhat different standpoint the play has at least two other centers of gravity. The first, which emerges from what is now called "the choral ode in praise of man," is that of humankind itself;[35] the second, the Athenian audience.[36] To insist on at least four such centers allows one to move outside the polarities that have come to define virtually every reading of the play. If the various antinomies of the play collapse or are reconfigured, then the usual representations upon which they rely—Creon "stands for" reason, the city, maleness, culture, innovation, and Antigone for their opposites—do not work.[37]

[33] See Sara Ruddick, *Maternal Thinking: Toward a Politics of Peace* (Boston: Beacon Press, 1989); and the commentaries by Mary Deitz, "Citizenship with a Feminist Face: The Problem of Maternal Thinking," *Political Theory* 12, no. 1 (1985): 19–35; and Joan Scott, "Gender a Useful Category of Historical Analysis," *American Historical Review* 91, no. 2 (1986): 1053–75.

[34] Both Goheen (*Imagery*) and Segal ("Sophocles' Praise of Man and the Conflicts of *Antigone*," *Arion* 3, no. 2 [Summer 1964]): 46–66, reprinted in T. Woodward, ed., *Sophocles: A Collection of Critical Essays* [Englewood Cliffs, N.J.: Prentice Hall, 1966]) use the phrase.

[35] See Martin Heidegger in *An Introduction to Metaphysics* (New Haven: Yale University Press, 1959), pp. 146–65.

[36] There is a sense, of course, in which every subsequent audience is also a center of gravity.

[37] See Saxonhouse's discussion of Antigone in *The Fear of Diversity*, pp. 63–76, and S. Benardete,

ANTIGONE AND THE LANGUAGE OF POLITICS • 153

In fact, it is Creon who insists on rigid distinctions that inscribe hierarchies. Since he is a highly problematic figure, the structure of the oppositions he promulgates is politically and interpretatively suspect. Once freed of them we can see how divisions between are also divisions within; how animus is heightened by affinity, how love isolates as well as unites, and how characters speak for principles and positions they undermine at the very moment they pronounce them. And if the usual signposts that provide interpretative and political security are lacking, then the play throws us into a world that is determined neither by a unified logic nor a transcendent telos.

In the remainder of this chapter I will offer four readings of the play, each corresponding to a center of gravity. Each reading will explore the languages of politics from a somewhat different perspective with the aim of generating a series of interpretative and political possibilities. Section IV, the first and by far the longest, is on Creon. Section V is on Antigone, Section VI on the choral ode, while Section VII is on the productive tensions between mythical Thebes and contemporary Athens.

IV

The Creon we first meet seems moderate and reasonable. His patriotism has led him to use his authority to secure order after a disastrous and fratricidal civil war. If he has had to take the extreme measure of forbidding the burial of the traitor Polyneices, he was just doing what had to be done. Moreover, he is admirably anxious to have the legitimacy of his rule rest, not only on his right of succession and kinship with the dead, but with his adherence to publicly proclaimed rational principles of leadership. "To know thoroughly the soul [*psuchēn*], intelligence [*phronēma*], and judgment [*gnōmēn*] of any man one must see his skill [*entribēs*] in the exercise of power and law" (195). A sign of such skill is the willingness of even the most absolute ruler to speak his thoughts openly, and actively seek the best available counsel. Since the highest virtue is civic virtue, the greatest friend is a friend to the city, and the best counsel is that which speaks honestly and publicly for the city's benefit. Because the city's security makes all else possible, everything of value depends upon loyalty to it. Elaborating an image he uses in his opening line and that will haunt him later, Creon likens the city to a ship: "If she is upright and we sail on her, friends will be ours for the making" (209).[38] All this is context and prelude to his pronouncement, the decree banning burial of Polynieces.

We are assured by virtually all critics that this speech and Creon himself would have been well regarded by an Athenian audience of male citizens (and that they

"A Reading of Sophocles' *Antigone* I and II," *Interpretation* 4, no. 4 (1974–75): 148–96 and 5, no. 1: 148–84.

[38] I have relied on David Grene's translation of Antigone in *Sophocles,* vol. 1 (Chicago: University of Chicago Press, 1991) but with my own emendations.

would have been aghast at Antigone's disobedience).[39] Indeed, many of these critics suppose that the audience's sympathy would continue until the exchange with Tiresias, where it becomes clear that while it was fine to dismiss women, the young, and even disobedient citizens, it is not fine to dismiss Apollo's prophet. We are also assured that Creon's position is that of the assembled male citizenry (and of Sophocles), such that he "stands for the city," more precisely democratic Athens, and so his first words, referring to the restoration of order, can be characterized as an "admirable exemplification of democratic patriotism."[40] If true, then we either ought not challenge what he says because it does not fit *our* view of politics, democracy, and gender or acknowledge that the deficiencies of his arguments are the deficiencies of democratic politics.[41]

But as I have already indicated, I do not think Creon can be identified with "the city" or maleness, still less with democracy, and only problematically with reason and reasonableness. Indeed, I think it more accurate to regard him as "standing for" a corrupt view of politics and the city, the excesses of hypermasculinity and an irrationalism that animates an aggressive commitment to reasonableness. Hints of this are already present in the highly praised first speech. For one thing, Creon is involved in a contradiction,[42] since his power to issue the edict comes from his family ties to the dead, yet he uses that power to ignore those ties. In these terms his insistence on "rational" criteria of leadership is a self-serving deracination that permits him to simplify the claims on him and the consequences of the actions he undertakes.[43]

---

[39] Thus Christian Meier (in *The Political Art of Greek Tragedy,* trans. Andrew Webber [Baltimore: Johns Hopkins University Press, 1993]) assures us that most of what Creon says "would have been quite acceptable and in line with the thinking of the day, the diatribe against anarchy, the disorder which women threaten and the necessity of male rule and of obedience" (p. 191). Christiane Sourvinou-Inwood insists that "there can be no doubt that Antigone's action would have been perceived by the Athenians as illegitimately subversive of the polis." They would have been appalled at a woman disobeying the head of her *oikos,* who extends her arrogance to the public sphere, and who claims to know what the unwritten laws (*nomina*) of the gods are better that "the city" does. Because "Sophocles was a solid citizen who held some important polis offices and was very popular with the judges of the tragedies who award him many victories," he could not possibly have written anything subversive. See her "Assumptions and the Creation of Meaning: Reading Sophocles' *Antigone,*" *Journal of Hellenic Studies* 109 (1989): 134–84. Similarly B.M.W. Knox (in *Heroic Temper: Studies in Sophoclean Tragedy* [Berkeley: University of California Press, 1964]) regards Creon's speech as a classic text of Athenian patriotism, William M. Calder III (in "Sophokles' Political Tragedy, *Antigone,*" *Greek Roman and Byzantine Studies* 9 [1968]: 404) insists that siding with Antigone "implies an historical anachronism," as does, though more cautiously, R. P. Winnington-Ingram, *Sophocles: An Interpretation* (Cambridge: Cambridge University Press, 1980).

[40] Sourvinou-Inwood, "Assumptions," p. 142.

[41] Saxonhouse argues that Creon (and Sophocles?) identifies reason and speech with the polis as against Antigone who "from the opening moments of the play denies the efficacy of human speech, scornfully dismissing the spoken decrees of the city's leader" (*Fear of Diversity,* p. 41).

[42] See the argument of Matt Neuberg in "How Like a Woman: Antigone's 'Inconsistency,'" *Classical Quarterly* 40, no. 1 (1990): 54–76. I find Neuberg's argument on this and on *Antigone* in general very persuasive.

[43] As Neuberg argues, Creon has essentially killed his son and wife. Thus he is punished by having his own most immediate blood and marriage ties perverted in death, the very thing he did to Antigone.

For another thing, though Creon makes much of a good ruler needing to seek counsel, he takes none when considering the decree he proclaims, which means that he is violating his own principles at the moment of their enactment. He asks the assembled elders not for their advice, but for their loyalty and assistance in instituting what he has decided on his own. And their response to his request (which they see as more of a threat and command) is equivocal at best. While they acknowledge his power to make the decree, they do not endorse it, and indeed seem to pull away from it in a move that begins a process of isolating Creon from others. They demur when he asks them to enforce the decree and give their support because they know he would kill them if they resisted, hardly a reassuring response to a man who celebrates fearless speech as indispensable to proper governance of the city.

Then there is the decree itself. If not extreme in substance—public stoning is an unusually cruel punishment—it is in extent. Given Polyneices' treachery, it is perfectly appropriate that he be forbidden burial within the confines and jurisdiction of the city. But Creon's decree extends everywhere, including, presumably, those places outside the city which belong to the gods. In his passion for order, he brings as much and as many as possible within the order he would rule—even a dead man lying outside the city's walls. Yet the order to leave the body unburied is precisely what creates disorder in nature and the city. It is what opens Thebes to an untamed animality that threatens to return humankind to some "pre-civilized" state.[44]

Finally the decree can be read in more than one register. Though Creon begins by setting out principles by which he himself wishes to be judged (principles he systematically violates), they can also be seen as a loyalty oath intended to ferret out traitors whom we already have reason to suspect from his speech will be many, everywhere, and defined by him alone.[45] By insisting that the city makes all good things possible and identifying himself with the city, he prepares for the security of one becoming coterminous with the security of other.

Even if the male citizens in the audience were initially outraged at Antigone's audacity and Haemon's defiance of his father, when Creon's "Shall I be ruled by a woman?" and "Shall I be ruled by the young?" becomes "Shall I be ruled by the people" and a claim that he owns the city and must be obeyed in all things,[46] their outrage might well become redirected. They might even reflect back on what they now saw as a precipitous agreement about gender and age. If one suddenly

His *philoi* are dead—he is robbed of his marriage—and the deaths of his son and wife spring from their cleaving to the very ties which Creon has sought to deny Antigone the chance to cleave to (ibid., pp. 74–75).

[44] See Segal's discussion of this in "Sophocles' Praise of Man."

[45] See the discussion by Lane and Lane in "The Politics of *Antigone.*"

[46] Creon does not deny he is alone in his views about Polyneices and Antigone; he denies he needs the town. In this he is, of course, contradicting his own principle of good leadership. When, in line 737 Haemon says *polis gar ouk esth' hētis andros esth' henos,* it can mean a city belonging to a single man (genitive of possession) or a city composed of one man (genitive of content). See the discussion in Joan V. O'Brien, *Guide of Sophocles'* Antigone (Carbondale: Southern Illinois University Press, 1978), p. 89.

discovers that a line of argument issues in an utterly repulsive conclusion, one might reexamine the premises that got one there.

Creon values order above all and so misunderstands the nature of *political* order as well as political power, political knowledge, and political thinking. One of his favorite words is *orthōs* and its cognates, meaning setting things straight, fixing them (in both senses), making them singular and commensurate in terms of a single coin.[47] He is intent on making what he controls as orderly as possible and, as we have seen, to bring as much and as many as possible into his orbit of security. Expanding the definition of what and who must be policed, warred against, and excluded to secure security, he even turns those closest to him into strangers and enemies. Even acknowledging the fact that political and military leaders were, at least until the fourth century, usually the same person, Creon confuses political and military order, regarding the absolute obedience and need for command necessary for the one as appropriate for the other. When the unruliness of politics is assimilated to the discipline of an army, the polis becomes, as Haemon says, "a barren desert."

Of course, order is a value. But Creon's drive for linguistic, political, and even metaphysical mastery is a category mistake like the one Aristotle says is made by those who value wealth and property above all else. While it is true that a good life requires a certain amount of wealth, it does not follow that the more wealth one has the better the life one leads. Indeed, there is a point at which wealth comes to control the wealth seeker, so that instead of being liberal, the virtue wealth makes possible, the rich man becomes ungenerous, and all his other human capacities become instruments in the pursuit of it.[48] Creon assumes that, because some degree of order is necessary for politics, the more order he can establish the more secure politics will be. But there is something distinctive, even paradoxical, about a *political* order, as I suggested in arguing that what is political is itself a political question. Politics requires insecurity and rests on contingency in a way that makes political order both a necessity and an oxymoron. The messiness and transformative dimension to politics, particularly democratic politics, cannot be contained either by the singularity of Creon's world or the opposition to it, which remains implicated in that world because of its opposition.[49]

Similar things can be said about loyalty and patriotism. Both are admirable political virtues. But what this means in practice is obviously contestable: Socrates regards himself, with only a trace of irony, as the true Athenian patriot, and one could make a similar case for Antigone. More than that, men and women cannot be identified with their place within a political order or civic ideology in

[47] See Nussbaum in *The Fragility of Goodness,* p. 58. It is true, as critics of Antigone remind us, that she comes from a cursed family. But if we think of Oedipus's crime of incest politically as indicating a community that has turned back in on itself, thereby becoming too homogenous and unified, then Creon's insistence on order and singularity mark him as a member of the family.

[48] Aristotle, *Politics* 2.1263a–b, 1265a.

[49] For an argument about democracy as a transformative culture, see Sheldon S. Wolin's "Norm and Form: The Constitutionalizing of Democracy," in J. Peter Euben, John R. Wallach, and Josiah Ober, eds., *Athenian Political Thought and the Reconstruction of American Democracy* (Ithaca: Cornell University Press, 1994), pp. 29–58.

the way Creon does. And the more power he uses to enforce this identity, the louder his silencing of alternative speech, the more aggressively he banishes presence to absence, the more what is banished and silenced returns to the center, to haunt the "wise," "sane," "rational" king with "rememories"[50] of things past.

Creon is not only antipolitical; he is antidemocratic as well,[51] a fact that would likely have been recognized by the Athenian audience, since his claim to have the exclusive right to speak the truth for the city is taking place in front of an audience that, in its own deliberations, stressed the communal definition of *alētheia*.[52] Indeed, tragedy itself presupposed such a view. In the theater the vision of each character is limited, as opposed to that of the audience, whose members' more encompassing perspective enables them to compare, criticize, and gradually assemble a composite vision of the whole denied the actors on stage. If meaning exists in the ensemble of characters and points of view, the claim to exclusive knowledge and absolute truth Creon makes in the play is undercut by the conditions of performance of the drama in which he makes it.

Creon's antipoliticalness—his assimilation of politics to the command and obedience of an army, the hierarchy of a rigidly patriarchal family, and to the

---

[50] The word is Toni Morrison's; see, for instance, her novel *Beloved* (New York: Knopf, 1987).

[51] Saxonhouse (*Fear of Diversity*) argues that Creon's crude response to Ismene—there are other fields for him to plow—echoes "democracy's emphasis on interchangeability rather than particularity" and that his tyrannical ways of "equalizing all without attention to family background" is "an embodiment of the democratic ethos as it came to be understood in Athens." This is perhaps true of Plato but hardly of democrats themselves. Although sortition and rotation in office presumed *isonomia,* an equality under and through the law, and ties of marriage (as distinct from blood ties) involved a certain interchangeability, the assumption that all citizens possessed sufficient wisdom to share in the opportunities and responsibilities of power did not rest on the claim of sameness but on difference. This took the form of two complementary presuppositions, one negative, the other positive. The negative one argued that whatever inequalities of status and wealth might exist, no citizen was so superior or inferior to another that their differences could translate into substantial inequalities of political power. All citizens must, in form and in public, treat each other with respect and dignity. More positively, it was precisely the fact of individual differences within a shared culture that made deliberation and debate necessary as well as possible. If only one point of view mattered, then only one person need speak. But where there were distinct points of view about what should be done, and each was involved in the doing, then all might have something worth saying whether in the smaller political units of the deme, or in the city *boulē* juries or, less frequently in Assembly. The idea of *isēgoria*—the right to speak freely to power—embodies both these negative and positive notions of equality. It was a right not to be intimidated by power and to participate in the collective determination of policy, both of which Creon repudiates. Even ostracism, which did temporarily banish those thought to be oversized for the polis, and the *graphē paranomōn,* which seems to have replaced it, presumed individual accountability, as of course did the *dokimasia* and *euthunai* discussed in chapter four. And while it is true that in a patrilineal society brothers or even uncles and cousins could be expected to marry and replace a dead husband, Creon's statement is nonetheless crude given what seems a relationship based on affection. Evidence for her argument is Demosthenes' oration *On the Embassy,* which specifically relies on Creon's speech. But by the fourth century, speeches from tragedies had become rhetorical tropes without particular regard for context, much as quotations from Lincoln are for us today.

[52] See Josiah Ober, "How to Criticize Democracy and Late Fifth- and Fourth-Century Athens," in Euben et al., *Athenian Political Thought,* pp. 149–71, and Richard Emil Braun's introduction to *Sophocles'* Antigone (New York: Oxford University Press, 1989).

sway humans have over beasts of burden—is not simply driven by some perverse desire to rule, but includes a desire to secure his new authority and master the disorder experienced in the just concluded civil war. The desire and so the mistakes are, as I have suggested, linguistic and epistemological as well as political. In each linked domain Creon would be absolutely sovereign. Though he counsels and sees himself embodying receptivity to advice and straight speech, he does not listen, hears only what he wants to hear and commands others to speak only when and in ways he thinks acceptable, and erases their presence (in both senses) by linguistic fiat. He is sure he knows all that needs to be known with a knowingness that transforms advice into disloyalty, pluralism into anarchy, and the sharing of power into a personal affront and incipient civil war. "Real" politics requires that things, events, and people be or become measurable and commensurable, and action be or be made calculable (a view explored in Plato's *Protagoras* and chapter nine). This demands that differences such as those of gender, age, and power be conceptualized as polarities, themselves recast as hierarchies and entered in a ledger as a security debit or asset. What does not fit is exorcised, what does not conform is silenced, what resists entry in a security index is banished to the house, to a living death in the darkened cave, or to oblivion.

When Creon hears that the corpse has been buried despite his decree, he is furious at the act and at the chorus's mere suggestion that some god might have a hand in it. It is the doing of those in the city who disapprove of his actions and refuse to "bow justly beneath the yoke and submit to me" (323). These men have bribed the perpetrators. But he will pay them back for what they have been paid to do. Yet he quickly discovers that the threat is closer to home and more dangerous than the shameless pursuit of profit; it involves a principled public defiance of his edict by his own niece. Antigone assures Creon that she knew about the decree, and so her public admission of defying it is a public challenge to which Creon swears "that she not I am the man if she can triumph and not pay for what she has done" (484–85). So he banishes her from the public world, sending her back inside the house where women belong so she will know her place (in both senses). And he forbids anyone to speak of her; "she no longer exists." Such is the power of a king's words that it can erase a life.

It has been argued that Creon's actions toward Antigone mirror the sequestering and silencing of women in Athens; that his control of her is also a controlling of female reproductive power, and that he is simply giving voice to the common male fear that, as Roger Just puts it, "the love, the passion, the emotionalism which such women as Antigone introduce into the affairs of men [are] destructive forces."[53] While the actual historical picture is more complicated, none of these complications alters the radical inequalities of power and cultural inferiority women suffered in ancient Athens. But it is not clear that the play endorses that policy. Certainly the men in the play are no less emotional and passionate than the women nor, surely, any wiser or saner. And if Martha Nussbaum is right, that

---

[53] Roger Just, *Women in Athenian Law and Life* (New York: Routledge, 1991), p. 205.

the chorus regards seeing and passionate weeping as intimately connected such that a purely intellectual (male?) reading of events (and the play) would be a partial one, if "impeding the flow of tears inhibits getting all that the text offers,"[54] then those lacking passion and emotion—Just's men—cannot understand the world they would master. Then there is the simple "fact" that the silencing of this woman leads to disaster for the polis, and that the only chance the city had to save itself from calamity is to listen to a woman who would not accept her place.

Creon is not merely seeking to erase "a woman" who also happens to be his niece; he is also trying to obliterate his future daughter-in-law. He is utterly unmoved by his son's love for Antigone since, as he crudely puts it, "there are other fields for him to plow," after saying which, he orders all to be silent about the marriage as he turns, uncertain of what awaits him, to confront his son.

Haemon enters and assures his father that he comes not to protest the decree or the death of his betrothed. He proclaims his steadfast loyalty to his father, the man whose excellent judgment shows him the right path to follow (*kai su moi gnōmas echōn chrēstas aporthois, hais egōg' ephepsomai*) (635–36). No competing obligation, including that of marriage, will move him to disregard the wisdom of his father. Creon is, of course, delighted with this response of absolute obedience, even though he had previously regarded the unconditional family support he now expects as undesirable. Sons who make everything else secondary to their father's will are an answer to a parent's prayer since they insure that he will have allies to stand with his friends and against his enemies. In the specific context the enemy is Antigone, both her evil act of disobedience and her evil speech that justified it. So Creon takes his son's sentiments as legitimating his own—that because Antigone has disobeyed the head of her *oikos* and polis, she is doubly condemned[55] and he is doubly threatened if she escapes.

> [I]f I nurture those of my house
> to be rebellious and disorderly,[56]
> surely I will encourage the same outside it.
> For he who is in his household an upright and useful man
> will also be found to be just in regard to the city.
> But he that oversteps the law or does it violence [*huperbas ē nomous biazetai*]
> or thinks to overrule his rulers
> shall never receive a good word from me.
> The man the city sets up in authority
> must be obeyed in great and small just and unjust things alike.
>
> (659–67)

Creon is sure that only such a man can be a good ruler (or subject), and that standing as a loyal friend to one's city against those vile transgressors who would destroy it by their disobedience is the height of justice and righteousness.

---

[54] Nussbaum in *The Fragility of Goodness*, p. 70. She is glossing lines 802–5.

[55] So, too, is Polyneices, who is killed twice.

[56] The word used here—*akosma*—means unruly and anarchistic.

The chorus approves of this speech as it did not Creon's opening one, though it will also approve of Haemon's which has a quite different purpose and tone and offers a radically different view of politics, language, and political knowledge. Haemon is exceedingly deferential and, given what we have seen and heard from Creon, we know why. Only protestations of unequivocal obedience can establish one's right to speak and stay Creon's rage. Only extraordinary tact will enable one to speak to one who only wishes to speak, to counsel one who only wishes to command, and to disagree with one who takes any sign of disagreement as life-threatening disloyalty. (Creon does thank the chorus for reminding him that Ismene is innocent.)

So Haemon begins cautiously and modestly, suggesting that someone else might have something useful to say, and that there are other voices than that of the ruler. What those voices say in private whispers is not what Creon wants to hear, which is why they are afraid to say it in front of the man who purportedly endorses straight speech but whose reaction to the sentry and the chorus's wondering about a god burying Polyneices indicates otherwise. What the people are intimidated from saying in public is that Antigone is dying undeservedly. What she insists on doing—burying her brother so he will not be food for wild animals—merits glory, not censure for a woman.

Creon only sees this as a threat to his authority and to the order he is committed to achieving. What he does not realize is that his inability to hear what is being said and the alacrity with which he dismisses contrary views as the product of impure motives (in contrast to his own unsullied principles) make him a threat to himself. He has built a political, moral, and epistemological moat around himself that seals off the complexities of his actions and his world. What need is there to listen to those who are bribed (the sentry and Tiresias), consumed by lust (his son), and mad (Antigone); or to those, such as women and the young, who are naturally inferior.

Political wisdom, Haemon argues, cannot be singular and monological or set in a discourse of command and obedience appropriate to an army but is, rather, plural and multiple. Similarly, political knowledge is, to recall Ober's phrase, constituted and reconstituted "through collective practices of public communication rather than being given by an external authority or discovered through intellectual effort." In these terms political knowledge is political not only because of its subject matter, but because of the way it is constituted and expressed. To strive for political and intellectual mastery, as Creon does, is to act antipolitically in the sense that it will destroy the city as well as the household upon which the city depends. While knowledge does bring power, political knowledge comes from yielding to other voices and positions, sharing public space with others rather than consigning them to shadows and whispers (the people of Thebes) or caves and houses (Antigone and Ismene).

Haemon uses two similes to convince his father to yield some of his anger and benefit from the counsel of others (which is what the king promised to do in his first speech).[57] In the first, he likens the passion for order to a tree that refuses to

---

[57] Haemon's similes are similar to the story of Niobe and to Tiresias's way of knowing. In all these

bend in a torrent and is, because of its rigidity, uprooted and swept away. In the second, he compares Creon's intransigence to that of a ship's captain who fails to slacken his sail in a storm and so capsizes the boat. It is an image that comes to haunt this captain, who boasts of guiding the ship of state into safe harbor. But to the extent that the sea was a symbol of elemental forces (including human passions) and that Athens was a sea power, the warning it represents may have had particular force.

Creon finds this view of political power, political knowledge, and wisdom intolerable. It complicates what he has tried to make simple, and challenges his authority to establish the parameters for what counts as knowledge, wisdom, and reason. Where he wants things calculable and certain, Haemon has introduced complexity and uncertainty. Where he seeks the power to rule (in both senses) and a political arithmetic of security,[58] his son insists on the plurality of political life, which makes such a search difficult if not self-defeating and unreasonable. So it is unsurprising that Creon is as impatient with the chorus's admonition to listen to his son as he was to its suggestion of a god's involvement in the burying of Polyneices. Learning that the people do not support him, he dismisses them as well as his son who reported it. He, not they, rules; it is his judgment that matters and their loyalty to him that constitutes civic virtue; he owns the city, not they. To Haemon's "there is no city possessed by one man only," Creon protests that the city is thought to be and does indeed belong to the ruler.[59]

The exchange between father and son becomes vituperative. The father accuses the son of partisanship, effeminacy for being a woman's slave, and presumptuousness for daring to offer him counsel and plans to exact his revenge by ordering Antigone brought out and killed before him.[60] For his part, the son lectures his father and insists that the father's acts are mistaken and unjust, that his edict dishonors the gods, calls his father's judgments senseless (or insane), and admonishes him for only wanting to talk but never to listen (*Boulei legein ti kai legōn mēden kluein*, 757).[61]

What makes the escalating animosity disconcerting is that each assigns radically different meanings to a shared vocabulary. In successive couplets in the stichomythia (726–65), "each responds by recapitulating a word or phrase from the previous line in order to call its usage into question or to redefine

cases, man does not dominate nature but learns from it sympathetically. This is distinct both from Creon's view and the celebration of *technai* in the choral ode in praise of man.

[58] See the discussion in Dillon, *Politics of Security*.

[59] See note 41.

[60] Van Nes Ditmars is less sympathetic to Haemon. Haemon starts by being conciliatory but ends condescendingly by lecturing his father, "This young man is too clever by far for his own good." His eloquence comes from "strong convictions and his support of abstract principle bespeaks a confidence in the power of reason to solve even the greatest difficulties, a confidence whereby youth falls afoul of age" (*Sophocles' Antigone*, pp. 101–2).

[61] "Creon's attempt to be first in Thebes is expressed primarily through his efforts to control speech. His reaction to the prophet is not an isolated incident, but the climax of his effort to speak with a king's voice, and eventually with the voice of a god" (Rebecca W. Bushnell, *Prophesying Tragedy: Sign and Voice in Sophocles' Theban Plays* [Ithaca: Cornell University Press, 1988], p. 50).

it."[62] Each challenges the other on a range of terms from abstract to concrete, from metaphysical to literal, and from religious to secular in an effort to establish a political discourse according to their respective views of the polis. Each tries to capture the honorific status of justice, wisdom, judgment, and honor in order to legitimate his own view of public life. For Haemon such contests are part of public life. But for Creon the very contest of terms is a sign of rampant anarchy that must be suppressed. So he orders Haemon to speak to him in a certain way as he had ordered the guard, the chorus, and Ismene; all this remember from a man who had offered fearless speaking as a criterion of patriotism.

But this demand for a single way of speaking does not create the unity and order he wishes but further fragments Thebes in a way that precludes the possibility of repairing the divisions that have set citizen against citizen, and brother against brother. The struggle over words mirrors the struggle over how to rebuild a shattered city, and as the war of words becomes more violent, it recalls Thucydides' description of the fate of language at Corcyra.

The exchange between Creon and Haemon suggests that sameness and interchangeability can mask different features (as with theatrical performances)—more specifically, that repetition of terms can obscure incompatible principles and interests. What seems to be or should be a firm basis for deliberation, shared language and culture, turns out to be divisive. Moreover, the person who strives most for transparent discourse is Creon. Yet his commitment to reason is intended to close off and close down what does not fit in his world and with his words. It is a complement to his drive for mastery, order, and the establishment of a speech about security within which "legitimate" speech can take place.

It is just as disconcerting to realize that the one seemingly unproblematic moment in the play—Haemon's defense of collective wisdom, reasonableness, and democratic deliberation—stands inside the play's action rather than outside it. When Haemon praises the man who is wise because he is never so rigid that he shuts others out, will not yield to sound advice, and refuses to be flexible in changing circumstances, it is not only an obvious condemnation of his father but an oblique one of Antigone (as well as his own subsequent actions). What would happen to Antigone (and *Antigone*) if she was "reasonable," flexible, sensible and yielded easily to circumstances rather than being in love with the impossible? "Moderation" may not be a vice, but it can be bad advice, and its invocation too easily ignores the fanaticism of order, the cruelty of the normal.

Haemon also uses reason strategically to disarm his father, who cannot be talked to any other way because of his power. More than that, this man of reasonableness is subject to uncontrollable rage, which though provoked by the callousness of his father, nonetheless indicates a connection between reason and unreason, passion and knowledge. What he says and does is framed by *erōs* (his love for Antigone) and hatred (of his father). The connection is elaborated in the juxtaposition of the chorale ode in praise of man's celebration of human intellect to the violent outbursts that precede it. In the ode man claims control of nature;

---

[62] Slatkin, "Sophocles' *Antigone*," p. 5.

yet the play suggests he cannot control himself, an irony present in the words used to describe man's civic and legal temper (*orgas*), which also means anger, and thought (*phronēma*), which also means pride.

After the exchange with Haemon, Creon leaves the stage only to return for a brief final confrontation with Antigone, whose lament he takes to be a death-delaying ploy, which he impatiently silences. He will not, as he had previously announced, have her publicly stoned to death—a prudent retreat given what we have heard about public sentiment in her favor—but will send her instead to a walled cave in which she can choose a buried life or death. In that way no stain of guilt will be upon him; or so he thinks.

As Antigone is led off, Tiresias is led on, unsummoned. The prophet seeks assurance of Creon's forbearance since he knows that what he will recount will be unwelcome. The story he tells is of what cannot be told, of unspeakable things unspoken, in Morrison's phrase. He tells of signs that paradoxically signal lack of signs, of the unintelligible screams of birds, gorged with the flesh of Polyneices, driven to a frenzy of mutual destruction that mimics both the civil war and the mutual destruction we are witnessing among men and women on stage. All he knows is that the sacrifices he offered to the gods were aborted by sputtering fires. This can only mean the presence of some mortal sickness in the city of which Creon, its leader, is the cause. With equal urgency but more authority, Tiresias repeats Haemon's advice about taking advice. That Creon has, like other men, made mistakes is no disaster. But failing to acknowledge them is. The king is poised upon a "razor's edge" (*xurou*).

By allowing the city's altars to be contaminated with Polyneices' flesh, Creon has blocked communication between mortals and gods, silencing the latter as he does the citizens of the city and Antigone. The murderous conflict among the birds extends the civil war into nature, with their songs intelligible only as signifiers of violent disorder.

Creon at first responds to Tiresias in his usual fashion. Tiresias is bribed, is only pretending to be giving good counsel, and is seeking his own profit. He will no more be ruled by the pious platitudes of a money-mad seer than he would by the words of women (who happen to be his niece and future daughter-in-law), by a young man (who happens to be his son), or by the people of Thebes (who happen to be his fellow citizens).

But when Tiresias recounts the king's transgressions in confounding the lower and upper worlds by burying the living and refusing to bury the dead, lists the punishments that await such deeds—the death of his child, the collapse of his city, the revenge of all those cities whose sons will be unable to receive proper burial because Polyneices does not—and when the chorus reminds him that the prophet has always been right in the past, Creon reluctantly "yields"[63] as a dreadful necessity.

---

[63] Creon's words here (*eikathein, paraikathein* from the verb *eikō*) not only mean to draw back or give way, but also to submit, obey, and follow. So his yielding would mean giving up his entire conception of politics and the "ontological" structure by which he has organized his life and rule.

Though Creon agrees to follow the chorus's advice and release the girl[64] and bury her brother, it is too late. The man who would save the city has destroyed it and turned himself into a breathing corpse like the niece he has condemned. The ruler once blessed with power is powerless to save the city he was dedicated to protect and the *oikos* he headed from the consequences of his own deeds. Creon had claimed a monopoly of wisdom and rationality but it is he who is "ill-minded" (*kakophron*), thoughtless (*aboulia*), and driven to condemn his own mistaken counsel (*dusboulia*).

The chorus says Creon has "come to know (or see) justice" (*dikēn idiein*). Yet there is something perfunctory and brittle about his acknowledgment of insufficiency and his defeat.[65] Though he echoes Oedipus (in *Oedipus Tyrannus*) in calling himself "nothing more than nothing," the collapse is too quick and complete, and the final figure lacks the dignity of that accursed king. Perhaps the difference lies in the way they have been wrong and the purposes to which their heroic obstinacy has been put. If I am right, Creon has been wrong from the beginning, wrong in general and in particular, wrong in his conception of politics and language, wrong in his strategy and his epistemology. He has, one could say, been mastered by his drive for mastery, defeated because he sought to measure all variation and diversity by a single standard and so drives the ship of state straight into the path of a death-dealing storm. However noble or necessary the effort to establish order(s) without contradiction and contest may be, there is no single measure within which differences can be assayed, compared, and domesticated. This incommensurability, rather than being a threat to politics, seems to be part of its substance.

V

But if Creon is wrong, is Antigone right[66] and is there all that much difference between them? She seems as single-minded as he is, as hard on Ismene as he is on her, as unyielding in her commitment to kin and Polyneices as he is to the city and Eteocles, as indifferent to the claims of culture as he is to those of nature. Oedipus's daughter is, after all, Creon's niece. It is enough to give family resemblances and family values a bad name.

Antigone's first words express an intense loving identity with her sister. She invites Ismene to join her in a plan to bury the body of their dead brother despite Creon's edict, thus proving worthy of their noble line. No one, she says, no human power, can "keep me from my own" (48) and if she must die for this "pious crime," she shall die loving him as he loved her. Nor can any human power keep her from

---

[64] The few references to Antigone in the last third of the play are equally indirect and abstract.

[65] Thus A.J.A. Waldock (in *Sophocles: The Dramatist* [Cambridge: Cambridge University Press, 1950]) regards Creon as "an uninteresting man," while Cedric Whitman (*Sophocles: A Study in Heroic Humanism* [Cambridge, Mass.: Harvard University Press, 1951]), Brian Vickers (*Towards Greek Tragedy*), and G. M. Kirkwood (*A Study in Sophoclean Drama* [Ithaca: Cornell University Press, 1958]) regard him as shallow and superficial.

[66] Winnington-Ingram (in *Sophocles*) suggests that the answer is more interesting than the question.

proclaiming her deed once done. She will not be silenced by fear or paralyzed by suffering, but will act with the nobility befitting a daughter of Oedipus.

Yet this loving sister turns on the sisterly object of her love with an implacable fury that shatters the just posited identity into chards. In its ferocity and in its radical transformation of a too loving unity into a too fierce hatred, the turning is an unsettling echo of incest and patricide, reminding us, as if we needed reminding, of exactly the noble line from which Antigone comes. To live up to *her* parents' deeds and honor their memory is, to put it mildly, a morally ambiguous ambition. But perhaps her repeated invocation of her parents and, by extension, of their transgressions explains her intransigent piety; as if it can somehow compensate for the family crimes and so finally end the curse upon the house.[67] Perhaps her death is a sacrifice to restore honor to and unite her dishonored and divided household.

It also reminds us that the just concluded fratricidal war is far from over. The conflict that pitted brother against brother now pits sister against sister, and, more significantly, niece against uncle. The form their battle takes is a war of words where each is locked in their respective semantic codes. Their inability to communicate with each other is made all the more vivid by their emphasis on verbal accord, their agreement on what has taken place, and on the way to describe it. In part, they are at cross purposes and talk past each other. But, in part, their effort to establish competing definitions for crucial terms such as friend, law, piety, honor, and even life and death means that their lexical antagonism represents incompatible values and points of view.

Ismene does not see Antigone as restoring honor to their house. Given their history, one must be leery of such dark thoughts. She reminds Antigone of their parents' violent deeds and dishonored deaths and of how their brothers killed each other, thus implying that Antigone is repeating the family curse at the very moment she supposes herself to be acting independently of it. Besides, it is "unnatural" for women to disobey and so try to rule men. They are too weak and men too strong. Given the forces arrayed against them, their natural inferiority, and their past, "extravagant action is insane."[68] Still, if Antigone persists in her headstrong action of loving what is impossible, Ismene will not cease loving her. We know already that the reverse is not true.

Given what is proposed (a death-bringing defiance of the commander/king), who says it (a woman who is also the progeny of a perverse family), where it is

---

[67] Winnington-Ingram talks about "the heroic feat of Antigone, who is determined to cancel the hatreds of her house" (ibid., p. 132).

[68] A number of critics think Ismene right about Antigone, or at least that the latter's singular focus on burying her brother is a kind of madness. "In her effort to justify her sacrifice of marriage by making it consistent with her willingness to dismiss the political meaning of her action of burying Polynieces," Sheila Murnaghan writes, "she adopts the same limited perspective of which Creon is guilty, seeing marriage only as an impersonal institution and neglecting its personal dimension" (which is why she ignores Haemon). The "sterility of her logic expresses the sterility of her situation" ("Antigone 904–920 and the Institution of Marriage," *American Journal of Philology* 107 [1986]: 204–5). I think Murnaghan only partly right for reasons suggested by Neuberg. (On the issue of madness, see Annie Pritchard, "Antigone's Mirrors: Reflections on Moral Madness," *Hypatia* 7, no. 3 [1992]: 77–93.)

said (outside the prescribed places for women), and how it is said (conspiratorially), there seems little doubt that Antigone's "proposed behavior and action would have been perceived by the Athenians as illegitimately subversive of the polis."[69] Having strayed from the culturally prescribed roles and spheres of activity, she seems an an-archic force,[70] threatening to breach the polis's defenses by opening up the city to the destructive passions it has supposedly banished. Such a threat must be "silenced, nullified, or destroyed."[71]

The transgressive quality of Antigone's unwomanliness is emphasized by the contrast with Ismene "who seems indisputably a 'woman' in her weakness, her fear, her submissive obedience, her tears, madness, hysteria." Where Antigone speaks her mind in public, defying Creon's claim to legitimate power, Ismene exemplifies the quintessentially "feminine" virtue of obedience.[72] Where Antigone does extreme things by acting beyond her proper sphere and being overvaliant (*perissa prassein*) and in love with the impossible (*amēchanōn erais*), Ismene is willing to endure women's weakness.[73]

But Athenians regarded women not only as threats to be shut up but as representatives of enduring more "natural" values than those by which men live. In these terms, what is wrong with Antigone is not her appeal to the unwritten laws, her love for her *philoi* and desire to bury her dead brother, but the unwomanly way she goes about doing these "womanly" things. Even at their most sympathetic, the chorus reads Antigone's deed this way. No one recognizes why and how her defense of family and private life has led her into the public realm (which is from one point of view the private realm of men), and why she is a "political actress," a peculiarity in English that captures the Greek oddity of a woman making a public challenge to male authority. This woman is a threat not only to a male in power but to the hypermasculinist conception of politics and security, which constitutes his regime and discourse.

No one recognizes the public dimension of her challenge except Creon. Whatever his myopia, and however excessive or self-serving his responses and definitions may be, he sees the public nature of Antigone's act and the ramifications of her defending it in public. His fierce insistence that she be silenced, closed up, and isolated (*mēd' aneimenas*) is due to his fear that she will "contaminate the citizens' opinions."[74] It may well be that "demands for equality and autonomous self-representation improved woman's lot only at the expense of further entrenching a male norm."[75] But that is not how Creon perceives it or the play

[69] Sourvinou-Inwood, "Assumptions," p. 139.

[70] There is a democratic and genealogical reading of "anarchy" insofar as the word means without an *archē*—that is, a beginning or leader—and suggests the possibility of many leaders and beginnings.

[71] O'Brien, *Guide*, p. 17.

[72] Irigaray in *Speculum of the Other Woman*, trans. Gillian C. Gill, (Ithaca: Cornell University Press, 1986), pp. 217–18. Irigaray argues that Antigone is "shut up" in both senses of the phrase.

[73] *Peisomai* means I shall obey, but also I shall endure.

[74] See Bushnell, *Prophesying Tragedy*, p. 66.

[75] Rosalyn Diprose, "In Excess: The Body and the Habit of Sexual Difference," *Hypatia* 6, no. 3 (Fall 1991): 156–57.

presents it. In fact the play confounds the norms. After all it is the male Creon who makes the polis vulnerable to "womanly" vices, and the "woman" Antigone who would have saved it if she had prevailed, which is not to say that this was her explicit aim.

Antigone does *begin* by doing what women are expected to do. But because Creon's decree politicizes love of family and the rootedness of the city in the household, she is forced to valorize what she would otherwise have taken for granted. But "forced" is misleading on two counts. First, she has a choice despite the family curse. Ismene and Antigone are two sisters with the same heredity and experience, confronted by the same situation. But the past dictates submission to the one and fierce opposition to the other.[76] Second, despite the fact that her action is initially a reaction to Creon's decree, there is a sense in which Antigone chooses what had been declared "natural" for women, in the same way that a woman can be said to "choose" to have children now in a way that is quite different than forty years ago. This is not to deny the costs of the choice or the significance of what she chooses against, both of which Antigone seems to recognize in her final speech. It is to suggest, with Orlando Patterson, that "her condition as a woman has forced her, in shame and isolation to defy, to *make* a choice and in the process to create something new: the energizing of these values, once so passively assumed, and their recruitment as the special object and content of the newly discovered and idealized capacity to choose."[77]

To choose to reaffirm what had been simply prescribed, and, by that choice, to act rather than react suggests a "manly" courage others in the play lack. It is a woman who stands up to Creon and to his conception of political order, political wisdom, and political power. It is a woman who contests the discourse he insists is rational, and who refuses to be silenced, as she talks past him to the gods and anyone, including the audience, who can hear her through Creon's clamor. This is not to ignore her harshness toward Ismene, or her unyielding opposition between *philoi* and *echthroi*. Indeed I want to insist that her intransigence is what enables her to challenge Creon and his conception of politics; it is what underlies her effort to restore (or create) the integrity of public discourse and life. But I also want to insist that the radical inequality of power between Creon and Antigone distinguishes what is usually regarded as the common obstinacy that marks them both as members of the same family. It is one thing to be intransigent in the face of tyranny, another for the tyrant to be intransigent toward his subjects, and it is the simple failure to differentiate one from another that helped inspire Marx (especially in *On the Jewish Question*) and Martin Luther King Jr. (especially in a *Letter from a Birmingham Jail*). It is because of who she is socially and dramatically that what she says and does—her drive to see things through to the end, her rejection of life as compromise, and her acceptance of death when life ceases to measure up to her heroic standards—acquires such depth and power, not only in its challenge to Creon, but to the Hobbesian imperative to even out the cob-

---

[76] See the discussion in Winnington-Ingram, *Sophocles,* p. 128.

[77] Orlando Patterson, *Freedom in the Making of Western Culture* (New York: Basic Books, 1991), p. 130.

blestones in order to make transportation more efficient over the flattened landscape.

I do not mean to romanticize heroism,[78] dismiss the ideal of democratic deliberation, or ignore Antigone's narrowness, hatreds, or exclusive love for Polyneices, whose peculiar intensity seems a desperate grasp for moral ballast in a world where civil and familial wars have left her without standing. Yet it is this harsh woman who speaks against power unafraid, exemplifying two defining principles of Athenian democracy, *isēgoria* and *parrhēsia*.[79] True there is something incongruous about a woman being "the true citizen,"[80] but I am not sure it was any more incongruous than Socrates' claim for philosophers being such, or any more oxymoronic than the "pious crimes" for which Antigone is condemned to death.

The Antigone who appears for the last time speaks with the chorus alone, "stationed" as one critic puts it "in the full light of the city proper, in dialogue with its citizens."[81] Her first "dialogue" was with Ismene, the second with Creon, while this one is with the citizens of the polis. Thus her path is from the enclosure of the most immediate family, to a somewhat larger realm of kinship, to the public world. Though she never renounces the family in which murder and incest have defiled kinship and indeed reaffirms her acceptance of its "perverse" institutions,[82] whatever she says has a public dimension because of where and to whom she says it. Moreover, though she has not changed her mind about the rightness of her deed, the immanence of loss and isolation drive her to a new level of reflection and anguish.[83] Recognizing now what she has been forced but also chosen to exclude, she speaks in a more complex but equally intense way about herself and the world—familial, political, and cosmological—she is leaving behind.[84] Never will she hear the marriage song or the cries of her children silenced by the sacrifice she makes for her brother. Never again will she see the sun or the

[78] See Bernard Knox, *The Heroic Teacher: Studies in Sophocles* (Berkeley: University of California Press, 1964).

[79] See Lane and Lane, "The Politics of *Antigone*." Goheen argues that "every time women are not controlled," even when their protest is justifiable, "havoc ensues" (*Imagery,* p. 206). I am suggesting that it is Creon who creates havoc. For us, the question raised by the play is how to link action and publicity where institutionalized public spheres are deeply compromised, and the definition of what is properly public is hotly contested.

[80] "Antigone is denied personal and political autonomy in the city of Thebes—what she cannot have as a woman; yet at the same time Antigone maintains her freedom of speech in public, which was the essence of freedom in Athens, where the worst punishment of exile was considered the loss of parrhēsia or free speech" (Bushnell, *Prophesying Tragedy,* pp. 64–65).

[81] Marilyn Katz, "The Character of Tragedy: Women and the Greek Imagination," *Arethusa* 27, no. 1 (Winter 1994): 92.

[82] Ibid., p. 95.

[83] In her final speech, Antigone "does not exemplify the eternal feminine figure who foregoes the political for the human and religious. She is the true citizen, male or female, whose philia leads her to see and perform her moral duty despite the consequences. She is in charge of her own destiny and yet submissive to the greater power of the gods" (O'Brien, *Guide,* p. 115).

[84] I have said little about what seems Antigone's perverse focus on burying Polyneices, because I find Murnaghan wholly persuasive about how, when, and why Antigone comes to the view and action she does.

faces of her fellow citizens or the sacred waters and groves of her beloved city. Never will she gain old age or an end to suffering except in her perverse marriage to death.[85] She thinks herself utterly alone—a metic bereft of fellow citizens, a pious woman without any sign of approval from the gods she has championed; reviled by the king and castigated by a chorus of men.[86] What can it mean for a woman who defines herself by *philia* and *erōs* to find herself completely alone? What must it feel like for one dying for the honor of a family she hopes to join to find her punishment changed from public stoning, which would have meant immediate death and a reunion with parents and brothers, to a living death in a desolate cave apart from the living and the dead?

Yet true to this new complexity, Antigone appeals to her fellow citizens and expresses the love for her city that had been largely absent and certainly unspoken until now and which seemed to justify saying she "stands for" the household. In her final speech she brings these loves into juxtaposition if not loving reconciliation, expressing the sense of their mutual dependency that seems part of the play's point. Of course, dramatically this just heightens her isolation. Here is another affiliation she must leave behind. Every attachment affirmed defines another dimension of loss. Still, appealing to her fellow citizens confirms the publicness of her act which had appeared inadvertently political but now seems purposely so.

Before she exits the stage and the play, leaving Creon in power, she repeats, now as much in desperation as in righteousness, that her suffering is due to reverencing things that deserve it.

> If this proceeding is good in the gods' eyes
> I shall know my sin, once I have suffered.
> But if Creon and his people are the wrongdoers
> Let their suffering be no worse than the
> injustice
> they are meting out to me.
>
> (981–85)

It will be: but not yet.

At this point Creon's victory seems decisive. He is the dominant presence in the play and power in Thebes. He has far more lines than Antigone, enjoys all the official trappings of authority, and sets the terms of discourse and action to which others must respond and react. Moreover, he has isolated his niece from her living *philoi* and denied her marriage and family, which constituted much of the social definition of women in ancient Greece. And he has shunted aside the

---

[85] R. Seaford ("The Tragic Wedding," *Journal of Hellenic Studies* 107 [1987]: 16–17) talks about the ritual and social similarities between a woman's death and her marriage. In both she was "conveyed on an irreversible, torchlit journey accompanied by song, to be abandoned by her king to an unknown dwelling, an alien bed, and the physical control of an unknown male." It was common for an unwed girl who died to be buried in her wedding attire.

[86] She does not even have a chorus of women to give her comfort as so many heroines do.

public nature of her act, denying this "unwomanly woman"[87] a voice within his jealously guarded language. In the end she seems dissolved and fragmented, a self "riddled with complications dispersed into the chards of a broken mirror," to use Luce Irigaray's phrase.[88]

But it is her voice, not Creon's, that finally triumphs. Of course, she has powerful allies in the gods, though she receives no sign of approval from them. And Tiresias does vindicate her action, at least to the extent that the failure to bury Polyneices is the cause of Thebes's afflictions. Yet that does not exhaust her power.

Joan O'Brien finds Antigone's power in her androgyny, in her directing traditional masculine qualities—daring, hunting for the impossible, acting on one's own initiative, seeking glory in death—"to the feminine act of love."[89] Better, I think, to see her as figuring the unsettled arithmetic of self and security that defines men as well as women. Seen in this light her "loneliness is not a disease to be cured but a necessary element of all heroism, indeed, of all self-knowledge."[90] This is, I will argue in the next section, one implication of the chorale ode in praise of "man."

If I am right about Antigone, then the polarities between household and city, nature and culture, woman and man, *erōs* and reason, divine and human law are no more persuasive as an interpretive scaffold from the standpoint of the characterization of Antigone than they were from the standpoint of Creon. In part, this is a matter of each principle generating its own antithesis or revealing an erotic attachment to its contrary. But in part, it is a question of the language or opposition being too tied to and so implicated in the language of order delegitimated by Creon's endorsement of it. As I shall suggest in the next section's consideration of the choral ode in praise of man, this way of thinking about politics and the play lacks fluidity and dimension.

As Antigone is led off, Creon remains behind triumphant. Yet his words dismissing her are inadvertently building a case against himself far stronger than the case he thinks he is building against her. When he predicts the fate of those whose hardness makes them break all the more completely, he anticipates Haemon's advice to him (which he ignores) of having his own life shattered. And when he moves from likening Antigone to iron to seeing her as a slave and animal appropriately yoked to his power, he is positing transgressive inequalities whose consequences we can infer from the preceding choral ode and see displayed in the subsequent action. Penultimately, when he proudly proclaims that no ties of kin will deter him from issuing rightful sentences of death, he is, like Oedipus calling down fierce imprecations on the killer of Laius, unaware of his guilt, since in sentencing Antigone to death, he is, in effect, pronouncing the

---

[87] What Clytaemnestra is called in Aeschylus's *Oresteia.*

[88] In Richard A. Cohen, ed., *Face to Face with Levinas* (Albany, N.Y.: SUNY Press, 1986), p. 238.

[89] O'Brien, *Guide,* pp. 5–6. The problem with calling Antigone androgynous or endorsing androgyny where there is a radical inequality of sexes and unequal validation of genders is that, as Marx recognized in *On the Jewish Question,* what seems to be an equal partnership is, in fact, an inscription of inequalities made more insidious by the abstract denial of their existence.

[90] O'Brien, *Guide.*

same punishment for his son and wife. Finally, while Creon may regard Antigone as the amorphous anarchic symbol of womanly power, it is worth recalling that conservatives regarded Athenian democracy the same way.

This reminds us that Antigone is not alone. We have heard from others in the play that the citizens do honor her, and we have reason to suppose that even the male citizens in the audience would find much to admire in her words and deeds no matter how unenthusiastic they would be about anything approaching the full political equality of women. But there are the audiences since, women as well as men, who move with and are moved by Antigone. For them it is she, not Creon, who has the last word.

Creon had sought to erase the (for him and perhaps most Greek men) disturbing fact of female procreative power and permanently preclude the transfer of that power into public space and action. Yet when Hannah Arendt uses the metaphor of natality to elaborate her notion of action, she makes just such a transfer. Action initiates what is new in the world, beginning what cannot be given final definition because intentions can only be accomplished with the active support of others who are themselves actors. Antigone, as play and character, is such an action. And when Arendt goes on to speak of action as a miracle because it cannot be predicted from any prior set of conditions (though analysts looking back on it necessarily see it as such), she provides another layer of meaning to Antigone's being in love with the impossible, with those moments or incidents that, like the democracy demonstrations in Tiananmen Square, seem "too unlikely, too accidental, too erratic, or coincidental to carry any real history with them."[91]

Of course, all this seems pure romanticism. At the end of the play Creon returns without Antigone's body, and no one mentions her, either in the final kommos or even in the earlier scene when the messenger reports the deaths of Haemon and Eurydice. "She lies at the play's end in a climate of total neglect."[92] Yet the play's ending is hardly the end.

VI

The choral ode in praise of man provides an "ontological" dimension to the conflicts that define the play while simultaneously redefining them. It does so by providing a third center of gravity, that of humankind itself.[93] From this point of

---

[91] The quotation is from Greil Marcus, *The Dustbin of History* (Cambridge, Mass.: Harvard University Press, 1995), p. 9. For Arendt's characterization of an action see *The Human Condition*, pp. 8–9, 177–78. In *Money, Sex and Power: Toward a Feminist Historical Materialism* (New York: Longman, 1982), Nancy Hartsock appropriates Arendt for a feminist politics against critiques of her by Mary O'Brien and Adrienne Rich. Arendt has received a second incarnation as an inspiration for feminist theory though the present emphasis is often on her early, less philosophical works.

[92] O'Brien, *Guide*, p. 114.

[93] But even here a note of caution is necessary. The chorus is not necessarily a spokesman for Sophocles, and as Michael Santirocco has pointed out (in "Justice in Sophocles' *Antigone*," *Philosophy and Literature* 4 [1980]: 180–98), *all* three choral odes leave the identity of their referents in doubt.

view, the passion for security and order is seen as a denial of the "strangeness" of man, a refusal to countenance a metaphysical homelessness which is a fact of mortal existence and a precondition for freedom, agency, and responsibility. That strangeness, signified by the Greek *deinos* and its cognates, is not only developed by what the chorus says in the ode, but by the ode's place in the play; by what comes before and after it, and by the way it draws together and deepens the drama's images of birds and seas, plowing and yoking, storms and disease.

The ode can also be read as a commentary on the relationship between politics and language, at least given that the ode presents most impressive civilizing achievements as the acquisition of language and the "disposition" (or "temper") that regulates citizens. These achievements are not represented as successive stages in a process of becoming civilized but as complementary aspects of a single dynamic.[94] This fact together with the bivalent meanings of *deinos* is another reason why I entitle this chapter the languages of politics.

> Many the wonders [*deina*] but none
> is more wondrous [*deinoteron*] than man.
> He crosses the sea in the winter's storm
> making his path through the roaring waves.
> It is the Earth, the oldest of gods
> ageless and unwearied that he wears away
> as the ploughs go up and down from year to year
> when he works with the breed that comes from horses.

$$(332–41)$$

Deinon and its cognates can mean that which inspires awe and wonder, such as the brilliance of the human mind and technical ingenuity, both of which allow men to create an earthly home. In this tonality, *deinon* indicates mastery and control, resourcefulness and daring, culture and civilization. But it can also mean what is terrible and fearful, monstrous and evil, self-annihilating and powerlessness in the face of implacable fate. In this tonality, it is the other and under side of achievement, the transgression that shadows progress and power, the hatred inside love and the passions inside reason, and the untamed wildness at the center of the city.[95]

Men and women are out of place and sequence, ill-fitting even when at home. That is because, unlike all other creatures, they are unnatural. They disturb the earth to make themselves a home and modify their own nature to become speech giving and polis living. For Heidegger, *deinon* denotes the violence of power which refuses conventional compromise, mutual aid, and security, the sinister uneasiness (*das unheimliche*) which casts humans out of the home their unnatural nature creates out of culture. This refusal of the customary, familiar, and secure,

---

[94] Slatkin, "Sophocles' *Antigone*," p. 1.

[95] In his essay on the ode, "Sophocles' Praise of Man," Segal argues that when Creon allows the body of Polyneices to be devoured by birds and dogs he is "reversing the process of civilization itself." "The exposed corpse," he continues, "is a possible cause . . . of the outbreak against man of all the uncontrollable mysterious forces on which his survival depends" (p. 48).

and the self-division and self-exile it bespeaks, is, he argues, implicit in the life of consciousness and our capacity to think outside or even against ourselves.

If Heidegger is right that this "stranger in the house of being" sets "forth into the un-said," "breaks into the un-thought, compels the unhappened to happen and makes the unseen appear,"[96] then we can be our own worst enemy and there is an ambivalence present in the drive for security that reflects that of *deinos*. To begin with, the passion to be secure(d) means both being safe and being tied down, which makes the imagery of snares and nets double-edged. Moreover, the passion for order stimulates a resentment against needing and desiring it. Yet both impulses seem constitutive of political life, even providing its dynamic and movement. Finally, the desire to be secure against that which is alien and other, unknown and uncontrollable, whether it be women, the young, the citizenry, or even the gods, is a desire to master oneself, since, at the very least, we are implicated with these others who, because they already constitute our lives, are permanently inside the moat.

It is "man" who tames the sea despite its turbulence and uses the earth for his own purposes despite its divinity. Given the sea as a symbol of the elemental forces of nature and equally elemental human passions, to master the sea is no mean boast or achievement. But the play's images of Creon as a captain steering the ship of state, his furious rejection of Haemon's advice to slacken sail, and the image of Thebes as a harbor of death indicate the exaggeration of the claim and the double edge to man's triumph. The edge is present in the assault on the goddess necessary for life, what Heidegger translates as the "unceasing incursion [*Einbruch*] into the indestructible power of the earth."[97] This is no simple celebration of technical mastery but suggests that life itself is parasitic on transgression, and nurturance on violence, all of which adds dimension to Creon's crude suggestion that Haemon will have other furrows to plow after Antigone is dead.[98]

This cunning man snares birds, domesticates animals, and catches fish in "the close spun nets of his own devising." With unbounded ingenuity he invents contrivances[99] that allow him to yoke the power of animals for his own purposes and enable him to teach himself speech, thought, and the temper for political life. This temper shelters him from the destructive forces around and inside him as the houses he builds do from the cold and driving rain. And though he cannot escape death, he can, because of his intelligence and technical mastery, escape from what were once death dealing diseases.

> With some sort of cunning, inventive
> beyond all expectation
> he reaches sometimes evil
> and sometimes good.

---

[96] Heidegger, *Introduction*, p. 161.
[97] Ibid., p. 154.
[98] See the gloss by O'Brien, *Guide*, p. 58–59.
[99] See Heidegger's discussion of *edidaxato, Introduction*, pp. 156–57.

sophon ti to mēchanoen
technas huper elpid' echōn tote men kakon,
allot' ep' esthlon herpei.

(365–67)

But as with first part of the ode, the action and imagery of the play complicate, qualify, and sometimes undermine the ode's claims for man's intelligence, ingenuity, and mastery. It is man who casts his snares, nets, and traps into nature, snatching living creatures out of their order, disrupting the rhythms of their lives in order to yoke, use, and wear them away. More particularly, Creon has woven a twisted net of ruin for himself and Thebes, and would yoke those (especially Antigone) who refuse obedience. In this, he links the tyranny of king over subjects (particularly women) to the tyranny of man over nature. And Antigone herself is likened to a bird. Birds are integral to the art of prophecy, which, by sympathetic listening to the voice of nature, allows men to read the will of the gods in contrast to the arts of control and self-taught devices, which Creon embodies and the ode extols. Birds are perched upon the dead body of Polyneices pecking away at the boundaries that separate humans from animals, untamed nature from the civilized city.

We have already seen how Thebes, like Corcyra, became, not a shelter against violence, but a sealed room in which the "tempers" that can make for political life are compressed into an ungovernable rage. And the action after the ode will reveal how quickly speech and communication degenerate into ranting and insult masked by claims to wisdom and charges of insanity or corruption against those who differ. What we see and hear is speech silenced or silencing what is seen as unfit to say, thought that is thoughtless in its suppression of those who think differently (passionately and intuitively), and reasonableness in the service of power.

Nor is it clear that the characters in the play have done what the ode says they can: invented and mastered language. It is not only that the Greek can be read as suggesting that men find their way to language rather than purposely invent or teach it to themselves, though that is significant enough. It is also that there are too many times in the play when language seems to have mastered men, when they are themselves caught, snared, or swept along on lexical currents that dissipate only in disaster.

Finally, there is disease and death. Men are said to have found a cure for disease, yet the city on stage is sick and the king who is the cause of the illness proclaims everyone else afflicted with the disease of deficient reason he himself is spreading. As for death, Creon is the cause of it, yet defeated by it—by the corpse and by Antigone, who, choosing death, retains a power denied her by Creon and the male polis. Against the claim that the accumulation of human arts can lead to emancipation, that *technai* provide the tools for a domination of nature and freedom from want and the arbitrariness of natural calamity, that the development of rational forms of social organization, such as the polis, and rational modes of thought grant permanent power, there is human mortality and the weight of history from whose specific gravity we cannot escape. No insight provides sufficient strength to unbind us from the past. Birds fly, but humankind walks toward a horizon limited by its vision. Because history is unforgiving, every step is paid for, every oversight tallied and punished, the unperceived injustice along with the desperate crime.

> When he weaves together [*pareirōn*] the laws of the land
> and the justice of the gods confirmed by oaths
> then high is he and his city [*hupsipolis*]; but no city [*apolis*]
> has he who binds himself to dishonor
> prompted by reckless daring.
> He who is so, may he never share my hearth
> may he never share my thoughts.
>
> (368–75)

But the play suggests how difficult it is to weave a life into a whole and justly honor what is just. It is not clear how warring gods, distinct spheres, and divergent obligations could be reconciled, let alone be mutually enhancing at least in the world on stage. And, given the problematic status of the passion for order as that is articulated by and embodied in Creon, it is not clear whether the unraveling is a coming apart or a beginning that is a reweaving of the fabric into new shapes and patterns; most likely it is both at once.

At the ode's conclusion, Antigone appears under guard as the violator of Creon's decree. Seeing her, the chorus, which can hardly believe, see, or bear it when it does, responds with a phrase (*es daimonion teras amphinoō*) which can be translated (as it is by Wycoff) as "my mind is split at this awful sight," or (as by Nussbaum) "looking at this strange portent I think on both sides." The immediate referent, of course, is Antigone. But the more general one is the naturally unnatural strangeness of human life captured by the word and idea of *deinos*.

My reading of the ode (and so of the play as a whole) is an overreading in two ways. By exaggerating if not romanticizing transgressiveness, it threatens to turn the ode in praise of man into one condemning him, thus sacrificing the tragic tensions in the play. Second, it identifies Thebes too closely with Athens.

The ode does praise "man"'s intelligence, technical ingenuity, and power even if it denies that his achievements are determined by either a transcendent telos or a unified logic. In addition, the chorus and no doubt Sophocles himself do not deny the existence of nature or the gods; indeed, without the contrast with them, the human condition would lose its distinctively tragic dimension. But the presence of the gods hardly insures purity of intent or result. Thus the temper that can explode into an ungovernable rage is also the temper that grounds the city. Creon's denial of plurality—his depoliticization of order, power, knowledge, and thinking and establishment of an arithmetic of security as the thought within which thought must take place—does not cancel the value of patriotism, loyalty, and order.

Similarly humans do need a home, an identity, and a collective sense of shared space, history, and rule. Yet because they are "thrown" into conditions they cannot escape, and into a world they did not entirely make and cannot ultimately determine, they cannot realize the need, cannot establish some impermeable place or identity without denying their capacity for action and freedom.

VII

But what does this have to do with Athens if Athens is an anti-Thebes where perversity, fragmentation, and excess are presented in the confines of the theater so it will not be present outside it? The characters on stage may not understand each other, but the audience presumably understands the play and each other sufficiently to allow us to call it an "audience" in a sense stronger than when we talk about a contemporary audience at a movie. Or to put the issue in terms with which I began, how pathological is the world of the play, how specific to Thebes is the human condition we see displayed there as encapsulated in the choral ode?

If the distance between mythical Thebes and contemporary Athens is too great, then Thebes is simply an object lesson and *Antigone* a morality play. If the characters on stage directly represent historical figures and events so that Thebes becomes Athens, then it is unclear how Athens could exist and why the playwright could be regarded as a political educator. Clearly the power of the play rested for a contemporary audience (as for us) on both proximity and distance: proximity because what the audience saw and heard on stage resonated with recognizable contemporary events, characters, and situations; distance because, though elements of the excesses on stage were present in Athenian life, they did not define it.

In the end I do not think we can specify how much mythical Thebes is or is not Athens in particular or in symbolic terms. Nor do I think we can say with finality whether the play represents reason as defective or as misused by characters who use the semblance of reason to mask their intransigence. The very terms of the distinction presuppose a Platonic epistemology opposing seeming and real upon which a rejection of theatricality, drama, and masks rests. Nor, for analogous reasons, am I thoroughly convinced of the more plausible assertion that Creon enunciates valid principles of leadership even if he does ignore them at the very moment he says them. Yet such indeterminacy need not be seen as a deficiency to be made up, but as a generating political and theoretical provocation.

This means that we cannot arrive at firm answers to the initiating questions of this chapter about politics, language, and public reason, and that there continue to be reasons to speak languages of politics. It also means that we must be wary of Habermasian distinctions between rhetoric and logic, philosophy and poetry, communicative discourse and the language of disclosure, the strategic and substantive dimension of speech, politics as the art of the possible and as the pursuit of the impossible, and the will to truth and the will to power. The wariness is necessary not because these distinctions make no analytic sense, but because, for political and dramatic reasons, they are too easily made. This is not to say we must give up the ideal of deliberative democracy. That remains a worthy aspiration, particularly if we mean by it an activist citizenry sharing power and respon-sibility but even if we mean the less demanding procedural sense of public reason advocated by Rawls and Habermas. But without confronting the play of power and desire as the Athenians do in the theater, reason and reasonableness become the bludgeon it is for Creon, and deliberative democracy loses its agonistic edge to an overly Apollonian vision of political life.

When the Athenians looked down at mythical Thebes, what they saw was a polis perched on the razor's edge, not only because it had just experienced a civil war, but because its response to that war took the form of a Creonic arithmetic of security where everything that could not be measured and controlled was defined as other and banished from the public realm. "In modernity," William Connolly writes, "the insistence upon taking charge of the world comes into its own." Nature becomes a deposit of resources for the potential use of humanity. "But ironically, in a world governed by the drive for mastery, any absence of control is experienced as unfreedom and imposition. . . . The drive to mastery intensifies the subordination of many, and recurrent encounters with the limits to mastery make even masters feel constrained."[100]

If I am right in my analyses of play and context of performance, the audience might achieve a self-awareness that mediated the play's tensions and paradoxes less dramatically present in their lives as members of household, as citizens, and as mortals. They could see wars between entities such as family and city that ought to be mutually sustaining, but also conflicts between young and old, men and women, citizens and strangers that are too easily erased by celebrations of reasonableness and deliberation. Watching the movement of the play might en-able them to track the interplay of attraction and repulsion among people as well as principles, to recognize how we often stand opposed to what we stand with, and to see how easy it is to misunderstand and misdescribe even those who share our worship, language, and remembered pain.

As spectators of the action rather than participants in it, they can see the irony in the praise of man with a clarity denied the characters on stage until the end when all is already lost. This might well make them even more skeptical of anyone claiming to have a monopoly of wisdom and increase their commitment to the communal basis of truth, which their experience in the theater (where meaning is derived from the ensemble of characters) already commends. Learn-ing what can happen when the passion for order becomes all-consuming and all-encompassing, they might appreciate more the necessity and pleasures of disor-der, of knowledge and wisdom that cannot be captured or snared. Finally, they might, after leaving the theater, be more likely to recognize that, though politics is a realm of decision and the common ground for it must be sustained, each decision and the ground it rests upon may establish a pattern of necessity where purposes harden, and institutions become fixed in a way that constricts public space and turns political discourse in on itself.[101]

---

[100] Connolly, *Political Theory and Modernity,* p. 2.

[101] There is a more complicated dialectic at work here as Derrida argues in his discussion of Hegel

All of this is possible, perhaps even likely. But it remains unclear exactly what practical consequences flowed from this self-awareness and larger perspective. I have argued that Antigone vindicates its heroine against a hypermasculinist construction of politics, and I have implied that her erasure in the last third of the play is "Sophocles'" point rather than a point that can be made in criticism of him. Yet I know of no firm evidence that the play increased the dignity accorded women or increased their power, even if it might have limited their indignity and powerlessness.

Of course, there are other audiences for *Antigone* (and many other Antigones). I have tried to suggest how our engaging "the" play could become a ground for our collective inquiry and reflection about political ends as well as for exploring theoretical debates about security and reason and gender. This presumes that the human condition the chorale ode describes in terms of *deinos* is not specific either to mythical Thebes or contemporary Athens.

I have talked about the response of the elders in the chorus to seeing Antigone brought before them as a prisoner immediately at the conclusion of the ode in praise of man. In Wykoff's translation, their mind is split "at the awful sight" they see before them. I would change that in one respect; their mind is divided at the awful and awesome sight they see before them: a woman who has defied a tyrant, and who in her speech and action reminds us, with exquisite power, of the gift and obligation of freedom.

---

on Antigone. Antigone is "an impossible figure, a figure inadmissible in the system, an unclassifiable instant that would escape the ringlike unfolding of thought." Yet this "leftover remainder that cannot be digested, this unassimilable indigestible nonetheless plays a fundamental role in the system, fundamental precisely because of its absolute indigestibility." Since it assures the systems space of possibility, it, in fact, supports it "from the outside and underneath." See *Glas,* pp. 151, 166.

Oedipean Complexities and Political Science: Tragedy and the Search for Knowledge

If oxen and horses and lions had hands or could draw with hands and create works of art like those made by men, horses would draw pictures of gods like horses, and oxen gods like oxen, and they would make the bodies (of their gods) in accordance with the form that each species itself possesses.[1]

—Xenophanes

The dead haunt the living. The past: it "re-bites" [*il remord*]. History is "cannibalistic," and memory becomes the closed arena of conflict between two contradictory operations: forgetting, which is . . . an action directed against the past; and the mnemic trace, the return of what was forgotten. . . . [A]n autonomous order is founded upon what it eliminates; it produces a "residue condemned to be forgotten." But what was excluded . . . re-infiltrates the place of its origin. It resurfaces, it troubles, it turns the present's feeling of being "at home" into an illusion, it lurks—this "wild," this "ob-scene," this "filth," this "resistance," of "superstition"—within the walls of the residence, and behind the back of the owner (the ego), or over its objections, it inscribes there the law of the other.[2]

—Michel de Certeau

IN THE *Apology* Socrates admonishes his fellow citizens for caring more for power and wealth than for truth, wisdom, and the goodness of their souls. If he corrupts the youth, it is by this insistence that excellence or virtue is a necessary condition for knowing what is valuable in private and public life and living by it. He himself is an example of his argument since he neglects those public and private goals valued by most men so he can pursue conversations with all he meets (but especially his compatriots) about why they should honor some things more than others.

The whole enterprise sounds quaint at best illiberal at worst. Most political philosophers talk about "thin" theories of the good and see those committed to "thick" theories as misguided communitarians. Those who do talk about public morality are most often associated with the religious right, and they, either para-

---

[1] Kathleen Freeman, *Ancilla to the PrēSocratics* (Oxford: Basil Blackwell, 1948), p. 22.

[2] Michel de Certau, *Heterologies,* trans. Brian Massumi (Minneapolis: University of Minnesota Press, 1986), pp. 3–4.

doxically or inadvertently given their political alliance with free-marketers, often value wealth and power above all things.

Socrates sounds less quaint and dangerous insofar as what he values most is the examined life. Properly limited by time, place, and circumstance, examining one's life seems a useful thing to do. It is why some people go to college or, more likely, something that may happen when they do.

In the culture wars each side accuses the other of failing to examine the implicit commitments that animate their arguments. Canonists see multiculturalists as indulging in a form of political correctness that curtails free debate while jettisoning reason in the name of ideology. Multiculturalists see canonist disclaimers about their own cultural power as self-serving evasions. Although canonists extol the virtues of rational exchange of views, they do not seem willing to defend their own intellectual or political positions but indulge in polemics, often, as I suggested in chapter one, of the kind Socrates' accusers used against him.

There is a surprising lack of critical examination of the idea of "reason" and reasonableness in the culture wars, though the more academic debate between modernists and postmodernists (say Foucault or Lyotard and Habermas or Judith Butler and Seyla Benhabib) is very much about that. That is unfortunate because, as the preceding chapter argued, reason is, to use Hobbes's phrase, often "scout to the desires." Indeed it is Hobbes's notion of instrumental rationality and his assimilation of reason to calculation that has shaped how reason and rationality are so often understood in public life. Socrates (as well as Athenian political thought generally, not to mention Aristotle) may have tried to separate economic from political thinking and activities, but much social science assimilates them such that strategies in the pursuit of wealth are seen as analogous to strategies in the pursuit of power. In rational choice theory (as well as among many empirical political scientists, for whom such theory purchases analytic elegance at the price of empirical fruitfulness), the voter is simply a consumer in drag.

Rational choice theory as well as the more generalized commitment to a science of politics, seen by its practitioners as the most sophisticated and "advanced" form of political theory, is remote from the assumptions and sensibility of the texts treated in this book. It is indifferent to anything like Socratic political philosophy and is largely skeptical about democracy, seeing it as involved in paradoxes and inconsistencies that make it impracticable except in a highly attenuated form. Moreover, it embraces the kind of high-flown speech Aristophanes ridicules and it lacks the tragic sense of the world found in *Antigone*. Here is Vernant in a passage I quoted in chapter two:

> In the tragic perspective, acting, being an agent, has a double character. On the one side, it consists in taking council with oneself, weighing the for and against and doing the best one can to foresee the order of means and ends. On the other hand, it is to make a bet on the unknown and the incomprehensible and to take a risk on a terrain that remains impenetrable to you. It involves entering the play of supernatural forces . . . where one does not know whether they are preparing success or disaster.[3]

---

[3] Jean-Pierre Vernant and Pierre Vidal-Naquet, *Tragedy and Myth in Ancient Greece,* trans. J. Lloyd (Atlantic Highlands, N.J.: Humanities Press, 1981), p. 37.

In this world things cannot be enclosed in theories, grasped by understanding, or assimilated to what has been. The abyss of the unprecedented and inexplicable Hannah Arendt saw in Nazism cannot be covered over by facts, goals, numbers, incidents, and results.[4] To think they can is to live and think like Oedipus; it is to be "rebitten" in de Certeau's image.

In this chapter I want to use Sophocles' *Oedipus Tyrannus* as an occasion to reflect on some of the epistemological and methodological claims made by political scientists in general and rational actor theorists in particular about their object of study and about themselves as studiers.[5] I shall suggest that the play's themes of incest and patricide can illuminate the relationship between the premium that method places on being analytic, rigorous, scientific, objective, and parsimonious[6] and the object domain of the goal-directed utility maximizing (or "satisficing") individual of rational actor theory[7] that the method constitutes for study. I also will suggest that the admirable traits found in Oedipus are also those posited by many political scientists (most vigorously by rational actor theorists) about political actors and themselves and that, as a result, the king's myopia parallels their own. He proclaims himself an independent agent free of fate and history, self-made and self-generated, and so able to see the world rationally. But in fact his knowledge comes with ignorance and so the meaning of his acts remains bifurcated in a way he only comes to understand in the scene where, significantly enough, he blinds himself. Penultimately, I will offer a reading of the play and an interpretation of its original conditions of performance to indicate a balance between proximity and distance worthy of emulation by political scientists if they are to avoid a method that mimics the culture they are studying and engaging in recondite abstractions that ignore the cultural specificity of their claims to universality. Most rational choice theorists read a particular historical and ideological configuration into "nature," a construct that then becomes the premise for a historical narrative that justifies it as either the telos of human development or the unacknowledged assumption of all previous (and subsequent) human behavior. As a certain stage of liberal capitalism becomes elaborated into a social ontology, rational choice theory becomes the thought within which all thought must take place. As with Hobbes it functions both as a postulate and a

---

[4] See Hannah Arendt, *Eichmann in Jerusalem: A Report on the Banality of Evil* (New York: Viking, 1964), and Greil Marcus, *The Dustbin of History* (Cambridge, Mass.: Harvard University Press, 1995), pp. 59–63.

[5] I do not distinguish rational actor theory from rational choice theory, public choice theory, and social choice theory. On the common assumptions of these theories and the disagreements within and between them, see Donald P. Green and Ian Shapiro, *Pathologies of Rational Choice Theory: A Critique of Applications in Political Science* (New Haven: Yale University Press, 1994).

[6] The enthusiasm for "parsimony" might be less if the authors celebrating it knew its original Latin and Middle English meanings. The issue of maximizing one's material advantage is raised in the play by the Greek word *kerdos,* which means both a search for material advantage and crafty or shrewd. Oedipus accuses Tiresias of being out for his own material gain when the seer tells him the truth.

[7] See the discussion by Kristen Renwick Monroe in her editor's foreword and "The Theory of Rational Action: Its Origins and Usefulness for Political Science," in her edited book *The Economic Approach to Politics* (New York: Harper Collins, 1991), pp. xiii–xxiii, 1–30, and Jon Elster's discussion of the ideal rational choice explanation in his introduction to his edited *Rational Choice* (New York: New York University Press, 1986), pp. 16–17.

projection, a description and prescription. When its advocates acknowledge its circularity, limited empirical successes, opt for "thin" rather than "thick" rational accounts, accept multiple equilibria and segmented rationality, conclude that rational choice explanations are more likely to hold where the options agents confront are relatively fixed and the decisions are not urgent, and accept the need for other theoretical perspectives, their admirable modesty compromises the claims made for its power and promise.

Finally, I will argue that the role of a spectator in the theater is as fruitful a model for political theory and political science as one based on economics or the physical sciences and that a tragic sensibility provides a needed antidote to the *hubris* of rational choice theory.[8]

I

Alone among mortals, Oedipus was able to solve the Sphinx's riddle and so save the city of Thebes. The riddle, "What creature walks on four feet, two feet, and three feet all in a single day?" The answer, "man,"[9] required a kind of abstract knowledge available to Oedipus because he was ignorant of the concrete circumstances of his birth.[10] The intellectual achievement that enabled him to see the changing nature of man and to discern what was continuous and similar amid change and diversity disabled him from solving the riddle of Laius's death and saving Thebes from a second plague. He did not "see" that and how the particular circumstances of his own life made him an exception to what he took to be a universal statement.

Having had a child despite an oracle that warned him that he would be killed by his son, Laius bound his infant's feet and exposed him to die. Thus Oedipus, unlike the generic crawling baby, walking adult, and cane-using old man, never walked "normally," never moved through any of the stages of life but was him-

---

[8] In Greek *hubris* suggests the unlimited violence that comes from passion and pride. It is licentiousness as well as insolence, legally a gross personal insult and assault. I will generally rely on David Grene's translation of the play in *Sophocles,* vol. 1 (Chicago: University of Chicago Press, 1991).

[9] "Long afterward, Oedipus, old and blinded, walked the roads. He smelled a familiar smell. It was the sphinx. Oedipus said, 'I want to ask one question. Why didn't I recognize my mother?' 'You gave the wrong answer,' said the sphinx. 'But that was what made everything possible,' said Oedipus. 'No,' she said. 'When I asked, what walks on four legs in the morning, two at noon, and three in the evening, you answered Man. You didn't say anything about Woman.' 'When you say Man,' said Oedipus, 'you include women too. Everyone knows that.' She said, 'That's what you think.'" Muriel Rukeyser, "Myth," in Sandra Gilbert and Susan Gubar, eds., *The Norton Anthology of Literature by Women: The Tradition in English* (New York: Norton, 1985), pp. 1787–88.

[10] The earliest form of the riddle was "there is on earth a being two footed, four footed and three footed that has one name [literally one voice]; and it alone changes its form. But when it goes propelled on most feet, then is the swiftness of its limbs weakest." This version is given by Charles Segal in his *Oedipus Tyrannus: Tragic Heroism and the Limits of Knowledge* (New York: Twayne, 1993), p. 56. See also the version and discussion in Thomas Gould's translation and commentary on *Oedipus the King* (Englewood Cliffs, N.J.: Prentice Hall, 1970), pp. 18–20, and Hugh Lloyd Jones in *The Justice of Zeus* (Berkeley: University of California Press, 1971).

self an unnatural unity who married his mother and sired his sisters.[11] Walking on three feet as an adult he used that third foot, his staff, to kill his father. Thus did he unknowingly fulfill the oracle he thought to escape and take revenge on the man who had sought his death.

Ignorant of what was closest and nearest, Oedipus did not know that he was the answer to the second riddle, Who killed Laius? and so the "cause" of the plague.[12] Not only is he ignorant of the conditions of his birth and origins, of who his father, mother, and people are, he does not even know his own name, which is a series of puns on *oida* meaning "know" and *pous* meaning "foot." For Oedipus, and perhaps for all mortals, seeing is also blindness, success hides terrible failure, strength is a source of defeat, and delusion most pervasive when we think ourselves most wise and in command. Oedipus's triumph in solving the first riddle was short-lived because his solution unraveled into yet another one. "Between the certainty I have of my existence and the content I try to give to that assurance," Camus wrote, "the gap will never be filled. Forever I shall be a stranger to myself."[13] Even worse, what escapes what one constructs is often a violence barely hidden by the surface calm of normal life, common sense, and established identity.[14] As the play suggests, the civilizing hero cannot banish the savagery in himself.

What makes the dilemmas of the play so relevant and disturbing for political scientists is that the characteristics that define Oedipus and make his triumph a tragedy are those traits political scientists find admirable in political leaders and in themselves. Oedipus is an astute politician and a beneficent and responsible

---

[11] Segal, *Oedipus Tyrannus,* p. 87.

[12] When Creon returns from asking the oracle (who has said that the plague afflicting Thebes is due to the city's harboring the murderer of Laius), the problem-solver king instantly starts the search: "Where is it to be found this obscure trace of an age old crime?" (*pou tod' heurethēsetai / ichnos palaias dustekmarton aitis;*). As Bernard Williams points out, though *aitias* refers to a crime it belongs to the language of diagnosis and rational inquiry. "Oedipus plans to conquer the problem by the same means he used in overcoming the sphinx, by gnōmē, rational intelligence." *Shame and Necessity* (Berkeley: University of California Press, 1993), p. 58.

[13] *The Myth of Sisyphus and Other Essays,* trans. Justin O'Brien (New York: Knopf, 1955), p. 14. See the discussion of the point in Jeffrey C. Isaac, *Arendt, Camus and Modern Rebellion* (New Haven: Yale University Press, 1992), pp. 110–25.

[14] In a recent essay, William Connolly argues that Foucault both challenges conventional morality in the pursuit of a higher ethical sensibility and is aware of the danger inscribed in the effort to shift the terms and bases of moral doctrines. Foucault (along with Nietzsche, Arendt, and Todorov) sees that "systemic cruelty flows regularly from the thoughtlessness of aggressive conventionality, the transcendentalization of contingent identities, and the treatment of good/evil as a duality wired into the intrinsic order of things" ("Beyond Good and Evil: The Ethical Sensibility of Michel Foucault," *Political Theory* 21, no. 3 [August 1993]: 365–66). Each one of these themes is dramatized in the play. I am not suggesting that Sophocles comes down on the same side as Foucault, though I think such an argument could be made on the ground that, though Sophocles believed there is a natural order of things and boundaries that had to be observed to avoid pollution (*miasma*), humans are, as historical beings, unable to fathom that order fully or adhere to it if known. I am suggesting that for Sophocles good and evil lie in the heart of their putative opposite, as rationality and irrationality do. Such polarities are evasions as well as inscriptions, desperate attempts to categorize under the rubric of normal.

leader. He is solicitous of the views of others and for the people, confident in his
abilities, and decisive in action, yet concerned for the view of the gods. His pride
in his achievement, prominent in the opening lines and tableau where he is being
supplicated by his afflicted people as if he were a god, is balanced by his piety.
Moreover, he is an acute problem solver, an enlightened man who promises to
reveal what is hidden, bring all to light, dissipate confusion and uncertainty, and
dispel superstition and ignorance. Thus critics describe him as "a questioner,
researcher and discoverer," a "calculator" who brings a quantitative sensibility to
the empirical world, and one who demonstrates, investigates, examines, questions, infers, knows, finds, reveals, makes clear, learns, and teaches.[15]

But the logic of noncontradiction does not apply to this man, who is one and
many and in whom opposites coexist.[16] For all his insight he is utterly blind to
the reality of his life (or lives) and identity (or identities) and so of the meaning(s)
of his actions. He thinks he is escaping his past, fate, and history and boasts of
being a self-made, self-generated, freely acting individual even as he fulfills it.
Having been told by a drunken companion that he was a bastard and then been
dishonored by Apollo when he sought to confirm what he had heard—the
priestess told him he would kill his father and marry his mother—Oedipus flees
Corinth and his "parents" who have in fact adopted him, to Thebes, which
"adopts" him though it is his original home. Later hearing that his Corinthian
"parents" have died, he boasts of being a self-made man and a child of fortune
and the gods, all this just prior to his discovering exactly who his parents are and
what he has done to them.

By marrying his mother Oedipus became an unnatural unity, too much one and
singular, too close to home, too implicated in his past: by killing his father he
became too much alone and too isolated, too divorced from his past. The crimes
of incest and patricide can stand for both the "unnaturally" intimate connection
between the way political scientists in general and rational actor theorists in
particular constitute their field of study, the method they use to study it, and the
political culture they are studying, as well as their tendency to reject precisely
those shaping features of the past that provide a justification for their rejection of
the past.

"A social theory that adopts the same means-end individualistic rationality that
the modern economy imposes," Michael Shapiro writes, "helps that structure
operate rather than effect a theoretical distance from it."[17] Using the entrenched
language of power and authority to study democratic politics reifies that authority
and power while muting the very possibility of radical critique. As this implies,
there is no morally neutral language because as accounts of social phenomena are

---

[15] See especially Bernard Knox, *Oedipus at Thebes* (New Haven: Yale University Press, 1957),
chap. 1, and Alister Cameron, *The Identity of Oedipus the King* (New York: New York University
Press, 1968).

[16] See Segal's discussion of this point, *Oedipus Tyrannus*, p. 118.

[17] "Politicizing Ulysses: Rationalistic, Critical and Genealogical Commentaries," in *Reading the
Postmodern Polity: Political Theory as Textual Practice* (Minneapolis: University of Minnesota
Press), p. 29.

accepted by social actors they become part of the social world itself, unpredicta-
bly altering the very institutions and practices that are being described.[18] One
could even say that we become the language we use insofar as "the languages we
speak and the cultural practices they at once reflect and make possible, mark or
form our minds by habituating them to certain forms of attention, certain ways of
seeing and conceiving of oneself in the world."[19] Every language encourages
speakers to think and act in some ways rather than others, creates and sustains
different kinds of characters with different understandings of human agency and
action.[20]

Such theoretical incest may explain the often tautological nature of rational
actor (or choice) theory[21] and, appropriately given my choice of Sophocles, lend
a certain irony to Riker's preference for "the simplicity" of the rationality assumption that people or things "behave in regular ways." The rationality model
allows one "to arrive at the regularity necessary for generalization" whereas
"simple observation" or induction is too "inefficient" an alternative. What matters is "the easy generation of hypotheses" and a "single efficient parsimonious
explanation of behavior" that allows "much of the complexity to disappear."[22]
But this seems nothing less than a prescription for ignorance premised on the
contradictory assumptions that the choice of method is arbitrary in the sense of
being indifferent to the subject matter but that it can, nonetheless, reveal nature
and human nature. More than that, the preoccupation with regularity and clarity
easily leads to regarding what is irregular and opaque as a threat. There is too
much diffidence for desperation here, yet there is, nonetheless, a Hobbesian attachment to method because it can maintain political as well as epistemic order.

Given Oedipus's generation, his unnatural singularity, his imposition of order
and simplicity, and the fact that he puts out his eyes when he finally recognizes
how wrongly he has read the meaning of his life, Riker's statement of preferences
becomes deeply problematic.

Such theoretical patricide focuses on the way traits attributed to individuals by
rational actor theorists (which are also the traits they claim for their theory)
presuppose a rejection of the past, the salience of traditional wisdom, and a mini-
mizing if not a disregard for the shaping hand of culture. To be rational, actors
and theorists must (or do) disregard what has fathered them even as the un-

---

[18] J. Donald Moon, "Political Science and Political Choice: Opacity, Freedom, and Knowledge,"
in Terence Ball, ed., *Idioms of Inquiry: Critique and Renewal in Political Science* (Albany, N.Y.:
SUNY Press, 1987), p. 239.

[19] Quoted in Terence Ball, "Educative vs Economic Theories of Democracy," in Diane Sansbury,
ed., *Democracy, State, and Justice: Critical Perspectives and New Interpretations* (Stockholm: Alm-
qvist and Wiksell International, 1988), p. 19.

[20] Ibid.

[21] See Gabriel A. Almond, "Rational Choice, Theory and the Social Sciences," Harry Eckstein's
"Rationality and Frustration in Political Behavior," and Mark P. Petracca, "The Rational Actor Ap-
proach to Politics: Science, Self-Interest and Normative Democratic Theory," all in Monroe, *The
Economic Approach to Politics*.

[22] W. H. Riker and P. C. Ordeshook, *An Introduction to Positive Political Theory* (Englewood
Cliffs, N.J.: Prentice-Hall, 1973), chap. 1, especially pp. 11–13.

acknowledged background of history and sentiment give texture and concreteness to the lives of the former and the claims of the latter.[23]

For instance, the aim of objectivity is to rid oneself of partiality by escaping those ties to place and people that compromise the neutrality of one's findings. Marx thought that such claims are almost always ideological, Nietzsche and Foucault that they are self-serving, self-defeating, and bad faith, Tocqueville that the rejection of past and tradition was distinctively American. To be antitraditional, he argued, *was* our tradition, a fact that perhaps explains the extraordinary deracination present in the casual but confident insistence that "*no* goals that are pursued with tolerable consistency can be called irrational."[24]

Given the challenge the play presents to rational actor and rational choice theories (even when they are modified by numerous "side assumptions," which make them more modest but less what they would like to be), as well as to the scientific aspirations of political scientists as a whole, it may be time, if not to renounce the Sisyphean quest for method and theories that ape natural science, then to "deprivilege" their status. It is true that Oedipus solved the Sphinx's riddle, and to the extent the knowledge political scientists seek is analogous to that, it is clearly worthwhile. But what is one to do about the ignorance of that knowledge?

One could begin by recognizing the "literary" dimensions of political science texts, the fact that how one writes, the texture of the prose—the use of equations or models, metaphors, the rhetorical structure of an argument—is itself a claim about how one can know and represent the world. Form or style expresses a sense of life and value, of what matters and doesn't, of what learning and communication and knowledge are, just as how one teaches may be as "substantive" as what one teaches. Life is never simply presented by a text, whether that text be Plato's *Republic,* Downs's *An Economic Theory of Democracy,* Elster's *Ulysses and the Sirens,* or *Oedipus Tyrannus.* It is always represented as something; there is always a choice involved, however constrained it may be by canons of academic professionalism.[25] More pointedly, it may be that a work of "literature" like the *Oedipus Tyrannus* is more alert to the moral complexities of action and actors,

---

[23] See Petracca, "The Rational Actor Approach to Politics."

[24] (Emphasis supplied.) I am quoting Ronald Rogowski, "Rationalist Theories of Politics: A Midterm Report," *World Politics* 20 (October 1977–July 1978): 299. See also Downs's seminal *An Economic Theory of Democracy* (New York: Harper and Row, 1957). For an argument as to why the substance of the goals must count as much as the preference for them, see Hanna Pitkin's discussion of consent as a ground for legitimacy in "Obligation and Consent II," *American Political Science Review* 60, no. 1 (March 1966): 39–52. For an argument that no human community can or could live with such stricture, see part 3 (on Aristotle) of Martha Nussbaum's *The Fragility of Goodness* (Cambridge, Mass.: Harvard University Press, 1986). Tocqueville's argument is most explicit in volume 2, part 1, chapter 1 of *Democracy in America.*

[25] See Martha Nussbaum, "Form and Content: Philosophy and Literature," in her *Love's Knowledge* (New York: Oxford University Press, 1990), especially pp. 3–5. In the same way rational choice and actor theorists tend to present choices of agents as the product of mentalistic acts by free-floating individuals, they present their own choice of method. In both instances they often ignore cultural constraints, including the definition of the profession and the desire for academic prestige and power that shapes their enterprise.

more alive to the variety of allusiveness and flawed beauty of the world than the hyperanalytic prose that characterizes rational actor theory and the fetishism of method that characterizes political science as a whole.[26] It is at least worth asking what a style "so remarkably flat and lacking in wonder" does to the world it studies and the students it teaches. It is at least worth asking what is lost when the tale of Ulysses becomes an analysis of calculation and measurement by an individual mentality trying to reduce risk and achieve end states that are completely detached from social and institutional forms of valuing, or when mythic time is transformed into the logical grammar and temporality of t_1, t_2, t_3.[27] Measuring and counting time is one of Oedipus's talents. He too organized time into logical patterns. But the patterns collapse in the terrible uncertainty of his life. "Go inside and reckon these things up," Tiresias taunts Oedipus after being provoked by the king to tell him who he really is. But anger prevents Oedipus from hearing. "And if you catch me as one who's false," the prophet adds, "then say that my intelligence in prophecy is nil" (461–62). Analysis, reason, logic, the penchant for precise speech and the passion for method is as much biography as conscious choice. Whether we know it or not, we write our lives into a world that has already inscribed itself in our souls.

But my criticism is ungenerous and overstated: ungenerous because Elster's use of a literary text to dramatize the substance and limits (or costs and benefits) of rational actor and choice theory has stimulated my obverse strategy; overstated because political science, like Oedipus, does provide important knowledge. Still, I want to insist that a work like *Oedipus Tyrannus* can help us see where political science in general and rational actor theory in particular are blind, bring clarity and depth where they are obtuse, and be winged and moving where they are dull and heavy.

As I suggested, one way the play can help is by indicating the need for methods to maintain a balance of proximity and distance toward the subject matter rational actor theorists are constituting and studying.

As I have argued, Greek drama was a political institution analogous to the Assembly, Council, and courts.[28] During the festival of Dionysus, playwrights competed for prizes before an audience of the entire citizenry. What that audience saw before itself on stage were plays that dramatized the decisions (about democratization or empire) it had taken in other forums and the cultural accom-

---

[26] See Sheldon S. Wolin's discussion of "methodism" in "Political Theory As a Vocation," reprinted in Martin Fleisher, ed., *Machiavelli and the Nature of Political Thought* (New York: Atheneum, 1972), pp. 23–75.

[27] In *Reading the Postmodern Polity,* Shapiro is sharply critical of Jon Elster's transformation of mythic art into rationalistic time (in the latter's *Ulysses and the Sirens* [New York: Cambridge University Press, 1984]). Cf. Segal's discussion of time as an active agent in his *Oedipus Tyrannus.* Rather than serving as something Oedipus can find out and know with certainty, time "becomes an active force that finally found him out. . . . Rather than being an aid to human understanding time seems to have a kind of independent power that blocks knowledge" (p. 87).

[28] The idea of tragedy as a political institution is explored in my introduction to *Greek Tragedy and Political Theory* (Berkeley: University of California Press, 1986), and in chapter 2 of *The Tragedy of Political Theory: The Road Not Taken* (Princeton: Princeton University Press, 1990).

modations (concerning sexuality, public and private life, and the relations between generations) by which it had defined itself as a community and a people.
The mythical settings for these decisions and accommodations provided both
distance from the urgency of immediate decision necessary in the Assembly,
Council, and lawcourts, and proximity to it since the sufferings of the characters
on stage resembled the audience's own. In this way the theater became a place
and experience in which democratic citizens could reflect on the significance of
their everyday lives and particular decisions in an arc of understanding more
comprehensive and theoretical than was otherwise possible. In it they could see
the problematic aspects of cultural hierarchies and distinctions which otherwise
defined their collective and individual lives. In these terms, the qualities Oedipus
displays on stage are the talents and temperament Athenians most prized in their
democratic leaders, such as Pericles, and that they idealized in themselves.[29] "To
attend a tragic drama," Martha Nussbaum writes in language that echoes Knox's
description of Oedipus, "was to engage in a communal process of inquiry, reflection and feeling with respect to important civic and personal ends."[30] From what
we can tell, that engagement provoked responses of extraordinary emotional
power and intense critical reflection, which, together, provided the ground for the
political judgments the audience would make when it brought the experience in
the theater to the Assembly, Courts, and Council as it had brought the experience
of being an active citizen to the theater. This is a representation of democratic
deliberation that is almost unintelligible within the individualistic premises of
rational actor theory.

What is clear from this and from Knox's argument about Oedipus and Athens
is that the talents of the king and audience were both political and intellectual. It
was this combination that the Athenians came to identify as unique to their own
democratic culture. No play dramatizes the greatness and limits of this combination more provocatively than the *Oedipus Tyrannus*. It does so in the context of
the fifth-century enlightenment during which, as we saw in chapter two, the sophists challenged the "natural" status they saw as conventional notions of education, law, religion, justice, and the polis while suggesting that man, not god, is the
measure of all things.

Given this, the idea of being a spectator in the theater is as rich and generative
a model for political theory and science as one based on economics and the
physical sciences. At a minimum it compensates for the limits of what Sheldon
Wolin has called "methodism" and provides a way to democratize political wisdom against the presumptions of professional expertise, political economism, and
technical jargon.[31]

---

[29] See Knox, *Oedipus at Thebes* (New Haven: Yale University Press, 1957), and "The Freedom of
Oedipus," in *Essays Ancient and Modern* (Baltimore: Johns Hopkins University Press), pp. 45–62.
While I think Knox's argument provocative, there is a danger in turning theater into history. For why,
see Froma Zeitlin's "Thebes: Theater of Self and Society in Athenian Drama," in Euben, *Greek
Tragedy and Political Theory*, pp. 101–42. This idea of theater should not be wholly alien to us, given
such works as Arthur Miller's *The Crucible* and Tony Kushner's *Angels in America*.

[30] *Love's Knowledge*, pp. 16–17.

[31] See note 26.

While the actors on stage are, by definition, bound to play the parts assigned them, a spectator can see what they can't: how those parts form a whole. Whereas the actor is, and enacts, his part, the spectator puts the parts together; he or she (it is probable that women attended the theater) was literally less part-ial and part-isan. But the truth attained by the spectator was inaccessible and invisible to the actors on stage only as a matter of position, not of nature. By extension and analogy ordinary citizens were limited in their capacity to judge not because they were incapable of Arendt's "representative thinking" (discussed in chapter two) but by circumstance.[32] Figuratively there is nothing stopping the characters on stage from being spectators at a different play. And, of course, when members of the audience left the play, they exchanged the near omniscience of spectators for the role of actors in public life.[33] Having seen what Oedipus did not see, knowing all along the shaping hand of circumstance where he had thought himself a self-made independent agent, they know that they might, individually or collectively, be like him, not because they will commit his horrendous crimes, but because they also may too confidently assume they have a method to master the empirical world and define human nature, which only a god could do. Impartiality, an ability to see more than one part and from one standpoint, is one thing; objec-tivity in the sense that one is outside or above all parts is another. The spectator in the theater (unlike the philosopher in the *Republic* or Parmenides) does not with-draw to some higher region, but remains a member of the audience, at once disengaged from the particular characters on stage, yet deeply affected by the sufferings they bear and the ignorance that plagues their lives.

But could they (can we) learn from the play so they (and we) would not live through the experience depicted in it? If the tragedians were the political educa-tors of Athens (the Greek word for producing plays is the same as the word for educating) did Sophocles think, or does the play suggest, that the audience could be spared the experience of Oedipus because it had seen *Oedipus Tyrannus?* Could the same be said of rational actor theory and methodism? To put it in a thoroughly unliterary way, if Oedipus had seen *Oedipus Tyrannus,* would he have acted differently? Could he have "escaped" his fate and achieved the free-dom of which he wrongly boasts?

What makes answering these questions so difficult is that the play provides no single vantage point on itself, no resting place where one can confidently say here I stand, I can see no other. Instead, it dramatizes the questions in ways that leave us with a deeper sense of the problems rather than with solutions to them. I offer three examples.

The first concerns the play's dramatization of the theatrical experience of it-self. In its preoccupation with sight, insight, and blindness, the *Oedipus Tyrannus*

---

[32] Arendt introduces the contrast between actor and spectator as a way of understanding philoso-phy with a parable attributed to Pythagoras. At a festival "some come to compete, others to sell things but the best come as spectators *(theatai),* so in life the slavish men go searching for fame and gain while the philosophers search for truth." (See *Life of the Mind,* vol. 1: *Thinking* [London: Secker and Warburg, 1978], pp. 129–31.)

[33] Men did but women did not since women were excluded from the central political institutions of the culture.

makes the audience self-conscious about the experience it is having. Yet the play itself presents important events (such as Jocasta's death and Oedipus's self-blinding) as outside the field of vision, accessible only in verbal fragments, which the audience must make coherent just as Oedipus must with the pieces of his life. In calling attention to its withholding of visual experience in favor of verbal description, the play evidences a consciousness of the theatrical spectacle as a narrative mediating between what is inside and outside, internal and external vision, physical acts and the emotional world they reveal.[34] But in the *agōn* between Oedipus and the blind Tiresias, the mediation breaks out into a conflict between the analytical empirical knowledge possessed by the king and the prophetic knowledge of the seer.

Second, the play suggests that the careful seeing and hearing it demands of the audience is too much and not enough. There are things no man should see, boundaries no man should cross, truths about ourselves that are unbearable to hear, times when anger, fear, or confidence prevent listening. And there are times when understanding the world requires the use of all the senses, not just the intellectual ones. Near the end of the play, in a scene of excruciating poignancy, Oedipus, now blind and equal to nothing, calls for his daughters so he can touch them in a gesture of love, loss, and contrition.

Third, though the play warns us about our penchant for coherence, order, and logic, it itself has what Bernard Knox calls "a ferociously logical plot." But then how does the knowledge Sophocles or the play possesses fit the dramatization of knowledge in the play? Does it resolve the tensions it portrays between the ways of knowing represented by Oedipus and Tiresias? Or does it leave us (as I think it does), with a framework within which various interpretative communities recast the resolutions it provokes in their own context of performance?

All this is very "literary," probably abstract, and no doubt frustrating if one is concerned with the real world of political decision, and policy. Yet I am not so sure contemporary political science approaches such as rational actor theory are any less abstract or, for that matter, any more forthcoming with solutions. And the frustration of having problems deepened rather than solved may be precisely the right antidote to policy analysts who have more solutions than a chemistry lab, rational actor theorists with their preference for parsimony, and political scientists preoccupied with methods and methodism.

All I shall do in the following pages is look at five moments in the play as a way of dramatizing my claims about the significance of *Oedipus Tyrannus* for political scientists in general and rational actor theorists in particular.

II

The Oedipus we see in the opening scene is a man of generosity and intelligence. Compassionate toward his suffering people who appear as suppliants before him,

---

[34] See the discussion in Segal, *Oedipus Tyrannus,* pp. 150–52, and my *The Tragedy of Political Theory,* chap. 4 ("Identity and the Oedipus Tyrannos").

open and collegial in the exercise of his kingly power, he is quick to analyze a situation and take appropriate action. He is proud of his achievements, comfortable commanding others, and confident of his ability to control events. He is, after all, the man whose intellectual prowess saved Thebes from the death-dealing Sphinx, and enabled him, a stranger, to become king.[35] Where others saw only discontinuity, difference, and plurality in the riddle about what walks on four feet, two feet, and three feet in a single day, he perceived unity in difference, identity in discontinuity, singularity in plurality, and coherence rather than fragmentation. They saw the parts but not the whole, but his abstract, analytical, generalizing intelligence enabled him to pierce the veil of illusion and uncover the solid ground of truth. Or so it seemed.

Since the legitimacy of his rule and the health of the city he rules depends on his superior intelligence[36] the plague and new riddle (Who is the murderer of Laius?) is a threat he must meet to exhibit anew the qualities of mind necessary to sustain his authority. The plague is a particularly complex challenge since it is at once a reminder of the unpredictability of events, the limits of reason, the connection of mind to body, and of politics to nature. In Thucydides the plague at Athens (which is contemporaneous with the play) follows and is juxtaposed to the Funeral Oration of Pericles. Where the latter is a paean less to the fallen dead than to Athenian power—the city is represented as a collective Achilles able to make the sea and land the highway of its daring—the plague destroys mind and body, city and family. Appearing out of nowhere, it kills with a randomness that mocks any assumption that nature is an inert object to be mastered by human intelligence and design. Instead, the plague reminds us that human beings are part of an organically connected network of animate beings whose delicately balanced mutually responsible relations are violated at the risk of disaster.[37]

Not only do the opening lines mention the plague, the very first phrase of the play—"Oh children, sons and daughters of Cadmus's line"—is cause for unease since it addresses the assembled citizenry as if they were children. The phrase represents a collapsing of generations which, while it enabled Oedipus to solve the Sphinx's riddle, also recapitulates his committing of incest. Apparently Oedipus's admirable qualities of mind are plagued by the unnatural acts, which have so far defined his life without his knowledge. At the heart of his rationalism, animating his confident assertion of self and order is his biography, paradoxically played out in the deracinated intelligence that allowed him to solve one riddle but that disallows him to solve the new one concerning Laius's death.

Thus the first four lines of the play with their reference to plague and incest introduce a theme that will be elaborated in the symbolism of Oedipus's self-

---

[35] Of course, no one is less a stranger and more at home than Oedipus.

[36] Again no one could be a more legitimate king. Oedipus is a *tyrannos* not so much because he acts tyrannically as because he has come to power through extraordinary means. "Tyranny" was a contested notion until the fourth century when it came to have most of the connotations we attribute to it. (The idea that intelligence is the prime condition for ruling is central to Plato's idea of the philosopher-king.)

[37] See Segal's discussion, *Oedipus Tyrannus*, pp. 6–9.

blinding: political meaning and order as well as the construction of character and self are neither a rational nor an irrational process. They derive neither from the purposive decisions of self-conscious individual actors seeking an efficient means for recognized goals nor in an incomprehensible way by actors who are victims of external forces and other agents. Oedipus moves within a pre-constituted reality that constitutes the terms of his identity. He acts within a script that provides meaning and structure for decisions, which are nonetheless his own. When the chorus asks what spirit drove him to put out his eyes, Oedipus answers: "It was Apollo, friends, Apollo that brought this bitter bitterness, my sorrows to completion. But the hand that struck me was none but my own" (1329–33).

To aid him in solving the new riddle Oedipus summons the blind seer, Apollo's prophet, Tiresias. He greets the old man with great deference as a savior who knows what only the gods know. For reasons obvious to the audience Tiresias does not want to be there and at first refuses to talk. For Oedipus such recalcitrance at first seems like ungratefulness toward Thebes, but then, when the old man speaks the truth, which Oedipus in his anger and certainty cannot hear, the king accuses the prophet of being part of the conspiracy that murdered Laius and would now murder him. Provoked by Oedipus's false accusations, Tiresias proclaims Oedipus the city's pollution and the murderer of Laius. "You have eyes but see not where you are, in sin, nor where you live, nor whom you live with. Do you know who your parents are?" (413–15). As his fury mounts, he heaps abuse on the man he believes is abusing him and boasts of his brilliance in solving the Sphinx's riddle, reminding Tiresias of his failure to do so.

Tiresias's second mention of Oedipus's parents stops Oedipus in his tracks. To the king's "What parents. Stop! Who are they of all the world?" the prophet answers with his own dark riddle: "This day will show your birth and will destroy you" (437–38).

From this moment on the play takes a turn away from a concern with the city's pollution to the king's origins. All of Oedipus's energies and intellect are turned toward the riddle of his own life. It is a riddle that will disclose the grounds for his reason and will, in fact, reveal the murderer of Laius. From now on every step forward in the discovery of who Oedipus is will be a step backward as present facts and distant memory forge inexorably toward a narrative of horrific violation.

The contest between Oedipus and Tiresias is a contest over ways of knowing and ways of presenting knowledge in language. Oedipus is impatient with Tiresias' riddling answers to his cross examination. He wants clear, unambiguous answers to direct questions, not allusive evasions that "darken" rather than enlighten. He wants language to embody meaning appropriate to a notion of truth and enlightenment as something one is conscious of having achieved, uncovered, and disclosed. Oedipean meaning comes from what he can see, from things subject to his will and captured by his categories. Yet despite his insistence on clear speech, his emotions—anger, suspicion, pride, and fear—prevent him from hearing even when Tiresias does speak clearly. Apparently hearing and speaking are as much a matter of subtext as text, of the dynamics between speakers as what it is that is said, as discussions in class often reveal. Even the simplest exchanges are less and more than they appear to be. Because truth is embedded in the disturbances of language and passion, it retains an opacity and is subject to contests shaped as much by the will to power as by the will to truth. If so, the "vague" phrases, oracular pronouncements, and poetic transcriptions that capture this dynamic may more fully represent "the" world and our exchanges about it than the more precise language Oedipus and political science demands.

Insistence on precision, rigor, and analysis presumes the world is of such a sort that it yields its deepest secrets to those who speak and think that way. It presumes too that, with the right language as part of the right method, mortals can pierce the veil of illusion. But this may itself be part of the myth of rationality that is so much part of the Oedipus story. The one character who speaks reasonably and lucidly throughout is Creon and he "has no drives except those which he can consciously control, and no relationships except those which bring an advantage, no qualities except those which can be calculated and entered on a balance sheet." But if he, rather than Oedipus, is taken to be the ideal rational actor and theorist then we are truly lost. For Creon is neither capable of receiving nor needing further self-knowledge through suffering. He shrinks from every risk and danger, regards self-protection as foremost, is satisfied with profit, and is reasonable in an utterly mediocre way. If he is the alternative, we are better off with Oedipus.[38]

But what attitude does the play take toward the two kinds of knowledge it dramatizes: the empirical, analytic, "academic" knowledge of an Oedipus and the inspired prophetic reading of signs of Tiresias? Obviously the play respects both enough to provide a stage for their *agōn*. Less obviously it speaks in both voices, manifests both kinds of knowledge, and refuses to make any final judgment as to their ultimate value, except perhaps to suggest that no final answer is possible for men and women living human lives. Thus the play shares the deciphering knowledge of prophets who speak in the poetry of parables. In this it respects the gods in whose honor drama was performed and acknowledges the depth of a world that will not yield to the identities and categories humans impose on it. But the play also shares the logical, analytic, investigative spirit that defined Athenian democracy as well as the enlightenment project of arriving at clear truths and firm answers. For all the suffering his trials bring, Oedipus perseveres in his search for truth and does solve the riddle of Laius's death and his own birth. And though the oracles prove true, and the gods stand vindicated against presumptuous men who suppose they may escape the forces that shape their destiny and character, the man we see at the play's end returns to something like the sense of command and power he showed at the beginning. Human knowledge, despite its propensity to take the part it sees for the whole it cannot, retains its majesty.

---

[38] The quotation and argument are from Reinhardt in his *Sophocles,* trans. Hazel Harvey and David Harvey (New York: Barnes and Noble, 1979), pp. 111–12. I think Reinhardt exaggerates but it is a provocative point nonetheless, especially for a discussion of rational actor theory.

To reassure her "husband" that Tiresias is indeed lying, Jocasta tells him of an earlier time when prophecy proved false; when Laius was told he would die at the hands of his son. But the reassurance she thinks to render by detailing the circumstances of Laius's death and the "killing" of the boy has the opposite effect on Oedipus. As the truth rises slowly out of its dark confines, so does madness. But there is still one thread of hope, and upon it the king clings for his very life. Laius was killed by robbers but Oedipus was alone when he murdered the man on the road. But before the sent-for shepherd can arrive to corroborate the plurality of the murderers, another messenger arrives from Corinth bringing news he expects to cause much pleasure and a little pain. Polybius, Oedipus's "father" has died of old age and Oedipus has been chosen king of Corinth. (Oedipus supposes Polybius to be his natural father which was why he fled Corinth to avoid killing him when Apollo responded to his questions about his parentage with a prophecy of incest and patricide.) Jocasta, who hears the news first, exults in the pain, for it confirms her belief that oracles are of no account. Hearing the news himself Oedipus joins her in trumpeting their triumph over prophets and, by implication, Apollo, the god of prophecy.

It is Jocasta who first draws the "existential" conclusion from the "fact" that if oracles are false and the gods do not exist, all is chance and opportunity. Men can do as they like without worry about the future, for it is all random, unstructured by history, institutions, or meaning beyond whatever we choose to provide for the occasion. Best then to live for the moment and at ease, discarding dire thoughts and fearful prophecies which disturb sleep to no purpose. But it is also Jocasta who first recognizes that their belief in the falsity of oracles may itself be false. For as the Corinthian messenger assures Oedipus that he need not fear killing his father because Polybius was not his real parent and goes on to detail how he saved Laius's son by receiving the doomed child from the Theban shepherd who could not bear to carry out his master's orders and let the boy die, she pleads with the man who she now knows is her son as well as her husband to desist from his investigation. But Oedipus is constitutionally unable to stop his relentless pursuit of his origins or give up the search for truth even to save his sanity. And so his mother/wife ends with what, given his character, she knows to be a futile future prayer, "god keep you from the knowledge of who you are." Oedipus does not listen. Given the kind of man he is, he cannot listen. Instead he presses forward in the hunt and the queen, in desperation and despair, goes inside the palace to commit suicide.

So intent is Oedipus on solving the mystery of his birth, and "bringing all to light," so adamant is he not to let go "the chance of finding out the whole thing clearly" that he completely misreads what Jocasta says and why she says it. He thinks her ashamed of his lowly birth and in a final fantasy of escape before the trap door closes, he imagines himself Fortune's (Tuchē's) child, self-made and self-generated, unencumbered by past or culture, a free individual agent who lives by his wits and mind.

This fantasy was not the king's alone, for the sophistic enlightenment whose beginnings coincide with the play's performance, emphasized the power of rea-

son to confront and resolve the problems of existence without recourse to supernatural or mysterious forces. In this shift,[39] abstract and conceptual modes of
thought largely replaced mythical and symbolic forms, as the world was now
seen as operating through impersonal processes that followed "scientific" laws.
Where the earth had been an all-giving mother, it was now a measurable surface
that could be mapped. Where the sun had been a god driving a blazing chariot
across the heavens, it was now a huge molten rock. And while the gods were not
wholly dismissed, they were increasingly understood as psychological forces
within man or as allegorical expressions of nature. Finally, the laws of cities
came not from the gods but from the deliberations of human assemblies and
councils, while the cities themselves were human institutions, not the seat of
divine powers rooted in a sacred landscape.

But Oedipus is not the child of chance but of Laius and Jocasta. He is not a
self-made, self-generated individual who produces meaning and decides his own
fate, but a man whose identity and character has been subject to meaning and
forces spatially and temporally beyond him. We might say that humans are partly
in life what Oedipus fully is as a character in a play: scripted figures whose freely
chosen action manifests an, at best, half-glimpsed character. Even a glimpse will
elude anyone who stubbornly adheres to the myth that he is an actor whose
behavior springs from individual self-interest and conscious choice, that he possesses extensive and clear knowledge of the environment and a well-ordered
organized stable system of preferences and computational skills that allow him to
calculate the best choice (given individual preferences) among the alternatives
available.[40]

Since human beings are never the disembodied creatures that Oedipus wrongly
supposes himself to be, they can recognize their human condition of mortality
(that they are born, live, and die) but they cannot know their own nature. To
possess such knowledge would be like jumping over one's own shadow. Even the
distinctive condition of being human is ambiguous, changing, and historical. Because thought cannot fix the essential meaning of our condition, it cannot define
human nature. Only a god who left the theater entirely could do so. For Sophocles the nature of man is as much a theological problem as the nature of the
gods.[41]

When Oedipus sees the truth, he puts out his eyes. The self-blinding is an act
of compensation and recognition. It acknowledges that the pride he took in his
far-seeing intelligence was unfounded since all his life he was blind to the realities that plagued his identity and action. It also reconciles him to Tiresias, whom

---

[39] As I have suggested in previous notes, the danger of such evolutionary stories is that they slight
the degree to which what seems overcome by events or thought remains the ground for everyday life.
The old ways did not disappear and in fact became more aggressively asserted as chapter five
suggests.

[40] See Kristen Monroe's summary in *The Economic Approach to Politics,* p. 4, and Herbert Simon's discussion of bounded rationality in his two-volume work with that title (Cambridge, Mass.:
MIT Press, 1982), especially chap. 1.

[41] See Arendt's discussion in the *Life of the Mind,* vol. 1, and *The Human Condition* (Chicago:
University of Chicago Press, 1958).

he had ridiculed for his ignorance and obscure speech, but whom he now joins as a blind prophet in a shared vision of the truth. And it honors Apollo, the god he had scorned, and the existence of an oracular structure of significance which remains opaque for even the most discerning eyes of the most enlightened human.

But the self-blinding is also an act by someone we recognize as Oedipus, someone we have known through the description of his acts by others as well as by what we have seen before us. In its forcefulness and excess, it is typical of the man and expressive of a character who killed another in anger, impetuously left his "native" Corinth when he wrongly presumed to know the meaning of Apollo's oracle, was quick to find hostile conspiracies among men who wished him no harm, who physically tortured the shepherd into talking, and who called down such fierce imprecations upon the killer of Laius (who happens to be himself) at the beginning of the play. Here is a fit son of Laius who would not yield (either to the oracle who said that if he had children his son would kill him), or on the road to a man (who turns out to be his son) and of a mother who commits suicide.

While Jocasta's suicide takes place in the palace and so remains a private act, Oedipus insists that he be made what the play as a whole is: a public spectacle. When he appears, the elders of the chorus asks him what madness (*mania*) it was that came upon him, what diabolical spirit it was that leaped so savagely upon his life that he should come to this. But they shudder at the sight of him and at the prospect of an answer to their questions not only because of their love for Oedipus but for themselves. If a man of such consummate intelligence and courage, if the savior of their city, can be so wrong, what about the rest of us?

Oedipus answers that he and Apollo are the joint authors of his life. Apollo may have set the course, but then as now in the act of self-blinding, he, Oedipus, was the one whose action realized that fate. He may have acted in ignorance, but everything he did was his, in the sense that it belonged to him and expressed his character. This discovery about himself "is scarcely less crucial than the discovery of his identity."[42] In fact the action of the play is not about the deeds he was fated to perform but about his discovery that he has already fulfilled them and this discovery is due entirely to his own actions.[43]

The play dramatizes the darkness inside enlightenment, a darkness whose exposure leaves men blind to the world they (thought) they knew so well and in which they felt comfortable and in control. The most far-seeing of men and women, those deemed most rational and most empirically grounded, live with an ignorance proportional to the certainties of their theories and the stable identities they impose on others and themselves.

As the paths of Oedipus's life come together, his double identity becomes one and the tension between the surface and deeper meaning of his deeds is resolved.

---

[42] Cameron, *The Identity of Oedipus the King,* p. 115. I have discussed this theme at length in *The Tragedy of Political Theory,* chap. 4.

[43] See the discussion in Knox, "The Freedom of Oedipus."

Yet the ambiguities of his life are not erased but rather recast in the play's final "vision" of its chief protagonist.

On the one hand the man who thought himself to be (and was thought to be by others) the equal of the gods and the supreme calculator, is now equal to nothing. The proud king once confident in speech and of his clear-sighted vision expostulates in a series of monosyllabic cries and scarcely coherent exclamations.[44] The rational man who prided himself on being an independent agent is now, like Tiresias, a blind beggar dependent on everyone for everything. "To the extent to which a man's fate is dependent on other men," Simone Weil has written, "his life escapes not only out of his hands, but also out of the control of his intelligence; judgment and resolution no longer have anything to which to apply themselves. Instead of contributing and acting, one has to stoop to pleading or threatening; and the soul is plunged into a bottomless abyss of desire and fear, for there are no bounds to the satisfaction and sufferings that a man can receive at the hands of other men."[45] At the heart of the play, the classicist Karl Reinhardt believes, is "illusion and truth as the opposing forces between which man is bound, in which he is entangled, and in whose shackles as he strives towards the highest he can hope for, he is worn down and destroyed."[46]

But that is only on one hand; there is another. It is suggested by Oedipus's exchange with Creon, now king of Thebes, with which the play concludes. He begs the man he had "used most vilely" to drive him into exile so he may never hear another human voice. But a moment and few lines later, referring to the burial of his dead mother/wife he commands (*episkēpto*)[47] and begs (*prostrepsomai*) Creon to do the deed and he continues issuing orders until Creon has to remind this man, who should need no such reminder, that he must not "seek to be master in everything, for the things you mastered did not follow you throughout your life" (1522–23). This sense of command is consistent with the way Oedipus not only takes responsibility for fate, but seizes it, proclaiming that the deeds

---

[44]   aiai, aiai, dustanos egō
        poi gas pheromai tlamōn; pai moi
        phthonga diapōt'atai phoradēn;
        iō diamon, hin' etēlou

        Where am I going? where on earth?
        where does all this agony hurl me?
        where's my voice?—
        winging, swept away on a dark tide
        O dark power of the god, what a leap you made!

                                                        (1441–45)

This is the Fagles translation as modified by Segal.

[45] *Oppression and Liberty,* trans. Arthur Wills and John Petrie (Amherst: University of Massachusetts Press, 1958), p. 96.

[46] Reinhardt, *Sophocles,* p. 134.

[47] One meaning of *episkēptō* is to make, lean upon, throw light upon, or impose upon. Another is to lay a strict charge upon someone or command them to do something. A third is to prosecute or indict. Given the themes of the play, the word, like the act of self-blinding, brings the parts into a whole.

done are his alone. The old Oedipus is not dead. Chastened, blind, and dependent he may be; but that is not all he is. His search for the truth and the knowledge he has, however dearly bought, gives him the strength and courage to persevere amid his misery.

And that is perhaps the most important thing: Oedipus did solve the riddle of his birth and Laius's death; he remained committed, single-mindedly so, to the hunt for the truth even when he had premonitions of the disaster that awaited its capture. If no man has suffered as he has, which is the boast he makes now, then no man has learned so well the lessons of mortal life. Knowledge not borne of suffering, which does not touch the soul as well as the mind, which does not remain in the company of passion, is abstract, uneventful, sterile, intellectualized—perhaps not knowledge at all. A recent critic of rational actor theory's dependence on the economic approach to the analysis of political behavior argues that a "great deal of human conduct occurs under circumstances that are insufficiently similar to those postulated by the rational actor approach for that method to be of great use for the purpose of explanation. The highly touted virtues of elegance and simplicity are very attractive in the abstract. They are less so when their application to real world explanation is achieved at the price of implausibility,"[48] or I would add, of surface plausibility.

III

There is no conclusion to the *Oedipus Tyrannus,* if by conclusion one means a final scene that sets all things right and in place and in which some irrevocable synthesis of opposing views is achieved. While it is true that, in some respects Oedipus becomes Tiresias, the opposed views of knowing they represent and literally embody remain, in Mikhail Bakhtin's terms, "a plurality of independent and unmerged voices and consciousnesses, a genuine polyphony of fully valid voices" where each is a rejoinder in a continuing dialogue about enlightenment.[49]

Given the play's stance toward the riddles it dramatizes and the way it itself becomes riddling, this is hardly surprising. Indeed it would be strange if there were one integrating conclusion that answered all the questions raised by the play. If we are, as the play suggests, caught in a web of local meanings which necessarily leave us riddles to ourselves if not others, then reducing the play to a single term would endorse what it seems to warn against.[50] In these terms the aim

[48] David Johnston, "Human Agency and Rational Action," in Monroe, *The Economic Approach to Politics,* p. 106.

[49] See his discussion in *Problems of Dostoevsky's Poetics,* trans. Caryl Emerson (Minneapolis: University of Minnesota Press, 1984) pp. 6–7, 32, 97.

[50] Indeed, Frederick Ahl would suggest that this is precisely what I have done. He argues that Oedipus's assumption that he did indeed kill his father and our presumption that he is right is precipitous, given that those upon whose testimony he (and we) relies to prove his guilt often have "vague identities and questionable motives" and that the king's conclusions are based on words that are "notoriously elusive and prone to ambiguity." *Sophocles' Oedipus* (Ithaca: Cornell University Press, 1991), p. 28.

of producing lawlike statements about measurable phenomena, adhering to the virtues of coherent parsimonious deductive theories or, more generally, anxiously purging contradiction, seems naive and self-defeating.

Certainly any obvious conclusion would cause the play to lose its capacity to disturb the alliance of reason, science, method, and progress that continues to flourish as the dominant conceit in political science. Political science may be able to provide essential perhaps even saving knowledge on occasion. But it can do so only if it honors what it cannot do, recognizes that every way of seeing is a way of not seeing, and avoids both incest, the cozy accommodation with dominant discourses and structures of power, and patricide, a deracination that denies the shaping hand of the past, discards inherited habits, beliefs, and institutions, and regards memory as an irritant.[51]

Drama and poetry do not make arguments or offer logically consistent truths informed by a rigorous collection of data. Their power lies in surprise and disruption, in shocking excess and in provocations that push us often against our interests and inclination to deeper and wider understanding of who we are, what we know, and how these are related. They teach by ellipsis and revelation, dramatizing "unspeakable things unspoken," making darkness visible without dissipating its terror. While Jocasta's suicide takes place offstage, the narration of her violent deed by the messenger (1237–1378) calls attention to what is not seen by withholding it. In this the play creates a counterpoint between events seen in the clear light of day in the theater's orchestra and the hidden events offstage, which acquire an added dimension of horror, mystery, and fascination because they are present but unseen. The offstage place is the interior of the palace, a space of the irrational and demonic.[52] What are we to say of a theory that steps over the abyss with no recognition that it is there or anywhere? Will we regard humans as organisms who generate layers of meaning that lie beneath the surface of understanding or as self-transparent as Oedipus supposes? Aristotle said philosophy begins in wonder; Sophoclean tragedy (or rather this one) begins in wonder that the opacity of events and character do not create more wonder.[53]

If life does indeed present such depth and complexity, then creativity is not the exclusive prerogative of the divinely inspired poet or individual hero but is an aspect of ordinary existence. If Freud is right in locating the unconscious inside the psyche, then "everyone is poetic, everyone dreams in metaphor and generates symbolic meaning in the process of living. Even in their prose people have unwittingly been speaking poetry all along."[54] Perhaps that helps explain certain

---

[51] See John H. Schaar and Sheldon Wolin, *The Berkeley Rebellion and Beyond* (New York: New York Review of Books, 1970).

[52] The argument and some of the language is taken from Charles Segal, "Spectator and Listener," in Jean-Pierre Vernant, *The Greeks,* trans. Charles Lambert and Teresa Lavender Fagan (Chicago: University of Chicago Press, 1995), pp. 206–7.

[53] Jonathan Lear, "The Shrink Is In," *New Republic* 82 (December 25, 1995): 24. Though I find some of Lear's points persuasive and his formulations helpful, I do not endorse his overall defense of Freud.

[54] Ibid., p. 25.

tensions in *Leviathan* and suggests a moment where the classicist Hobbes remembered Greek drama.

How is one to capture such depth or, if not capture it, at least honor its presence and generative capacities for good or for ill? The question leads back to Nietzsche's *Wir Philologen* discussed in chapter two and to Martha Nussbaum's concern for stylistic choices dictated by habit and convention, by "Anglo-American fastidiousness and emotional reticence," and by the "academization and professionalization of philosophy."[55]

IV

Even if Nussbaum is right about all texts (including those written by rational actor theorists) expressing a particular sense of life and possibility and representing choices that have as much to do with academic fashion and prestige as with truth, of what use is her polemic for political scientists concerned with the parameters of decision and policy? Indeed, as I asked in chapter two, of what "use" is a fifth-century B.C. drama for understanding political life in a modern nation-state? There are so many historical differences between then and now, between them and us; so great a transformation of scale and sensibility between ancient Athens and contemporary America; so many disjunctions between theater and university, stage and classroom, drama and political science that to suppose that some Greek play could retain its distinctive power to provoke and "enlighten" seems a gross exaggeration.

Yet the burden of this chapter as of this book as a whole is that it can and does; that if we wish to avoid drawing our political and methodological gods too much in our own likeness or wrapping ourselves in them as a form of mental prosthesis, we could do worse than make *Oedipus Tyrannus* companion reading for political science texts, methodological primers, and arguments about rational actors and theory.

Perhaps there are political and moral standards that exist somewhere in the mind of God or in the totality of the universe. Perhaps we need to believe there are if we are not to lose something of value (however it is we came to value it). But as *Oedipus Tyrannus* suggests, none of us lives in the mind of God (or the gods) or the totality of the universe, but in "specific places demarcated in their configurations and in their possibilities for action . . . by transient, partial, shifting, and contingent understandings of what is and what should be."[56] This is not to deny that some understandings are less partial and transient or that we can give reasons for our political judgments, or that some visions of the future and constructions of the past are better, fuller, or truer. It is to reiterate the conclusion of the *Antigone* that the world is not made for us or we for the world. Our history

---

[55] *Love's Knowledge,* p. 20.

[56] Stanley Fish, "The Common Touch, or One Size Fits All," in Darryl J. Gless and Barbara Herrnstein Smith, eds., *The Politics of Liberal Education* (Durham, N.C.: Duke University Press, 1992), p. 251.

tells no purposive story and reveals no teleology. There is no Archimedian point from which we can confirm or authenticate our activities, no "redemptive Hegelian history or universal Leibnizian cost-benefit analysis"[57] to show that it will all turn out well in the end. What does exist is evidence that our fondest achievements, including reason, critical intelligence, and the capacity for reflection, however admirable, are "plagued" by a darkness that no enlightenment can wholly dissipate

Socrates of course is seen as repudiating this tragic sensibility in the name of reason, critical intelligence, and self-awareness. There are grounds for this claim. Yet his insistence in the *Apology* that he has human as opposed to divine wisdom and the kind of teacher he is dramatized as being speaks in a less optimistic register, one that, like comedy and tragedy, encourages democratic citizens to maintain a certain humility in the face of their power and self-importance. At least in that dialogue the world does not yield its meaning(s) to reason, and the commitment to an examined life is necessary because our partialities are never dissipated but are continually being reconfigured even as we are constituted by them. It is for this among other reasons that Socrates' project sometimes seems less a matter of disinterring the deep features of our reality than showing us, as Sophocles does, how hard it is for us to obtain a clear sense of what we already know. In these terms the trouble lies for "us" as for Oedipus (and Wittgenstein) in our inability to see what is before our eyes, in the fact that we sometimes fail to see the truth not because it is so hard but because it is so familiar.

Plato is a more complicated case, as I will argue in the next two chapters on the *Gorgias* and *Protagoras*. Both dialogues present us with reason's hope being disappointed by dialogue floundering on rocks of power and interest. What is uncertain is whether the disappointment is due to a misunderstanding of reason or because "we" are too corrupt to live up to its demands and realize its promise. The answer has much to do with the relationship between Socrates and Plato and everything to do with the question of philosophy's relationship to democracy.

---

[57] The phrase is Bernard Williams's. See *Shame and Necessity* (Berkeley: University of California Press, 1993), p. 166.

The *Gorgias*, Socratic Dialectic, and the Education of Democratic Citizens

> We cannot assume today that men must in the last resort be governed by their own consent. Among the means of power that now prevail is the power to manage and manipulate the consent of men. That we do not know the limits of such power—and that we hope it does have limits—does not remove the fact that much power today is successfully employed without the sanction of the reason, of the conscience of the obedient.
>
> —C. Wright Mills[1]

I

The question of who corrupts the young obscured what is perhaps a prior question, one that frames the *Apology* even though it is not explicitly raised in it: how can one know what effect one has on others? There are so many contingencies even in the relationship between two people, say a teacher and student or a parent and child, that the idea of knowing how to educate one's fellow citizens politically seems daunting to say the least. We know that reading the "right" books does not always form the "right" action, that taking courses in moral philosophy or professional ethics does not necessarily translate into ethical behavior, and that one of the most cultured peoples in the West committed perhaps the worst atrocities in the West. So the question remains, How do "we" "make" someone better, "make" them into good citizens? An issue in totalitarian regimes where the intentions of all but a few are subject to constant "reeducation," it is even more of one in a democracy where the "we" must be inclusive (or at least the burden falls on any exclusion), and the idea of "making" someone anything seems inherently antidemocratic. What the *Apology* implicitly raises the *Gorgias* explicitly does when Socrates criticizes Gorgias and Pericles for having "made" people worse rather than better and suggests that he, having the political art, would not.

From chapter two on I have emphasized the ways in which Socrates' vocation can be seen as an elaboration of Athenian democratic practices even when he is explicitly critical of democracy. But even if I am right about the *Apology* providing evidence for such continuities, my claim is counterintuitive (to say the least) in regard to virtually every other dialogue in the Platonic corpus, none more so than in regard to the *Gorgias*. If Socrates' criticisms of democracy in this and

---

[1] C. Wright Mills, *The Sociological Imagination* (New York: Oxford University Press, 1956), pp. 40–41.

other dialogues are of such a nature that he can plausibly be seen as antidemocratic, then my case for his being a democratic political educator and my distinction between a political and a politicized education that depends on it seems far-fetched. True, his criticism of democracy may be useful for democrats to take seriously, but that, while significant, is something different and leaves the opposition between philosophy and democracy I am challenging intact. One of the burdens of this chapter is to show the ways in which Socrates is democratic and how thinking of him in that way illuminates aspects of dialogue that are often elided.

In chapter three I offered a general argument that Athenian politics made political theory possible and necessary. In the following chapter on accountability I looked at two specific practices that Socrates could have, or more strongly did, build upon when he demanded that his interlocutors render an account of their lives. While the chapter on Salamis talked about a cultural dialectic, the chapter on accountability was concerned with specific institutional practices. In this chapter I want to make an argument that complements that of chapter four while further illustrating that of chapter three. I will do this by exploring how elements of Athenian democratic culture and politics shape both the substance and form of the *Gorgias.* Whereas my response to Walzer (as well as Bloom and Barber) in chapter four rested on moving from practice to philosophy, my response here moves from philosophy to practice.

With the help of Thucydides and Hobbes, chapter six on *Antigone* defined the issue of political corruption in terms of the corruption of speech and language. That formulation reappears in the *Gorgias* as a debate over the purposes of rhetoric. More specifically, I ended chapter six by asking how much the corrupt world of mythical Thebes was a mirror of or an object lesson for the audience in the theater. Given the world on stage, any hope for a Habermasian project seemed partial in both senses. But insofar as the world on stage was another place in Zeitlin's sense, the experience of watching the play may have contributed to the possibility of such a project in the sense of contributing to the Athenians' ability to deliberate about politics. Though they surely never lost sight of the necessarily strategic dimensions of language as Ober has repeatedly emphasized, the contrast between persuasion and violence implicitly recognized the need for speech to be something more than strategic. It was some such distinction that lay behind Thucydides' characterization of how language became "defamed" during the civil war at Corcyra. This chapter reposes the question raised in the concluding sections of the *Antigone* chapter by exploring the tension between Socrates' (or Plato's) proposal that philosophical dialogue can be seen as paradigmatic for political deliberation and the degree to which philosophy itself is politicized.

As in the *Clouds,* the issue of political corruption is posed largely in generational terms. It is posed specifically in the relationship between Gorgias and his young student Polus, in Socrates' relationship to Alcibades, and in Socrates' charge that Pericles has made the Athenians worse. (Except for his comments on Aristides Socrates is no more respectful of the older generation of leaders.) More generally it appears in Socrates' pointed question of what will become of the

Athenians when they can no longer glory in the empire, power, and wealth they now celebrate as their noblest achievements.

II

The *Gorgias* is not a very promising dialogue if one wants to make a case for a democratic Socrates. The dialogue presents him as contemptuous of the multitude and the idea that it could have its own will and voice, as rejecting jury pay and majority rule, as indifferent to the question of who enjoys the political rights and prerogatives of citizens, as endorsing expert political knowledge, as regarding leadership as a form of "psychic engineering," and as perversely disparaging the revered democratic leaders of Athens,[2] all as part of a misbegotten project of substituting philosophical truth for the contingencies and uncertainties that mark all politics but democratic politics most of all.

While I have no desire to explain away these antidemocratic sentiments or dismiss the conventional readings of the *Gorgias,* I will read the dialogue against the grain[3] to complicate the picture of Socrates as antidemocratic. At a minimum I will argue that Socrates is more of a democrat than he seems and that much of what he says about democracy in the *Gorgias* is directed at the way democracy is being construed by the interlocutors in the dialogue and those in Athens who agree with or honor them. If such putative friends are in fact enemies of democracy, then Socrates' critique of them raises the question of who are democracy's true friends and whether the real friend may be the seeming enemy. This question has special urgency in a society which, as Ian Morris has emphasized,[4] citizens thought of themselves as tied together, restrained, and made equal by *philia*. If, like Polemarchus in the *Republic,* one is confused about who one's true friends and enemies are, then such ties and any politics based upon them become deeply problematic. And unless one is clear on this, it will be difficult to distinguish between critics of democracy attempting to recall or inspire their fellow citizens to the highest possibilities of their culture[5]—whether it be by argument, example

---

[2] See Neal Wood and Ellen Wood, "Socrates and Democracy: A Reply to Gregory Vlastos," *Political Theory* 14, no. 1 (February 1986): 68, and Brian Vickers, *In Defense of Rhetoric* (New York: Oxford University Press, 1988), chap. 2.

[3] I have done such a reading in much more detail in "Democracy and Political Theory: A Reading of the Gorgias," in J. Peter Euben, John R. Wallach, and Josiah Ober, eds., *Athenian Political Thought and the Reconstitution of American Democracy* (Ithaca: Cornell University Press, 1994), pp. 198–226.

[4] Ian Morris, "The Strong Principle of Equality and the Archaic Origins of Greek Democracy," in Josiah Ober and Charles Hedrick, eds., *Demokratia: A Conversation on Democracy, Ancient and Modern* (Princeton: Princeton University Press, 1996).

[5] It is perhaps worth remembering that radical democratic movements were often generated by attacks on the dominant culture for failing to adhere to their own declared principles or to extend them to all. (That is one lesson of E. P. Thompson's *Making of the English Working Class* [New York: Vintage, 1963] as well as C.L.R. James's *Black Jacobins* [New York: Vintage, 1963].)

or provocation—from those who are antidemocrats.[6] Let me take Socrates' criticism of Athens's political leaders as an example of why the distinction is not as obvious as it seems. Later I will argue that this criticism involves a contest over how Pericles—and so Athenian democracy—was to be understood.

There is no question that Socrates' criticisms of the Athenian leaders are ungenerous at best, simple-minded and moralistic at worst. In assuming that leaders are in complete control of events, he ignores the contingencies that accompany all collective endeavors, and the inevitable discrepancy between intentions and results. But let us suppose Socrates (or Plato) knows that such revisionist representations, though they might find favor in a few militantly conservative circles, would be taken as provocative. Suppose the point is to stimulate argument and debate, to have Athenians become more thoughtful about what they had done and could do in the future. In this regard consider Sheldon Wolin's argument[7] that during the Peloponnesian War the connection between power and place was attenuated as Athens became a naval base from which power was projected rather than embodied in internal deliberations, policy decisions, and decrees. Should we regard sharp criticism of such developments and the leaders responsible for them as being antidemocratic? Perhaps, if the critiques go far enough. But how far? Though I am not sure of the answer, I am sure that the *Gorgias* poses the question with unique force and subtlety and that a case can be made that part of Socrates' critique is directed against the unforeseen consequences of Athenian imperialism.

Those consequences are foregrounded when Socrates pointedly asks Callicles what will happen to him, to Athens, and by implication to his assessment of Athenian leaders when the city loses its empire, as of course it had by the time the dialogue was written. The tension between the dramatic and historical dates of the *Gorgias* presents Socrates as more politically prescient than the more "realistic" and pragmatic Callicles.[8]

There is another way of getting at the complications involved in making a sharp distinction between sympathetic critics of democracy and antidemocrats. Socrates dismisses majority rule as an absurd way of deciding on the best way or life or even the best policy. Since such rule is seen as essential to if not distinctive to democracy, such rejection seems strong evidence of Socrates' hostility to the equality and antifoundational epistemology democracy presupposes. But majority rule is not distinctive to democracy and so Socrates' criticism is not directed just at democracy but at any regime—including oligarchy—in which some

[6] For reasons elaborated by Josiah Ober in *Mass and Elite in Democratic Athens: Rhetoric, Ideology and the Power of the People* (Princeton: Princeton University Press, 1989), such a polarity misdescribes the complicated ideological negotiations between elites and nonelites.

[7] Sheldon S. Wolin, "Transgression, Equality, and Voice" in Ober and Hedrick, *Demokratia*, pp. 63–90.

[8] E. A. Havelock, in *The Liberal Temper in Greek Politics* (New Haven: Yale University Press, 1957), argues that Plato lacked any understanding of the practical world with which the rhetoricians dealt. It is this political stupidity masked by high-flown pronouncements that Havelock suggests alternately annoy and enrage Callicles. I am suggesting the dialogue offers an implicit response to such charges (though they are only implicit and not conclusive).

group of citizens, no matter how exclusive, decide things by majority vote. What is distinctive to democracy is who is part of the majority when it does vote. More than that, even democracy's friends have often worried about what majority rule can mean in the face of elite manipulation, as Mills does in the epigraph for this chapter.[9] For all the dangerous notions that claims about manufactured consent can lead to (such as false consciousness and democratic centralism), for all the reconceptualization of power due to Foucault, and for all the attempts by writers on popular culture to find local resistance where Mills finds manipulation, his concerns remain salient and echo Socrates' concerns about rhetorical manipulation[10] and manufacturing of consent.[11]

I offer one final way of complicating the distinction between being a sympathetic if critical friend of democracy and being antidemocratic as it applies to Socrates in the *Gorgias*. Although there are obvious and significant dissimilarities between modes of communication employed in the relatively face-to-face society of classical Athens and our own electronic mass media, Socrates' concern with democracy's susceptibility to rhetorical manipulation anticipates contemporary concerns about the debasement of public discourse, the disappearance of public spaces, and the danger of the "system world" cannibalizing the "life world."[12] In its indifference to truth, our political discourse has become, in Neil Postman's view, "dangerous nonsense." "By favoring certain definitions of intelligence and wisdom and by demanding a certain kind of content," television has created "new forms of truth-telling."[13] When he goes on to insist that television fosters "misplaced irrelevant fragmented superficial information that creates the illusion of knowing something which in fact leads one away from knowing," we can hear Socrates' response to Gorgias's claims about the power of rhetoric overwhelming truth about medicine or politics.

[9] See Steven Lukes's discussion of "the third dimension of power" in his *Power: A Radical View* (London: Macmillan, 1974) and John Gaventa's elaboration of it (and of manufactured consent) in his *Power and Powerlessness: Quiescence and Rebellion in an Appalachian Valley* (Urbana: University of Illinois Press, 1980).

[10] John Fiske, *Understanding Popular Culture* (New York: Routledge, 1989).

[11] In *All Consuming Images: The Politics of Style in Contemporary Culture* (New York: Oxford University Press, 1988), Stuart Ewan talks about the "engineering of consent" where public relations experts "conflate ideological management techniques with the idiom of social and political liberty" and goes on to quote Edward Bernay to the effect that "the engineering of consent is the very essence of the democratic process, the freedom to persuade and suggest." The various freedoms in the Bill of Rights—speech, press, petition, and assembly, "the freedoms which make the engineering of consent possible"—are among the most cherished guarantees of the Constitution of the United States (p. 267).

[12] There is the added similarity of each dealing with the promises and danger of "enlightenment." The phrases "life world" and "system world" are Habermas's. He first introduced them in *Legitimation Crisis,* trans. T. McCarthy (Boston: Beacon Press, 1975) but develops them at great length in *The Theory of Communicative Action,* vol. 1, trans. T. McCarthy (Boston: Beacon Press, 1981).

[13] See his provocative but overstated *Amusing Ourselves to Death: Public Discourse in the Age of Show Business* (New York: Viking, 1985), p. 108. A similar argument is made by Roderick P. Hart in *Seducing America: How Television Charms the Modern Voter* (New York: Oxford University Press, 1994). Ewen argues that advertising, public relations, and other "industries of image and hype" are creating "a jerry-built material world with provocative, tenuous meanings suggesting fathomable value, but occupying no clear time or space" (p. 159).

For Socrates, rhetoric as practiced by Gorgias is committed to manipulation and misinformation since his power (and that of the kind of rhetoric he practices) depends on the ignorance of the people.[14] In this sense Gorgias is antidemocratic while Socrates is someone who reveals that fact and who, moreover, suggests in contrast that a participatory egalitarian politics requires that people be able to judge the character of the speaker and the general veracity of what is said, as well as distinguish between speech that is narrowly strategic[15] from speech that is not. Such a view is hardly antidemocratic, even if it is asking too much.

The political deficiencies and dangers of rhetoric do not lead Socrates into a wholesale rejection of it for at least two reasons. One is the fact that philosophy too is rhetorical, even manipulative, a fact Socrates implicitly and the dialogue explicitly acknowledges (as I shall argue). The other is the need each has for the other, as when Socrates ends the dialogue with a rhetorical display—the telling of a myth—intended, among other things, to convince the dialectically unpersuaded Callicles of the benefits of philosophy.[16] Nor do the deficiencies drive him into an epistemologically rather than a politically grounded notion of knowledge and wisdom. Rather he explores, both by what he does and what he says, the possibilities of a philosophically informed, politically grounded rhetoric that could help constitute a political education for a democratic citizenry. At least in this dialogue Socrates does not transform politics into a theoretical object requiring elaborate education as a prerequisite for the sharing of power as he is said to do in the *Republic*. He does not separate democracy from theory and intellect. What Socrates (or Plato) does do is what I suggested Salamis accomplished (in chapter three)—detach aristocratic values of the sort Callicles embraces from social class and reattach them to intelligence and philosophy while holding out the possibility that knowledge like power might be widely distributed. It is this vision of an aristocratic democracy as discussed in chapter three that Socrates explores persistently though inconclusively in the *Gorgias*.

As this implies Socrates assumes democracy as a context for his argument, and his criticisms of politics would be beside the point and unintelligible if the *dēmos* was not a significant political actor. The assumption is manifest in the *Gorgias*'s thematic preoccupations with freedom, power, and empire, in its stress on the need for open frank speech, accountability, and responsibility, and in its insistence on assessing what someone says by the merits of advice rather than on his birth, status, or wealth. It is also present in the dialogue's intellectualism (by which I mean a concern for the precondition for what it is doing)[17] and in the way

[14] Michael Berubé argues that the persuasiveness of critics like Kimball and D'Souza depend upon the ignorance of its audience. See his "Public Image Limited: Political Correctness and the Media's Big Lie," in Paul Berman, ed., *Debating PC* (New York: Dell, 1992), pp. 124–49.

[15] I say narrowly and primarily because I do not think one can, practically speaking, establish a hard line between strategic and nonstrategic, manipulative and nonmanipulative.

[16] James L. Kastely argues that rhetoric and philosophy are partners because the former can help us distance ourselves from what we are most attached to and therefore assist the dialectic examination of our lives. See his "In Defense of Plato's *Gorgias*," *PMLA* 106, no. 1 (January 1991): 96–109.

[17] See Martin Ostwald's discussion of the evolution of *nomos* in his *Nomos and the Beginnings of the Athenian Democracy* (New York: Oxford University Press, 1969). One can see the same self-

these thematic preoccupations become the stated preconditions for successfully engaging in philosophical dialogue. And it is evident in the dialogue's commitment to and dependence upon the idea of what Robert Dahl calls a strong principle of equality, where all members of a community are regarded as sufficiently well qualified to participate in making binding collective decisions on all issues that significantly affect their good or interest. (Though Socrates proposes the idea of expert political knowledge, the dialogue he has with his interlocutors in the *Gorgias* neither illustrates nor claims it.)[18] As I read the dialogue, no one (including Socrates) is presented as so superior that he or she should be entrusted with making the collective decisions about what to talk about or who is entitled to speak about what, to whom, how.

Socrates not only assumes democracy as a context for his critique of politics; he elaborates democratic practices discussed in previous chapters into a philosophical-political vocation. As I have argued, both the form and content of his criticism of Athenian democracy could build on a tradition of democratic self-critique found in drama and in the demand for accountability represented by the *dokimasia* and *euthunai.* If, as Benjamin Barber argues, reflexivity conditioned by civic education turns out to be democracy's greatest virtue, if democracy is debate about what democracy is, then what better example can we have than the *Gorgias* and of Socrates who embodies, or at least helps constitute, a democratic culture of this kind? It is for these as well as other reasons (set out in chapter two) that I believe that Socrates of the *Gorgias,* like Socrates of the *Apology,* remains a teacher for how to politically educate a democracy democratically, even if, as I would not deny, he remains skeptical of certain practices we regard as essentially democratic.

Finally, I want to offer a way of reading the *Gorgias* that opens up its democratic possibilities against the confluence noted in chapter one between conservative canonists who find congenial political pronouncements in classical texts and multicultural critics who accept their readings and condemn Socrates because of it. I argued there that such agreement relies on a deflationary reading of the dialogues. Here I want to offer an example of an alternative reading as a way of substantiating my criticism that such readings ignore the riddles posed by the way Socrates' knowledge is, to repeat Gregory Vlastos's words, "full of gaps, unanswered questions," "invaded by unresolved perplexity in a way that makes Socrates strange" (*atopos* is what Callicles calls him), as well as the need to keep faith with Socrates assertion of ignorance and his implicit denial of it.[19] I will argue that such interpretations tend to miss how the tensions, contrasts or even contradictions between text(s) and context(s), argument and drama, form and movement, and characters (such as Socrates and Callicles) create generative

---

consciousness in Pericles' preamble to his Funeral Oration (in Thucydides) when he reflects on why the institution he is about to embrace came to be and whether it should continue to exist.

[18] See Paul Woodruff, "Plato's Early Theory of Knowledge," in Stephen Everson, ed., *Epistemology* (New York: Cambridge University Press, 1990), pp. 60–84. Notice that Socrates drops the discussion of *technikou* almost as soon as it is raised at 500a.

[19] *Socrates: Ironist and Moral Philosopher* (Ithaca: Cornell University Press, 1991), p. 3.

spaces from within which the issues and conclusions of the dialogue are continually reframed. This is not so much a contrast between surface and depth or low and high (as in the *Republic*), as between shifting points of reference and view on the surface. And this means that questions of consistency and inconsistency are fluid and multiple for the same reason that a moment such as the Funeral Oration in Thucydides' *History* reads differently depending on which other speeches it is compared with, which other Athenian leaders he is compared with, and which incidents (Melos, the plague, the Mytilenean debate) are juxtaposed to it. If, as I will argue, these multiple points of view remain unresolved by any "normalizing" narrative, then the dialogue contains a superabundance of energy and transformative impulses ancient critics and modern defenders associate with Athenian democracy.[20]

I have already referred to Carol Dougherty's argument that the Athenians did not try to resolve the multiplicity of narratives by which they represented themselves as Athenians but allowed competing narratives about the origins of democracy, about Athenian identity, and even contradictory views of specific historical events to remain unrationalized. She goes on to suggest that the competition over origins was part of a contemporary controversy over the construction of citizenship and civic identity. As she puts it, "foundation tales of all kinds tend to respond to needs of the present as much if not more than they adequately record the past."[21] Her point applies to the *Gorgias* and helps us make sense of the debate over Periclean leadership, which is not only about whether he was a good leader but about how "Pericles" is to be represented and what sort of politics various representations legitimate. Her point also helps us make sense of how and why the contest over "Plato" and "the" Western tradition he comes to stand for is involved in contemporary debates over democratic citizenship and American civic identity.

III

Socrates' antidemocratic sentiments in the *Gorgias* seem clearest in his disparagement of the revered democratic leaders of Athens and in his conception of leadership as "psychic engineering." His most vehement criticism is aimed at the most democratic leader, Pericles, who is accused of making his fellow citizens worse by indulging their desires rather than educating their souls. How can someone who made those in his charge lazy covetous chatterboxes, who had a worse reputation among those he led at the end of his tenure of office than in the beginning, and who complained about his unjust treatment at the hands of the people he purportedly led be considered a good political leader? If he was a horse trainer who trained his horses to be even more unruly than they were before, or a

[20] See Sheldon S. Wolin, "Norm and Form: The Constitutionalizing of Democracy," in Euben et al., *Athenian Political Thought*, pp. 29–58.

[21] "Democratic Contradictions and the Synoptic Illusion of Euripides' *Ion*," in Ober and Hedrick, *Demokratia*.

doctor whose prescriptions made his patients worse, would we praise their art and accomplishments? Why not use the same standards for Pericles?

As an alternative Socrates offers the true political art (*alēthōs politikē technē*) and himself as the one living practitioner of it. This political art aims at improving the souls of citizens, transforming their ill-formed aspirations and ill-informed unselfconscious commitments. In its assumption of a radical inequality between the competent authority of the true statesman and the actual lives of people, in the discrepancy it posits between the judgment of the people and the knowledge necessary for moral self-knowledge, which is itself a necessary condition for participation, it is a view of leadership incompatible with even a tepidly liberal view of democracy. The case against Socrates as democratic seems both powerful and closed. But, as is by now obvious, I do not think it is either.

It isn't because, for one thing, it depends on a kind of reading the dialogue itself warns against. The *Gorgias* is concerned with deception and self-deception and shows Socrates using tactics he explicitly excoriates and failing to achieve what he repeatedly says he must in order to answer the central question of the dialogue ("Which is the best life?"). Moreover it incessantly calls attention to what is absent or problematic in the argument and drama such that the preconditions for dialogue become the dialogues' subject. And finally it leaves the great dialectician talking to himself.

For another thing there is the question I posed earlier of when being a critic of democracy makes one antidemocratic rather than a prophet recalling his or her people to what is best in their past and most promising in their future. This is a particularly pressing question if, as the juxtaposition of the dramatic and historical contexts of the dialogue suggests, that democracy has become so corrupt[22] that critique must be systemic and a particularly difficult one if we read the *Gorgias* against the background of Euripidean or Aristophanic drama, whose criticisms of Athenian democracy can make Socrates' criticisms of his native city seem relatively tame.

The dialogue, like the *Antigone,* presents the general corruption as one of language, a corruption of particular significance in an oral culture and in a democracy which relied on speech as a mode of political education, common deliberation, and judgment. It is in this regard that Socrates appears more committed to democratic culture than the popularly acclaimed Gorgias and the putative democrat Callicles. For the Gorgias of this dialogue[23] language is a form of manipulation and the necessary as well as sufficient condition for power, freedom, and happiness. The rhetorician's mastery of language enables his students to master anyone, any time, any place and for any ends.[24] It is the consequences of this which Socrates brings Gorgias to see and which brings the rhetorician to take Socrates' side later on.

---

[22] Though I think this is Plato's (or Socrates') argument, I am not endorsing it.

[23] If we regard *Gorgias* as a prismatic focus then the danger to democracy lies less within him than with the cultural forces that have made him popular and powerful. We make similar analyses of our political leaders when we see them against larger cultural frames.

[24] There is a wonderful example of this in the "gene industry" as analyzed by Ruth Hubbard and Elijah Wald's *Exploding the Gene Myth* (Boston: Beacon Press, 1993).

Where speech becomes mere words, when, as with Callicles (and some contemporary political leaders), protestations of affection and respect for the *dēmos* disguise contempt for them,[25] democratic citizens may well become cynical, passive, act impulsively or in ignorance, all of which then justifies elite claims to superiority. When masters of speech like Gorgias are disconnected from a living community of fellow citizens so that their sons will not have to fight in a war their words may have helped begin, the separation of words and things becomes the separation of power and responsibility.[26] If political judgment rests on the anticipated communications with others with whom I share a world and with whom I have to come to some agreement, then "distorted communication" of which Gorgias boasts and perpetuates is a threat to it. That he is uninterested in listening to what others say (he claims he has already heard every question that could possibly be asked him) and that he is a foreigner make him less aware of the highly contextualized discriminations and attention to particular ties of place and time that remind a people of their shared past and future. But he also dissolves the enlarged mentality political judgment requires, a mentality that enables citizens to think in place of others, to consider their perspectives. To quote Arendt yet again, "The more people's standpoints I have present in my mind while I am pondering a given issue and the better I can imagine how I would think and feel if I were in their place, the stronger will be my capacity for representative thinking and the more valid my final conclusion, my opinion."[27] This does not entail any erasure of self, interest, or will (or reifying them either). Nor is it a matter of altruism, following the dictates of an ontology or adhering to a stable vision of community. What it does entail is political and moral imagination, the ability to at least momentarily take the part of others, to see as they see and so see more of the world one shares with them. Like an actress one has to play more than one role to avoid "type-casting." Like a member of an audience one is able to see how the parts make up the whole. This is not a claim for objectivity or universality but for impartiality, in which we think as fellow actors, in representative ways.

The example Gorgias sets, the view of politics as domination he assumes or espouses, and the sort of citizens likely to emerge from that example and view (i.e., Polus and Callicles) endanger the always fragile negotiations that character-

---

[25] In his second speech in favor of natural superiority, Callicles hardly disguises his contempt for the *dēmos* and later calls it a "mob of slaves" and a "rabble of worthless men" (489c).

[26] Rhetorical ability *is* a necessity for a democratic political leader but it must be linked, Thucydides' Pericles tells us, with the ability to discern the appropriate policy, patriotism, and integrity (2.60.5). If one "despises rational argument and wishes, like Gorgias, to win fame and fortune by some other means, what more convenient doctrine to espouse in the process than Gorgiasic view that there is no truth anyway and it's all a matter of manipulation, more or less like drugging? Then one's failures to exhibit the traditional relational virtues will look daring rather than like sloppiness" (Martha Nussbaum, "Sophistry about Connections," in *Love's Knowledge* [New York: Oxford University Press, 1992], p. 221).

[27] Hannah Arendt, "The Crisis of Culture," and "Truth and Politics," in *Between Past and Future: Eight Exercises in Political Thought* (New York: Penguin, 1968), pp. 219–24, 227–64. She draws her notions of judgment from Kant and Aristotle. On the ambiguities of her argument, see Susan Bickford, *Listening, Conflict and Citizenship* (Ithaca: Cornell University Press, 1996), chap. 3.

ize democratic deliberations. But this is not a matter of undistorted communication since the *Gorgias* presses the ubiquity of power upon us even in philosophical discussions where it seems least present and most inappropriate. Nor, given
the contest over the representations of Athenian democratic leaders and Socrates
own manipulations, does it permit a sure line between fact and fiction.

One could say that the dialogue presents two principles in tension if not at war
with each other: one's a Habermasian ideal of a communicative reason in which
dialogue and deliberation are governed by ideas of frankness, mutuality, consensus, and rational argument derived from the formal structure of communication itself. The other is the Foucauldian suspicion that such discursive practice is
a particularly insidious way of concealing power's regime of truth with its normalizing productions and perpetuation of exclusions and hierarchies, both of
which problematize any ideal of manipulation and coercion-free "conversation."
For the former dialogue provides a paradigm for an emancipatory political theory
and politics. For the latter it is another instance of hiding power amid the rhetoric
of rationally motivated agreement.[28]

Thus the *Gorgias* holds out the hope and vision of dialogue as an exchange
which excludes extraneous concerns beyond the desire to understand, clarify,
reflect, and achieve agreement on the animating questions of individual and collective life. Here is a need for frankness and precision, friendship and consistency. But the dialogue challenges that vision by politicizing philosophy
through its own semantic complexity. Here is Mikhail Bakhtin.

> The words, directed toward its object, enters a dialogically agitated and tension-
> filled environment of alien words, value judgments and accents, weaves in and out of
> complex interrelationships, merges with some, recoils from others, intersects with
> yet a third group: and all this may crucially shape discourse, may leave a trace in all
> its semantic layers.[29]

There is a third complication about Socrates being antidemocratic, this one involving his criticism of Pericles.

By the time we get to Socrates' critique, Pericles has been assimilated to tyrants. For Gorgias the connection is implicit, emerging from his definition of
politics as deceit and domination for selfish ends. In these terms no political
leader, including Pericles, could have shared responsibility with relative free and
equal citizens since all leaders aim to be powerful, free, and happy and above the
law, doing what they want, when they want, to whomever they want. What is
implicit with Gorgias is made explicit by Polus who identifies the democratic
leaders with the tyrant Archelaus. It is left to Callicles to provide a metaphysical
justification for it and to praise Xerxes and Darius as having acted according to
the nature of what is just (483e2)—in their attacks on Greece! So when we get to
Socrates' critique of Pericles, the latter's democratic sympathies are portrayed as
a particularly ingenious cosmetic ploy to insinuate himself with the *dēmos* in

---

[28] See Habermas's "Further Reflections on the Public Sphere," in Craig Calhoun, ed., *Habermas
and the Public Sphere* (Cambridge, Mass.: MIT Press, 1992), pp. 421–61.

[29] *The Dialogical Imagination* (Austin: University of Texas Press, 1981), p. 276.

order to better dominate it. But if Socrates is criticizing *this* Pericles then it is not so clear that his criticisms of the Athenian pantheon is a criticism of "democracy" rather than of the way democracy and leadership have come to be construed by men like Gorgias, Polus, and Callicles (and the society that has called them forth). If I am right, then the contest over "Pericles" is a contest over how to represent the Athenian past as a way of legitimating a contemporary political agenda.[30]

In addition, despite the claim that he alone possesses the true art of politics which should presumably insure that his students are just in the way Gorgias's are not, Socrates was tried for corrupting the young and blamed then as he is now (by I. F. Stone) for having taught students who were responsible for a violent antidemocratic coup. Thus the accusations he levels at Gorgias were brought against him and the question becomes why he was as inept at "educating" his students as he accuses Gorgias and Pericles of being.[31] What makes things even more peculiar is that Socrates prominently invokes Alcibiades who was both one of those people he was accused of corrupting and a ward of Pericles. Thus Socrates and Pericles share responsibility for their students' excesses. And that creates a certain kinship between Socrates and the man he accuses of being the worst political leader of all and against whom he offers himself as corrective. To top it off there is Socrates' own inability to "control" Callicles. In the end he is left talking to himself, which is, Callicles implies, what he has been doing all along.

But what about the charge of "psychic engineering," the claim that Socrates endorses the idea of a political *technē* and rule by experts whose special unshared knowledge entitles them to tell others how to live or, at a minimum, establishes a relationship of teacher and student Arendt insists is inappropriate for the citizens of a democratic polis?

There is no question that such an idea is present in the *Gorgias*. If politics is a *technē* as shoemaking, horse training, or medicine is and those who possess the political art can "make" people better, prescribing for their souls as a physician does for their bodies in accordance with some agreed upon procedures and ends, then political issues can be dealt with rationally by professionals indifferent to the blandishments of men such as Gorgias. If there is such an art, no accidents of character or situation can thwart its success, since it is the absence of such an art that leaves someone like Gorgias unable to control the consequences of his teaching as they appear in the form of unjust actions by his students.

As with Socrates' criticisms of Pericles we confront complications which leave us less certain of Socrates' endorsement of any such political *technē*. Of

---

[30] None of this is meant to deny that there is a real contest between Socrates and Pericles over who (if either) possesses the true political art. On this see the discussion by Stephen Salkever in "Socrates' Aspasian Oration: The Play of Philosophy and Politics in Plato's *Menexenus*," *American Political Science Review* 87, no. 1 (March 1993): 133–43.

[31] Thomas Pangle sees the depth of the irony when he notes that "Socrates thus predicts his doom at the hands of the citizenry soon after having laid it down as *the* criterion of an effective statesman that in the course of his rule he make those he rules more tame and submissive to his rule than they were before he undertook to rule them!" ("Plato's *Gorgias* As a Vindication of Socratic Education," *Polis* 10, nos. 1–2 [1991]: 6).

course any such uncertainty affects the degree to which Socrates' arguments for a *technē* can be grounds for his being considered antidemocratic.

To begin with, it is worth noting that Socrates presents his claim as a counter to Gorgias's assertions about the power of rhetoric to give one absolute domination over everyone and every situation. The old rhetoric promises mastery over others as a means to achieve the satiation of desires. It persuades by flattery rather than on the basis of facts or common deliberation since its success depends on manipulation. And it magnifies the divisions within the soul and city. But the new philosophic rhetoric, the true political *technē* Socrates claims to practice, promises mastery for shared ends, treats others as ends, convinces these others on the basis of knowledge and dialogue and lessens the divisions within the soul and city. Making a man a friend to himself is, for Socrates, the precondition for making him a friend to others, and so a good citizen.

However strategic Socrates claims for a political *technē* may be, he does make them. Of the three analogies Socrates introduces by way of justifying his art/ artisanship—shoemaking, horse training, and medicine—the latter is the most plausible and most invoked. A political educator or leader is like a doctor of the soul who prevents or cures political and psychic illness as the doctor does physical ones. Unlike inert materials (leather or wood) that artisans work on or the irrational beasts that concern trainers, in medicine the "material" participates in its own physical regeneration. The question is, How? It had been one of Gorgias's boasts that the rhetorician is more powerful than the doctor even on medical matters since if a patient refuses to heed a diagnosis or take a prescription all the doctor's skill goes for naught, whereas a rhetorician can convince someone to do what makes him worse because of *his* skill with words. This is the ground upon which he claims rhetoric to be the master art. But for Socrates a good doctor-patient relationship entails the doctor persuading his patient to accept treatment by explaining the cause of his symptoms and the reasons why he is making the prescriptions he is. More significantly a healthy man would do whatever he wants and so the political authority of the expert would be at most temporary.[32]

But this is still a *technē*. What evidence is there for the stronger claim that, despite all appearances, Socrates does not endorse even this kind of a *technē* for politics?

If there is any ultimate authority in the dialogue, it is not a *technē* as Socrates has defined it but dialectic or dialogue itself. But this is a peculiar form of authority. For one thing it is neither personal, contained in a body of knowledge, nor derivable from transcendent norms but is, like politics, constituted and reinterpreted by the participation of human agents in ways that do not happen even in a doctor-patient relationship. For another thing, even dialectic or dialogue is contested and politicized, either by Callicles who challenges it directly, or indirectly

---

[32] As Terence Irwin notes in his translation of Plato's *Gorgias* (Oxford: Clarendon Press, 1990), p. 216.

by Socrates who pointedly departs from it, again unlike medicine.[33] Finally, Socrates' criticisms of Callicles' elitism suggest the possibility that dialectic, unlike *technai* (including medicine), could be taught and practiced by anyone. If that is indeed his belief, if he is hoping to create a citizenry capable of thinking for itself and thus immune to rhetorical manipulation, a citizenry moreover that is willing or even anxious to accept the responsibilities of power democracy requires, then the criticism of "Pericles" may constitute a general warning against democrats relying too much on *any* leader. Then the point of Socrates' philosophical rhetoric would not be to educate a few great leaders but to educate every Athenian to be a leader, at least to the degree that he will not have his judgment deformed by a Gorgias or a Callicles.[34] In these circumstances philosophical education becomes political education and Socrates' concern is with us as choosers rather than with any particular choice.

Consider the parallels between this view of a democratic political "leader" and Socrates' own role as a "teacher" and dialectician.[35] Socrates does not want us to think what he thinks or as he does unless we persuade ourselves by thinking for ourselves. There can be no passive acceptance of doctrinal instruction, whether the source be philosophers or political leaders. Thus the *Gorgias* finds Socrates questioning the authority of tradition, the many, self-styled political experts, pretenders to moral superiority, and self-proclaimed aristocrats, all the while insisting that he has "no more knowledge than you do when I ask and speak but rather join in a common search with you" (506a) and that he does "not know how it is that these things (the subject of the dialogue) are so" (509a).[36] Rhetoricians and sophists tell people what they want to hear as a way of gaining power over them. Socrates calls even the most obvious things and accepted views (about Pericles, wisdom, power, happiness) into question as a way of sharing power with them, whether in the dialogue or city.

---

[33] Medical relations too are "politicized." See, for instance, Barbara Ehrenrich and Deirdre English, *For Her Own Good* (Garden City, N.Y.: Anchor Books, 1979), and Burton J. Bledstein, *The Culture of Professionalism* (New York: Norton, 1978).

[34] "Too long have the workers of the world waited for some Moses to lead them out of bondage," wrote Eugene Debs. "He has not come; he will never come. I would not lead you out if I could; for if you could be led out, you could be led back again." This is quoted by Mark E. Kann in "Challenging Lockean Liberalism in America: The Case of Debs and Hillquit," *Political Theory* 8, no. 2 (1980): p. 214. At the end of the dialogue (527a–b) Socrates both insists that only one *logos* is left standing and that his conclusions are as temporary as the next contest.

[35] Socrates denied he was a teacher. The fact that he became one of the great moral teachers in the West is an irony subtlety discussed by Alexander Nehamas in "What Did Socrates Teach and to Whom Did He Teach It," *Review of Metaphysics* 46 (December 1992): 279–306. (Hereafter, page references will be given in text.) Most commentators consider Socrates' role as demurrer ironic. I think he was opposing himself to the sophists who claimed to have a doctrine they could give to their students. Socrates did not "have" a doctrine in the sense they claimed to have it, was very much aware of the disjunction between intentions and consequences, and thought teachers were supposed to have students who thought for themselves. (See the discussion of these issues in chapter two.)

[36] As Vlastos points out (*Socrates: Ironist and Moral Philosopher*), he often says this after what seems unambiguous victories and compelling arguments.

Or consider the way philosophical conversation as a common search for a shared good that enhances an individual's and dialogical community's good stands as an ideal of political deliberation as well. In these terms Socrates' insistence that "if my opponent has any substance in what he says I will be the first to acknowledge it" (506a) provides a standard for a political debate over the best policy. Moreover, as participants in the dialogue should take responsibility for what they say and are in this respect educators of each other, so should citizens. To be a good citizen requires that one be a friend to oneself, which is a precondition and end of dialogue. When Socrates argues that truth is larger than particular interests of those engaged in its pursuit or claims he cares for the argument that is their shared enterprise rather than being victorious, he is proposing a political as well as philosophical ideal. In these terms "philosophical" choices have direct consequences for how one acts politically, indeed for how one thinks about politics and action. Finally, the process of talk in both philosophical discussion and political deliberation changes how one talks. In both instances there is a move from what is private, selfish, or merely taken as given to a situation where reasons in terms of common purposes must be offered and defended. That participation in dialogue or deliberation changes those who participate in them is one reason why Benjamin Barber can describe what he calls "the civic bond" as "dialectical."

> Individuals become involved in government by participating in the common institutions of self-government and become involved with one another by virtue of their common engagement in politics. They are united by the ties of the common activity and common consciousness—ties that are willed rather than given by blood or heritage or prior consensus of beliefs and that thus depend for their preservation and growth on constant commitment and ongoing political activity.[37]

With appropriate substitutions (e.g., of dialogue for government) this is true of philosophical argument as well.

Now this suggests that the question of whether and how Socrates is a democrat is not only a matter of what is said but of how it is said, not only a question of explicit argumentation but of dialectical "method" and of the dramatic movement of the dialogue. Thus, it would be possible for the way criticisms of democracy are made—provocatively, frankly, inconsistently, ironically, dialectically, polyphonically—to be "democratic," even as the particular argument was not.

I want to elaborate this claim by articulating three voices in the *Gorgias*. Each voice is also a way of considering the relationship between philosophy and politics. I then want to recast these voices and these relationships as they are played out in the drama between Callicles and Socrates, which will lead to the question of Plato as a democrat and the third part of this essay.

The first, which I have called "Habermasian," is the possibility of philosophical dialogue as an idealized analog for democratic deliberation. The idea that political debate should emulate dialectic as Socrates celebrates it stands as a

---

[37] *Strong Democracy: Participatory Politics for a New Age* (Berkeley: University of California Press, 1984), p. 223.

rebuke to Callicles' view of politics as a war of all against all, against the idealization of tyranny, and against the equation of power with domination. Here "communicative rationality" would be free from deceptions and self-deception, strategic manipulations and domination. The second is what I called "Foucauldian," which politicizes philosophy, making it clear that establishing a dialogic community no less than a political one involves fiercely contested negotiations of power. Politicized philosophy confronts power as much as reason, and its search for truthfulness, in the sense of a mutually established ground for speech against rhetorical debasement, is disrupted by the play of interest and advantage within the dialogue, which echoes a similar play outside it. In this voice dialogue, like the democratic polis, rests on consent that is continually reworked and perpetually liable to politicization. If the first is the will to truth, the second confronts truth with the will to power, in the sense of both a suppressed instinct and generative possibilities.

There is a third voice that problematizes any analogy between philosophy and politics—a voice that reminds us of Socrates' death and anticipates the animus between philosophy and politics. Occasionally foregrounded, as when Callicles pointedly warns Socrates that his preoccupation with philosophy will leave him politically helpless and susceptible to false accusations that may well lead to his death, it mostly exists on the margins as frame, or at the center as subtext.

IV

Fifty years ago Werner Jaeger wondered whether "we have not given enough thought to the possibility that in his own character Plato had so much of that unruly will to power as to find, and fight, part of himself in Callicles." Though such a will to power lies "deeply buried" in Plato's other writings, its presence in the *Gorgias* may explain why Socrates was so powerful an influence on him. For if Plato "had by nature been only a second Socrates, the real Socrates would hardly have had such an overwhelming effect on him as he had."[38] Though I would quarrel with parts of this formulation, Jaeger is right to emphasize the singular energy and passion of Callicles' challenge to Socrates and philosophy, and the deep ambivalence toward politics this challenge portends.

Callicles is bewildered by his reaction to Socrates. "I do not know how it is that your speech attracts me Socrates. Yet I share the common feeling [*pollōn pathos*] of being unconvinced" (513c). On the one hand he admires Socrates' courage and tenacity, his independence and largeness of sensibility in adhering to something beyond petty pleasures and mundane preoccupations. If not convinced, Callicles seems at least worried by Socrates' argument that tyrants and those who would advise or support them are the least powerful, free, and happy because they must necessarily exhibit a slavelike hypersensitivity to what others think and might do. One could say that it is Socrates not Callicles who demonstrates a natural superiority the latter so admires.

[38] *Paideia*, vol. 2 (New York: Oxford University Press, 1945), p. 138.

Yet for Callicles what makes Socrates powerful also makes him vulnerable to unjust accusations and prey for any ambitious politicians. While Callicles respects philosophy as an essential ingredient in the education of a good man, to *be* a philosopher in the sense of making philosophical considerations paramount is a kind of insanity. It trivializes one's talents, marginalizes one's significance in life,[39] is ultimately self-defeating, and leaves one with a severe case of vertigo. At the very outset of their conversation Callicles recognizes that if Socrates was serious in his arguments with Gorgias and Polus human life "will have to be completely turned upside-down [*anatetrammenos*]" and "everything we do seems the exact opposite of what we should do" (481c).

"One chooses dialectic," Nietzsche wrote in *Twilight of the Idols,* "only when one has no other means. One knows that one arouses mistrust with it, that it is not very persuasive. Nothing is easier to erase than a dialectical effect; the experience of every meeting at which there are speeches proves this. It can only be *self-defense* for those who no longer have other weapons."[40] Perhaps Plato shared some of Nietzsche's sentiments and so Callicles might have had the same effect on him that Socrates had on Callicles. Perhaps Jaeger is right in assuming that the *Gorgias* is a dialogue between two parts of Plato's soul (which would give yet another dimension to the *Republic*). What we would need to know to answer these questions is Plato. But in the most obvious ways we don't.

I begin with a simple but sometimes unappreciated fact: nowhere in any dialogue does Plato speak in his "own" name. This makes the charge that Plato is an authoritarian, antipolitical, or antidemocratic, indeed the attribution of any doctrine to him, deeply problematic, unless one believes that Socrates is Plato's mouthpiece or that there is a straightforward way of distinguishing the democratic Socrates from the authoritarian Plato. Let me suggest why I do not think Socrates is Plato's mouthpiece, why, even if he is, it will not advance the argument for the latter's authoritarianism, and why, even if we could establish such a separation, it is not very consequential for the question of a democratic Socrates or Plato.

In a recent essay Michael Frede distinguishes various forms of Platonic dialectic.[41] One form is didactic, where the respondent, ignorant of certain truths as shown by his false statements, confronts a questioner who already knows the answer and asks questions that will induce him to give the right one so they can proceed to the next step of the argument. In these exchanges the respondent has no influence on the course of the argument since the questioner will not go on until she has received the right answer. This view of dialectic assumes that Socrates is "advancing an argument he already has and espouses, because it is an argument Plato has and endorses and which Plato just puts into Socrates' mouth;

---

[39] See the discussion in Nehamas, "What Did Socrates Teach," p. 279.

[40] Nietzsche, "The Twilight of the Idols," in Walter Kaufmann, ed., *The Portable Nietzsche* (New York: Viking Press, 1968), p. 476.

[41] "Plato's Arguments and the Dialogue Form," in James C. Klagge and Nicholas D. Smith, eds., *Methods of Interpreting Plato and His Dialogues,* supplementary volume in Julia Annas, ser. ed., *Oxford Studies in Ancient Philosophy* (Oxford: Clarendon Press, 1992), pp. 201–19.

an argument" in which the participant has no real power or influence "except that, for dramatic purposes, he can be represented as stubborn or misguided and thus as making it more or less difficult for Socrates to get to the conclusion of his argument" (209). This is how most undergraduates understand the Platonic "dialogues" on first reading, and how some of their teachers understand them after many.

But this form is never present in the early dialogues and absent in the *Gorgias.* All are aporetic, representing Socrates as engaging in "elenctic, rather than didactic, dialectic" (210). An *aporia* is a situation in which one no longer knows what to say or do about an issue or question.[42] Like Callicles, one is befuddled, torn between the conclusions one has reached and what seems to be the case, at a loss as to how to get out of the difficulty presented by the contradiction between one's original claim and the conclusion of the ensuing argument. If it was a situation where Socrates provided a proof for the contradictory claim, then Callicles would be embarrassed as were Gorgias and Polus. But being at a loss as to what to say and do is a different matter.[43]

How does elenctic dialectic do this? Take Callicles as an example. Callicles presents himself as an expert on politics and human nature. Socrates proceeds to test the knowledge upon which this claim to expertise rests. If Callicles (or Thrasymachus or Protagoras) contradicts himself on the very subject on which he claims expertise then his authority is in question. Socrates is less concerned to refute directly any particular answer or claim than he is in refuting Callicles himself. Indeed we might go further and argue, as I have in respect to leadership, that no claim to authority seems to withstand Socratic critique, that expertise itself is suspect. (The situation is analogous to the one in which we find equally reputable experts testifying on the opposite sides of an issue in a lawcourt. It is not so much their individual expertise that gets called into question but the very idea of expertise itself.)

If Frede is right about elenctic dialectic and I am right in applying it to the *Gorgias,* then Callicles contributes significantly to the movement and substance of the dialogue. It is true that Socrates poses the equations and in that sense shapes the argument. But since he does so to clarify the views and life of his interlocutor, "it does not matter in the least what the questioner himself knows or believes to be the facts about the subject in question" (212). Thus even if Plato were to identify with Socrates, he is committing himself only to the elenctic dialectic itself, not to any particular argument, which means that if we are to make any inference about the position of the character Socrates or Plato, it has to be highly indirect. Even in what are regarded as nonaporetic dialogues as differ-

---

[42] Frede (ibid.) is too parsimonious in his description of *aporia.* According to Liddell and Scott, *aporia, aporeō* and *aporos* can mean being left without resources, being in difficult straits, having trouble passing through some place, or difficulty in dealing with someone, embarrassment and hesitation, scarce or hard-to-get, and can refer to people who are intractable or in need.

[43] This is one reason why I think Richard McKim may overstate his case in his otherwise insightful essay "Shame and Truth in Plato's *Gorgias,*" in Charles L. Griswold Jr., ed., *Platonic Writings, Platonic Readings* (New York: Routledge Chapman and Hall, 1988), pp. 34–48.

ent as the *Phaedo, Timaeus,* and the second part of the *Parmenides,* the commitment of the questioner is often qualified, and even where it is not "nothing follows about the commitment of the author." So even in his most dogmatic dialogues "Plato" maintains "a radical distance from the views and arguments of the characters of the dialogue," which is a work of fiction anyway.

But why does Plato take such pains to avoid being committed to particular arguments of the dialogue and how and why do dialogues achieve this purpose? Surely one thing is to impress upon us how hard, even impossible, it is to legitimately speak with authority, how few of us are justified in our confidence about the meaning of our actions and speech, how easy failure of understanding is especially in those matters which effect and affect us most deeply. Human knowledge seems unable to master any subject, let alone subjects such as virtue, reality, justice, power, happiness, and freedom. These are not issues that are easily bounded by disciplines for they help to determine our whole life as citizens and individuals.[44]

Perhaps this is the kind of ignorance that led Socrates to characterize himself as someone who cannot pronounce on the questions he is inquiring about and who denies that he is a teacher in the sense of being an expert or an authority. But what about Plato? Did he have the knowledge Socrates claimed not to have? Certainly nothing prevented him from presenting his arguments as treatises, which would have amounted to a claim to speak as the author and from authority.[45] But he doesn't. At a minimum, dialogue seems to have afforded Plato the opportunity to present his views without endorsing them more strongly than he thought justified. But it affords something more. The dialogues, Frede points out, go "to great lengths to specify a fictitious context out of which the argument arises: it is individuals with a certain character, general outlook, a certain social position, certain interests, ambitions and concerns, individuals in a certain situation, who enter the debates, and this background noticeably colors their views" (p. 216). What we see in the *Gorgias* (or *Protagoras* or *Republic*) is that to know about power, justice, friendship, happiness, freedom, or courage entails knowing about one's character, outlook, social position, interests, ambitions, and concerns; that beliefs and experiences are deeply yet unobviously connected; that arguments emerge out of and remain more or less embedded in one's way of life; and that philosophy is tied to interest. What we see is, again, the politicization of philosophy in counterpoint to the *Apology's* vision of philosophical politics.

Frede concludes by indicating how the relationship between respondent and

---

[44] Frede, "Plato's Arguments," p. 215. See Martha Nussbaum's parallel discussion of the way the choice of *technē* reconstitutes what it means to be human in her chapter on the *Protagoras* in *The Fragility of Goodness* (Cambridge: Cambridge University Press, 1986), chap. 4.

[45] Charles L. Griswold Jr. argues that "if reflection on the 'beginnings' of philosophy is unavoidable, if the fundamental question of metaphilosophy concerns the 'quarrel' between the proponents of philosophy and its various critics, if philosophy cannot be attacked or defended directly, and finally if the defense of philosophy requires a conversation with the critics of philosophy (and not just with abstract formulations of their 'positions'), then it makes sense for a philosopher who agrees to all this (which Griswold thinks Plato does) to write *dialogues*" ("Plato's Metaphilosophy: Why Plato Wrote Dialogues," in his *Platonic Writings, Platonic Readings,* p. 157).

questioner in the dialogue anticipates and is paradigmatic for the relationship between reader and author outside it. If Plato's concern is for our becoming clear about our ideas, commitments, and lives, then he must thwart our temptations to adopt his views for the wrong reasons; for instance that an idea comes from a great mind like Plato's. Instead Plato pushes us to sort out our own views in order to come to what Frede calls "the correct view" (p. 217). If there is any lesson teaching or moral in the Platonic corpus this is it: "nothing but our own thought gains us knowledge."[46]

Yet most of us do not think for ourselves, at least not in the way Socrates commends we must. Socrates is no more successful with us than he is with Callicles in the dialogue or Critias, Alcibiades, and Charmides outside it. Nietzsche is right when he dismisses dialectic as the last refuge of resentful impotence. Most of us most of the time agree with him and Callicles that philosophy "emasculates" those of exceptional abilities by seducing them away from public life where there are real stakes to "live out their lives skulking in some corner, whispering with three or four boys, never saying anything worthy of a free powerful and notable man" (485d). It is not only that philosophers are useless in terms of their own moral or moralistic principles—as Vlastos asked, Where was Socrates when the Athenian assembly debated the fate of the Mytileneans?—but that in the end we simply walk away from them. At best we are like Crito, who acquiesces to arguments he has no doubt heard many times before and which manage to silence rather than convince him. Or we are like Protagoras, who (as we shall see in chapter nine) praises Socrates as an excuse to get away from him (all other stratagems having failed). Or like Euthyphro, whose last words, "for right now, I am in a hurry to get somewhere, and it is time for me to leave" (15e), are astonishing given that *he* initiated the discussion and is continuing with an action whose morality and motives have been shown to be profoundly suspect. In these terms Socrates' concluding myth in the *Gorgias* is a monologue whose impact is emblematic for us who read the Platonic dialogues. Even when we do not accept all of Socrates' arguments we almost always accept the superiority of his position to those of vanquished interlocutors like Crito, Protagoras, Euthyphro, or Callicles. Yet it makes little or no difference in our lives. Having taken Socrates' side we close the book and, like the interlocutors, proceed to go about our business, perhaps amused by Socrates' cleverness, or feeling edified in an abstract way that allows us to be self-righteous and amoral at the same time. What we do not do is doing what agreement with Socrates should entail: living the examined life by devoting ourselves, as he did, to the search for the good life.

No doubt what Socrates and Plato ask is extremely difficult. But if we agree that the search for goodness, justice, and truth is the right thing to do and not to do it, if we know that it constitutes a better life than the one we lead yet continuing to live as we do, we are, as Plato's readers and Socrates' admirers, in what

---

[46] Frede, "Plato's Arguments," p. 219. Frede argues that because dialectical debate has a "public character," it assures an amount of rationality "which is not guaranteed when the soul is left to discourse with itself. Left to itself, the soul is not only hampered by its idiosyncratic views, it is also too easily derailed in its reasoning" (p. 218).

Alexander Nehamas calls "a very peculiar situation indeed." For "to believe that Socrates' effect, either on his own interlocutors or on the readers of the dialogues is generally beneficial is to be taken in by Platonic irony and to show ourselves to be missing the point in our very claim to see it. It is nothing other than displaying our ignorance of our ignorance" (p. 298).

But perhaps Plato could succeed where Socrates failed even if that success entailed abandoning Socrates in his name, a not unfamiliar theme from anyone familiar with Dostoevsky's *Legend of the Grand Inquisitor.* Perhaps he could take Socrates' paradoxical ignorance and systematically articulate the view that the life of knowledge and philosophy is the best life for humans to live. Perhaps he could take Socrates' goodness, his motivation, character, and activity, and make it more than a matter of luck or "divine accident"[47]—make it the product of a *technē.* If there were a way to ensure that there would always be a few Socrateses around who would be honored for what they are, then one would likely turn to systematic education to "produce good people and the ability in those who are not good to recognize them" (p. 304). One would produce the *Republic* as a response to Socrates' failure with Callicles, Protagoras, Euthyphro, as well as Alcibiades, Critias, and Charmides.

On Nehamas's account Platonic philosophy entails the separation of knowing from doing and the adoption of a method that makes the kind of political *technē* Socrates of the *Gorgias* sometimes endorses, but which elenctic dialectic ultimately undercuts, a real possibility. Plato wants to show us what the good life is while separating the ability actually to live that life from the lesser, but still admirable ability, to recognize the superiority of that life and of those who live it. Not only could he define what the good life was, he became "rapt" with "a method of learning which itself does not depend on luck and good will, but only on ability and persistence—a method which offers no choice, but imposes the obligation to accept its conclusions once you begin to follow it." It was on this basis that he devised a system for the direct education of every person's soul. The method, Plato's method, is "in its higher reaches mathematical" (305). We can have a political *technē* that produces the right kinds of students and citizens. Here is the missing ground for Socrates' criticisms of Gorgias's inability to control his students, and Pericles inability to control the citizens he leads. It is also the way a future Socrates can control a future Callicles or Alcibiades, thus exonerating philosophy from the charges of failure and complicity leveled at Socrates.

But all this is, Nehamas suggests, premised on a belief that philosophy constitutes the best way of life. Where this sense is lost, as it now is, the "idea that philosophers are particularly qualified to understand the nature of the good life and show it to others must lose much of its hold" (pp. 305–6).

But I am not wholly convinced by the undemocratic Plato that emerges from Frede's and Nehamas's readings. I am not sure "Plato" wanted us to come to "the correct view," which sounds more didactic than elenctic. Nor am I sure that he regarded dialectic as instrumentally as Frede seems to when he sees it as

---

[47] *Republic* 492a.

a way of arriving at truth rather than a way of representing it. If the choice of writing dialogues (and arguing dialectically) "expresses a sense of life and of value, of what matters and what does not, of what learning and communicating are, of life's relations and communications,"[48] if life is never simply presented by a text but always represented as something, then dialogue becomes exemplary and intrinsically valuable. A dialogue like the *Gorgias* then is a way of expressing the surprising variety, complexity, and impenetrability of the world, its flawed beauty and furtive orders, which, however revered or longed for, yield to fissures and contingency. It suggests that even the most ingenious schemes of political and linguistic containment cannot erase division and conflict and that any mode of philosophical prose less allusive and attentive to particularity than dialogue is would flatten the political and intellectual landscape. The rhythm of dialogues like the *Gorgias* and *Protagoras,* with their inversions and subversions, their movements of attraction and repulsion, of friendship and enmity, trust and suspicions, embodies a surplus that exceeds any single position or interpretation.

This does not preclude Socrates from holding particular views that Plato may have shared, at least in the aporetic dialogues: views about the good life, about it being better to suffer injustice than commit it, about virtue being knowledge and sufficient for happiness. That he holds these views matters to the success of dialectic, whether it is the dialectic within the dialogue or between the dialogue and its readers. But what also matters is how he came to those views, the sense in which he "holds" them, and whether he risks them in a dialogic encounter. Unlike Frede and Nehamas, I think he does.

In part this has to do with the fact that a position's survival through every examination in the past does not guarantee it in the future; it may have been proved false in the very next one after that.[49] But in part it has to do with something that emerges from Socrates' discussion with Callicles about whether it is better to suffer or commit injustice, something which bears both on Socrates' criticism of Pericles and the issue of political expertise.[50] Doing and suffering injustice are ineradicable features of human life because the consequences of any action—whether done by Pericles or Socrates himself—escapes prediction and containment. Since none of us can live in a completely controlled environment and are thus likely both to (inadvertently) cause suffering and to experience it, the issue is how to live, politically and philosophically, in a world where our best efforts must partially fail.[51] In these terms Callicles' defense of the tyrannical life is also a Nietzschean insistence that only by cultivating the widest range of passions most intensely can one live life to the fullest. This endorsement of the sublime over the ordered life, this impiety toward conventions that impose unnatural limits on the forces of desire, this celebration of the sheer joy of imposing

[48] See Martha Nussbaum, "Introduction: Form and Content, Philosophy and Literature," in her *Love's Knowledge,* pp. 3–53.

[49] Vlastos, *Socrates: Ironist and Moral Philosopher,* p. 114, and *Gorgias* 527a–b.

[50] *Gorgias* 509c–510a, which elaborates 469a–c.

[51] Kastely, "In Defense of Plato's *Gorgias,*" pp. 100–101.

one's own order on that which is other are what Callicles admires both in Socrates *and* in Pericles.

As this implies, it is not only particular views that are at stake in Socrates' dialectic counters. Something far more is at risk even for Socrates, more likely for Plato—the status of dialectic itself. As I have argued, the *Gorgias* dramatizes the contest of power present in the constitution of discourse, how winners erase what they have triumphed over even as they deny there has been a war. Whatever Socrates' protestations about dialectic operating above the fray, he and it are portrayed as very much part of it. This is true not only of the *Gorgias* but as we shall see in the next chapter of the *Protagoras,* where the sophist argues that Socrates' insistence on dialectical argument is his way of forcing an opponent to fight on unfavorable ground. In these dialogues, as elsewhere, Socrates departs from his own dialectical strictures, using the antidialectical tactics of his opponents.[52] This is usually seen as Socrates showing that he can play his opponent's game better than he can so that his choice of dialectic is really not aimed at vanquishing his opponent since he can do that without dialectic. I think something more than that is at stake: the status of dialectic and of Socrates. Dialectic demands that one is willing to open oneself up to a refutation of one's life and character as well as to the arguments that manifest it. Few are willing to do so— certainly Callicles isn't, though he recognizes that not doing so is a kind of cowardice—because one could discover that one is not who one thinks one is and is not doing what one thinks one is doing. The courage required to face the risk of discovering commitments acquired inadvertently and wrongs done unintentionally is not only something Socrates displays in regard to his exchanges with the interlocutors in the dialogue, but something Plato is also undertaking in regard to Socrates. This means that in the *Gorgias* (as in other dialogues such as the *Protagoras* and *Republic*) Plato may be discovering the commitments he has more or less inadvertently made to Socrates as well as the injustice he has suffered or is perpetuating as Socrates' student and rival.

Nor am I convinced that Plato "provides the sort of Final Answer and Full Disclosure that can resolve doubt by submitting all problems to the regime of a mathematical world model."[53] Even in the *Republic* these arguments are embedded in a dramatic context that persistently challenges its readers to reexamine not only its particular theses but the frame within which they become claims to be true or false. What we make of any such claim depends on what we make of the fact that Socrates interrupts the discussion to warn the interlocutors that they have been hasty in their agreement, gullible in their confidence, and impatient in argument and failed to recognize the significance of what they ask and fail to ask. It depends too upon what we make of the dialogue criticizing what it is (poetry and drama) and extolling virtues it ignores (that one should play a single role in

[52] Perhaps most bizarrely is Socrates long, contrived interpretation of Simonides' poem in the *Protagoras,* as we shall see in the following chapter.

[53] The language is Harry Berger Jr.'s in "Levels of Discourse in Plato's Dialogues," in Anthony J. Cascardi, ed., *Literature and the Question of Philosophy* (Baltimore: Johns Hopkins University Press, 1987), p. 78.

life or as Socrates ventriloquizes the voices in the dialogue), and posits analogies between soul and state it gives ample evidence to reject.[54] Sometimes Socrates is explicit about these interruptions, but not always. Insofar as Socrates is a character in a drama written by Plato, there is a set of signals Plato provides readers which seem unavailable to any of the interlocutors including Socrates. Interpretations that fail to materialize within the imaginary encounters of what Harry Berger calls "the field of dramatic play" are conspicuously featured in the "field of textual play." Thus the *Gorgias, Protagoras,* or *Republic* like other dialogues (Berger's example is the *Ion*) can be read as a dialogue or *agōn* between its speakers and its text. "For the text tells us something about itself in adumbrating the limits of a form of discourse—Socratic logos, constrained by its oral conditions—which only textual representation can recuperate, or supplement, or transcend."[55]

If the Platonic dialogues abound in so many contradictions and inconsistencies then trying to elicit the "presence of the master, the coherence of his meaning and the disclosure of his mind"[56] seems a daunting if not impossible task. Impossible unless one is as confident as Terence Irwin is that on the basis of textual evidence one can readily distinguish the views of Socrates from those of Plato, document the successes and failures of Plato's defense, rejection, and revision of Socratic ethics, and recognize that many of those views are "false, confused, vague, inconclusive and badly defended."[57] Or, by contrast though similarly, if one believes that rigorous attention to the dramatic context of an argument is a "key to Plato's intentions." Then an "attentive reader" can reveal Plato's intentions and provide us with Plato's teaching.[58]

If I am right about the *Gorgias* and Plato, then I was wrong to begin by saying Plato does not appear in his dialogues. He is all over them. "Perhaps," Aryeh Kosman writes, "we should not be discussing Plato's silence but his ventriloquy; the displacement of speech, its projection into a created other, a dummy, a mute substitute who is truly a silent partner in the act despite the fact that it is he who 'speaks.'"[59] These voices remain unstilled, provoking, and inspiring, repellent yet seductive even for Callicles and Nietzsche "in spite of themselves" (in both

---

[54] See Diskin Clay, "Reading the Republic," in Griswold, *Platonic Writings, Platonic Readings* pp. 19–33, and my chapter "Justice in the Republic," in *The Tragedy of Political Theory: The Road Not Taken* (Princeton: Princeton University Press 1990), pp. 235–280.

[55] In "Levels of Discourse," p. 83. Like Berger I think Plato is aware of the kinds of criticisms Derrida makes of him.

[56] Ibid.

[57] Terence Irwin, *Plato's Moral Theory* (Oxford: Clarendon Press, 1977), chap. 1, p. 3. For reasons why the rigorous attention to dramatic context of an argument by an "attentive reader" will not provide a "key to Plato's intentions" and reveal Plato's teaching either, see Berger's discussion in "Levels of Discourse." I think Kosman overstates his case insofar as he excludes the possibility that Socrates (but not only him) also creates the "author" or text that creates him.

[58] See Berger's critique of Stanley Rosen in "Levels of Discourse," pp. 87–89.

[59] "Silence and Imitation in the Platonic Dialogues," in Klagge and Smith, *Methods.* In Harry Berger Jr., "Facing Sophists: Socrates' Charismatic Bondage in *Protagoras,*" *representations* 5 (Winter 1984): 66–89.

senses of the phrase).[60] This is an astonishing fact given the general rejection of Socratic intellectualism as defined by a trust in reason, a belief that ignorance is the ultimate evil, an identification of virtue with knowledge and happiness, and an indifference to the affective side of human life and the need for habituation. Surely Socrates has his feet planted firmly in the *Clouds.* And yet he moves us even as he fails to convince us, perhaps because Plato's dramatization(s) of Socrates' life transmutes his teacher's intellectualism into something more arresting and affecting.

Nehamas and Nietzsche are right when they claim Socrates was unsuccessful in persuading friends and enemies alike of the truth of the statement that it is better to suffer injustice than to commit it. But when he staked his life on that truth by refusing to escape the death sentence,[61] that became, in Plato's hands, a story of passion and pathos and Socrates became a man of Achillean courage who died for the life he led. This myth of a man who was at once a courageous citizen of a democracy, and an independent thinker in part because of it, frames the arguments of the *Gorgias* and continues to agitate those who think of themselves as educators in a democratic polity. Mostly these are philosophers and political theorists whose professional responsibilities include teaching classical authors. But sometimes the question of whether Socrates (or Plato) was a democrat matters to them more than usual and to more people than usual. I think that is true now because of the ongoing debate between multiculturalism and canonists over the meaning(s) of America, a conflict that, not coincidentally, mirrors that between Socrates and his interlocutors in the *Gorgias* over the meaning of Periclean leadership and Athenian democracy. The peculiarities of this debate discussed in chapters one and two suggest a need to recast the terms of my argument.

V

Suppose we ask not about Socrates or Plato being a democrat but about the resources for democratic readings and culture contained in dialogues like the *Apology, Crito, Gorgias, Protagoras,* and *Republic.* Such a shift would, to begin with, turn our attention away from the historical Socrates and authoritarian Plato to the interplay between an evolving text and the generation of sometimes divided interpretive communities who care about and for them. Then analysis of "the" text would include some study of how these interpretive communities are constituted and sustained, their place in the larger culture, how they "use" the text while learning from it. When, as in the nineteenth-century debate over the reform laws in Britain or now in the controversy over Great Books and core curriculum

---

[60] As Nehamas suggests, Nietzsche's "repugnance for Socrates" was "indissolubly mixed with admiration" ("What Did Socrates Teach," p. 279).

[61] See Arendt's "Truth and Politics," in *Between Past and Future,* pp. 247–48, where she argues that this teaching by example is the only form of persuasion that philosophical truth is capable of "without perversion or distortion." She goes on to suggest that it is the only way such truth can become practical and inspire action "without violating the rules of the political realm."

in the United States, these communities are wider than the academy, the issue of the relationships between democratic readings and democratic citizenship has more salience than it otherwise might.

Historicizing a text does not absolve us from making arguments for our interpretations of them; closely reading passages, contesting translations, detailing the interplay of what used to be called form and content, text and context. It means that, as Socrates suggests in the *Apology,* mortality inflects any understanding of events and texts and eternal verities are always worked out in local circumstances.

Attending to the democratic potentialities and democratic readings of works like the *Gorgias* affords the chance to return to some themes of chapter one. I suggested there that some of Plato's most implacable critics are in fact his allies, while some of his most strident defenders turn out to be the wolves in sheep's clothing. If what makes texts like the *Gorgias* (or *Republic* or *Protagoras*) "great" is their capacity to generate the kinds of moral and political controversies canonist defenders such as Bennett and Cheney would silence or circumscribe, then feminist, postmodernist. and Marxist critics of "Plato" may be giving his texts the life and energy his friends exhaust (providing, of course, that the critics do not themselves come to form a new orthodoxy). Clearly conflicting views of human nature and goodness in dialogues like the *Gorgias* are inscribed in the very plots, themes, arguments. and dramatic settings of canonical texts in ways that undercut their "usefulness" in any politicized education.[62]

Thus the *Gorgias* is polymorphous—exactly what Plato objects to about democracy in the *Republic* when he describes it as a bazaar of constitutions. If so, then the hearers most likely to respond to Jaeger's tensions and Bakhtin's semantic complexity are likely to be "democratic" readers. Readers committed to a single interpretative methodology, political standpoint, or philosophical approach and who aggressively insist that each character and term are fixed are deaf to the kind of irreducible paradoxes the *Gorgias* sustains and which are so often the substance of Greek tragedy. They play over the polyphony of shifting meanings (including those of democracy, politics and philosophy) and miss the degree to which the interlocutors push each other (or us) to continual reassessment of our political and philosophical commitments, and how the dialogue pushes democratic citizens to be alternatively if not simultaneously political educators of each other. Such readers are like those individuals who embrace what Stuart Hampshire calls "a morality without perpetual regret, because it is without any sense of the possibilities lost, unnoticed."[63]

If I am right, then Callicles is not just a villain. Nor is he erased by what can be construed as Socrates' victory over him. He lives on as an agitating presence and thematic counterpoint waiting for restitution or revenge, for Nietzsche or Grote, for Foucault or Lyotard to take up his cause. Indeed the very difficulty of the

---

[62] See Kenneth R. Johnston in "The NEH and the Battle of the Books," *Raritan* 12, no. 2 (Fall 1992): 118–132.

[63] Stuart Hampshire, *Thought and Action* (New York: Viking Press, 1959), p. 241, and Barber's discussion in *Strong Democracy,* pp. 258–59.

effort to defeat him makes him a live cultural option and constitutes part of the power and provocation of the *Gorgias*.

But Callicles is no friend of democracy despite Socrates ironic (or spiteful) punning of his love for a man named Dēmos. That he is not is a useful reminder to those who romanticize the quasi-Nietzschean arguments he makes. We would not want him to rule either within a dialogue or in the world outside it. Yet for all this his voice disrupts the comfort of conversation in a way that creates an interpretative space, incites us to participate in the construction of the dialogues' meaning(s), and pushes us to reinvent Socrates and Plato as contemporary interlocutors.

The presence of Callicles does one more thing; it makes theorizing an activity and resists its becoming an artifact. Twenty-five years ago Frederic Jameson argued that every "theory about the world, in its very moment for formation, tends to become an object for the mind and to be in itself invested with all the prestige and permanency of a real thing in its own right, thus effacing the dialectical process from which it emerged."[64] I am suggesting that the *Gorgias* keeps the dialectic process conspicuous.

VI

The contest over who Socrates and Plato were, like the contest in the *Gorgias* over who Pericles was, is partly a contest over the identity of democracy, including the role of philosophy for a democratic citizenry. Some philosophers are contemptuous of democracy, despising it for its ordinariness and grossness, its lack of grace and virtue. But I do not think that describes Socrates in the *Gorgias*, for as I have argued there is evidence that he is critiquing those he cares for so that they will not rest content in an unreconstructed understanding of who they are, but will take the risk and find out what they could become.[65]

I have quoted the Corinthians in Thucydides that the Athenians were "born into the world to take no rest themselves and give none to others" several times already. The daring innovation and constant transformation they attribute to this most democratic of cities are imitated by the generative power of Platonic dialogues, whose resilience lies less in the prescriptions they offer or the harmony they commend than in the way their irreconcilable tensions keep open the question of what it means to be human. It is the responsibility of those citizens in a democracy charged with the care and teaching of such works to insist that this openness to struggle is one of the most valuable parts of a legacy we need to pass on to our citizen students.[66] Doing so we can help recover the cultural heterogeneity of the West in ways that can ease the rigid polarities that mark the contemporary cultural wars and enhance the political education of our compatriots.

[64] *Marxism and Form: Twentieth-Century Dialectical Theories of Literature* (Princeton: Princeton University Press, 1971), pp. 57–58.

[65] Kastely, "In Defense of Plato's *Georgias*," p. 107.

[66] Johnston, "NEH," p. 132.

The *Protagoras* and the Political Education of Democratic Citizens

Though Zeus had received from me
Such services, the tyrant of the gods
Rewarded me thus foully, with punishment;
For tyranny somehow contains within itself
The sickness of suspicion aimed against its friends.

Listen to the miseries of mortal men, their helpless state before
I placed awareness within them and the use of mind. . . .
At first, though they had the power to see, they saw in vain and
hearing heard not. In the manner of such forms as move through dreams,
they spent their lives confusedly with aimless actions.

—Aeschylus, *Prometheus Bound,* 221–25, 442–50

I

Virtually every political, theoretical, and pedagogic issue broached in the previous eight chapters is reprised in the *Protagoras.* That fact, together with the fact that the dialogue is explicitly focused on the relationship between democracy, education, and philosophy, makes it an appropriate subject for this concluding chapter. As Protagoras is Socrates' interlocutor in the dialogue, so is the *Protagoras* mine.

It is often said, by both sympathizers and critics of Athenian democracy, that there was no theoretical defense of democracy by an ancient Greek. Even if I am right that political theory was shaped by a democratic culture it exemplified even in critique, that there were "theoretical" dimensions to democratic practices such as tragedy, and that Socrates' democratic sympathies are often ignored (as in the *Gorgias*) or underestimated (as with the *Apology*), the very lengths to which I go to make this argument attest to the initial plausibility of the claim. Perhaps the self-transformative impulse of democracy is incompatible with theory's commitment to order and coherence. If so, then there would be a "natural" antagonism between democracy and theory regardless of the content of the latter, and the animus against democracy we find among the first political theorists would be due more to the imperatives of theorizing than to the class status or lack of philosophical sophistication of the theorist.[1] But if my argument about the aporetic, polyphonic, and generative qualities of dialogues like the *Gorgias* (and *Protagoras*) is right, then this view of theory is too "Creonic."

Perhaps there was no theoretical defense of democracy because those who lived it had no reason to theorize about it, beyond the reflection we find in pre-philosophical literature such as drama and history. In these Hegelian terms political theory arose when the practices that had made it possible became systemically and systematically corrupt. Thus theory emerges as an epitaph and initiatory moment of transcendence. Though my argument in chapter three has some affinities with this view, the view does not sufficiently explain why the "cradle of democracy" was unable to produce a theorist for democracy to match the stature of its critics.

There is one frequently cited exception to these generalizations: Protagoras and his defense of democracy in Plato's dialogue. Though they also rely on evidence outside the dialogue, most critics think Socrates (or Plato) sufficiently respectful of Protagoras, and Protagoras enough of a democrat and theorist, to conclude that he was "the world's first democratic theorist,"[2] offered "the first defense of participatory democracy," and provided "the only more or less systematic statement of democratic political theory that has survived from ancient Greece."[3] If true, then the terms in which I have urged reconsideration of the relationship between democracy and political theory or philosophy have, to say the least, been tendentious.

Protagoras's defense of democracy comes as a response to Socrates' claim that the practices and attitudes of the Athenians prove that virtue cannot be taught. In asserting that it can and is in fact being taught, not only in Athens but in all civilized cities, Protagoras provides a theory of democratic political education and a justification of his role as an educator. This has led critics to proclaim him "the first professor," the "father of higher education,"[4] the "first outcropping . . .

---

[1] See for instance the discussion of self-predication and abstract nouns in Michael Frede's introduction to Stanley L. Lombardo and Karen Bell's translation of the *Protagoras* (Indianapolis: Hackett Publishing, 1992). Nicole Loraux has argued that we have no written theoretical defense of democracy because writing typified oligarchic *apragmones* (see my discussion in chapter four) as against the essential orality of democracy. (See her *The Invention of Athens: The Funeral Oration in the Classical City,* trans. Alan Sheridan [Cambridge, Mass.: Harvard University Press, 1986]). R. Brock has argued *pace* Frede that the Athenians' "concentration on abstract nouns to the exclusion of personalities" suggests that they had arrived at "the beginning of abstract political theory" and "were perfectly capable of justifying democracy in theoretical terms" ("The Emergency of Democratic Ideology," *Historia: Zeitschrift für alte Geschichte* 40, no. 2 [1989]: 169).

[2] Cynthia Farrar, *The Origins of Democratic Thinking* (New York: Cambridge University Press, 1988), p. 77.

[3] Neal Wood and Ellen Wood, "Socrates and Democracy: A Reply to Gregory Vlastos," *Political Theory* 14, no. 1 (February 1986): 68. Here is G. B. Kerferd, "For Protagoras has produced for the first time in human history a theoretical basis for participatory democracy," in *The Sophistic Movement* (New York: Cambridge University Press, 1981), p. 144.

[4] C.C.W. Taylor's characterization of Protagoras in his commentary on the edition of the *Protagoras* he edited in the Clarendon Plato Series (Oxford: Clarendon Press, 1976), p. 61.

of the academic mind,"[5] and "a professional man for whom teaching was an occupation whose commercial success bore witness to its intrinsic value and social utility."[6] Even if such claims are overstated, they help redress readings of the dialogue that focus on virtue at the expense of teaching. To consider it as concerned with both issues entails attending to who Protagoras is and what he does as well as to the arguments he makes. It also invites us to reconsider Socrates as a teacher, especially given how often the dialectical mode he endorses is undercut by his praise of the art of measurement and his rhetorical extravagances.

Concern with teaching returns us to the first two chapters. As I argued in chapter two, in the *Apology* Socrates says that he is accused of corrupting the youth because he supposedly makes the worse argument appear the better, is an atheist who speculates about matters better left alone, pretends to be wise when he is not, and, in general, encourages the young to challenge the authority of their elders and the laws. In the course of defending himself, Socrates insists that Meletus say who improves rather than corrupts the young. Meletus answers that the laws, norms, and practices of the city do; indeed that everyone and everything does except Socrates. Protagoras too was accused of corrupting the young[7] and may have been exiled from Athens because of it. Yet he makes an argument *similar* to the one made by Meletus in the *Apology*. In response to Socrates' claim that there can be no political *technē* since Athenian practices presume that no one can teach virtue, Protagoras argues that no one teaches it because, to a lesser or greater degree, everyone does; parents, teachers, friends, judges, fellow citizens, the laws, and the culture as a whole. Every aspect of living in a polis is a form of political education.

The conception of political education he expounds seems to quiet Arendt's concerns about the illicit importation of hierarchic models of authority from the educational to the political realm. If all citizens have a share in political virtue such that they teach virtue to each other as they do a common language, then "political education" need not be a contradiction in terms, as it is for her. It appears that Protagoras may be a far more appropriate model of a democratic political educator than Socrates.

---

[5] Susan C. Jarratt regards the sophists as the "first public intellectuals in a democracy," in *Rereading the Sophists: Classical Rhetoric Refigured* (Carbondale: Southern Illinois University Press, 1991); and Christian Meier, *The Greek Discovery of Politics* (Cambridge, Mass.: Harvard University Press, 1990), p. 197, calls them trained experts.

[6] H. I. Marrou, *A History of Education in Antiquity*, trans. George Lamb (Madison: University of Wisconsin Press, 1956), p. 49. For Marrou this is a condemnation since he regards the Protagoras's aims as overly practical and philosophically superficial.

[7] Because of Plato's perverseness, Grote argued, the sophists "came to be seen as ostentatious impostors, flattering and duping the rich youth for their own personal gain, undermining the morality of Athens public and private, and encouraging their pupils to unscrupulous prosecution of ambition and cupidity. They are even affirmed to have succeeded in corrupting the general morality, so that Athens had become miserably degenerated and vicious in the latter years of the Peloponnesian War, as compared with what she was in the time of Miltiades and Aristeides." *A History of Greece*, vol. 8, new ed. (London: J. Murray, 1883), p. 156.

Protagoras can be seen to replace Socrates in yet another way. Eric Havelock has argued that in bringing to light the habitual unconscious practices of education, Protagoras cultivated a critical self-understanding of how citizens came to be the kinds of people they were, act as they did, and spoke about what they spoke about as they did.[8] His Protagoras helps constitute the tradition of self-critique I have celebrated as the cultural imperative which provided the substance and form for Socratic political philosophy. It may even be that the self-awareness Protagoras provides offers a more explicit, and ultimately more useful, ground for distinguishing a political from a politicized education than anything one can find in Socrates.

Like Socrates, Protagoras provides a mediating position between conservative canonists who rely on classic texts, and multiculturalists who challenge that reliance as part of a hegemonic cultural power. On the one hand Protagoras seems to have been regarded as subversive, not only because he offered a form of higher education outside the "normal" social structure, but because his cosmological and historical narratives, such as the one in the great myth in the *Protagoras,* contravened traditional ones. Yet, as he states, and as his invocation of Simonides' poem indicates, Protagoras relied on what might be regarded as the classic texts of his own time as a way of illustrating his teachings and legitimating his teaching. In terms of the contest between New and Old Education in the *Clouds,* he stands aside from the polarities each endorses. Whether that is for strategic or moral reasons or some combination of the two, and why that matters, we will see later on.

One way to see the radicalism of Protagoras's "theology"[9] is to contrast it with that of tragedy, more specifically with that of *Antigone* and *Oedipus Tyrannus* as presented in chapters six and seven. *Antigone's* choral ode in praise of man celebrates humankind's possession and development of various *technai*. These distinguish man from the beasts, and allow him to challenge the gods in all respects save that of death. The culmination of that praise is the invention of language and the polis. Yet the equivocations created by the imagery and surrounding context of the ode, together with the impiety and transgression that shadow each step of progress, embodied in *deinos* and its cognates, is absent from Protagoras's myth. But it is not absent from the *Protagoras.* The optimism of the myth and Protagoras's confidence is challenged not only by Socrates, but by the tension between the dramatic and historical dates of the dialogue.

---

[8] In *The Liberal Temper in Greek Politics* (New Haven: Yale University Press, 1957). Jarratt (*Rereading the Sophists*) argues that sophistic "discourses disrupted stable historical narratives," David Steiner (*Rethinking Democratic Education* [Baltimore: Johns Hopkins University Press, 1994], chap. 2) that rhetoricians aimed "not only to advocate a policy but to unpack the oratorical devices of rival arguments which meant that each speech served as a warning to the citizen that rhetors can manipulate words and that language is far from a neutral tool of deliberation" (p. 49). Kerferd (*The Sophistic Movement*) makes a similar argument.

[9] I put quotation marks around theology because Protagoras was most probably an atheist. On which, see the discussion in Farrar, *Origins,* and in Miles Burnyeat's introduction to his edition of the *Theatetus* (Indianapolis: Hackett, 1990).

The dramatic date is two years before the outbreak of the Peloponnesian War, three years before the plague. It was a time of enormous confidence in the promise of human intelligence and power to sustain a realm immune to the inhuman forces that otherwise leave men victims of chance and necessity. In this world Protagoras's art and his version of political theory seem sensible and appropriate. There is no urgency, or need to go much beyond current beliefs and practices. Small advances are enough, reform more than enough.

The historical context is different. Athens had experienced a seemingly endless war it eventually lost, and undergone several oligarchic coups, a fact emphasized by the presence of Alcibiades and Critias in the audience. This "other" context is evoked by the dialogue's reference to the sophists as the blind leading the blind back into the world of the past and to Hades and by the "allusions to plague metaphors of disease."[10] All this compromises, if it does not undercut, Protagoras's case for his art, whose plausibility depends on a confident consensus that no longer exists. Prudence based on experience may not be much help after violent coups, lost wars, and lapsed agreement on the terms in which experience should be represented.

Among other things *Antigone* and *Oedipus Tyrannus* dramatize the contestable character of what counts as reason, sanity, knowledge, and wisdom. We see how claims to possess such qualities are less innocent than their claimants suppose or want others to believe them to be. In many instances such claims are compromised by the aggressiveness with which they are asserted, and by the dramatic context in which they are made, which frequently gives an entirely new or other meaning to what is being said. The question of what reason or wisdom is and who if any of the characters possess it is reiterated in the proximity/distance between the corrupt world portrayed on stage and the world of the theatergoers.

The *Protagoras* exhibits similar preoccupations. Once more claims to wisdom or reason are seen as self-serving maneuvers to gain status or reputation. Like the role of *deinos* in *Antigone*, the *Protagoras* asks whether virtue, and so the goals of human life as a whole, is singular or plural, and if the latter, whether reason can negotiate between them or provide some measure of their relative merit. In the dialogue as in the dramas, claims to be wise are compromised by the tone in which they are made and by the dramatic structure which sometimes undermines them. For instance, reason unites Socrates and Protagoras when they jointly champion it against the generally held view that people who know what is right but cannot do it because they are overcome by irrationality. Yet the rancor between them suggests that dialogue is war by other means. Protagoras's myth speaks of Zeus's gifts, which purportedly stilled the violence that had left men vulnerable to each other. But the discursive coda on punishment is more of a contradiction than an elaboration of the myth. Finally, whereas the initial argu-

---

[10] Martha Nussbaum, "The 'Protagoras': A Science of Practical Reasoning," in her *The Fragility of Goodness* (Cambridge: Cambridge University Press, 1986), pp. 104–5; and Harry Berger Jr., "Facing Sophists: Socrates' Charismatic Bondage in *Protagoras,*" *representations* 5 (Winter 1984): 66–91.

ment about whether virtue can be taught relied on a notion of *technē* close to common practices,[11] by the end of the dialogue Protagoras and Socrates endorse an art of measurement remote from those practices. We are told that only this art can save man from irrationality, which implies that Zeus's gifts have failed to do so. Such an art promises (though it also presupposes) moral certainty and political control. With it *Antigone*'s Creon could attain the singularity, order, and security he sought, and heal the wounds of civil war, which would not have occurred in the first place if such an art was available. And just think of what such an art would do for Oedipus and those rational choice theorists who honor calculation, measurement, and predictability; or for those educational reformers anxious to generate blueprints to reshape students; or for Pericles' efforts to "make" the Athenians better.

Questions about what reason, knowledge, or wisdom are, how they operate in the world, and who can rightly claim to possess or manifest them, is another way of asking about the relationship between philosophy and democracy, a theme posed first in chapter two. There I argued that the *Apology* expresses the necessity of philosophical citizenship for a radical democracy. The *Protagoras* reconsiders this possibility. It does so not only through the dialogue between Socrates and Protagoras, but through the tension between a "Socratic" and Platonic voice in the dialogue. Let me pose the general issue of philosophical citizenship and the particular stances the *Protagoras* takes to it by employing Walzer's idea of "connected" critics.[12]

In what may be a modification of his discussion of philosophy and democracy set out in chapter two, Walzer praises those critics who give voice to the common complaints of their people or elaborate the values that underlie them, as against those who express their disenchantment by political withdrawal, disinterest, or escapism.[13] Standing sufficiently close to their audience and sufficiently confident of that standing, such critics render a recognizable account of everyday experience on the "assumption that what is actual in consciousness is possible in practice" and then "challenge the practices that fall short of these possibilities."[14]

Walzer regards his connected critics as general intellectuals who have something to say about both the whole of society and the critical enterprise generally, as opposed to both critics who survey the whole world, are dismissively critical of "modernity, popular culture, mass society, bureaucracy, science and technology, the welfare state, and "anything else that turns up," and specific intellectuals who are in practice critics in the little world of their (usually academic) profession. His kind of critic does not stand on mountaintops, master of all they survey, claiming authority and issuing commands. They are "participants who work at a certain difficult distance, balancing solidarity and service, finding their way in the

[11] See John Wallach, *Plato's Political Art* (forthcoming); Nussbaum, *The Fragility of Goodness;* and W.K.C. Guthrie, *The Sophists* (New York: Cambridge University Press, 1971).

[12] In *The Company of Critics: Social Criticism and Political Commitment in the Twentieth Century* (New York: Basic Books, 1988).

[13] Ibid., pp. 9, 16.

[14] Ibid., p. 19.

little battles as well as the big ones, seeking to be faithful to the hopes of popular revolt, to outlast the defeats, to sustain a form of criticism internal to, relevant to, loyal to democratic politics."[15]

The preoccupations of what Walzer calls "the Ancient and Honorable company of Critics"—how does one stand vis-à-vis others, what sort of authority can one claim, how much distance does criticism require, where does one find the standards for such criticism, what language is appropriate for it, and what motives drive one to be a critic in the first place—are also the preoccupations of the *Protagoras.* From one point of view the different answers to these questions that Socrates and Protagoras give define their respective views of philosophy, democracy, and political education. But from another point of view, they are both "connected critics," and their agreement defines their deficiencies. The first view is that of the *Apology,* the second may be that of the *Protagoras.*

How connected Protagoras is, and what one makes of the ways and to whom he is connected, depends on how "conservative" he is taken to be. There are two views on the issue, and they, again, help define what is at stake in the debate between Socrates and Protagoras and between them and "Plato."

The conservative Protagoras accepts the laws and norms of whatever polity he happens to find himself in on the assumption or conviction that there is no standard of judgment and justice beyond whatever is current in a specific society. Thus his claim to teach virtue is a claim that he can discern and teach the actual tradition of a particular society better than can its own members. Of course, this also means that his expression of democratic sympathies at the beginning of the dialogue is strategic rather than principled, an implication that gains plausibility by the alacrity with which he changes those sympathies. It may well be that democratic societies are more likely than others to allow him the opportunity to teach (which gives added point to Socrates' wonderfully absurd claim that the secret of Spartan power is its welcoming of sophists). But, like management's inclusion of workers in corporate planning because it increases productivity, should democracy become inhospitable to sophists, Protagoras would (as Socrates does not) simply go somewhere else. He may well take his cues from the people, but who the people are and what their traditions happen to be are of no particular interest to him.

Insofar as Zeus's gifts of *aidōs* and *dikē-* provide a universal standard that the legal and moral code of any polis must meet, Protagoras is less conservative than he seems. But Zeus and his gifts largely disappear in the great speech (punishment replaces them), as well as in the dialogue as a whole. Besides, once a polity satisfies this requirement, whatever it regards as justified is so until it is changed. This leaves little ground for criticizing the institutions of any city no matter how cruel or unjust they may be if the city has enough social cohesion to ensure survival.[16] This position may be defensible especially if one repudiates universal norms and general intellectuals (in Foucault's and Deleuze's sense),[17] but it is a position that needs defense.

The case for Protagoras's "radicalism" rests on the claim that he, like Socrates, brings the Athenians to think critically and comprehensively about what they are doing. Though he emphasizes the power of custom and law to dominate the student through all levels of education, by bringing such acculturation to consciousness he "implies the possibility of a critical relation to that process—an ability to stand outside of and perhaps to control aspects of it."[18] Moreover, if rhetoricians not only advocated policies but sought to unpack the oratorical devices of rival arguments such that citizens could become aware of and thus turn around rhetorical attempts at manipulating them, and if Protagoras contributes to this, either directly through his public displays or through his students, then he has made a major contribution to the process of democratic deliberation.[19]

Though there is much to be said for these arguments as a general characterization of sophists and rhetoricians, there is less to be said for them as a characterization of Plato's Protagoras (or in Cynthia Farrar's neologism "Platagoras"). For one thing who are the people being brought to self-consciousness if most of his teaching is done in private rather than public, and all of it is addressed to the sons of wealthy Athenians (even if Protagoras does offer a money-back guarantee)? For another thing, the contest between the sophists we witness in the dialogue seems less a matter of unpacking rival rhetorical devices than competing with each other in ways just as likely to create confusion as clarification for an audience. Indeed it is Socrates rather than Protagoras who does this within the dialogue (and Plato who unpacks various rhetorical strategies—including that of Socrates—of the dialogue). But most disconcerting of all is that his notion of education is too much like socialization, his conception of the political art too accommodating and functionalist, his teaching too ready to accept whatever moral imperatives or organization of power happens to exist. With the distance between the ideal function of the *nomoi* and their actual practice all but erased, it is unlikely that a student of Protagoras would discover a reason for ignoring an order to arrest an innocent man such as Leon of Salamis.

What might be called Protagoras's "functionalism" is a product and manifestation of his complacency or, more germanely, given Prometheus's importance in the dialogue, of his lack of foresight. The discrepancies between the historical and dramatic dates of the dialogue reveal the limits of both his optimism (about human progress) and his "realism" (his emphasis on punishment as a fundamen-

---

[17] See their "Intellectuals and Power," in Donald Bouchard, ed., *Language, Counter-Memory, Practice: Selected Essays and Interviews,* trans. Donald Bouchard and Sherry Simon (Ithaca: Cornell University Press, 1977).

[18] Jarratt, *Rereading the Sophists,* p. 104. Harold Barrett makes a similar argument: the "sophists directed the power of their writing and teaching toward raising people's consciousness of their attribute as social creatures and of their identity as individuals," in *The Sophists: Rhetoric, Democracy and Plato's Idea of Sophistry* (Novato, Calif.: Chandler and Sharp, 1987), p. 36.

[19] See Steiner, *Rethinking Democratic Education,* chaps. 1 and 2; Peter Nicholson, "Protagoras and the Justice of Athenian Democracy," *Polis* 4, no. 2 (1989); and J. S. Morrison, "The Place of Protagoras in Athenian Public Life," *Classical Quarterly* 35 (1941): 1–16.

tal mode of education) in times of crisis like those faced by Creon and Oedipus and described by Walzer in his brilliant characterization of the English Civil War quoted in chapter two.

But Socrates too seems to lack foresight and, as Nietzsche repeatedly argued, was optimistic most obviously in intellectualism. If so, then the dialogue not only shows why Socrates is superior to Protagoras but how what they share despite their disagreement is somehow insufficient and flawed. Is there a "Platonic" sense of systemic crisis that provides a skeptical voice about Socratic dialectic and dialogue as well as Protagorean myth/discourse? If so, then Socrates' collapse into Protagoras and their fluctuating identification with the *dēmos* may signal Plato's disenchantment with Socrates' way of theorizing and political project. But, of course, I share that vision of theorizing and political project, which means that the *Protagoras* becomes, as I mentioned, the interlocutor for this book.[20]

II

The view of Platagoras as a paradigmatic educator of democratic citizens rests on a particular reading of this dialogue of extraordinary complexity. One can admire such complexity, as Paul Shorey did, when he wrote that "a greater variety of topics and literary motives is combined in the artistic structure of the *Protagoras* than in any other dialogue except perhaps the *Phaedrus* or the *Republic*."[21] Or one can regard the dialogue as an "irritating patchwork,"[22] in which the discussion "wanders from verbal sophistries and elentic examination through extravagantly ornate literary criticism and lengthy epideictic, ending in an admission which makes such wandering seem pointless."[23] But in either case it is clear that the dialogue is richly, if not prohibitively, polyphonic.

For instance, there are two Socrates: the one now telling the story and the one who engaged in the previous day's events, which are now retold. Then there is the voice of an ill-mannered, aggressive, questioner Socrates ventriloquizes, who prevents him from criticizing the argument for hedonism he seems to endorse, though it contradicts the ethical injunction (that it is worse to do injustice than to suffer it), by which Socrates lived and for which he died.[24] In addition, there is the Socrates who identifies with Prometheus, even though it is that god's lack of foresight that allowed his forgetful brother to jeopardize human existence, and

---

[20] It is for this reason (among others) that I shall largely ignore the views and portraits of Protagoras found in other sources.

[21] Paul Shorey, *What Plato Said* (Chicago: University of Chicago Press, 1933), p. 119.

[22] The phrase is from W.K.C. Guthrie. But we think this only if "we look to the *Protagoras* for philosophical lessons. . . . But read as a play in which the most outstanding and individual minds of a brilliant period meet and engage in a battle of wits, it will give a different impression" (*A History of Greek Philosophy* [Cambridge: Cambridge University Press, 1975], vol. 4, p. 235).

[23] Clyde Lee Miller, "The Prometheus Story in Plato's *Protagoras*," *Interpretation* 7 (1978): 27.

[24] Berger, "Facing Sophists," and Roger Duncan, "On Courage in the Protagoras," *Phroneses* 23 (1978): 216–28.

despite the fact that Prometheus's fate and his conflict with Zeus is a present absence in Protagoras's myth. In addition, there is the fact that the dialogue ends with Protagoras collapsing into the voice of the many from whom he has contemptuously distanced himself, as Socrates collapses into Protagoras (as if defeating him required that he become him or speak his words), all of which make the surface polarities of the dialogue radically unstable. Furthermore, there is the tension between the dramatic and historical dates of the dialogue.

Then there is a general complexity suggested by Socrates' claim in the *Theaetetus* that the arguments in which he engages never come from him but from the person with whom he is speaking, since he is after all only a midwife. Refusing to impose his own knowledge in a way that would reduce his auditors to disciples he draws their own wisdom from them. It is the model of teaching that underlies his claim that he was not a teacher and the fact that he was an exemplary one. He does not teach because he will not let himself be constructed as a master who seeks and creates *epigonoi*. But he is a teacher beyond compare because he helps each person bring his wisdom to birth. Yet there is something disconcerting about the claim and the process as it appears in the *Protagoras*. If the arguments come from the person to whom Socrates is talking (such as Protagoras), and if, as the dialogue's conclusion indicates, he becomes the other, then the arguments do come from him and he is always talking to himself. Moreover, the self he talks to must be divided, and multivocal. *This* teacher is not a single self, but is bound to his interlocutors and so divided from himself, uneasily driven by the logic of the argument and the community of discourse.[25]

Penultimately there are his attempts at irony, including the ornate overinterpretation of Simonides' poem, which often seem, to use Gregory Vlastos's phrase, "clumsy and heavy handed."[26] Finally there is the startling discrepancy between Protagoras's reputed gifts and power attested to by Hippocrates' breathless anxiety to meet him, and his utter helplessness against the much younger Socrates, who easily demolishes his arguments and punctures his pretensions. The victory is somehow too easy, and the pleasure Socrates takes in humiliating Protagoras not once (at the time of the discussion), but again in the telling of it, is, to put it bluntly, unattractive. If Socrates is merely cutting Protagoras down to size, he seems to be doing it with a chainsaw.

Obviously all this raises serious questions about Socrates' protestations of respect for Protagoras and my portrait of him. They are questions that remain with us at the end when Socrates says he has an urgent appointment for which he is long overdue. Since he winds up being easily distracted by an anonymous friend to whom he retells the entire story of his previous conversation with Protagoras, we know better.[27] They are also questions about Plato's respect for Socrates, and whether, as I have already suggested, the *Protagoras* prefigures a distancing between teacher and student (even if the art of measurement can be construed as an anticipation of the theory of the forms). This would add yet another dimension to

---

[25] Berger, "Facing Sophists," pp. 66–67.

[26] See his introduction to the Jowett and Ostwald translation of the *Protagoras* (Indianapolis: Bobbie Merrill, 1956), p. xxxi.

[27] See Joseph Cropsey, *Plato's World* (Chicago: University of Chicago Press, 1995), chap. 1.

the issue of teaching, and complicate my argument about Socrates and Plato in the concluding sections of the previous chapter.

All this instability of argument and persona means that positions, alliances, and characterizations in the dialogue are kaleidoscopic. Spaces for expression are unexpectedly opened up and just as abruptly closed down, unsought identities are insisted upon, and moments of resentment and reconciliation follow each other in quick succession. It is as if the *aporia* that so often characterizes the endings of Plato's dialogues here suffuses the whole, a fact that confounds various claims of characters that they possess a political *technē*.

On the one hand, there is the waywardness of the dialogue and the fact that everyone seems to lack foresight. On the other hand, there is the claim that an art of measurement can eliminate contingencies of circumstance and character, inversions and reversals that mark the dialogue. Such an art is, we are told, necessary for human salvation. But if, as I shall argue, the dialogue form speaks against its efficacy if not existence, then we cannot be "saved" and the tragic sensibility purged at the level of argument reappears in the dramatic structure.

III

Plato presents the *Protagoras* as a conversation between Socrates and an anonymous friend about events that occurred the day before. From the look on Socrates' face, the friend assumes that he has been with Alcibiades, the most beautiful man in Athens. But the friend is wrong; Socrates has been with a far more seductive man, Protagoras, the wisest and thus the most alluring man in Hellas. The friend is as anxious for the gossip about Socrates' encounter with Protagoras as he had been for Socrates' being with Alcibiades. So he invites Socrates to take the seat now used by his slave and entertain him with the retelling of the previous day's philosophical encounter.

Socrates tells of how Hippocrates[28] was so impatient to meet Protagoras that he burst into his bedroom at an ungodly hour, willing to pledge everything he owned and risk the bankruptcy of his friends for the chance to study with such a great teacher. Yet, as becomes immediately apparent, Hippocrates has never seen or heard Protagoras. All he knows is the latter's reputation for being a remarkably clever speaker, which means he knows next to nothing. His unqualified enthusiasm for relinquishing himself to the sophist suggests a significant lack of foresight. He could only come to recognize the disaster of studying with Protagoras as an afterthought if at all, a vulnerability that parallels mankind's after Epimetheus's disastrous maldistribution of capacities.

Socrates' strategy is to make Hippocrates self-conscious (both aware and awkward) about his ignorance, and temper the young man's unreflective attachment to Protagoras. This he does in three ways or steps, which together suggest the kind of teacher he is (as opposed to Protagoras), and the difference between a

---

[28] Hippocrates is the namesake of the renowned Greek physician whose works celebrate the progress made by medical science. This gives impetus to the claims to expertise by Protagoras as a doctor of the soul for the patient Hippocrates and anticipates the narrative of progress in Protagoras's myth.

politicized and a political education. The first way is to substitute himself for Hippocrates, pushing the young man to the wings as he takes center stage. The second is to deflate the godlike authority Protagoras claims for himself and that is attributed to him by Hippocrates. This he does by likening Protagoras to a vender who, in the interest of selling himself to make money, indiscriminately extols all of his products to anyone willing to pay the price. When, Socrates argues, we buy food for the body, we can take it home in containers and consider its nutritional value (and so whether it is good for us) in conversations with those, such as dietitians, who are expert in such matters. But education is not like food. There is no comparable separation of ends and means, no time or opportunity to think afterward about what we have ingested, since we have become different people because of what we learn, and cannot return to the person we were before. "You cannot," he tells Hippocrates, "carry teachings away in a separate container. You put your money down and take the teaching away in your soul by having assimilated it and off you go, either helped or injured" (314b).

There is a third way Socrates substitutes himself for Protagoras as he teaches Hippocrates about being a teacher and a student and us about the dangers of academic vanity. Socrates must defeat Protagoras without taking his place as the godlike authority to whom unreflective yet potentially powerful men ignorantly entrust themselves. If we regard Protagoras as a prismatic focus[29] for the institutional, cultural, and social structures that have allowed him to attain the status and power he has, then Hippocrates' near worship of him suggests a need left by the demystification of the gods to which the sophist himself has contributed. Thus Socrates must deal with both the cynicism that accomplished such demystification, and the still living but sublimated desire for the divine. Or, more concretely, he must substitute himself for Hippocrates without becoming a substitute for Protagoras until the end when, with the latter's reputation now tarnished, Socrates can collapse into Protagoras, leaving us and Hippocrates without cynicism or a need for the divine. At least that is Socrates' hope. Whether it is Plato's is another matter.

Of course there is a paradox here. To avoid the danger of precipitous commitment to ruinous teachers a student must already have knowledge, if only about whom to consult and which claims to expertise are warranted, even though one becomes a student in order to know. In these terms a "good student" is not one who is obedient or restates what has been taught or mimics the teacher, but one who is able to make some independent judgment about what he is likely to become when "remade."[30]

While this paradox helps explain the prominence of foresight and measurement as themes in the dialogue, it still leaves us uncertain about what is involved in being a good student and teacher. Is it possible to be one without being the other, or is reciprocity an essential aspect of being either and their conjunction a predicate for the transmission of virtue and for *political* education? Commenta-

---

[29] As Berger does in "Facing Sophists," p. 77.

[30] Protagoras uses *epistatēs* (from the verb *ephistasthai*) which means control, master, stand over, and puns on the verb *epistasthai*, to know, which allows Socrates to give *epistatēs* the sense of "one who is control by virtue of his knowledge." See Taylor's discussion, *Protagoras*, p. 67.

tors agree that the *Protagoras* is about whether virtue can be taught. But they take this to be a question about virtue rather than about teaching, and so focus on the argument about the unity of the virtues rather than the disagreement over teaching which is often implicit in the dialogue's dramatic structure. The operative assumption, I think, is that knowing what virtue is can be divorced from, and is philosophically and politically prior to, the understanding of what is entailed in teaching and learning. But if they are coeval or conjoined or even fold into each other, and if what distinguishes Socrates from Protagoras (and Gorgias) is the kind of teacher he is as much as any doctrine about virtue he espouses,[31] then failure to reflect upon the different ways Protagoras and Socrates teach misses half the argument and the whole point.

As we saw in chapter two Socrates often disclaims being a teacher. He does not have the sort of knowledge others claim to possess. Nor does he have a finished doctrine which he expects others to learn. Because he is willing, even anxious, to be a student of his students, he does not share Gorgias's complacency that he has heard everything worth hearing and so, by implication, need not listen to anyone, a stance that leaves the rhetorician unable to foresee the consequences of his teaching. Insofar as Socrates is committed to and actually able to hear challenges to his views and vocation, he is committed to a reciprocity Gorgias and Protagoras reject. And to the extent their rejection is tied to the undemocratic sentiments they both express, Socrates' exposure of this tie becomes part of his vision of democratic political education.

But that is too neat and one-sided. Socrates' commitment to reciprocity and ability to hear what others say is imperfect and suspect. In one sense, this must be the case. If, as I believe, Socrates is presented in a more compromising light in this dialogue than in most others, that may be because Plato came to understand that this ambiguity is a necessary implication of Socrates being the kind of teacher he was. (I will suggest later there are other ways to read the unflattering aspects of Socrates.) As I argued in the preceding chapter, if we simply agree with Socrates and are confident we understand him, we cannot be the kind of students he apparently wants us to be, and so he cannot be the kind of teacher he wishes to be. Indeed, if we too readily and easily agree with him, we would be imitating Hippocrates. With Socrates we have in Alexander Nehemas's words, "someone who, precisely in disavowing ethical knowledge and the ability to supply it to others, succeeded in living as moral . . . a life as anyone ever did who belonged in a tradition he himself initiated. And he does not let us know how."[32] That seems to me the point, in the sense that it establishes a reciprocity and distance that is a necessary condition for Socrates being a "teacher" of virtue and a political educator of democratic citizens.

That there is something disreputable about being a sophist is indicated by

---

[31] See the discussion of Socrates as a "teacher" in Alexander Nehemas, "What Did Socrates Teach and to Whom Did He Teach It?" *Review of Metaphysics* 46 (December 1992): 279–306, and Michael Frede, "Plato's Arguments and the Dialogue Form," in James C. Klagge and Nicholas D. Smith, eds., *Methods of Interpreting Plato and His Dialogues,* supplementary volume in Julia Annas, ser. ed., *Oxford Studies in Ancient Philosophy* (Oxford: Clarendon Press, 1992).

[32] Nehemas, "What Did Socrates Teach," p. 296.

Hippocrates' embarrassment when Socrates suggests he will become like Protagoras if he studies with him, and by the contemptuous refusal of Callias's eunuch to admit Socrates and Hippocrates to his master's house because he thinks them sophists. When they finally do gain admittance, they are greeted by perhaps the most wonderfully comic scene in the Platonic corpus, one unlikely to increase our esteem for Protagoras and his students, or reduce the distance Socrates is establishing between him and Hippocrates and us. Anxious to hear their master's every word, Protagoras's students follow so closely at his heels that they must part every time he turns around, only to reform and divide again with his every turn. Moreover, the house is infested with sophists, each with his own smaller entourage. To complete the picture and give political urgency to the comedy, Alcibiades and Critias arrive.

To get Protagoras's attention, Socrates, who apparently knows and is known by him, introduces Hippocrates as a member of a "great and wealthy" family and a youth of unsurpassed "natural" ability,[33] anxious to become a man of public repute by studying with him. But then Socrates asks what seems a non sequitur: should the discussion of what Hippocrates is likely to learn from associating with Protagoras take place in public or private? It is less curious when we recall Hippocrates' embarrassment at the prospect of becoming a sophist, and hear Protagoras thank Socrates for his foresight[34] and consideration in asking since he, like all other sophists who go into great cities and try to persuade the best of the young men to follow him rather than their friends and relations, creates substantial jealousy, hostility, and intrigue. But why should this be so if sophists bring such great benefits to their pupils? Are the people who suspect them wrong, or are they more perceptive than Protagoras wants them to be? Is there something about the teaching of wisdom that estranges citizens from the sophists, or something distinctive about their conception of wisdom or teaching that does so?

Protagoras's defense against such animus relies on a claim that he is more traditional than his accusers and more honest than his fellow teachers. He is more traditional because what he does is what all the great teachers and poets of the past did.[35] They were all sophists.[36] But they got into trouble because they tried

---

[33] *Oikas megalēs te kai eudaimonos autos de tēn phusin dokei enamillos einai tois hēlikiōtais.*

[34] *Orthōs promethēi hupes emou.* The literal translation is "You are being thoughtful on my behalf," but it could also be read as "You are playing Prometheus on my behalf." (See the discussion by Miller in "The Prometheus Story.")

[35] Protagoras mentions three poets, Homer, Hesiod, and Simonides. On first meeting Protagoras, Socrates likens the situation in Callias's house to the Homeric house of Hades, quotes Odysseus, compares Hippias to the shade of Heracles, Prodicus to Tantalus, and Protagoras himself to Orpheus. In Berger's words, all three are likened to dead leaders of souls, "the blind leading the blind back into the world of the past, purveyors of the conventional and archaic wisdom of the poets who created Hades" ("Facing Sophists," pp. 74–75). It is in Hesiod that we get the story of Prometheus, Epimetheus, and Pandora that surrounds Protagoras's story and it is a poem by Simonides that provides Socrates with the opportunity for the longest most contrived speech in the dialogue (outside of Protagoras's "Great Speech").

[36] There are few occurrences of the noun *sophistēs* in the surviving literature before the end of the fifth century. For the history of the word, see Martin Ostwald, "The Sophists and Athenian Politics," unpublished manuscript, and *From Popular Sovereignty to the Sovereignty of Law* (Berkeley: University of California Press, 1986), chap. 5.

to disguise what they were doing to avoid ill will. But since the powerful saw through them (though the many[37] understood nothing on their own but aped whatever their leaders said), they confirmed the initial suspicion and made themselves, putative teachers of wisdom, look stupid. But he, unlike those who have preceded him, proclaims who he is: a sophist who teaches wisdom to others. So *he* has no qualms about giving his lecture before all the assembled company. Indeed, it would give him great pleasure.

Yet there is something disconcerting about Protagoras's protestations of honesty, since he mentions, but never specifies, that he takes other precautions. Since we do not know what they are, we cannot be sure when an argument is part of a strategy to allay suspicion and maintain his authority. This is not necessarily to damn him—the *Protagoras* like the *Gorgias* continually reminds us of the necessarily strategic dimension of speech—but it is a warning.

With all now assembled, Socrates asks Protagoras what Hippocrates will get for his money. The great teacher responds with a cliché: "every day, day after day, you will get progressively better and better" (318a). Pressed by Socrates for particulars and justification, Protagoras assures everyone that he, unlike other teachers (some of whom he pointedly says are in the room), will not force students to study conventional subjects that do not interest them. Instead he will teach them what matters most to them and in general: political judgment or "sound deliberation [*euboulia*] in his own affairs and in those of the city and how to maximize his power in political debate and action" (319a). In effect, he claims to possess and to teach the art of citizenship.

Though respectful, Socrates doubts such an art exists and so, naturally enough, that Protagoras can teach it.[38] When Socrates denies that there can be a political art, what is he denying and what questions about politics and teaching is he raising as he does so? Any answer must consider what *technai* were and whether Socrates regarded dialectic as a kind of *technē* or whether it stood in opposition to them.

The evolution of the word *technē* and its range of meaning is complex and contested, not only in general, but in this dialogue itself. Most generally, *technai* were systematic activities in which thought and action were linked by the skilled use of intelligence.[39] By systematizing experience, *technai* could anticipate future events and limit the waywardness of natural materials or forces. Mastering some part of nature meant being able to bound and measure a part of the world in ways that subjected it to human design. One who possessed a *technē* could craft an object, realize a form, or carry out an idea. One who taught a *technē* relied not only on precept but on a form of apprenticeship, suggested by the idea of studying with someone.

The question is whether political education is or can be such an art. Clearly

---

[37] The Greek suggests a contrast between those of exceptional ability who rightly are leaders as opposed to those ordinary people who are rightly followers.

[38] Kerferd suggests that Protagoras "is confronted with a choice of admitting that virtue cannot be taught and that his profession is a fraud and that the theory of Athenian democracy is false and his patron Pericles is ignorant of the true nature of political virtue" (*The Sophistic Movement,* p. 133).

[39] On this see Guthrie, *The Sophists,* and Wallach, *Plato's Political Art.*

such education is not random. But the question being posed in Athens during the middle to late fifth century was whether the process of education now emerging as a distinctive activity could be made into an art so that people could "make" others into something as they molded inanimate materials. Protagoras claims that there is such a *technē,* that he is in possession of it, and that he can teach it to others. Socrates denies that there is such an art, and so the issue of whether it can be taught is moot. But it is not clear how specific his skepticism is. Does he think Protagoras does not know what it is and so he cannot teach it, or that Protagoras has no idea of what it means to be a teacher, particularly of democratic citizens? But Socrates' skepticism is present not only in his explicit criticisms of Protagoras, but in the dialogue's implicit opposition between *technē* and dialectic (as discussed in chapter eight). When Socrates opposes dialectic to political *technē,* he is also contrasting the notion of making men good as a *praxis* to one of making men good as a form of *poiēsis.*

But at this point Socrates' skepticism about the teaching of virtue derives from another source; his experience with the practices of the Athenians whom he, like everyone else in the Hellenic world, regards as wise. While these wise men rely on the expertise of craftsmen to advise them about how to build ships and walls or any other technical matter where no one doubts the skill can be taught, and ridicule anyone who lacks the requisite education and *technē,* in the Assembly anyone can offer advice without ridicule or prior training. Either the Athenians are not wise and politics is an art that can be taught but they don't know it, or they are wise, in which case politics isn't and can't be. Moreover, the wisest of Athenians, such as Pericles, make no effort to teach their sons wisdom or have them taught the political art in which they themselves excel. Either they were derelict in their responsibilities, an unlikely situation given their wisdom, or they believed it could not be taught. Since Protagoras has declared himself old enough to be the father of everyone in the room, Socrates' example has the effect of making the dialogue a test of whether Protagoras can do what Pericles can't.

Socrates' question further emphasizes Protagoras's strategic dilemma. Protagoras can hardly deny the wisdom of the Athenians in whose city he is and in which he seeks students. Yet he cannot simply agree they are wise since that would make him superfluous. Given his previous admission, he must also show that political education is a *technē* that is not the possession of all, but that there is, nonetheless, a very small group of which he is the only contemporary representative, who possesses this *technē* to such a degree that they can help others (who are also exceptional) possess political skills more fully. He must be sufficiently democratic not to offend, and sufficiently elitist to attract the sons of the wealthy who can afford his fees and gain advantage over those who cannot.

Given Protagoras's age, learning, and experience, Socrates is reluctant to contradict him. Yet he remains confused about these issues and so invites Protagoras to do in the present company what he claims to do in general: teach them that virtue is teachable. Protagoras accepts the challenge, and asks how Socrates would prefer him to teach, by story (*muthon legōn*) or argument (*logōi diexelthōn*). Left to decide for himself, Protagoras chooses a story because it is more pleasurable (*chariesteron*), the ground upon which he made previous decisions and upon which Socrates builds in his defense of hedonism. This story is regarded as the heart of Protagoras's theoretical defense of democracy.

IV

There was a time, Protagoras begins, when the gods, but not men, existed. As the moment came for the genesis of humans, the gods put Prometheus and Epimetheus in charge of assigning to each race its appropriate powers and abilities. Unfortunately for mankind, Epimetheus (afterthought) convinced his brother Prometheus (forethought) to allow him to make the preliminary distribution of capacities. So involved did the former become in distributing power so that no nonreasoning species could overwhelm another that he had nothing left for humans when they, shaped by the gods inside the earth, were ready to take their place upon it. Confronting this desperate situation, his own poor judgment, and his brother's narrow vision, Prometheus was driven to steal fire and wisdom in the practical arts from Hephaestus and Athena so men could at least survive. But he was again shortsighted, since men need something more to survive than animals do: they require political wisdom. Without it the Promethean gifts are useless. Though these enable men to speak and satisfy their material needs, they leave humans in a debilitating dilemma. To be powerful enough to defend themselves against stronger animals they have to live in cities. But lacking the political art (*ouk echontes tēn politikēn technēn*) their attempt to do so ends in the committing of gross injustices against each other which forces them to scatter (*skedannumenoi*) and again become victims of animal (rather than human) predators.[40] In this war of all against all, "men" live as brutes but without their strength, their passions distorting their view of the good and blocking its effective pursuit. Only the power made possible by the political art can save them.

Seeing their plight and this dilemma, Zeus sends Hermes to bring justice and shame (*aidō te kai dikēn,* 322c)[41] to make "friendship and political order" (*poleon kosmoi te kai desmoi philias*) possible. But the precondition for both is that all men share in the political art, which means that this art, unlike the others that are divided among men, is unique. "For cities would never come to be if only a few possessed these. . . . And promulgate this law [Protagoras has Zeus say] as coming from me: death to him who cannot partake of shame and justice. For he is a plague upon the city" (322d). This does not entail all having an equal capacity for justice and shame, only that all must have a sufficient share of it to live among others.

As further "proof" that all humans have a share of civic virtue (which is appar-

---

[40] The word Protagoras uses to describe the destruction of the flawed communities prior to Zeus's gift is the word that was used in charging Socrates with corrupting the young.

[41] *Aidos* can mean conscience, self-respect, shame, modesty and respect or regard for others. On this, see Taylor, *Protagoras,* p. 85.

ently what justice and shame constitute), Protagoras cites the obvious "fact," that,
while we ridicule anyone who pretends to be a flute player but isn't, with the
political art we are incredulous at those men who confess their lack of it. That is
because he is, in effect, admitting that he is inhuman. While we have to accept
natural deficiencies as givens, we punish and reprove insufficiencies that can be
remedied by education. And the "we" here includes everyone, or at least every
citizen. Since every city relies on civic virtue (which now includes temperance and
piety as well as justice and shame), all teach this all the time in order to avoid
reverting to a "state of nature." Thus every polity educates from childhood on,
using whatever means necessary; threats and persuasion, blows and admonitions,
poetry and punishment, anything that will make the young virtuous. After years of
school, the city "compels" the young to "learn the laws and model themselves on
them" since they have been given by the great lawgivers of the past. Thus education is ubiquitous. We are all teachers and students of virtue as we are of a common
language. Even the most unjust person raised in a just regime is a paragon of
righteousness compared with an individual who lacks any education at all.

   Yet while everyone is a teacher of virtue, which is why we cannot find any who
teaches it as we do with other arts, there are a few men who, having a bit more
virtue than others, may be called "teachers" of virtue. Such men must be cherished, not harassed, for they are "uniquely gifted to assist others in becoming
good and noble" (328b). Protagoras regards himself as such a man, and so worthy
of every penny he is paid, as his students confirm.

   It is an extraordinary performance and a compelling argument worthy of the
respect accorded it by contemporary democrats seeking classical antecedents.
What Protagoras says responds to Arendt's worries about "political education"
and provides a fusing of democracy and philosophy less extravagantly intellectualist and so more realistic than that endorsed by (my) Socrates of the *Apology*
and *Gorgias.* Perhaps Protagoras is fully deserving of the reputation that drew
Hippocrates to him.

   For one thing, the story makes the case for the significance of democratic
politics. Being a citizen may not be natural in the sense that physical attributes
are, but it is, nonetheless, constitutive of our being human. For another, there is
the defense of democratic political education. Protagoras supposes an equality
more fundamental than any inequalities that are found in the "nature" of things.
While virtue is not innate, it is universal in the sense that everyone has the
capacity to learn it and normally does so merely by living in a polis governed by
nomoi. Finally he prescribes a "radical" task for "professors" of political theory
who, because they know more of what we all know, can make us do better what
we already have the capacity and interest to do. Such teachers bring citizens to be
more explicitly and reflectively aware of the structure of their practices, the substance of their ethical commitments, and the possibilities of their common
deliberations.[42]

---

[42] See especially Steiner, *Rethinking Democratic Education,* chap. 2; Nussbaum, *Fragility of
Goodness,* chap. 4; and Miller, "The Prometheus Story."

Despite the unique ability such professors have of bringing clarity and self-understanding to our collective lives, they are not (at least at this stage of Protagoras's argument), experts immune to the judgment of others, or teachers whose authority is unquestionable because it derives from initiation into the mysteries, social status, or ontological claims about Being. Of course, there will be some young men of wealthy families who have a greater interest and natural propensity for civic virtue, and this will qualify them to lead the democracy. But they could not be, given Protagoras's account, men apart, like those oligarchs and tyrants who regard the people as lacking in any virtue and thus as qualitatively inferior to them.

But the performance is also extraordinary for what it reveals about Protagoras as a teacher, democrat, and thinker, and for what it elides but nevertheless presses in upon us. From this standpoint Socrates is right to warn Hippocrates of what will happen to him if he studies with Protagoras.

Given the state of war as the alternative to possessing civic art, and the fact that citizenship constitutes us as human beings, the man who teaches that art is god-sent. Since the quality of life in a political community depends upon the citizenry's sense of justice, the deterioration of which leads back to a state of war, the need for education is urgent and unavoidable, and the man who recognizes and fills that need deserves our highest praise. Protagoras, like Zeus, is such a "man." Like Zeus he saves us from ourselves, and, by preventing the natural diversity reflected in the diversity of skills from degenerating into disharmony, creates peace and unity as the god did. It clearly follows that those who accuse the sophists of dividing the community are excoriating their greatest benefactors. Indeed, proof of this lies in the way Protagoras used the story to place the question of teaching *aretē* in the context of a traditional myth and religion. In these terms Protagoras's initial modesty is belied by his evolutionary narrative in which he becomes the culmination of civilization and he and Zeus are presented as the chief benefactors of humankind.

There is a parallel shift of emphasis and mood from the myth's generous view of humankind to the discursive exposition that follows. In the myth, Zeus's gifts mean that men have a god-given propensity to be just and respect others. But what follows stresses the importance of punishment and coercion. This identity of punishment and education implies that justice may be no more than a conditioned set of behavioral responses sustained, if only as a necessary facade, by fear. But where the battle of all against all is contained by the punishment of all by all, politics becomes force and virtue an offer no one can refuse.[43] So too there is the suggestion that any means is justified if virtue is the end, a suggestion that, not so coincidentally, justifies any means Protagoras uses (such as duplicity and disguise) to teach virtue.

Penultimately there is the suspicion, planted by Protagoras earlier when he mentions without specifying the other precautions he must take, that what we

---

[43] Berger, "Facing Sophists," and Patrick Coby, *Socrates and the Sophistic Enlightenment: A Commentary on Plato's Protagoras* (Lewisburg, Pa.: Bucknell University Press, 1987), pp. 58–70. See also his comments on Protagoras's connection and punishment and calling to account, p. 63.

have heard is as strategic as substantive. Read this way the myth is wonderfully "crafty," no doubt a model to emulate for students wishing to disguise their politics. For the story legitimates his teaching of the wealthy few while endorsing equality, presents him as modest yet uniquely qualified to promote civilization, principled yet self-promoting, one of "us" yet a god-gifted foreigner, thoroughly traditional yet fashionably radical.

Finally, there are questions unanswered and issues suppressed. For instance, the myth does nothing to specify the content and status of Protagoras's teaching, though that was the question the myth was supposed to answer. We do not know precisely how what he teaches will make one better in private and public affairs, or whether he will teach his students to be more just or more successful, or whether success in private affairs is always compatible with success in public affairs. These uncertainties are all the more pressing since his own form of instruction, unlike that of Zeus, is restricted to the wealthy few. If the education Protagoras offers is distinguished by its nobility, value, and usefulness from the education required for the political participation of the *dēmos,* why should those who have received such superior instruction subject themselves to the rule of their inferiors who have not?[44] If politics *is* a matter of expertise in a stronger sense than initially stated, then political questions become technical ones to which Protagoras can provide answers. (Under the pressure of Socrates' challenge and argument, his growing distance from the *dēmos* will become contempt for it.)

The sophists in general, and this myth in particular, have been praised for providing a counternarrative, a countercosmology, and secularized theodicy to the one prevalent at the time. There is some truth to this, and some reason to praise the pluralization it engenders. Yet, in Protagoras's case at least, there is something politically problematic about the alternative. I begin with Aeschylus's version of the Prometheus myth.

In Aeschylus, Prometheus acts out of pity for humankind with the full knowledge that his beneficence will bring Zeus's implacable hatred and a terrible punishment. There is no failure to foresee the consequences of his deed here as there is in Protagoras's story. Indeed, it is because Aeschylus's Prometheus knows the future that his deed is so courageous and his concern for humankind so moving. In denying Prometheus's foresight and eliding the conflict between Prometheus and Zeus, Protagoras undercuts Prometheus's divinity, lessens his courage and concern, and suppresses the "ontological" significance of his act. Central for Aeschylus is the "fact," also present in *Antigone*'s ode in praise of man, that humans are saved by transgression. The arts that are the necessary conditions for human achievement and exercise of power come from theft.

These issues and the tragic sensibility found in Aeschylus never arise in Protagoras's story because the myth is optimistic and progressive. In it, human beings have wisdom and can teach it, have foresight and use it, can apply human intelligence to the world and control forces that might otherwise control them. Though some trace of the brutish primitivism of the past must remain to remind

---

[44] This is Steiner's question, *Rethinking Democratic Education,* pp. 34–35.

us of the saving aspect of Protagoras's art, we have achieved a level of civilization that leaves the older world of power, conflict, and transgression in the dark.[45]

For Aeschylus the darkness remains, only partially dissipated by the gift of fire, which is nonetheless life-giving and illuminating. But while fire provides humankind with material well-being and clarity of sight and insight, it also burns and blinds. In Hesiod's story of Prometheus, the gift of the practical arts is accompanied by a shrouding of the knowledge of death. This too is a "gift," but an ambiguous one. The last to escape Pandora's box is hope, which, by turning our eyes from death, allows us to think beyond the moment and plan for the future. Yet hope is also blind hope which leads to ruin, miscalculation, projection, and then despair. We are back to the tension between the historical and dramatic dates of the dialogue and being prepared for the "saving" art of measurement.

If, as Hayden White has argued in a way that recalls both Walzer's description of the English Civil War and mine of *Antigone*'s Thebes, myths and the ideologies based on them presume the adequacy of stories to the representation of the reality whose meaning they purport to reveal, then faltering belief in this adequacy means that the society's entire cultural edifice enters into a crisis. This is because not only is a particular system of beliefs undermined, but so too is the very condition of the possibility of socially significant belief.[46] This sense of crisis frames Protagoras's speech and the dialogue as a whole. It is this frame as much as the particular arguments that take place within it that reveal the inadequacy of Protagoras's understanding of his vocation. After all, what can it mean to make men more aware of their practices when the world in which they are situated and constituted is collapsing? This may also reveal the limits of Walzer's connected critic.

In this world, Protagoras's story and arguments (as well as Socrates' responses to them) can be understood differently, even ironically. Different times and altered circumstances mean different readers, displacements, and inversions; in other words, what is present in the dialogue itself.[47] In these terms the *Protagoras* becomes a story and myth whose necessary fate is analogous to the one Protagoras tells within it.

V

Socrates does not immediately respond to the substance of the story, or to Protagoras's extrapolation from it intended to prove that virtue is teachable and that

---

[45] I take much of this discussion from Miller, "The Prometheus Story," pp. 22–32. The emphasis on punishment provides a "realistic" subtext that is never integrated into the overall narrative.

[46] Hayden V. White, *Metahistory: The Historical Imagination in 19th Century Europe* (Baltimore: Johns Hopkins University Press, 1973).

[47] When we first see Protagoras, his students follow closely on his heels. With each turn these pupils part only to reform in a constant rhythm of displacement and reassertion of order. If we take this image as a frame for the dialogue, one might say that the dance becomes less coordinated and the parting a breaking apart. Or one could take it as a metaphor for dialogue itself with its rhythm of agreement and division. On the significance of the historical and dramatic date of the dialogue see Nussbaum, *The Fragility of Goodness.*

he teaches it. Rather his first words are a combination of ostentatious deference, false praise, and a deflationary speech about speech. He lauds Protagoras's "virtuoso performance" which has left him entranced, overwhelmed, and thoroughly convinced, except for "one small matter," which he is sure Protagoras will dispose of as easily as he has all other aspects of the subject. Must we, Socrates wonders, regard Protagoras's speech as analogous to political oratory performed by his friend Pericles who is no more able to ask or answer questions than a book? Or can the issue at hand be discussed in a different manner—one, presumably, that is more appropriate to the subject and the occasion? Fortunately Protagoras, unlike his friend, Pericles, is as adept at offering brief replies to questions as he is at performing speeches of the sort that has so overwhelmed Socrates.

The one little thing that worries Socrates, and so prevents him from being fully satisfied that the issue is settled and the discussion concluded, is the question of whether virtue is one thing or composed of many parts, and, if the latter, how the parts are related to each other. The question arises from the fact that Protagoras keeps adding elements to his original notion of virtue without specifying whether these are additions or elaborations. The question matters because Protagoras claimed to teach virtue. If he does not know what it is, or if virtue consists of many parts that may be incompatible with each other, then he cannot teach it, either because he doesn't know what it is or because there is no "it" to teach.[48]

Initially Socrates takes his stand with Protagoras against an anonymous interlocutor who is trying to show that the different parts of virtue are not distinct, but imply and presuppose each other, in a way that makes them a single whole. But Protagoras soon rejects the alliance. He can see no point in Socrates' logic chopping, though he does sense that it is distracting from his performance and may potentially embarrass him. Despite the fact that Socrates gets him to go on (later he will need the pressure of the entire audience to do so), Protagoras continues to be wary and unconvinced by Socrates' insistence that his primary interest is in testing the argument. The sophist's wariness becomes a refusal to answer and a long speech, which, if the following applause is any indication, recaptures his glory and the initiative. But now it is Socrates' turn to be unimpressed. Unless Protagoras cuts his answers short, Socrates will forget the point and will not be able to follow him. Since Protagoras claims equal adeptness at long speeches and brief answers, Socrates insists that Protagoras (who with justification regards it as an "order") display his talent at the latter. "Socrates," he says, "I have had verbal contests with many people, and if I were to accede to your request and argue as my opponent demanded, I would not be thought superior to anyone, nor would the name Protagoras be known throughout Hellas" (335a). For Protagoras this is a contest for standing and power, a battle in which he has no intention of yielding the superior ground to his enemy. Given the delight Socrates takes in puncturing Protagoras's pretensions, a delight that, as I have suggested, raises questions about the motives he denies, Protagoras is right to be leery. He understands that

---

[48] On the argument from 329a onward, see Kerford, *The Sophistic Movement*, pp. 136–37.

the issue is his life, that dialectic "forces" men to give an account of their arguments and lives, and that what is at stake is power as much as truth.

Since Protagoras refuses to engage in a dialectical discussion, and since Socrates readily admits he is no match for Protagoras in making long speeches, Socrates gets up to leave. He has no time for the sort of displays Protagoras prefers, though they might be pleasant to listen to if and when he has the time.

He is restrained by Callias and the others. It is the only time we hear much from those in the audience. What they say and how they say it gives us a sense of Socrates' task and how he is being understood. Their statements and posturing are also an oblique commentary on the questions of virtue's teachability and democratic political education that frame the dialogue. Here, after all, are the great teachers of Greece.

Callias wants the debate to continue, but thinks Protagoras right to insist that he has as much right as Socrates to set the terms of debate. Alcibiades disagrees, reminding Callias that Socrates concedes Protagoras's superiority in long disquisitions, but Protagoras won't concede Socrates' superiority in dialectic. If he contests this point, he can hardly defend himself by offering some long oration that, in addition to not being part of a dialectical discussion, avoids the issues, makes others (but never Socrates) forget, and allows Protagoras to avoid giving an account of his position. Critias sees Callias and Alcibiades as partisans, and enjoins the rest not to be, so they can appeal equally to both sides and continue the discussion. Prodicus gives a longer speech, making tendentious distinctions and urging amity instead of enmity, while Hippias makes an even more tendentious speech calling them all kinsmen, friends, and fellow citizens "by nature [*phusei*] not by convention [*nomōi*]. For by nature like is akin to like, but convention, which tyrannizes the human race, often compels us to act contrary to nature. Therefore it would be shameful [*aischron*] if we who understand the nature of things should—being as we are the wisest of all the Greeks and gathered here together in this veritable hall of wisdom, in this greatest and most august house in the city of cities—not produce anything worthy of all this dignity but bicker with each other as if we were the dregs of society" (337d–e). He begs Socrates and Protagoras to compromise by adopting a middle course, and allow themselves to be supervised by a moderator who will monitor the length of speeches.

Socrates is willing to stay, but unwilling to have an umpire, since such an umpire would have to be superior to the participants and no one is superior to Protagoras. (Given the posturing of Prodicus and Hippias, Protagoras is a model of directness and so there is, despite the irony, a point to this.) Instead, he suggests that Protagoras ask questions which he will answer to show why brief responses best advance the discussion. When he has answered Protagoras's questions, then it will be his turn to make Protagoras accountable to him in the same way. Though Protagoras wants no part of it, he has no choice but to accede.

He has no choice because he is trapped by his vanity. He must be supreme in all intellectual matters since his reputation depends on it. But this preoccupation with reputation makes him dependent on the judgment of others who give it, even when it conflicts with his own. So he is bound to stay. What he can do, or at least try to do, is shift the terms of discussion back to his earlier triumph with the myth. What he can do is put the question about the unity of virtue in the context of poetry. Since the poets were the political educators of Greece, his displacement returns us to the question of the political education of democratic citizens and to the legitimacy he claims for what others see as his dangerous novelty.

The poem Protagoras chooses to explicate is by Simonides, and its subject is becoming and being good. Protagoras's purpose in choosing it is to show that Simonides contradicts himself. Although there are serious issues raised by the poem, such as the impossibility of perfection, the unbridgeable gulf between gods and men, the vicissitudes of life, and the necessity of moderation,[49] Protagoras's tendentious, aggressively unsympathetic rendering of it and Socrates' even more elaborately contrived, combative counterrendition suggest that the poem is largely incidental to other purposes. Those purposes have to do with Socrates' ability to best Protagoras on any ground the latter chooses, the way canonical texts can be used to mean anything and are thus an unlikely candidate for saying anything significant about the unity of virtue, and the way invoking such texts are evasive retreats to an authority beyond argument. Of course, there is one complication to all this: the *Protagoras* is precisely such a text, and the argument of this chapter is about its "usefulness."

When Protagoras finishes his long exposition, Socrates reverts to what is by now a trope: he proclaims himself overwhelmed by Protagoras upon whom he lavishes great praise prior to attacking him. "At first I felt as if I had been hit by a good boxer. Everything went black and I was reeling from Protagoras's oratory and the others' clamour" (339e). To "stall for time," Socrates calls on Prodicus who is from Simonides' home town, to defend his compatriot from so lethal a critique (339e). But Socrates manages to recover soon enough to present an even more long-winded, showy, convoluted interpretation than the one offered by Protagoras. Indeed it is a speech almost as long as Protagoras's "great speech." And its major point has less to do with the teaching of virtue than with claiming that philosophy's most ancient roots are, counter to popular belief, in Crete and Lacedamon, which are, against all evidence, the cities most populated by sophists. Both places hide this fact by pretending that their strength lies in fighting, because they do not want their enemies to know that the real source of their strength is wisdom. As soon as Socrates finishes, Hippias renders some perfunctory praise as a prelude to offering his own speech on the same poem. Socrates quickly declines the offer.

The dialogue began with the assumption that the Athenians were the wisest of all people, a sentiment echoed later by Hippias in his intervention. But now we are told that it is the Spartans who are wise and Sparta and Crete where sophists congregate, even though sophists were probably banned at both places. If the Spartans are the source of philosophy, then laconic brevity is appropriate to its practice. But, of course, Socrates is hardly being brief as he extols brevity. And despite its parodic aspects, his speech is taken with such seriousness because in

---

[49] See Taylor's gloss, *Protagoras,* pp. 141–48.

the sophistic world speeches are speeches, nothing more or less. It is as if the substance of what is said is overwhelmed (as Socrates says he is by Protagoras) by the ingenuity and technical virtuosity of the speaker who can convince no matter how arbitrary his assumptions or how absurdly recondite his conclusions. Now we see that Socrates' objection to set speech is analogous to our frustration at presidential debates where candidates say what they have to say regardless of the asked question and without engaging the position of their opponents. The problem with the sophists, as presented in the *Protagoras,* is not simply that they make the worst argument appear the better, or that they cynically use traditional poetic education for their own ends. They do both, but so do others, perhaps including Socrates. What is distinctive to them is that they do not make an argument at all, if an argument requires the participants to have real personal and political stakes in it. As I have already suggested, sophists do not have to give an account of or take responsibility for what they say, because as foreigners, they do not have to live with the results of whatever decision an Assembly influenced by their students take. But what sort of political educators are men so situated likely to be? What conception of virtue are they likely to exemplify and propose?

No sooner is Socrates finished with his interpretative reductio ad absurdum than he dismisses odes and poetry about which he has been discoursing at such length. They are subjects for the "trifling" symposia of the marketplace types (347d).[50] Uneducated and unable to entertain themselves by conversation, these people pay for flute girls[51] and, what is presumably analogous, long-winded speech. Having nothing to say themselves, they rely on the extraneous voices of poets who remain silent to their questions, or indulge in the sort of endless and futile academic debates about the meaning of the poems, such as the one we have just heard. But in this company, such diversions are simply a childish distraction from carrying on a serious discussion that "tries to reach a conclusion" (348d).

Once more Protagoras is reluctant to participate; once more he is driven to do so by the entreaties of the assembled company and the potential embarrassment and loss of reputation if he does not heed them. Socrates tries to mollify Protagoras by assuring him that the only thing he cares about is examining things he finds perplexing, and that he has found that he, like all other human beings, is more resourceful in action, speech, and thought when he works collaboratively. And who better to work with on such subjects than Protagoras, whom Socrates regards as "the best qualified to investigate the issues that decent and fair men should examine, especially virtue"? Not only does Protagoras consider himself to be noble and good, but he is able to make others so as well, and has so much self-

---

[50] 347c–d. In addition to "trifling" (or trivial or petty) *phaulōn* can also refer to the worthless poor or the common as opposed to the sophisticated. Here as elsewhere Socrates is driving a wedge between Protagoras and democracy. But he is also identifying Protagoras with what is worst in democracy since the word *agoraiōn,* which I have translated "marketplace types," can have more pejorative connotations such as huckster and petty retailers as well as forensic speakers, all of which Socrates implies Protagoras is.

[51] The mention of hiring flute girls almost certainly means Socrates is *not* identifying the market types with the poor.

confidence that instead of concealing this skill as all others before him have, he advertises the fact that he is a sophist and teacher of virtue and was the first to charge a fee for this (348e).

Socrates goes back to the beginning, yet again asking about whether the parts of virtue—wisdom, temperance, justice, piety, and courage—are five names for some one thing, or separate powers or functions. Protagoras is now willing to agree that the first four are reasonably close to each other, but demurs at including courage because there are many who lack virtue but are courageous. But if, Socrates argues based on Protagoras's admissions, courage requires confidence, and if confidence requires knowledge of an action or practice such as diving or fighting, then those who were courageous without knowledge, or only confident out of ignorance, would in Protagoras's words be "contemptible" and "out of their minds."[52] But, Socrates concludes, since overly confident men are mad, the wisest are most confident and the most confident are the most courageous. If so then wisdom (and presumably all other virtues) are identical to or at least presuppose courage. Protagoras objects; his admission that the courageous are confident did not entail the obverse, for a confident person can lack wisdom and so act rashly. Confidence comes from skill and passion, but courage comes from one's nature and the proper nurture of the soul.

Socrates' response seems unusually oblique. He picks on what seems an aside which he uses to shift the entire discussion to a consideration of hedonism, and to make an implausible argument that being overcome by pleasure or passion is simply a matter of ignorance. But in fact the issue of pleasure has framed the entire dialogue, from the prurient curiosity of the friend to whom he relates the conversation, and the audience who views the discussion as a form of entertainment, to Protagoras's initial choice of myth over argument. So the question of whether pleasure rules knowledge or knowledge pleasure and other passions is central rather than tangential, since if what drives Protagoras is gaining and giving pleasure, then that, not knowledge, is what he teaches others. And if the subtext of his instruction is that knowledge is a means or instrument to pleasure, then it may be paradoxical to call him a teacher of virtue if virtue is knowledge. So this shift refocuses on the issues posed in the initial confrontation between Socrates and Protagoras. What is at stake is who Protagoras is, what he does, and whether he knows the answer to either question.

At first Protagoras objects to the equation of pleasure with goodness and evil with pain, which Socrates presents as the view of the many. He sees no need to take their argument seriously, since the many "say whatever occurs to them" or "comes into their head" (353a). But if one looks at life as a whole instead of living in and for the moment as the many do, one sees a qualitative difference between noble and ignoble pleasures. From this larger perspective one can easily recognize that some pleasurable things (such as overeating) are not good, other painful things (such as surgery) are not bad, and a third class of actions is neutral.

---

[52] The word *mainomenoi,* which I have translated "out of their minds," can also imply a more frenzied condition, like that of a "raving lunatic."

Protagoras quickly and easily changes his mind, agreeing with Socrates that the distinction between noble and base pleasures is in fact one between fleeting and longer-range ones. What has intervened to make him give up this larger view and accept the idea that everything which promotes a pleasant and painless life is automatically good?

One thing that has intervened is the argument where the ordinary man was made to accept the notion that pleasure is the only good. Either Protagoras regards the admissions of the common man as something that Socrates has shown to be true, in which case he is, for good or bad reasons, unable to distinguish between Socrates' views and those he elicits; or he has been forced by strategic considerations to continue his vacillation between contempt for the *dēmos* and ingratiating himself with the democracy. In any case, the ensuing exchange between Socrates, Protagoras, the ordinary man (or the *dēmos*), and an aggressive imaginary interlocutor, leaves us uncertain about who believes what and for how long. More than any other Platonic dialogue, the end of the *Protagoras* seems nothing more or less than a momentary frieze in an eternal circle dance.

In these revised terms seeing life as a whole entails having close to perfect foresight, which means, at the very least, that men cannot be overcome by passion or blinded by emotion from discerning what is truly or ultimately pleasurable and what seems to be but is not. That is not the view of the multitude who believes knowledge too fragile to resist desire, fear, immediate pleasure, or any other strong emotion. If reason is scout to the desires, then it is an inconsequential thing, as are the people who claim to possess and teach it.

Given the choice between acknowledging the rule of knowledge and his own importance, and that of pleasure and his own insignificance, Protagoras enthusiastically allies himself with Socrates and dismisses the thoughtless views of the many. Unsurprisingly, Prodicus and Hippias endorse the agreement reached by Socrates and Protagoras, especially when Socrates goes on to admonish the many for not honoring the sophists. "But you, thinking it [incontinence] to be something other than ignorance, do not yourselves go to sophists, nor do you send your children to them for instruction, believing as you do what we are dealing with is something unteachable. By worrying about your money and not giving it to them, you all do badly both in private and public life" (357d). This "refutation" of the many on behalf of the sophists echoes Protagoras's initial promise to Hippocrates and, for the moment at least, creates a community of interest among rivals.

But for foresight to be unerring (as it has not been in the dialogue), there must be a standard by which to compare present and future pleasures and pain so certain and compelling that men can agree on what virtue is, and be able to anticipate and control the consequences of their actions in conformity to it. Such a standard is provided by the "art of measurement" (*metrētikē technē*). Distinctions between noble and base pleasures are premised on this art's capacity to accurately weigh our fleeting false pleasures against long-term true ones. Thus the hedonism embraced by the many is not really wrong, but can only become right with the possession of such an art. With it we can know not only what is good for our body and soul but what conditions make for "the preservation of cities and power and wealth," which is what Protagoras claimed to teach and Hippocrates sought to learn.

The inventors of this "life-saving" art (*esōsen . . . bion*)[53] would rival or even surpass Prometheus and Zeus by supplying a more certain standard than shame and justice (which Protagoras largely ignored in the discursive epilogue to his myth anyway). This standard would be objective, in the double sense of being independent of time and place, even if particular circumstances dictated the "data" to be calculated, and of being something all men might accept once it was taught to them by experts. With the art of measurement there would be no civil wars for Creon to deal with and no failure of insight such as that which plagued Oedipus. Here there would be a set of prescriptive glasses that enabled humans to see through distortions and past the massiveness of the present. Here is a precise, even quantifiable, answer to the political and moral dilemmas that have so far stood in the way of order, an ethically rational universe, and the success of educational blueprints. With it human beings could do perfectly what Protagoras does so imperfectly: strategically weigh the costs and benefits of every action and choice. With it *deinos* would mean one thing.

The art of measurement is a prescription in more than one sense. Like the gifts of the gods, this one would change how we see ourselves and live in the world. Martha Nussbaum has argued that, in the guise of offering us an empirical description, Socrates' art of measurement in fact presents us with a radical proposal for the transformation of our lives. Like the other gifts mentioned by Protagoras, this science of measurement will enter into and shape the nature and attachments of the being who receives it.[54] As I argued in chapter seven, a method of study can itself become a norm for the behavior it supposedly describes.

Coming from Socrates, these are astonishing arguments. Not only does he hastily, even presumptively, endorse a hedonistic calculus that contravenes the life he has led and the death he has chosen; he extols the godlike gifts of the sophists against whom he defined his own vocation. More than that, the art of measurement seems to pretend to the kind of inhuman wisdom Socrates of the *Apology* denies he possesses and suspects is impossible. Finally, some of the other arguments in the dialogue, such as the one on courage to which I shall next turn as well as the dialogue's dramatic movement as a whole, suggest both the impossibility of attaining such an art and the danger of trying to do so.

It is not that the idea of a measure is alien to Greek thought or Athenian political practice. In Homer, for example, heroes often measure distances. But the distance that matters is not one between immediate and long-term pleasures,[55]

---

[53] *Esōsen* from *sōzō* and *sōō* also means to preserve and keep alive as well as to have in mind or remember. *Sōzō* is often used in the additional sense of motion to a place, as when we bring someone safely to somewhere, which suggests that the art brings us safely through the travails of our life to some haven.

[54] This is Nussbaum's argument in *The Fragility of Goodness*. But cf. Terence Irwin, *Plato's Moral Theory: The Early and Middle Dialogues* (Oxford: Clarendon Press, 1977), chap. 3.

[55] It is true, of course, that in choosing a short, glorious life over a long, inglorious life, Achilles is

but between the best life and culture have to offer—one's home and people—and war and death.[56] It is Achilles remembering his mortal father rather than his immortal mother, Odysseus choosing Penelope and Ithaca over Circe.

The seven sages whom Protagoras has identified as sophists like himself sought a measure that would make the symmetry, balance, and proportion of the cosmos the standard for relations between citizens and cities.[57] Without some such measure the world would be immeasurable—that is, boundless, elusive, and chaotic. Under these circumstances, humans would be buffeted by internal and external forces beyond their comprehension and control. With their intentions thwarted, and their lives threatened, driven by passions and indulging injustice, they would revert to the condition of humankind prior to Zeus's gift. Here measure is associated with political and intellectual power (themselves barely distinguishable from each other). Yet the human space the measure defined and defended was one of qualitative diversity and constant tensions, its variety and antagonisms embodied in Greek polytheism.

Finally, the significance of measure in fifth-century Athens was associated with the extension of the idea of *technai*. Communities of discourse defined the performance of these *technai* which could progress, but were, nonetheless, seen as objective, in the sense of being implicit in the activity and the quality of the thing or condition the activity aimed to bring into existence. But these were qualitative norms of excellence, not quantitative criteria of efficiency.[58]

But the art of measurement broached by Socrates, and eagerly embraced by Protagoras, is something more and different than this and from the dialogue's initial conception of being a good man and a good citizen.[59] Embedded in something like what Nietzsche called an Hegelian "idolatry of the factual"[60] (because all action can be fully explained by its place in a supramundane narrative of progress), the art of measurement stills the ethical anxieties and metaphysical discomforts that have defined the texts considered in previous chapters. Heidegger[61] argued that the basic achievement of science is the invention of a world to which prescribed rules and methods can be applied. Such a world, once established, would have the appearance of fixity and inevitability about it, something to be discovered and acted into, a bounded stage upon which real players per-

---

making a kind of calculation. But his set of concerns is so different that we could equally say that Achilles is the *least* calculating of the Greeks.

[56] Adrian Poole, "War and Grace: The Force of Simone Weil on Homer," *Arion*, n.s., 1, no. 2 (Winter 1992): 1–16.

[57] See Vlastos, "Isonomia," *American Journal of Philology* 74 (1953): 537–66, and "Isonomia Politike," in Jürgen Mau and Ernest Gunther Schmidt, eds., *Isonomia Studien zur Gleichheitsvorstellung im griechischen Denken* (Berlin, 1964), pp. 1–35.

[58] As Wallach argues in *Plato's Political Art.*

[59] "Socrates is now operating with a very different conception of excellence than that which underlay his original claim that excellence cannot be taught." Taylor, *Protagoras,* p. 213.

[60] Nietzsche, in *Untimely Meditations,* trans. R. J. Hollingdale, introd. J. P. Stern (Cambridge: Cambridge University Press, 1983), p. 105.

[61] In "The Age of the World Picture," in *The Question concerning Technology and Other Essays,* trans. William Lovitt (New York: Harper and Row, 1982), pp. 115–54.

form. The particular character of the future may not be known, but the world is prefigured in a way that makes the method used to approach it seem exact, rigorous, and uncontestably appropriate. As with rational actor theory, the art of measurement projects a world which invites calculation and measurement, and turns the studiers of that world as well as the objects of study into measurers and calculators.

The art of measurement not only recasts the idea of political virtue as conceived in the initial encounter between Protagoras and Socrates, it challenges the conception of political education that has animated this book. The kind of democratic politics, political philosophy, and teaching presupposed and implied by a commitment to its existence or, still more, the claim to actually possess the art is at odds with the argument of the previous eight chapters. That it is made by Socrates, and that my argument about the relationship between democracy, philosophy, and education is also made on the authority of Socrates, make the challenge all the more direct.

Insofar as the art of measurement makes the knowledge and practice of virtue available to all, it is more consistent with Protagoras's democratic claim that no one teaches virtue because everyone does, than with the fact that he taught it to a wealthy elite. But this democratization is achieved at the cost of transforming democratic politics. For the new political art makes public deliberation/debate/contestations unnecessary, perfunctory, or a matter of cost-benefit analysis. If there are no inescapably incommensurable demands, then there is no need to develop the intellectual habits equal to the task of discriminating among them.[62] And if there are not, then the complexities of living a human life as portrayed by drama and Socratic political philosophy as I have presented them are but temporary impediments to the good life. In this respect, the art of measurement is a rebuke to democracy, or at the least a rebuke to the ordinary man's and woman's capacity to deal with a more complicated world than the pluralizing calculus it entails. Such men (and women) could only participate in public life if hedonism was their morality, and the art of measurement their intellectual virtue. This is certainly the view Socrates puts forth with Protagoras's agreement and help. Whether it is also his view is another matter.

If the argument for the art of measurement as a saving *technē* is endorsed by Socrates for more than strategic pedagogic or dramatic reasons, then it would transform dialectic into didacticism of the sort I argued it was not in the preceding chapter. If we can in fact measure the future consequences of our acts with the exactness the art demands, educational blueprints become possible, and there would be minimal discontinuity between intentions and consequences and no need for dialogue.

Behind Socrates' insistence on dialogue as a mode of political education is the appreciation that moral character and citizenship are not created by a pure act of will, but involves reciprocity and respect, as well as conflict and power. His

---

[62] Steiner, *Rethinking Democratic Education,* p. xiii.

educational practice assumes that teaching is as much a gift as a program, as much a matter of accidents of affection and friendship as of having a plan. However much he may depart from his own announced strictures, Socrates understands this in a way Protagoras does not. This understanding would be made anachronistic by the art of measurement. Just ask: what would philosophy become, and who would Socrates be, if the art of measurement he enthusiastically champions defined political life?

But there is evidence, some of it adduced earlier, that there are indeed strategic and dramatic reasons why Socrates presents such a forceful case for the saving knowledge made possible by or as an aspect of the art of measurement. I argued earlier that the art of measurement is a radical recasting of a political *technē* as that is first debated between Socrates and Protagoras. But that is an overstatement. Indeed, the art of measurement may be understood as showing what Protagoras must believe to legitimate his early confidence that he possesses and can teach the political art. In these terms Socrates poses a Kantian question: what must the world be like for Protagoras to possess the political art as he understands it, to teach it as he understands teaching, and to be so certain about his success and the consequences of what he says?

As one commentator put it: "it should not be forgotten that the initial question of the dialogue is not whether virtue can be taught but whether Protagoras is a good teacher of it."[63] Nor should it be forgotten that the contest is over whether it can be taught to Hippocrates and, presumably, other Athenian youth in similar circumstances. What we see, or at least are supposed to see, is Protagoras's inadequacy as a teacher of virtue. One way of highlighting that inadequacy is to show just how extraordinary a reevaluation of the world within and outside the dialogue would be necessary for him to be successful. If Protagoras is repeatedly unable to foresee the course of the dialogue, how likely is he to foresee the coming crises that would confound the evolutionary process he posits with its supposition that social habit suffices for political life?

Socrates' endorsement of the art of measurement is made even more problematic by the fact that it is part of an argument refuting the many on behalf of the sophists whom he has ridiculed throughout the dialogue (whenever they did not do a better job on themselves than he could do). But perhaps the strongest evidence against accepting Socrates' endorsement of the art of measurement at face value is, as we shall see in a moment, the discussion of courage.

If I am right about all this, then the art of measurement is less Socrates' view than the implicit assumption behind Protagoras's claim to be the kind of teacher he is, teaching the kind of subject he supposes himself to teach. If I am right that the foresight it demands and would make possible is so exaggerated as to be an inhuman presumption, then the hope for it may, like hope itself, be the final plague released from Pandora's box. Hope blinds men to mortality and limitations, to exactly what Socrates of the *Apology* thought necessary for doing phi-

---

[63] Duncan, "Courage in the Protagoras," p. 221.

losophy and, I have argued, for doing politics as well. But hopelessness, the weary or resentful reaction to dashed hopes, is just as self-indulgent. The teaching of virtue requires both, and the teaching of courage requires both most of all.

VI

Whatever partnership exists between Socrates and Protagoras dissolves when the former asks whether courage is a part of virtue in the same way piety, justice, temperance, and wisdom are. Having gotten Protagoras's assent to the proposition that incontinence is nothing but ignorance, and that self-control is a matter of wisdom, Socrates is able to conclude (without Protagoras's cooperation) that wisdom is identical to courage. Since knowledge of what is and what is not to be feared is courage, no ignorant man could be courageous. Confronted with this conclusion, Protagoras is silent and sullen. Like Callicles, he tells Socrates to question himself, for he will no longer be coerced into answering. As usual, Socrates reassures him that he has "no other object in asking these things than my desire to investigate these questions about virtue, especially what virtue is in itself. For I knew if that could be made clear, then we would be able to settle the question about which we both have had much to say, I claiming that virtue cannot be taught, you that it can" (361a).

But why does the final impasse arise with the discussion of courage? Why do their differences over courage drive a permanent wedge between them, dissolving the agreement over hedonism that had united them in opposition to the many and to the ventriloquized voice that persistently blocks Socrates from criticizing hedonism?[64] Those differences come from the fact that, in terms Protagoras himself has endorsed, courage cannot be included in a utilitarian calculus. If the paradigmatically courageous act is steadfastness in the face of death, and if death is the cessation of all affective states as Protagoras seems to believe when he denies that courage can be pleasurable, then one cannot be both calculating and courageous. Something more than calculation and strategy must be present if courage in the face of death is to be accounted a virtue, and if it is not so accounted, then a significant dimension of a human life is left out. Since Protagoras seems unable to account for a fundamental political value such as patriotism, it is questionable whether his teaching can be trusted to make good citizens. Moreover, Protagoras's earlier preoccupation with the strategic considerations concerning his teaching and his present rejection of courage as an aspect of virtue raise questions about *his* courage, and whether the implicit, perhaps framing,

---

[64] Berger, in "Facing Sophists," argues this at length. There is a subtext to the discussion of courage involving the shift in modes of warfare from hand-to-hand combat to the disciplined collective power of the hoplite phalanx. The qualities necessary for success in the former—a heartless, frenzied possession (*astorgos*) that overcame fear and inspired courage was dysfunctional in the phalanx where success depended on maintaining one's place in line. The same kind of restraint and discipline was required in naval warfare. It was the sea where Athens was supreme and it was the courage of its citizen-sailors that provided a ground for their claims to greater power in the city as I have argued in chapter three.

lesson of the dialogue is a counsel of cowardice. Finally, Socrates' insistence that all parts of virtue are knowledge means that virtue is eminently teachable (though not by Protagoras who seems ignorant of what it is), while Protagoras's denial that courage is part of virtue and thus knowledge means that virtue is unteachable (except perhaps by Socrates, who thinks it knowledge).

This means that the argument has "turned on them,"[65] since they now defend positions opposite to the ones they endorsed in the beginning. If the discussion "had a voice of its own," it would mock the lack of foresight that led to getting things "topsy-turvy and thoroughly confused" (*atopoi*, 361a). Socrates would like to clear up these matters by continuing the discussion until they come to some conclusion about what virtue is and whether it can be taught. He does not want Epimetheus to "frustrate us by deception a second time in this inquiry, as he did in the distribution of powers and abilities in your story" (361D). Socrates prefers Prometheus.

Protagoras demurs, but only after generous praise for Socrates' enthusiasm and intelligence, predicting—now with genuine foresight—that he "would not be surprised if you gain among men high repute for wisdom" (361E). Socrates accepts the decision to end the conversation and rushes off to keep his appointment. "I stayed," he concludes, "only as a favor to our noble colleague Callias" (362A).

VII

This chapter began with an expectation that Protagoras (or Platagoras) would provide a theory of democratic political education that could reconcile expertise and equality, allay Arendt's worries about importing inappropriate modes of authority into politics, and further delineate the differences between a political and politicized education. It presumed that he himself could provide a model of how professors in a democratic polity should teach. But he has been a disappointment on each score. The elisions pressing in on the antiseptic atmosphere in Callias's house make Protagoras's attitude and views seem complacent. Just as disappointing is his evanescent commitment to democracy, his confounding of socialization and education, his inordinate reliance on punishment, and his vanity.

This book began with an expectation that Socrates could do all I have just said Protagoras could not. But what we read and see in this dialogue may make us as uneasy about studying with him as about studying with Protagoras. If we accept the perhaps exaggerated view that choosing a teacher is choosing a life, then there is much in the dialogue to make us wary of Socrates and of the arguments I have made on his authority.

Let me recall some of the ways the dialogue makes us uneasy about Socrates. First of all, there is his identification with Prometheus. Given Prometheus's fail-

---

[65] I have used Lombardo and Bell's translation (in *Plato's Protagoras*), here because it rightly echoes the initial view we get of Protagoras and anticipates the reversals Socrates is about to describe. For the same reason I follow their translation of *tarattomena* at 361c.

ure in entrusting the distribution of powers to his brother, an oversight that forced him to steal in order to save mankind, this is a deeply problematic identification. Then there is his own complacency in believing that dialogue and dialectic could actually accomplish some real world change. In the future already present in Callias's house, the commitment to leisurely conversation will be unhinged by political conflicts in which some of the company will be the victims of others. Socrates may not be as complacent as Protagoras, but he offers no vision of the future to help us ameliorate the present or even understand what to do about the past.[66]

Then there are Socrates' repeated protestations of concern for the state of the argument and the proclaimed indifference to reputation, both of which are belied by his intemperate pleasure in humiliating his sophistic opponent. Here even more than in the *Gorgias,* Socrates' repositionings seem those of a general choosing the terrain of battle, keeping an enemy offstride, and then setting up verbal trophies on the battlefield after victories. Harry Berger finds this similarity, together with Socrates' punctuation of his triumphs in each round with comments on his skill in sizing up his opponent and making arguments, a sign that "something troubles Socrates."[67] It surely troubles those of us who might be his students, including Plato.[68]

Penultimately there are the arguments hastily made, quickly abandoned or ignored, and elaborately ventriloquized even when they seem profoundly "un-Socratic." Whatever else is happening, Socrates seems to have lost all control, either because of what he has become or what he must now confront. Finally, there is the peculiar fact that as Protagoras collapses into the multitude whose views he little respects, Socrates collapses into Protagoras whose views *he* little respects.

Up to a point we can "save" Socrates by offering explanations (or excuses) for what seem his deficiencies (or perhaps his uncharacteristic honesty). We could regard his identification with Prometheus's failure as an identification with what is most human in the god in contrast to Protagoras'ss myth which implicitly assimilates his art with that of Zeus the savior. While Protagoras thinks he can save mankind as Zeus did, Socrates does not. We cannot be "saved" in the way Protagoras supposes because we remain, like Protagoras, flawed in our divinity.

Similarly, we could argue as I did earlier, that revealing the "unsavory" side of Socrates is necessary for him to be the kind of teacher who is not Protagoras. To simply accept what Socrates says because he says it, instead of coming to a position on our own in conversation with others, is to turn him into Protagoras. One could say that for Socrates to be a teacher he cannot teach or be "Socrates"; that he only is when he isn't; that his arrogance is a flashing red light which tells us to stop and look carefully before proceeding. It is essential that we approach

---

[66] See Tracy Strong, "On Revolution, Politics and Learning from the Past," *Polity* 12 (Winter 1979): 303–4.

[67] Berger, "Facing Sophists," p. 112.

[68] Given the fact that "Socrates" is a character in a dialogue written by Plato, this is an odd locution.

him with the suspicion and skepticism Hippocrates lacked when he approached Protagoras.

But this is too complacent about Socrates and about Plato's identification with *him.* The Athenian auditors in Callias's house are representatives of the finest aristocratic houses in Athens. Yet they fail to provide the city with the necessary leadership, which raises questions not only about Protagoras's ability to teach virtue but Socrates' as well. Is it a waste of time to listen to Protagoras and Socrates debating? Did the fate of those in the audience make Plato "wonder whether their generation of Athenians spent too much of their energy listening to sophists debate whether virtue can be taught and too little becoming men of virtue"?[69] Critias and Alcibiades were both traitors to the Athenian democracy. Did Plato think Socrates was as well? Is there evidence in this dialogue that he came to believe Socratic questioning too corrosive, Socratic assumptions overly intellectualist, and Socratic faith in remaking democracy as itself a myth no more convincing and no less optimistic than that of Protagoras?

In the "Platonic" voice, Socratic intellectualism represents the worst of two worlds. It is antidemocratic, but still closely tied to democratic practices, and its political logic points to an aristocracy of intellect it refuses to accept. The assertion that virtue is knowledge, that incontinence is ignorance, and that the pursuit of wisdom constitutes the best life is far from the experience of ordinary Athenians.[70] Indeed the exaltation of philosophical wisdom makes the conditions of its acquisition so demanding that it is practically as exclusive as a sophistic elite of wealthy students. Why not admit that the sharing of such wisdom and virtue is, in principle as well as in practice, tied to necessary inequalities of condition and natural endowment? Is there not something naive, even destructive, in Socrates both refusing to take his bearings from the cultural forms that constitute the practices of everyday life *and* attempting to transform that life by politically educating the citizenry to live it philosophically? Does not one have to recognize the enormous role habit and socialization play (as Protagoras does), while acknowledging that, for most men and women, this is their life. Given this, the examined life is ineffective or dangerous, except for the one man, Socrates, whose "truth" is the search for truth, or for those few potential philosophers who can be let loose from their moorings of habit because they will be reanchored in the refined art of measurement or in a theory of the Forms. In these terms Socrates did corrupt the youth.

This "Platonic" voice is echoed with a different moral valence in Bernard Williams's criticisms of what he calls the "characterless self." Williams regards this self as "distinctively modern and Kantian" with some anticipations in Plato. I am suggesting that, in the *Protagoras,* "Plato" may be criticizing Socrates in similar terms.

There are times, both in the *Protagoras* and elsewhere, where Socrates seems

---

[69] John Walsh, "The Dramatic Dates of Plato's Protagoras and the Lesson of Arete," *Classical Quarterly* 34 (1984): 101–6.

[70] It is just as far from the experience of ordinary oligarchs, though they at least would be sympathetic to claims of privilege and superiority.

to be arguing or assuming that no one is entirely free so long as there is any ethically significant aspect of themselves that belongs to them simply as a result of the process by which they were contingently formed. In Williams's words: "If my values are mine simply in virtue of social and psychological processes to which I have been exposed, then it is as though I was brainwashed and cannot really be a free rational and responsible agent." To avoid this, my whole outlook should, in principle, be exposed to a critique, as a result of which every value that I hold can become a consideration for me, something critically accepted, rather than merely something that happens to be part of me.[71]

The idea implicit in this aspiration to total critique is that the criticizing self can be separated from everything that a person contingently is, as Oedipus believes when he proclaims himself the child of chance. As long as my values have been acquired through mere contingency it is as if they were not really mine. But, Williams asks, who is the already existing self that is brainwashed by such a process? "In truth, however, it is not that such a self is misled or blinded by the mere process of being socialized; one's actual self, rather, is constructed by that process."[72]

There is surely much to this. At the very least it is a warning about the limits of intellectualism, including intellectualist considerations of intellectualism such as those in this book. Still, as I have argued in the previous chapters, it is important not to underestimate the "intellectual" dimensions of Athenian political culture. This is not to ignore the presence of class conflict and agonistic contests for power, or to reinscribe the "pure transcendence" of Greek culture. Still less would I deny the Dionysian play of desire or the "primitivism" of Greek religion, which so shock students acclimated to ancient culture by reading the Platonic dialogues purged of their erotic "excess" and dramatic depths, all of which ought to give an edginess to any discussion of "democratic deliberation" in classical Athens. It is to reemphasize that the ground, context, and inspiration for Socratic intellectualism and political philosophy are the democratic culture in which he lived, and that evidence for this can be found in the very commitment to critique and dialogue. In the *Crito* Socrates insists that since the laws of Athens (actually it is the laws of Athens as he constructs them), have made him what he is, he owes them virtually unconditional obedience. Implicit in his argument is that these laws are also father to the vocation he practices as well as to him as a citizen, so that his obedience to them becomes an acknowledgment that he owes what he is to what he criticizes. In Arendtian terms, he is being conservative because he has been radical.

If I am right about the relationship between democracy and philosophy in Athens and about Socrates, then what seems deracinated argumentation and a procedural commitment to deliberation and debate assumes a radical democratic politics at its center. This means that "characterless self" has (or had) a character, a democratic one.

Yet there is a complication having to do with what I noted earlier in consider-

---

[71] *Shame and Necessity,* pp. 158–59.
[72] Ibid., p. 159.

ing Socrates' claim (in the *Theaetetus*), that the arguments of a dialogue never come from him but from the person to whom he is talking. If true, then the other becomes internalized, in the sense that he or she becomes myself as opposed to I, and so I am always talking to myself as I talk to another. Conversely talking to another is also talking to myself, which is why Socrates was so concerned for Hippocrates, and why, in general, it is necessary for one to exercise foresight when choosing a teacher/interlocutor/student. For each encounter risks the self-division, self-opposition, perhaps self-contradiction that is a necessary condition for a "genuine dialogue." "We are bound to one another by the law of our face-to-face existence," Harry Berger writes, "but also each of us is divided from himself by the same law."[73] Thus the reciprocity between interlocutors entails a mediation of the self(ves) divided in the course of dialectical exchange. Any *political* community, and all *political* education, must take account of these divisions, rejecting both the mystical unity of all on the one hand and the isolated, autonomous, integrated, fully self-sufficient, unbreachable individual on the other. This is what the polyphony of the *Protagoras* (as well as the *Gorgias*) respects and represents. Each time one reads it, the performances are fresh, the voices newly modulated, the exasperations differently placed.

VIII

In the *Apology* Socrates is accused of corrupting the youth, thereby threatening the continued viability of Athenian democracy. The *Protagoras* offers both a vigorous defense of Socrates against the charge, and expresses a concern that his accusers may have been right.

I do not think that the *Protagoras* resolves the tension, any more than the close vote for Socrates' guilt does in the *Apology*. Indeed, as I have argued, its radically aporetic quality suggests that it may be for Plato part of the problem. Yet that quality is also continuous with the tragic sensibility that helped constitute Athenian democratic culture. Implicit in Aeschylus's play is that Prometheus includes Epimetheus; that the one who knows in advance becomes the one who knows afterward.[74] If we regard the Titan as representing human powers, then folly and cleverness, blindness and insight shadow each other. Any political education, and effort to cultivate the capacity for judgment, must take account of this fact.

One could say that the idea of an intellectual citizenry or philosophical democracy is a noble legacy *and* a seduction, the only aspiration worthy of political educators and sheer vanity. One could also say that it is our fondest hope, but given the Pandora story, that is an unsettling thought. Perhaps it is better to say, with Michael Walzer, that democracy is a wager and education the means of winning it.[75] No one played for higher stakes than Socrates. Whether he won or lost remains an open question.

[73] Berger, "Facing Sophists," pp. 80–81.

[74] Miller, "The Prometheus Story," p. 116.

[75] Michael Walzer, "Exclusion, Injustice, and the Democratic State," *Dissent* 40, no. 1 (Winter 1993): 60.

ABOUT THE AUTHOR

J. Peter Euben is Professor of Politics at the University of California at Santa Cruz. He is the author of *The Tragedy of Political Theory*, the editor of *Greek Tragedy and Political Theory*, and co-editor of *Athenian Political Thought and the Reconstitution of American Democracy*.